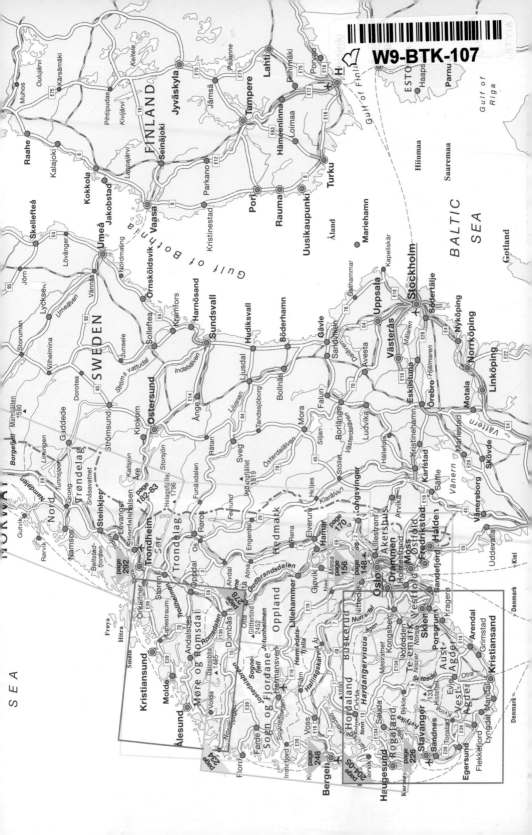

INSIGHT GUIDES

Norway

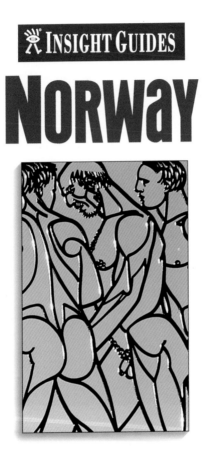

APA PUBLICATIONS

Part of the Langenscheidt Publishing Group

INSIGHT GUIDE
NORWAY

ABOUT THIS BOOK

Editorial
Project Editor
Simon Ryder
Managing Editor
Cameron Duffy
Editorial Director
Brian Bell

Distribution
United States
Langenscheidt Publishers, Inc.
36–36 33rd Street 4th Floor
Long Island City, NY 11106
Fax: (1) 718 784 0640

UK & Ireland
GeoCenter International Ltd
Meridian House, Churchill Way West
Basingstoke, Hampshire RG21 6YR
Fax: (44) 1256 817988

Australia
Universal Publishers
1 Waterloo Road
Macquarie Park, NSW 2113
Fax: (61) 2 9888 9074

New Zealand
Hema Maps New Zealand Ltd (HNZ)
Unit D, 24 Ra ORA Drive
East Tamaki, Auckland
Fax: (64) 9 273 6479

Worldwide
**Apa Publications GmbH & Co.
Verlag KG (Singapore branch)**
38 Joo Koon Road, Singapore 628990
Tel: (65) 6865 1600. Fax: (65) 6861 6438

Printing
Insight Print Services (Pte) Ltd
38 Joo Koon Road, Singapore 628990
Tel: (65) 6865 1600. Fax: (65) 6861 6438

© 2008 Apa Publications GmbH & Co.
Verlag KG (Singapore branch)
All Rights Reserved
*First Edition 1991; Third Edition 1999
Updated 2008*

CONTACTING THE EDITORS
We would appreciate it if readers
would alert us to errors or out-
dated information by writing to:
**Insight Guides, P.O. Box 7910,
London SE1 1WE, England.
Fax: (44 20) 7403 0290.**
insight@apaguide.co.uk

www.insightguides.com
In North America:
www.insighttravelguides.com

The first Insight Guide pio-
neered the use of creative full-
colour photography in travel
guides in 1970. Since then, we
have expanded our range to cater
for our readers' need, not only for
reliable information about their
chosen destination but also a
real understanding of the culture
and workings of that destination.
Now, when the internet can supply inexhaustible facts, our books
marry text and pictures to provide
those much more elusive quali-
ties: knowledge and dis-
cernment. To achieve
this, they rely heavily on
the authority of locally
based writers and pho-
tographers.

Fjords, midnight sun and Vikings
are the aspects most often identified with Norway. From the
spectacular scenery of the west
coast to the wilderness of the
frozen north, Norway is a country
that entices all those in search
of unspoilt nature. But to see
what else Norway has to offer
there is no better place to start
than Snorri Sturluson's chronicle
of the lives of the Vikings.

How to use this book
This book is carefully struc-
tured to convey an under-
standing of the country
and its culture, and to
guide readers through its
sights and activities:

◆ To understand Norway today, you need to know something of its past. The first section, headed by a yellow colour bar, covers the country's history and culture in lively **features** written by specialists.

◆ The main **Places** section, with a blue bar, provides a complete run-down of all the attractions worth seeing.

◆ The **Travel Tips** section is a convenient point of reference for practical information on travel, hotels, restaurants, shops and festivals. Information may be located quickly on the index printed on the back cover flap – and the flaps are designed to serve as bookmarks.

The contributors

Originally edited by **Simon Ryder**, this fully updated guide builds on earlier editions produced by the late **Doreen Taylor-Wilkie**, a Scottish broadcaster and travel writer, who was first inspired to write about travel by Norway. Taylor-Wilkie also wrote the chapters on the fjord country.

The history section was the work of **Rowlinson Carter**, who became obsessed during his researches with the tales recounted by Snorri Sturlusson. **Michael Brady** arrived in Norway in 1958 from the United States. As an outdoor man and specialist on skiing and fitness, he was well suited to writing about customs, sport and the outdoor life.

Other contributors included one of Sweden's most eminent journalists, **Inga Wallerius**, who has a deep interest in ethnic cultures and wrote on the Sami people. **Bobby Tulloch's** chapter on Svalbard was the result of an expedition there, while **Jim Hardy** contributed his knowledge on Scandinavian arts. **Karen Fossli** wrote on the oil industry, film and Norway's neighbours, and **Anita Peltonen** provided chapters on Oslo and its environs. **Robert Spark** contributed the Places chapters outside of Oslo and the fjord country.

Previously updated by Oslo-based **John Harley**, who described Norway as "one of God's best-kept secrets", the book was revised by **Lance Price** with help from **Lars Bevanger**. This version was updated by **Nina Berglund** and edited by **Jason Mitchell**, **Alexia Georgiou** and **Siân Lezard**.

Map Legend

▬ ▪▪	International Boundary
▬ ▬ ▬ ▬	County Boundary
⊖	Border Crossing
▬ • ▬	National Park/Reserve
▬ ▬ ▬ ▬	Ferry Route
Ⓣ	Metro
✈ ✈	Airport: International/Regional
🚌	Bus Station
P	Parking
❶	Tourist Information
✉	Post Office
✝ † ⊹	Church / Ruins
†	Monastery
☾	Mosque
✡	Synagogue
🏰 🏚	Castle / Ruins
∴	Archaeological Site
∩	Cave
𝟏	Statue/Monument
★	Place of Interest

The main places of interest in the Places section are co-ordinated by number with a full-colour map (e.g. ❶), and a symbol at the top of every right-hand page tells you where to find the map.

CONTENTS

Maps

Norway **142**

Central Oslo **148**

Oslo **156**

Around Oslo & its Fjord **170**

Heart of Norway **182**

Southern Norway
& its Fjords **204**

Stavanger **226**

Southwest Coast **234**

Bergen **248**

The Hurtigrute **262**

Møre and Romsdal **278**

Trondheim **292**

North, into the Arctic **302**

The Far North **316**

Svalbard **338**

Oslo T-bane **390**

A map of the whole country
showing the extent of the
area maps listed above is on
the inside front cover.

A map of Oslo is on the
inside back cover.

Introduction

Best of Norway **6**

Northern Contrasts **15**

History

Decisive Dates **18**

Beginnings **21**

Kings and Christianity **29**

The 400-Year Sleep **36**

Union with Sweden **43**

An Independent, Modern
Country **50**

Features

Who are the Norwegians? **67**

Epic Explorers **77**

Off-the-Shelf Monarchy............**82**

The Sami: People of
Four Nations **87**

Boat Builders and Engineers.... **93**

An Outdoor Life **101**

Sporting Passions **107**

Fishing: Sport and
Sustenance **112**

The Traditional Arts **117**

Tradition, not Haute Culture ..**123**

Why Does Everything
Cost So Much?................**130**

Travel Tips

Transport 348

Accommodation 354

Eating Out 360

Activities 363

A–Z 370

Language 377

Further Reading 378

♦ **Full Travel Tips index
is on page 347**

Information panels

A Viking Burial 27

The Great Exodus 44

The Heroes of Telemark 54

Norway and its Neighbours 59

Black Gold 97

The Great Ski-Jump 105

Morgedal and Telemark
    Revival. 108

Nobel's Peace Prize 160

Røros and the Old
    Copper Country 188

A Country Afloat 284

Stiklestad 297

Insight on ...

Folklore: Sagas and Folktales 80

Nature's Larder .128

Bio-diversity and Sustainability . .242

Land of the Midnight Sun 310

Places

Introduction 141

Oslo, Nordic City of Light 147

Around Oslo and its Fjord 169

The Heart of Norway 181

Peak and Plateau 193

Telemark and the South 203

Fjords 215

Rogaland 217

Stavanger 225

Hordaland. 233

Bergen 247

The Most Beautiful Voyage 261

From Sogn to Nordfjord 267

Møre and Romsdal 277

Trondheim. 291

North, into the Arctic 301

The Far North .315

Svalbard 337

THE BEST OF NORWAY

Stunning mountains, fabulous fjords, scenic coastal landscapes and thriving urban pockets in between make Norway a haven for those who enjoy both city life and the great outdoors. Here are some tips for seeking out the highlights.

BEST VIEWS

- **From Holmenkollen in Oslo** The classic old ski jump is being replaced in time for the Nordic Skiing World Championships in 2011, but the panoramic view over the city and fjord won't change. *See pages 105, 161.*
- **Kongens Utsikt** Literally "The King's View," it offers a unique vista over the Tyrifjord west of Oslo and the rolling farmland around it, towards the mountains to the west. *See page 171.*
- **From the Stalheim Hotell, Stalhei** You may feel moved to burst into song gazing at this symphony of mountains, valley and fjord. It's classic Norwegian scenery. *See page 241.*

- **From Reine, Lofoten** This old fishing village is nestled at the foot of mountains that shoot straight up from the sea. Sit out with a cold beer and a plate of codfish tongues (a local delicacy). *See page 317.*
- **From Verdens Ende, Tjøme** The tip of an island south of Oslo featuring barren rocks that slope down to the fjord. *See page 176.*
- **From the deck of a Hurtigrute ship** Just about anywhere along the coast from Bergen to Kirkenes, especially when the Midnight Sun is shining. *See page 261.*

BEST VALLEYS

- **Østerdalen** This long, slanting valley cuts dramatically through the mountains, with forests on either side and patches of farmland on the valley floor. *See page 185.*
- **Norangsdalen** This wild valley not far from Geiranger is best experienced by driving from Hellesylt up to Øye. There you'll find a car ferry over the fjord, from which there are outstanding views. *See page 280.*
- **Valdres** Midway between Oslo and Bergen lies Valdres, a valley of great contrasts, with fertile cultivated land, shiny lakes, wilderness and the high peaks of Jotunheimen. *See page 196.*

- **Romsdalen** Another Norwegian classic, the heart of which runs south from Åndalsnes to Dombås. Romsdalen feeds into the much larger and more famous Gudbrandsdalen. *See page 280.*

ABOVE: Hurtigrute ship views. **LEFT:** Holmenkollen sculpture. **BELOW:** on top of the world at Romsdalen.

BEST GEOGRAPHICAL POINTS OF INTEREST

- **Lindesnes Light-house** Perched on Norway's southernmost point, this classic old lighthouse is open to visitors and offers a wonderful walk alongside crashing waves from the North Sea. Queen Sonja brought her royal guests here for her 70th birthday in 2007. *See page 205.*
- **Stadlandet-Vestkapp** This western landmark offers windswept promontories with stunning scenery, long feared by mariners. Nearby is the coastal town of Selje with a spa hotel and the ruins of an ancient cloister. The West Cape is probably one of Norway's most underrated destinations. *See page 272.*
- **North Cape** Some complain that this

famous spot, at the top of the country, has been spoiled by high entrance fees and commercialisation. It remains a tourist magnet, especially when the Midnight Sun is shining. *See page 328.*
- **Grense Jakobselv** This unusual spot in the Far North stands at Norway's easternmost point, just over the border from Russia. There's a lonely stone church here, and views to the Barents Sea, all a short drive from Kirkenes. *See page 332.*
- **Galhøpiggen** Trails lead up to Norway's highest peak, but you'd better be in good shape to make the hike. Most Norwegians make the pilgrimage at least once. *See page 195.*

BEST MUSEUMS

- **The Petroleum Museum, Stavanger** Also known as "the oil museum", here is a modern, hands-on account of Norway's most important industry. *See page 227.*
- **Cannery Museum, Stavanger** Located in an old sardine canning factory, this intimate museum offers insight into what used to be the area's main industry. *See page 227.*
- **Norwegian Folk Museum, Oslo** A large, open-air museum of old, mostly wooden houses from all over the country, plus an original stave church and even an Oslo apartment building. *See page 162.*
- **Munch Museum, Oslo** Housing the vast collection of paintings that Norwegian artist Edvard Munch left to the city of Oslo. *See page 155.*
- **National Gallery, Oslo** If you don't

have time to drive around the country, stop here to see spectacular landscapes. There's also a room devoted to Edvard Munch. *See page 152.*
- **Maihaugen** Another open-air museum, in the former Olympic town of Lillehammer, with wonderful collections of handicraft and folk art. *See page 183.*
- **Lillehammer Art Museum** The building of this gem of a museum was designed by Snøhetta, the architectural firm who won praise for its library in Alexandria, Egypt. *See page 184.*
- **Norsk Skogmuseum (Forestry)** This museum in Elverum showcases Norway's timber industry and the history of hunting, fishing and trapping. *See page 186.*
- **Ringve Museum, Trondheim** The former estate of a Norwegian naval hero is now devoted to the history of music and musical instruments. *See page 295.*

ABOVE: the North Cape, still a surefire crowd-puller. **ABOVE RIGHT:** memorabilia on display at Stavanger's Cannery Museum. **RIGHT:** Munch's portrait of his sister Inger (1892) hangs in Oslo's National Gallery.

BEST DRIVES

●**Atlanterhavsvei**
Short but stunningly
sweet, this drive
offers an unforget-
table coastal link be-
tween the west coast
cities of Kristiansund
and Molde. There's a
great place to stay
along the way, on an
island off the coast
called Håholmen. *See
page 282.*

●**Fredrikstad out to
Hvaler** Another road
built right on the wa-
ter that connects a se-
ries of popular islands
off southern Norway
near the Swedish bor-
der. Drive all the way
out to Skjærhalden,
where it ends. *See
page 174.*

●**Valdresflya** Closed in
winter, this narrow
road (Highway 51)
runs north from
Fagernes over the
mountains to the his-
toric village of Lom,
famed for its stave
church and gourmet
food. You'll pass

some of Norway's
most famous mountain
trailheads, and there
are opportunities for
hikes along the way.
See page 197.

●**Trollstigen** Famed for
its hairpin bends, this
road remains a thriller
as it runs down a steep
mountain in the heart
of the beautiful county
of Møre og Romsdal.
See page 280.

●**Most highways in
Finnmark, Northern
Norway** Nothing quite
matches the wide-
open, often barren
landscapes of this area
far north of the Arctic
Circle. Watch out for
reindeer herds. *See
page 324.*

●**Highway 55 over
Sognefjell** A classic,
from Lom to the
Sognefjord. The high
country sprawls on
either side of this fa-
mous route over the
mountains from Gud-
brandsdalen to the sea.
See pages 189, 267.

ABOVE: Akershus Fortress, Oslo. **BELOW:** hair-raising
bends are the trademark of Tollstigen's mountain
roads. **BELOW RIGHT:** a Viking ship figurehead from
Oseberg, on display at the Viking Ship Museum.

BEST HISTORIC SIGHTS

●**Akershus Fortress &
Castle, Oslo** The
pride of Norway's
capital, perched on a
bluff overlooking the
harbour and fjord, this
thousand-year-old
complex is an absolute
must. *See page 148.*

●**Viking Ship, Oslo**
No visit to Norway is
complete without a
visit to these original
Viking Ships, housed
in a museum on the
Bygdøy Peninsula.
See page 162.

●**Oscarsborg Fortress,
off Drøbak** This his-
toric military complex
on an island in the
Oslo Fjord, famed for
firing the shots that
sunk a German battle-
ship in 1940, now
welcomes visitors
for overnight stays,
dinner, and cultural
events. *See
page 172.*

●**The Fortress at
Halden** Spread over
the hillside above the
town, the fortress
played a critical role
during border
skirmishes with the
Swedes. Great views,
and lots of cultural
goings-on all summer.
See page 174.

●**Røros** This perfectly
preserved old mining
town east of Trond-
heim is a UN World
Heritage Site. The
mines are open for
tours. *See page 188.*

●**Håkonshall, Bergen**
Norway's royal fam-
ily still holds events
at this legendary spot
on Bergen's water-
front, a major stop on
a visit to the old
Hanseatic capital. *See
page 250.*

●**Nidarosdomen,
Trondheim.** Nidaros
is the Nordic area's
best example of
a medieval
cathedral.
Present-day
pilgrims can still
follow the an-
cient path leading
from Oslo to Trond-
heim. *See page 291.*

BEST PLACES TO STAY

- **Engø Gård, Tjøme**
Rated as one of the best places to dine in Norway, this former farm and *pensjonat* on an island south of Oslo also offers elegant yet relaxed lodging. The swimming pool is located inside a glass pavilion, and it's just a short walk to the sea. Pricey but memorable. *See page 176.*

- **Kongsvold Fjellstue**
This historic lodge in the mighty Dovre Mountains was originally geared for royalty on their way from Oslo to Trondheim. Good accommodation is enhanced by fine dining, and trailheads lead off in several directions. *See page 190.*

- **Holmenkollen Park Hotell, Oslo** This old timber lodge right out of a fairy tale offers great views over the city, fjord and forests, and now has a spa facility in addition to elegant dining. *See page 356.*

- **Henningsvær Bryggehotel, Lofoten** Built on the water, you can't get much closer to the heart of a famous old fishing village than this. *See pages 262, 315.*

BEST MEALS

- **Hallingstuene, Geilo** A rose-painted haven of excellent Norwegian food in the heart of this mountain town, on Highway 7 near the gateway to the Hardanger Plateau. *See page 193.*

- **Fossheim Turisthotell, Lom** Launched to local acclaim by Norwegian chef Arne Brimi, this relatively modest hotel's dining room makes clear the importance of showcasing Norway's own natural ingredients in gourmet cooking. *See page 198.*

- **Bagatelle, Oslo** Considered by many to be the best restaurant in Norway, this super classy establishment has prices to match. *See page 361.*

- **Solsiden, Oslo** It's hard to beat this busy, casual summertime restaurant when it comes to Norwegian seafood, and you'd be hard pressed to get any closer to waterfront dining. *See page 361.*

ABOVE: seafood canapés. **LEFT:** the Kongsvold Fjellstue Hotel. **BELOW:** when driving, watch out for moose and other wildlife.

MONEY-SAVING TIPS

Norway is a notoriously expensive country, and visitors need to be mentally, as well as financially, prepared. Try to avoid spoiling your visit by comparing the prices of everything to those back home. There are also a few things that may ease the strain on your credit cards:

Hotel passes Hotel rates in Norway can actually be lower than in other countries, especially in the summer when the seminar- and conference-goers go on holiday. Several local chains like Rica and Thon also offer discounts or even free nights within their chain if you buy a pass.

City passes Most of Norway's major cities offer passes that give the holder access to all public tranport and many museums, as well as discounts on a wide range of goods and services. They can be pricey though, so before buying one do your own calculations to ensure you can make it pay off.

Taxis Single-fare public transport tickets are expensive, so four people sharing a taxi can save money on short hops. Be careful, though, as taxi rates jump in the evening, and on weekends and holidays.

Boat service There won't be a tourist guide on board, but commuter ferries are a cheap way of visiting the seaside cities.

NORTHERN CONTRASTS

Norway offers the visitor a beguiling mix of tradition and modern convenience, spectacular nature and city delights

The most accurate observation made about Norway is that it is a land of contrasts: the landscape is both beautiful and brutal, hospitable and hostile; barren rock submits to soft fertile plains, majestic mountains tower above mysterious fjords; harsh winters are relieved by often glorious summers; and long polar nights give way to the radiant midnight sun. One of the oldest civilisations in Europe has become one of its youngest nations. The Norwegians themselves have adapted rather quickly. The rapacious Vikings have turned into global peacemakers. It is a country where Grieg and Ibsen compete with Idol and Disney; where environmental concern challenges over-consumption. Norway has urban excitement and rural tranquillity: shopping malls and Mercedes rub shoulders with compass and rucksack; high technology parallels steadfast tradition.

A thriving offshore oil industry has brought prosperity, and as a consequence, social habits are changing rapidly, though, in a society where the divorce rate is high and co-habitation the norm, the home and family still remain important. Politically, democracy and debate pervade all levels of society, and a blend of national pride and an engaged electorate continue to ensure political independence. Murray's *Handbook for Travellers in Norway* described the Norwegians in 1874 thus: "Great patriotism and hospitality are two of the leading characteristics of the Norwegians; they are often cold and reserved, and combine great simplicity of manner with firmness and kindness. 'Deeds, not words' is their motto." – 125 years later, little has changed.

But where does all this place the visitor?

Most people are pleasantly surprised when they visit Norway. For a start, the people are friendlier and far more open than the stereotypical Scandinavian image would have us believe; and second, the scenery is even more breathtaking in reality than any guidebook could ever hope to inspire. Although the country is vast – it takes as long to fly from Oslo to northern Norway as it does to Rome – the main town centres are more than manageable with good public transport and everywhere within walking distance anyway. Add to this the fact that the infrastructure, communications and services are efficient, and that it is safe to go out at night, and you have all the ingredients for a pleasant stay.

As for prices, it all depends on the reason for your visit and how you spend your money. Surveys persistently place Oslo among the top 10 most expensive cities in the world, but the statistics tend rather to reflect the spending habits of businessmen with expense accounts than those of the selective tourist. ❑

PRECEDING PAGES: winter on the fjord; waiting for confirmation in Kautokeino.
LEFT: Norwegian fjords provide breathtaking views.

Decisive Dates

ICE AGE TO BRONZE AGE

10,000 years ago The first people appear in the territory of what is now Norway, following the retreat of the great inland ice sheets. They hunt reindeer and other prey as they gradually spread northwards.

5,000–6,000 years ago First agricultural settlements appear around Oslofjord.

1500–500 BC Agricultural settlements develop in southern Norway, while people in the north continue hunting.

ROMAN AGE

AD 0–400 Burial sites indicate links with the civilised countries to the south – utensils of bronze and glass have been discovered. Latin-based runic letters appear for the first time.

(The migrations of AD 400–550, including to coastal areas in the west, herald a restless period. Farmers are pushed into marginal areas. Forts have been found on Lake Mjøsa.)

AD 793 Norwegian Vikings loot the English monastery of Lindisfarne. They raid (or trade with) and colonise parts of west and southwest Europe. Vikings settle in the Orkneys, the Shetlands, the Hebrides, and on the Isle of Man (remaining there until 1405).

VIKING AGE

AD 800–1030 Our knowledge of this period is largely based on archaeological remains. Although written down some time later, the Norse sagas reveal that the Viking Age was the richest of all the early periods in Norway.

840 Vikings found Dublin, which remains under Nordic rule until 1171.

844 Dublin's Norwegian king exchanges envoys with Emir Abderrhaman II, the Moorish king in Spain.

861 Vikings sack Paris.

866 Vikings control most of England.

872 Battle at Hafrsfjord near Stavanger. King Harald Fairhair strengthens his position as ruler of large areas of the country.

1001 The sagas relate that it was Leiv Eiriksson who discovered Vinland (America).

1028 King Canute of Denmark invades Norway. King Olav flees, but later regains control.

1030 Battle of Stiklestad. Christianity arrives through trading contacts with the rest of Europe. This culminates with three missionary kings, Håkon the Good, Olaf Trygvasson and Olaf the Stout, who becomes St Olav following his death at the Battle of Stiklestad.

1050 Harald Hardråde founds Oslo.

1066 King Harald Hardråde is defeated at the Battle of Stamford Bridge, in England, bringing the Viking Age to an end.

MIDDLE AGES

1100 The first bishoprics appear, among them the see of Nidaros (Trondheim) in 1152.

1130 Start of civil wars which last until 1227. This period was also the start of the High Middle Ages. It was a period of population growth, consolidation within the Church and the development of towns. The monarchy dominates both Church and nobility. Farmers change from being freeholders to tenants.

1241 Saga writer Snorri Sturluson is put to death by the King of Norway's men.

1299–1319 Oslo becomes the capital during the reign of King Håkon V.

1319–43 Inter-Scandinavian royal marriages produce joint Norwegian-Swedish monarchy, later to include Denmark.

1349 Onslaught of the Black Death. Population (Oslo: 3,000; Bergen: 7,000; Trondheim: 4,000) reduced by 50 percent. Towards the end of the Middle Ages state revenues are inadequate to finance the desired expansion of the Crown and state. The king and the nobility seek revenues from neighbouring lands, leading to the growth of the political unions.

1380 Olav, son of Håkon VI (1340–80) becomes King of Denmark and Norway.

Trinity Sunday 1397 The union of the three crowns is formalised in the Swedish town of Kalmar.

1450 Union with Denmark set up by treaty.

UNION WITH DENMARK

1536 Norway ceases to be independent. Norway's Council of the Realm is disbanded. Danish noblemen start to take over the running of Norway.

1537 The Reformation of the Norwegian church is enforced by royal (Danish) decree. From the early 1600s Lutheranism is the sole creed of Norway.

1624 Oslo burns to the ground.

1645 The Danish king surrenders Jemtland and Herjedalen to Sweden. The fief of Trondheim is surrendered in 1658 (but is regained in 1660).

1660 Fredrik III is acclaimed heir to the throne by an assembly of the States General in Copenhagen and assigned the task of giving the kingdoms a new constitution.

1662 Town privileges are introduced to concentrate wealth from the timber trade in the hands of urban, middle-class merchants.

1807–14 Napoleonic Wars. Denmark/Norway ally with France, and the resulting blockade isolates Norway. Shipping and timber exports collapse, and famine and hunger spread.

INDEPENDENCE AND NEW UNION

January 1814 Secession from Denmark.

17 May 1814 The new Norwegian constitution is formally adopted at Eidsvoll.

10 October 1814 Treaty of Kiel places Norway in a union with Sweden.

1825 The great exodus to the USA begins.

1854 The first railway line is laid.

1872 The first trade union is formed.

1884 Norway's first political parties are set up.

August 1905 National referendum leads to the end of the union with Sweden.

NORWEGIAN INDEPENDENCE

18 November 1905 The Storting (Parliament) votes unanimously for Prince Carl of Denmark to become elected as King (Haakon VII) of Norway.

1913 Universal suffrage is granted to women.

1920 Norway joins the League of Nations. After

World War I, Norway retains its claim on Spitsbergen.

1939 Norway proclaims neutrality in World War II.

9 April 1940 German forces invade Norway.

7 June 1945 King Haakon returns from exile. Rise of the social-welfare state.

1957 King Haakon VII dies. Olav V is crowned.

1960s Oil exploration in the North Sea begins.

1972 Norway votes against EU membership.

1991 King Olav V dies. King Harald V is crowned.

1993 Norway brokers Israeli/Palestinian peace.

1994 Norway declines again to join the EU. The Winter Olympics are held in Lillehammer.

1997 Christian Democrat Kjell Magne Bondevikis is elected prime minister to head a centre-right coalition.

2000 Oslo celebrates its 1,000-year anniversary. Bergen is named European City of Culture 2000.

2001 Norway is elected to serve on the United Nations Security Council. Crown Prince Haakon controversially marries an unwed mother with a partying past.

2002 Explorer Thor Heyerdahl dies.

2004 Edvard Munch's *The Scream* is stolen in broad daylight from the Munch Museum, Oslo.

2005 Center-left coalition wins national election and gains majority in Parliament.

2006 Center-left government led by prime minister Jens Stoltenberg of the Labour Party takes office. Munch's paintings *The Scream* and *Madonna* are recovered. ❑

PRECEDING PAGES: Viking gold.

LEFT: the Stiklestad open-air play.

RIGHT: 1905, Danish Prince Carl, carrying his son, arrives in Norway to become King Haakon III.

BEGINNINGS

For two centuries the Vikings terrorised large parts of Europe, travelling far and wide in search of land, wealth and, when it suited them, trade

L ife in Norway has been influenced to an extraordinary degree by the terrain and the weather. The original inhabitants hugged the coastal areas which, warmed by the Gulf Stream, made life more bearable. With the gradual recession of the last Ice Age about 12,000 years ago, the hunters and fishermen inched northwards but again only along the coast because the interior remained inhospitable.

The thaw was followed by mild weather, unknown before or since. Around 500 BC, however, just as iron was beginning to replace bronze and the Athenians were getting ready to build the Parthenon, the climate inexplicably deteriorated. The impact of suddenly colder, wetter weather was dramatic.

Taking a step back

During the preceding Bronze Age considerable progress had been made in weapons, ornaments and utensils made out of metal imported from Britain and continental Europe. Contemporary rock drawings show boats that were capable of carrying 30 men (although not yet with sails), warriors on horseback and either two- or four-wheeled carts drawn by horses or oxen. These developments were thrown into reverse by the climate change and a large part of the population perished.

Survival in the new Ice Age demanded cultural adjustments. Men, who until then had usually worn a kind of belted cloak, pulled on underwear and trousers. Instead of a semi-nomadic existence, all had to settle on farms in order to secure winter fodder and shelter livestock, which had previously grazed outside all year round. People and animals occupied either end of the same house, an unhygienic but necessary form of early central heating.

In common with most of Europe, Norway was again struck by the weather in the 14th century. The economic decline that followed

was exacerbated terribly by the Black Death. The resulting acute shortage of labour led to the collapse of the aristocratic estates, demoting the owners to peasantry. The number of knights in Norway dropped from 270 to 60.

But who were these people? The recorded history of Norway begins remarkably late, only

in about AD 800, and the archaeological pointers towards specific events in earlier times are comparatively scanty. The ancient world had curious opinions about the ancient northerners: one, advanced by Pomponius Mela, was that, living on birds' eggs, the people had hoofed feet, and ears so large that they covered their bodies, thereby dispensing with the need for any clothing.

Another, Greek in origin and containing an element of truth, had the territory populated by Hyperboreans, a jolly race who lived in forests and sang and danced their way to incredible longevity. When eventually tired of life, they feasted, bedecked themselves with flowers and

LEFT: discovered in 1880, the Gokstad ship is now in the *Vikingskipshuset* (Viking Ship Museum), Oslo.
RIGHT: Odin, king of the Norse gods.

threw themselves off cliffs. Norwegians continue to live longer than practically anyone else in Europe. Furthermore, they remain energetic to the end. It is one thing for a foreigner struggling on skis to be overtaken by a blasé six-year-old, quite another if the speed demon turns out to be a venerable grandmother.

Lieutenant W.H. Breton, a 19th-century tourist, was amazed by reports of a man who married at 113 and lasted until he was 146. Another visitor commented on four peasants who were the principal dancers at an entertainment laid on for King Christian VI: all of them were well over 100. One Derwent Conway, in

about 1820, asked a fit 74-year-old in Telemark for the secret of his robust health. Pouring himself a fifth glass of home-made corn brandy, he replied that it was due to this excellent drink.

New blood

That the original inhabitants of Norway received infusions of new blood, probably from the east, is indicated by artefacts which have given their name to their respective cultures: Funnel-Beaker, Battle-Axe and Boat-Axe peoples. Changing burial practices are another reliable sign of influential immigration.

It was once thought that the Sami (Lapps of Finnmark) were the original inhabitants. Being Mongoloid and short of stature, they are very different from the familiar Scandinavian stereotype. However, it seems theirs was a relatively recent migration from Siberia, long after European types had moved in. The great majority of Norwegians are directly descended from the people who were occupying their territory long before 3000 BC, the date customarily taken as the beginning of Western civilisation.

Like a Nordic Rip van Winkle, Norway slept through the millennium in which Greece and then Rome flourished, although the runic alphabet did appear around the 3rd century AD. It was Latin in origin but dispensed with the curved Latin letters because, perhaps, straight lines were easier to cut into wood, stone and metal, as runic inscriptions invariably were.

Norway was ignored by the civilised world until the late 8th century, by which time the Muslim tide had been turned back and Charlemagne was building his empire. Nowhere in Pliny the Elder, Tacitus, Ptolemy or any of the celebrated descriptions of the then known world are the Norwegian people mentioned by name. Even the term "Scandinavia" is a misreading of a text by Pliny, who referred to the unknown land beyond Jutland as *Scatinavia*.

Development in secret

Foreign ignorance, however, did not mean that nothing was happening locally. The evolution of ship design was the most potent of these hidden developments. Although the Phoenicians had undertaken stupendous voyages very much earlier, they routinely stayed within sight of land. The Norwegians were working on vessels capable of crossing oceans.

The Gokstad ship, found in a burial mound near Sandefjord in 1880, was a masterpiece. Made out of oak planks, it was 25 metres (82 ft) long and 5 metres (16 ft) wide. It had a mast and 16 pairs of oars. The crew handled one oar each which left enough room for an equal number of marines. The *styrbord* or rudder, which hung on the right (hence, starboard) side, could be raised for fast beaching. A modern replica crossed the Atlantic in just four weeks. These ships represented a menacing mobility, and once the Norwegians had cause to take their unsuspecting neighbours to the south by surprise, they were able to do so with stunning efficiency.

The Norwegians introduced themselves to

the rest of the world with deceptive tranquillity. The *Anglo-Saxon Chronicle* of 787 contains the laconic entry: "In this year King Breohtric married King Offa's daughter Eadburge. And in his days came the first three ships of the Northmen from Hereoalande" (known today as Hordaland, on Norway's west coast).

The Vikings appear

In 793 the Vikings opened their account in earnest by plundering the monastery of Lindisfarne off the northeast coast of England near the

> ### BAD NEIGHBOURS
>
> In Arthurian romances the Vikings were described as being "wild and savage and had not in them the love of God nor their neighbours."

among their victims in the 9th and 10th centuries that it was synonymous with the term "pirate" or "sea robber". This is further confused by the tendency in English chronicles to call all Vikings "Danes", while many were actually "Northmen", "Norsemen" or, in present terminology, Norwegians. In contrast, in continental records Norwegians take all the credit (or blame) for what was usually the work of Danes. Swedish Vikings were busy too, but they tended to direct their attentions overland via Russia.

Scottish border, one of the great sanctuaries of the western Christian church. The next year they attacked the monastery of Jarrow further down the coast in Northumbria, and the year after that they arrived in South Wales and in Ireland with more than 100 ships. They were driven off by King Maredudd and that, together with the resistance they had encountered in England, persuaded them, for a period of 40 years, to turn their attention to softer targets in Ireland.

Various opinions prevail about the origin of the name "Viking", but there was no doubt

LEFT: early sailing equipment.
ABOVE: a set of Viking keys.

Proper outside investigation into the geography and demography of Norway began with King Alfred the Great of England, who had every reason to wonder about people who had become painful tormentors. He was enlightened by Ottar, a Norwegian chieftain from Hålogaland, at the same time as Alfred was waging war with other Viking chieftains. Ottar told the king that Norway was a very long and narrow country, full of rocks and mountains. The only places that could be pastured or ploughed were those close to the sea; the inhabitants kept sheep and swine and bred tame deer, which they called reindeer.

In reality, the Vikings were land-hungry

adventurers for whom rich and undefended coastal abbeys were irresistible business opportunities. They had no scruples about violating their supposed sacrosanctity; on the contrary, they saw Christianity as a heretical threat to their own heathen beliefs.

Truculent population

While Christians put their faith in the sign of the cross, the Vikings trusted the hammer of Thor the Thunderer, defender of heaven against giants, men against monsters, and themselves from the "Followers of the White Cross", as they called Christians. Small Viking raiding

parties faced with a large and truculent population found that a reputation for uncompromising destruction and cruelty served their purposes well, encouraging the enemy to flee rather than put up a fight. Viking victory celebrations – "[a] wild outburst of triumphant rejoicing" – included the proven intimidatory tactic of transfixing captured children with spears and drinking out of the skulls of fallen enemies.

The Vikings also have apologists who prefer to concentrate on their apparent managerial talents in occupied territory and an artistic streak manifested in the finely worked ornaments recovered from excavated ships. In the early

18th century, Baron de Montesquieu praised them as an army of free men in an age when armies were usually press-ganged.

The historian Snorri Sturluson is disarmingly indifferent to matters which others might consider to be grave flaws in their heroes. The royal pretender Harald Gille is summarised as "friendly, jovial, playful, unassuming, generous, accommodating and easily led". All this glosses over the fact, which Sturluson himself recounts, that he blinded and castrated a rival, hanged a bishop and died drunk in the arms of his mistress with his wife standing by.

The reason sometimes given for the sudden explosion of Viking activity abroad is that it was the result of another explosion, that of population because of uniform polygamy. Overpopulation was certainly the case in western Norway where agricultural land was so scarce, but the problem was less acute elsewhere.

Nevertheless, all sons, legitimate and otherwise, were entitled to equal shares of their father's inheritance, and as political power and social standing were invested in property, the aristocracy especially were reluctant to carve land up into smaller and smaller parcels. The surfeit of sons was thus encouraged to seek a fortune abroad.

The profits of piracy

Women and children often accompanied the men but they were usually parked in fortified camps while the men "harried". Occasionally they did join in and one of them – an Amazon who rose to command her own army in Ireland – was acclaimed as the fearsome Red Maiden.

When the Vikings came across unoccupied land or, as in the Orkneys, rendered it so by annihilating the natives, they were keen to settle it. If that proved to be impractical, a raid might at least produce some slaves who could either be sold or, increasingly, put to good use at home. When piracy could not be made to pay, however, the Vikings were willing to engage in conventional trade.

Profits from piracy and trade generated in Norway the nucleus of a merchant class which complemented the traditional structure of aristocratic earls, free men and thralls (or slaves). The pecking order was reflected in western Norway by *wergild*, a system which stipulated the compensation due in the event of murder. A slave was worth half the value of an ordinary peasant and a quarter of that of a land owner, who in turn was worth only a quarter of a chieftain and one-eighth of a king.

Slaves must have been worked hard because there was a provision in law which absolved owners of guilt if a slave died through exhaustion or ill-treatment. Owners were permitted, when slaves died, to throw their children into an open grave to die from exposure. They were obliged, however, to step in and rescue the last one left alive.

Some slaves, such as captured craftsmen, were prized, as were young women with whom masters could replenish or increase the labour pool. Unlike the custom in nearby Sweden, the child of the union between a Norwegian master and slave woman remained a slave.

Viking women made an impression abroad in a way that hints at the emancipated attitudes ascribed to them in the 20th century, albeit a reputation bestowed less frequently on Norwegian women than on the other Scandinavians. In 844 a Norwegian king ruling in Dublin exchanged envoys with Emir Abderrhaman II, the Moorish leader in Spain. Alghazal, a poet, was appointed to the court of the King of the Pagans and became enchanted by the queen. While keen to further their acquaintance, he was alarmed at the prospect of the king finding out.

The queen reassured him that "it is not customary with us to be jealous. Our women stay with their husbands only as long as they please, and leave them whenever they choose." She seems not to have added that Viking husbands reciprocated in kind.

VIKINGS ABROAD

The Viking kingdom on the Isle of Man lasted until 1263, when it was sold to Alexander III of Scotland along with the Western Isles.

Viking men traded wives, or even gave them away to friends, if they bored or displeased them.

Protection money

The renewed Viking campaigns were launched from the west coast of Norway, from strongholds on the Scottish islands or from the Norwegian kingdom in Ireland, centred on a castle built in Dublin in 841 by Torgisl. The Vikings were overlords rather than settlers in Ireland, although some intermarried. Norway might still have overseas territories today if a Danish king, as we shall see, had not mortgaged the Orkney and Shetland Isles to raise money for his daughter's dowry.

LEFT: a confrontation from the *Frithiof Saga* by E. Tégnér, illustrated by Knut Ekwall.
ABOVE: petroglyphs at Skjeberg, south of Oslo.

The Viking raids into Europe were conducted like annual summer holidays, and year after year the fleets grew larger. An alarmed Charlemagne threw up military posts along his northern borders to guard against them. The defence of Paris against the Vikings was led by another King Charles, known as Charles the Bald. The city was attacked in 857 and sacked in 861. Charles offered one lot of Vikings 1,360 kg (3,000 lb) of silver to go and fight some of their compatriots instead of him. In 885, however, both were back and it cost a further 318 kg (700 lb) of silver to get rid of them.

The most enduring Viking presence in France was in Normandy which, of course, was named after them. Over the years the Viking armies on the continent grew to massive proportions and were not finally driven off until 891, by the German emperor Arnulf.

Although geographical proximity recommended the British Isles, Vikings were active wherever the pickings looked good. At one point they laid siege to Lisbon and they penetrated the Mediterranean as far as Constantinople. Nor did they restrict their territorial ambitions to continental Europe. Vikings sailed west to Iceland, Greenland and eventually to the American continent. As many as 20,000

THE VIKINGS IN BRITAIN

The Vikings attacked the British Isles in earnest from 834. The most spectacular effort was in 851 when they took 350 ships up the Thames, stopping off to capture Canterbury before storming London, only to be finally turned back by Ethelwulf at the battle of Aclea. By 866 most of England was under their control with only Wessex, ruled by Alfred the Great, staying independent. After the initial success of a winter campaign in 878, they were defeated by Alfred, but continued to rule large parts of England and a kingdom based in York. All further territorial ambitions were curtailed with the arrival of William the Conqueror in 1066.

Norwegians emigrated to Iceland; by the latter half of the 10th century there were no fewer than 39 petty kingdoms established there.

This surging mixture of colonialism, plunder, trade and adventurism lasted for two centuries between the fall of the western Roman Empire and the First Crusade, and it nearly brought about the overthrow of Christianity in Europe (as the Muslims had been close to doing earlier). The benefits to those left at home were considerable. The period produced unprecedented wealth. ❏

ABOVE: a detail from a drawing by Halvfdan Egedins in Snorri Sturluson's *Sagas of the Norse Kings*.

A Viking Burial

In the year AD 921, a peripatetic Arab named Ahmad bin Fudlan came across Vikings who had settled on the banks of the Volga River. They were trading with Constantinople: furs and slaves for gold, silver ornaments and silks. A chieftain died while he was with them, and his account of the funeral is an antidote to some of the romantic nonsense that has been written about the Vikings.

When the chieftain died, Ahmad reported, his maidservants were asked: "Who will die with him?" The first to volunteer was immediately put under guard in case she changed her mind, not that she gave any indication of wishing to do so.

The elaborate formalities began with the division of the chieftain's estate into three equal parts. One went to his family, the second to cover the cost of the funeral, and the last on drink. The boat in which the chieftain was to be despatched was drawn out of the water and decorated with quilts and cushions. Ahmad then met "the angel of death"; he described her as "dusky, hale, strongly built and austere". Austere she might well have been, for it was her function eventually to kill the carousing maidservant.

The chieftain's body was removed from the temporary grave where it had lain for 10 days. Ahmad had a good look at it. "I saw that he had gone black, because of the cold", he said; but otherwise "the corpse had in no way altered." The body was dressed in finery and propped up on cushions in a tent erected on the boat.

"They now brought liquor, fruit, and herbs and put them by him, then they brought bread, meat, and onions, and threw them down in front of him. They brought a dog, cut it in half, and threw it into the boat, then brought all his weapons, and put them by his side. After that they took two beasts of burden, drove them along until they sweated, then cut them up with swords and threw their flesh into the boat. The girl who was to be killed, meanwhile, was going up and down, entering one tent after another, and one man after another had intercourse with her. Each one said to her, 'Tell your master that I only do this for love of him.'" The girl was later taken to the boat, where she handed over her bracelets and anklets to the "angel of death" and the two girls who had been guarding her. They were joined by men carrying shields and pieces of wood.

Farewell drinks and songs followed until, Ahmad wrote, "I saw that she had become bewildered and wished to enter the tent."

The old woman followed her into the tent, whereupon "the men began beating the shields with the pieces of wood so that the sound of her screams should not be heard. Six men then entered the tent, and all of them had intercourse with her. They then made her lie down by the side of her dead master, and two took hold of her hands and two her feet. The "angel of death" put a rope done into a noose round her neck, and gave it to two men to pull. She came forward with a large, broad-bladed knife and began thrusting it in and out between

the girl's ribs in place after place, while the two men strangled her until she died."

Walking backwards, the next of kin then went naked to the boat and lit kindling which had been placed beneath it. "At this moment, an awe-inspiring gale got up, so that the flames of the fire grew stronger." One of the Vikings chose to compare the funeral arrangements with what he had heard about Islamic rites. "You Arabs are stupid," he remarked to Ahmad, "because you take your dearest and most honourable men and cast them into the dust, so that creeping things and worms eat them. We burn them with fire in a twinkling and they enter Paradise the very same hour." Then, according to Ahmad bin Fudlan, "he laughed heartily." ❏

RIGHT: a romantic view of a Viking (1828).

KINGS AND CHRISTIANITY

Constant battles for the throne and the arrival of Christianity in a stubbornly pagan land were the unlikely precursors to Norway's "Period of Greatness"

With Snorri Sturluson, Norwegian history begins to speak for itself instead of relying on outsiders who observed or passed on fantastic tales about the land and its people. Sturluson's epic *Heimskringla (Sagas of the Norse Kings)* is a work of genius.

He visited Norway only twice, but working on his remote saga island of Iceland he compiled an almost inconceivable mass of information beginning in prehistory and continuing until 1177 (two years before he was born), by which time the Vikings had been tamed, Christianity had taken hold in Norway and the country had endured a century of civil war.

Amusing tale

Although Sturluson was himself a foreigner, he drew on the oral history of the skalds at the courts of the Norwegian kings. He was obviously a discriminating historian, although never one to exclude an amusing tale because he did not believe it: "It is the way of skalds, of course, to give most praise to him for whom they composed, but no one would dare tell the king himself such deeds of his as all listeners and the king himself knew to be lies and loose talk; that would be mockery, but not praise."

There are no fewer than 2,000 names of persons and places in his saga and he gives his readers a vivid sense of what was happening, as it were, at home. But Sturluson's unlucky recompense was to be put to death by the King of Norway's men in 1241.

Sturluson introduces the Norwegian royal line in the person of Halvdan the Black, a king troubled by his inability to dream. He consulted Torleiv the Wise, who said he had suffered from the same complaint and had cured it by sleeping in a pigsty. The king followed his example "and then it always happened that he dreamed."

More prosaically, Halvdan was descended from the Swedish Ynglinger family who ruled in Uppsala. His branch had moved to Norway

about a century before the Viking period, when the concept of Norway as an entity existed only in the term *Norovegr*, or North Way, the coastal stretch from Vestfold to Hålogaland.

A king dreaming in a pigsty might seem to belong to mythology rather than history, but he was real enough. The Oseberg ship unearthed in

Vestfold in 1904 proved to be that in which his mother, a Danish princess, was buried. When Halvdan died, his body was chopped up so that the pieces could be more widely distributed to bring good luck to the recipients.

Female demands

Halvdan's son, known as Harald Hårfagre (Fair Hair), was to become the first ruler of a united Norway. It was said of this subsequent unification that he was put up to it by a woman whom he wished to take to bed. Her reply to his proposition, conveyed by messengers, was that she could not possibly "waste her maidenhood" on a man who ruled over a kingdom that com-

LEFT: one of the oldest stave churches, Borgund.
RIGHT: Harald Hårfagre (*circa* 1200).

pared so unfavourably in size with those in Denmark and Sweden. His messengers nervously reported her comment but were relieved by the philosophical way in which he took it: "She has reminded me of those things," he said, "which it now seems strange I have not thought of before."

Harald advanced north from Vestfold to improve his conjugal prospects. He made contact with the powerful Earl Håkon, whose interests extended south from Trøndelag, the region surrounding what was eventually to become Trondheim. The cold facts, never as interesting as Sturluson's version, are that Harald and

Håkon saw the mutual benefits of trade but first had to suppress unruly Viking bands along the coast who would have disrupted it.

Harald needed assistance and set the precedent for cooperation between the Norwegian and English thrones by turning to Athelstan, King of England. As a pledge of friendship, accompanied by some mutual chicanery, he initiated what was to become another quite common practice: he sent his infant son Håkon to be fostered at Athelstan's court.

Harald's campaigns sent many of his dispossessed opponents into exile in Iceland, Shetland, the Orkney Islands and the Hebrides. The decisive battle was at Hafrsfjord, near present-

day Stavanger, in southwestern Norway in about AD 900. The victory made him, Sturluson says, the first king of the Norwegians, and also won him the postponed hand of the "large-minded maid", who proceeded to bear him five children. As a love story, however, the conclusion is not completely satisfactory. Sturluson writes: "They say that when he took Ragnhild the Mighty…, he had divorced himself from nine other women."

Too many children

The awesome number of royal progeny was to prove a constant source of havoc in the matter of choosing a successor. The English chronicler Roger of Hoveden wrote: "it is the custom of the kingdom of Norway… that everyone who is recognised to be the son of any King of Norway, even though he be a bastard and born of a serving wench, can claim for himself as great a right to the kingdom of Norway as the son of a wedded king and one born of a free woman. And so fighting goes on incessantly between them…"

Harald Hårfagre's umpteenth son, but the only one by Ragnhild, was the wretched Eirik Blood-axe, who advanced his succession in AD 933 by murdering all but one of his legitimate half-brothers. The exception was Håkon, the boy who had been fostered by King Athelstan. Eirik had none of his father's authority and the united kingdom quickly degenerated into squabbling petty kingdoms ruled by various of Harald's bastard sons. On Håkon's return from England, Eirik was forced to flee in the opposite direction, ending up as King of Northumberland.

First Christian

Håkon den Gode (the Good) was more successful than Eirik at holding hostile factions together. Before he died (about AD 960), he was acknowledged as king over the whole coastal area from Oslo to Hålogaland. He was a notable reformer of law and defence; he was also the first Norwegian Christian king, having been baptised while in England. He imported an English bishop and missionaries with a view to converting his countrymen; but that wasn't easy.

Nowhere was resistance to Christianity more forcibly expressed than in Trondheim, which was then against any form of imposed authority whether by Håkon or, as they had just convincingly demonstrated, by the rival King

Øystein of Oppland. Øystein, to some "the Mighty" and to others "the Evil", had offered them as king a choice between one of his thralls, known as Tore the Hairy, or his dog, Saur. They chose the dog. "Then they bewitched the dog with the wit of three men", sufficient to enable the hound to communicate through a mixture of barking and speech. It was into this unorthodox regal set-up that Håkon tried to introduce Christianity. He urged people to "believe in one God, Christ, the son of Mary,

SAUR, THE DOG KING

According to *the Sagas of the Norse Kings*: "The king lived in a palatial kennel and was carried 'when it was muddy' on the shoulders of its subjects."

ioners would drink themselves into extinction and, by instructing them in the cultivation of fruit and vegetables, hoped to persuade them to consume at least some solids. In the end the missionaries realised that pious sobriety was unattainable. The best they could hope for was to have the toasting converted to Christian saints rather than pagan gods. They provided a long list of saints' names and it seems that some of their parishioners were content to drink to them with undiminished frequency and pleasure.

and give up all blood offerings... and fast every seventh day". From the typical audience "there was straightaway a mighty uproar", followed by devious ploys to trick Håkon into eating a morsel of horse flesh on a day when he was self-righteously fasting or make him participate in a toast to one of their pagan gods.

Håkon's imported missionaries despaired. Their targets would not deviate from drinking to pagan gods morning, noon and night. They were concerned, too, that their potential parish-

LEFT: the monument at Hafrsfjord, where Harald Hårfagre first united Norway.
ABOVE: traditional Norwegian houses with turf roofs.

Missionaries' fate

The missionaries had less luck in suppressing traditions like blood sacrifices (usually animals but occasionally humans). In Trondheim the obdurate response to the message they preached was to send out four ships looking for tiresome missionaries: they "slew three priests and burned three churches; they then went home".

Even when Christianity was finally adopted in Norway, much of the old religion lingered until the Reformation and beyond. The early Christian clergy, for instance, ignored papal injunctions about celibacy. The medieval stave churches are another case in point. Their intricate construction resembles nothing if not the keel of a Viking ship, and they are festooned with dragon heads and scenes from heathen mythology. Many of these churches lasted into the 19th century, when they finally succumbed beneath a torrent of Pietism.

On the military front, Håkon was under constant threat from Eirik Bloodaxe's avenging sons coming over from Northumberland. In defeat they turned to their uncle, the Danish King, Harald Bluetooth, who wanted to regain old Danish territories at the mouth of Oslofjord. At a decisive battle in 960 Håkon was defeated and killed, paving the way for about 25 years of Danish rule, starting with 10 years under Eirik's son Harald II Gråfell.

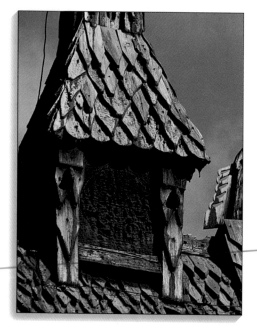

Unlikely convert

Christianity had to wait for Olav Tryggvason, later King Olav I (AD 995–1000) and a monument in Norwegian history, for its next champion. Sturluson says he was a great sportsman who could walk on the oars along the outside of a ship, "smote equally well with both hands" and could hurl two spears at a time. By the age of 12 he was a full-blooded Viking, cruising the Baltic in command of five longships and later moving west to terrorise the English coast. His personality changed through a chance meeting in the Scilly Isles, where he was resting after some strenuous atrocities. A wise old man took him to one side and explained the

True Path. Transformed overnight, Olav returned to England "and now went about peacefully, for England was a Christian country and he was also a Christian".

He was not so peaceful when converting his compatriots at home. Those who opposed him "he dealt with hard; some he slew, some he maimed and some he drove away from the land". In the circumstances, it is understandable that a man elected to argue theological niceties with the king stood up only to develop "such a cough and choking in the chest that he could not bring forth one word and he sat himself down".

Olav Tryggvason was unlucky in love. In proposing marriage to the wealthy Queen Sigrid of Sweden, he insisted she would first have to be baptised. She demurred: "King Olav was very wroth and answered hastily, 'Why should I wed thee, thou heathen bitch?'" reinforcing his point with a smack in the face. "That may well be thy death", she observed: so it proved.

She was a crafty enemy. Her wealth attracted a procession of proposals from minor kings, which she found irksome. King Swein Forkbeard of Denmark, son of Harald Bluetooth, was the type she preferred, and as soon as they were married she talked her husband into an alliance with the Swedish King Olav the Tax Gatherer against Norway. A great sea battle ensued, at the climax of which Olav, who was being assisted by King Boleslav of Poland, was forced to jump overboard. He was never seen again and the victors, including the gratified queen, divided the spoils among themselves.

First saint

The man who would soon restore Norway's integrity had, like Olav Tryggvason, embarked on a naval career at 12. Olav Haraldson, later St Olav, was in England when the same Swein Forkbeard landed his forces and was responsible for the then King of England, Ethelred, being castigated ever more as "the Unready".

Olav allied himself with Ethelred in an anti-Danish war which came to a head at London Bridge across the River Thames. The Danish forces looked, and probably felt, impregnable on their fortified bridge, but they reckoned without Olav's well-built Vikings. Having fastened ropes to the piles under the bridge, they heaved at the oars and brought the whole thing down. Several churches in England are still dedicated to St Olav for this remarkable feat.

A formidable enemy

Olav laid the foundations of the Church, even in petulant Trøndelag, but antagonised many potential rivals, none worse than the expansionist King Canute of Denmark and England, who invaded in 1028 with overwhelming forces. Olav fled to Kiev until he learned that the earl whom Canute had appointed to rule Norway was dead. He returned to regain his kingdom but miscalculated his level of support in Trøndelag and was killed.

Olav was elevated to sainthood and his body placed in the church of St Clement in Trondheim (later to be moved). In spite of his insensitive missionary zeal, the memory of Olav kept for the Byzantine emperor in Constantinople and saw service in Syria, Armenia, Palestine, Sicily and Africa. He was an enterprising warrior. During one siege he faked his own funeral and, emulating the Trojan Horse, his men persuaded the townspeople to open the gates to admit his coffin which, they promised, would work powerful magic to their benefit.

All of this was immensely profitable because the mercenaries were entitled to keep as much treasure from captured palaces as they could grab with both hands. An oblique memorial to Norwegians like Harald who served with the Varangians exists on the great Piraeus marble

alive the notion of a united and independent Norway through the troubled centuries ahead.

King Canute's kingdom fell apart after his death, the Scandinavian component reforming into three distinct and generally hostile kingdoms. Norway was later ruled by Magnus I and then by Harald Hardråde.

Noble mercenary

Harald was typical of the young nobles who were forced to look abroad to enrich themselves. He signed up as a Varangian mercenary

LEFT: detail of the carving on Borgund stave church.
ABOVE: runic inscription on a Viking monument.

lion which the Venetians carried away after their conquest of Athens in 1687 and which now stands at the entrance to the Arsenal in Venice. Very faded, but still visible, is an example of Varangian graffiti: a runic inscription etched into its flanks.

Harald consolidated the kingdom of Norway. Troubled as Norwegian kings invariably were by the people of Trøndelag and its capital, Trondheim, he founded Oslo in 1048 as a counterbalance. He provided the town with a patron saint, Hallvard, whose main claim to sainthood seems to have been the refusal of his body to sink after being thrown into a fjord with a stone around the neck.

Defeat in England

As King Canute's sovereignty over England (1017–35) was still within living memory, it was possibly inevitable that a confident Harald would develop similar ambitions. In any case, there had been so much toing and froing between the west coast of Norway and Britain that the affinities between them were as close, or closer, than those between scattered settlements in Norway. Harald therefore probably felt he was exercising a natural right in his invasion of England.

His approach was from the north but his army was stopped at Stamford Bridge, in present-day North Yorkshire. Some historians

minors. One died young, Sigurd went off to the Holy Land to earn his title, "the Crusader", and Øystein mixed Viking raids with improvements to fisheries, harbours and roads and the establishment of monasteries. Sigurd had the throne to himself after Øystein's death, though he continued to be confronted by the complicated rules of succession throughout his reign.

These battles to occupy the Norwegian throne went on and on. There were brilliant interludes under a king like Sverre, but more often than not the succession was a squabble between the powers behind official contestants who might be children not yet six years old.

argue that the English army's rush north to meet Harald weakened its ability to resist William the Conqueror when he materialised in the south.

After Harald's death in this abortive conquest of England, he was succeeded by his sons Magnus and Olav the Peaceful, the latter founding the towns of Bergen and Stavanger before ultimately being succeeded by his son – yet another Magnus, but in this instance unforgettably "the Bareleg" because, after visiting Scotland (which he dearly wanted to annex), he took to wearing a kilt.

Magnus's death produced the familiar pattern of multiple heirs, in this case three simultaneously acclaimed kings who were all

With the stability of Håkon IV's 46-year reign and that of his son, Magnus the Lawmender, however, Norway achieved its 13th-century "Period of Greatness".

Cultural awakening

Money was spent on cathedrals and churches, the arts flourished and Norwegians assiduously studied and followed European fashions. This cultural awakening was to some extent through the creation of a wealthy upper class and the consolidation of state and Church. It was not so beneficial for the peasants; riches were not evenly spread, and the number of independent farmers dropped significantly as they defaulted on mortgages, leaving the Church and big landowners free to repossess their land.

Norway's overseas empire contributed to a sense of greatness. Jämtland in Sweden was Norwegian, as were the Orkney and Shetland Islands. In 1262 Iceland accepted Norwegian sovereignty, as did Greenland. It was the period, too, which saw the growth of towns like Bergen with a rich trade in dried fish from the north. Foreign trade, to begin with, was mainly with Britain but it then tilted towards the Baltic coast, especially Lübeck and the merchants of the Hanseatic League. The Germans had plenty of corn but a shortage of fish; a perfect trade balance with Norway.

> **COURTLY BEHAVIOUR**
>
> The court of King Magnus the Lawmender was a polite affair, with a prescibed set of rules relating to court etiquette.

The Lübeck merchants grew ever more powerful because of Norway's almost total reliance on them. They were allowed to buy property in Bergen and settle there. If their demands were not met, they simply threatened to cut off corn supplies. Reliance on imported food was effectively costing the country a degree of independence, an unsettling vulnerability which persists in the current national obsession about subsidising agriculture wherever it is remotely possible (and refusing to join the European Union in order to continue to be able to do so).

The Black Death

A galley arriving in Sicily from the Far East in October 1347 brought the Black Death to Europe. Within a couple of years, a third of the European population was dead. The plague was carried north to Bergen in 1349 in the hold of an English ship. The effect on isolated Norwegian farming communities, especially, was catastrophic: farms which had been painfully created in conditions difficult at the best of times were reduced to waste, and in some cases remain so to this day.

The estates generating the wealth which was the necessary platform for general economic development could not be maintained while labourers dropped dead. The nobles who survived were reduced to scratching a living out of the land like everyone else. The effect of *force majeure* acting as a social leveller assumed a

pattern in Norwegian history which cannot be discounted in explaining the easy-going classlessness which remains today.

The decimation of the nobility removed the impetus behind the normally turbulent activity around the Norwegian throne. Unchallenged, two successive kings sat out long peaceful reigns, a foretaste of the comparative stability about to be foisted on all Scandinavia in the late 14th century through the cunning manipulation of Margareta, widow of King Håkon.

A Danish princess, Margareta was married to Håkon at the age of 10 and was thus steeped in the machinery of monarchy. She has been credited with "the greatest personal position ever achieved in Scandinavia" and was sometimes addressed as "Lady King". She first persuaded the Danes to accept as king her son Olav, then aged five.

With mother active behind the scenes, Olav also took over the crown of Norway at 10, and not long afterwards inherited the claim of the dispossessed Folkung dynasty in Sweden. He died suddenly at 17 and Margareta found a suitable substitute to don the united crowns in Erik of Pomerania, her five-year-old nephew. ❏

LEFT: the Ring of Brodgar, Viking remains on the Isles of Orkney off the northeastern tip of Scotland.
RIGHT: runic inscription in Orkney.

THE 400-YEAR SLEEP

A long spell under the control of its more powerful neighbours brought Norway mixed fortunes and, ultimately, something to celebrate – a constitution

The union of the three crowns was formalised at a coronation in the Swedish town of Kalmar, close to the then border with Denmark. The date, appropriately, was Trinity Sunday, 1397. The coronation was performed by the Danish and Swedish archbishops; Norway was represented by the Bishop of Orkney. Although

While taking steps to undermine the authority of the nobility, Erik also tried to squeeze the Hanseatic merchants for money. Their response included an attack on Copenhagen, where they were seen off by 200 examples of a new invention, the cannon. He was less successful when the merchants retaliated with a blockade. Those

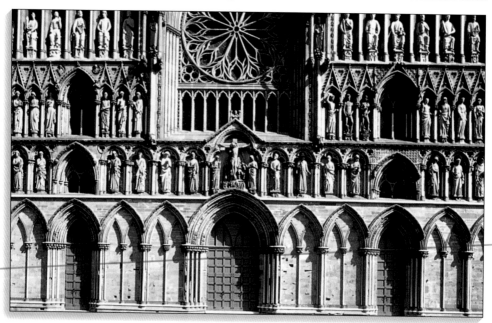

there may have been an attempt to draft a constitution which would have united the three realms forever under a single king, the rules of succession that were adopted left a gaping loophole. Erik of Pomerania was given full rights to dispose of the crown as he saw fit, a recipe for reversion to the old royal uncertainties after his death.

End of the union

In the event, the union collapsed in his lifetime. His greatest difficulty was paying for the court and administration in Copenhagen. The united crown had no significant estates of its own; the nobility did and was comparatively well off, but it was not inclined to surrender its wealth.

hardest hit were the nobility and wealthy merchants who, holding Erik responsible for their misfortune, conspired to dethrone him.

Erik retreated to the island of Gotland in the hope that they would change their minds. Norway would have done so, but the Danish nobles wanted to make a fresh start. The invitation went to Christian of Oldenburg, who thereupon rose from the title of count in an obscure part of Germany to found a dynasty which was to last for more than four centuries. Sweden resisted the choice, but Norway went along with it.

Christian I was almost as short of money as Erik had been. His attempts to make up shortfalls were notoriously at the expense of Norway, the weaker partner. Expected to hand over 60,000 guilders as a dowry for his daughter Margaret's marriage to the heir to the Scottish throne, he mortgaged the Orkney Islands to Scotland for 50,000. When the time came for the wedding, he was still 8,000 guilders short, and so mortgaged Shetland as well. To put 8,000 guilders into perspective, he spent three times that on a trip to Rome a few years later (which he had to borrow from the Hanseatics). The Scots gloated over the deal; not merely the trifling price but that Margaret "deemed it a greater thing to be queen in Scotland than daughter of a king who wears three crowns".

Treacherous murder

Norway's resentment at such exploitation eventually boiled over. On the turn of the 16th century, Knut Alvsson, a Swedish-Norwegian nobleman, led an uprising which created a potentially independent state stretching from Oslo to Bergen. Danish troops were sent to put a stop to it. The outcome, however, was thoroughly dishonourable. Alvsson had established himself in Akershus Castle in Oslo. He was invited to negotiate under a flag of truce and promptly murdered. In the poem *At Akershus*, Ibsen called his death a blow to Norway's heart.

Norwegian resentment at the treatment meted out to Alvsson was exacerbated by punitive taxes to pay for Christian II of Denmark's wars with the restless Swedes. Norwegians were not altogether sorry to see him toppled and bundled off into exile, but they were not ready to extend a welcome to his successor, Frederik I.

Norway was nominally Roman Catholic and there was little interest in the forces of the Reformation which lay behind the tussle for the Danish throne. The country did not have the urban bourgeoisie who elsewhere were the first to adopt Lutheranism. Norway's peasant culture was deeply conservative, not to say backward, so much so that many scholars classify Norway as "medieval" until the early 16th century.

It could be said that the Reformation, when it reached Norway, was the first of the great European cultural swathes that had any real impact on the country. Feudalism passed it by (never a

Norwegian knight in armour rescuing damsels in distress) as did the Renaissance. Most of rural Norway remained doggedly in its past, Christianity providing only a veneer on what were fundamentally old pagan ways.

A new leader

It was at this point that a new Norwegian leader emerged. He was Olav Engelbrektsson, the Archbishop of Trondheim (or Nidaros, as it was then known). Olav raised an army with a view to getting Christian II back. The exiled king was able to muster a fleet with Dutch help and in 1531 set sail for Oslo. A storm scattered the fleet so that

only a small part of it went into action against Akershus Castle. The attack was futile. Christian was captured and imprisoned, and the Norwegians were forced to acclaim Frederik I as their king.

Christian II was still in prison when Frederik died and was replaced by Christian III, a Protestant. He rounded up the Danish bishops and then ordered the Archbishopric of Trondheim to be abolished, if necessary by force. Olav thought of resisting but, having weighed up the likely repercussions, fled to the Netherlands.

Any further hope of Norwegian independence was squashed by Christian III's 1536 edict demoting the country to the status of a Danish

LEFT: the main entrance to Nidarosdomen (the cathedral), Trondheim.
RIGHT: Akershus Slott og Festning (castle and fortress), Oslo.

province: "and it shall henceforth neither be nor be called a kingdom in itself." The humbled status was intended to last in perpetuity; in the event it lasted for less than 300 years, culminating not in independence but in an 1814 takeover by Sweden after Norway had become a coveted prize bobbing between its more powerful neighbours.

The loss of political sovereignty under Denmark could not obliterate Norway's separate identity at once. People went on speaking the same language as before and local administration retained many traditional features, but the creeping effects of the Reformation, and Chris-

tian III's determination to "Danicise" Norway, could not be postponed forever.

The Danish influence

Most of the new Protestant clergy were Danes. The revised version of the Bible was in Danish and so were the hymns. Official jobs were invariably given to Danes, who conducted them in the Danish language and reported back to the administration in Copenhagen.

With the spread of schooling and therefore literacy in books imported, naturally, from Denmark (the first printing press was late in arriving in Norway), the anomaly arose of people speaking one language among themselves but

reading, albeit with characteristic Norwegian pronunciation, writing and conducting all official business in another. The result was a hybrid Dano-Norwegian and the genesis of a language dispute which has not been settled to this day.

Norway won a measure of Danish respect in the latter's frequent wars with Sweden, in which the Norwegian contingents acquitted themselves well. Denmark began to realise that Norway could only be governed in its own way. Sweden was forever peering enviously over Denmark's shoulder at Norway. Too much antagonism could result in Norway accepting a more attractive offer of union with Sweden.

A valuable asset

The Norwegian economy began to recover from its long decline, partly as the result of vast shoals of herring which materialised off the coast and partly because of the invention of the water-driven saw, which made exploitation of the timber forests lucrative. Christian IV was far more positive about Norway than his predecessors. He visited the country at least 30 times, making a special trip on learning of the discovery of silver at what is now Kongsberg. He supervised the founding of the town, hence the name, which translates as "King's Mountain". He founded and attached his name to Kristiansand, as he did "Christiania" to the new city built on the site where the former Oslo had burned down in 1624. Nevertheless, Christian ran the country as if it were a private company. He cracked down on the Hanseatic traders, making them take out Norwegian citizenship, if they had not already done so of their own accord, or leave. Foreigners from other parts were encouraged to bring to Norway their skills, enterprise and, best of all, their money. Under his encouragement, former trading posts became towns in places like Drammen, Moss, Larvik, Mandal and Arendal.

The Norwegians did not always receive these foreigners with uncritical joy. In 1700, for example, a simple fight between two men in Arendal escalated into a brawl which pitched all 900 resident foreigners against everyone else. It lasted a week. Nevertheless, a population which had been reduced by the Black Death to something like 180,000 picked up under Christian's energetic policies, reaching 440,000 in 1665 and nearly 900,000 by 1801.

Not all of Christian IV's successors shared his delicate touch with regard to Norwegian sensibilities. There were periods when the Danish crown was autocratically absolute, and respite depended on having an independently minded *Stattholder*, the crown agent with responsibility for Norway.

Ulrik Frederik Gyldenløve, the illegitimate son of Frederik III, conscientiously protected his Norwegian charges. He intervened to save peasants from the more rapacious taxes sought by Copenhagen, and he built up the Norwegian armed forces so that at Kvistrum in 1677 they were able to humiliate a far larger force of

THE DEVIL'S DRINK

The legacy of the zealous Pietism that arrived in Norway in the 18th century can still be felt today, especially when it comes to alcohol.

existence was actually abominably frivolous. Gripped by a kind of manic fundamentalism, they despised their folk culture and, particularly in the 19th century when Pietism was still going strong, were encouraged to tear down the ornately carved, wooden stave churches. Confirmation and attendance at church on Sunday were made compulsory.

Looking around them, the Pietists were appalled by the realisation that in their midst, or anyway within the national boundaries, there were still heathens. Thomas

Swedes. Peter Wessel Tordenskiold became a great naval hero for many daring feats, the best of which was sailing a small squadron up a fjord (Dynekilen) and destroying a Swedish fleet.

Hellfire and brimstone

As Norway belatedly shed the mantle of medievalism and got to grips with Protestantism, it adopted the faith as zealously as it had once defended paganism. The rural areas, especially, embraced Pietism, real hellfire-and-brimstone stuff which persuaded peasants that their austere

LEFT: an old rose-painted *stue* (living room).
ABOVE: a traditional, rural Norwegian Sunday.

von Weston, a superb linguist, took it upon himself to remedy the situation among the Sami (Lapps). Hans Egede went further afield to save souls in Greenland and, although he worked tirelessly, it took him eight years to win his first Innuit convert.

On the other hand, when a liberal wind blew in Copenhagen, it was also felt in Norway. For example, when Christian VII went mad the affairs of state fell into the hands of his physician, a German named Johann Friedrich Struensee. He believed in unrestricted trade, freedom of the press and so on.

Norway was gratified to see the abolition of a trading system which placed a fixed and artificially low value on Norwegian iron imported into Denmark, whereas Danish corn exports to Norway were sold at whatever the market would bear. Correcting the imbalance helped, but prospects of additional economic reforms ended abruptly when it was discovered that Struensee had been having an affair with Caroline Mathilde, wife of his deranged patient, and was executed.

One-man enlightenment

Against a backdrop of Pietism and the death penalty for sexual irregularity, one of the first rays of the Enlightenment shone through in the person of Ludvig Holberg. He was born in

Nelson attacks

Co-existence between Denmark and Norway was traumatised from the unlikely quarter of Napoleon Bonaparte. Britain had fallen out with Denmark (and hence Norway) over the Danish alliance with Prussia and Russia. A total of 149 Danish and Norwegian vessels were seized in British ports; in response, a Danish force marched into Hamburg and appropriated British property worth £15 million.

The British naval commander, Horatio Nelson, moved on Copenhagen with a powerful fleet. Danish and Norwegian crews manning a line of blockships put up a spirited defence, and

Bergen but later became a resident of Copenhagen; a playwright, historian and satirist (in Latin) who, according to the distinguished historian T.K. Derry, "in his own generation had no obvious superior in range of intellect except Voltaire". Holberg's impressive output included 26 plays for the newly founded Copenhagen Theatre between 1722 and 1727.

Holberg never returned to his home town of Bergen after leaving at the age of 21, and it is a pithy comment on the difficulty of drawing a clear line between specifically Norwegian and Danish history during the four centuries when the two countries were so closely tied that both countries now claim Holberg as their own.

after a six-hour battle Nelson urged the Danish crown prince regent to capitulate, failing which he would have to destroy the blockships "without having the power to save the brave Danes who have defended them". The prince agreed.

A few years later Napoleon insisted that Denmark-Norway join his continental system and close their ports to British ships. A large British fleet demanded the handing-over of the Danish Navy, which Napoleon sorely needed after losing his at Trafalgar, and when this met with refusal, Copenhagen was bombarded with at least 14,000 rounds over three days.

British troops occupied the capital for six weeks, after which they went home with the

Danish fleet and vast quantities of naval stores. The enormity of such an attack on what was a neutral country put Denmark and Norway firmly into Napoleon's camp, a position which required them to join him in attacking Sweden.

The division thus rendered between Sweden and Denmark was bound to have serious consequences. The impotent "pig in the middle" was Norway. The inevitable was set rolling in 1810 when Sweden's King Karl XIII appointed as his heir (of all people, considering

EIDSVOLL CONSTITUTION

On 17 May 1814 Norway became a "free, independent and an indivisible realm" according to the new constitution, but it would take a further 91 years for these words to become a reality.

let Norway have the national bank it had long craved. In the end, the decision did not rest in either Norwegian or Danish hands. Union between Sweden and Norway was imposed by the Peace of Kiel (following Napoleon's defeat at Leipzig) in 1814.

Battle for the throne

Christian Frederik was not going to surrender Norway without a struggle. He entertained the idea of getting himself popularly acclaimed as king (he thought his chances best in Trond-

the events which had just passed) Jean-Baptiste Bernadotte, one of Napoleon's marshals. Bernadotte improved his Swedish credentials by changing his name to Karl Johan and succeeded to the throne in 1818.

Karl Johan conceived a plan whereby Russia and Britain would support Swedish claims on Norway. They agreed, with the result that Norwegian ports were blockaded to secure a "voluntary" union with Sweden. The Danish Crown Prince Christian Frederik tried to rally Norwegian loyalty, among other things by agreeing to

LEFT: the old mining town of Røros, Sør-Trøndelag.
ABOVE: a northern graveyard on Andøya, Vesterålen.

heim) but the feeling among the population at large was that the Danish line had renounced its sovereignty and the Norwegians were now entitled to choose their own king.

In April 1814, an assembly of 37 farmers, 16 businessmen and 59 bureaucrats met in Eidsvoll to decide what that future should be. The constitution they prepared was signed on 17 May, still the biggest day of the year in Norway. On the same day a new king was elected; it was the tenacious Christian Frederik. Sweden would have none of it. The Norwegians fought well in a one-sided contest but Christian Frederik soon had to sue for peace. Karl Johan stepped forward to occupy his double throne. ❏

UNION WITH SWEDEN

Through such artists as Ibsen, Grieg and Munch, the voice of an increasingly
restless and independent-minded Norway could be heard beyond its own borders

Divorce from Denmark was followed by a quarrel over the division of joint assets and liabilities. The assets were Iceland, Greenland and the Faroes which, Norway claimed, were Norwegian colonies long before marriage with Denmark. The liabilities were the Danish-Norwegian national debt.

Who owed what? The Norwegian position was not only that Denmark alone should shoulder the burden but that compensation was due to Norway for centuries of exploitation. Assuming powers granted under the Treaty of Kiel which had brought about the new union, Karl Johan declared that Norway would pay off some of the debt. The matter of the colonies was not finally resolved until 1931, when the International Court at The Hague found in favour of Denmark.

Two kingdoms

Friction between Karl Johan and the Norwegian half of his kingdom was present right from the start: he envisaged a gradual merging of the two kingdoms, while Norway was determined to consolidate the independence ratified by the 1814 constitution.

A constitutional battle took place over a bill to abolish all noble titles and privileges. Again and again the Storting (Parliament) presented the bill – and the king refused to sanction it. The constitution said he could refuse a bill only twice; the third time it automatically became law. Karl Johan objected strongly to this limitation on his authority which did not exist in Sweden.

A fundamental principle was at stake and the dispute was not to be resolved easily. Indeed, it remained the biggest bone of contention for the life of the union and, as much as anything else, was the author of its eventual dissolution. Norwegian pride was prickly. Merchant ships could fly the Norwegian flag close to home but not in waters notoriously under the sway of North

African pirates. Sweden had bought off the pirates but the immunity extended only to the Swedish flag; if Norwegian ships wanted to take advantage of it, they had to switch flags.

Sweden's dogged refusal to allow Norway its own diplomatic and consular representation abroad was not only an insult but a practical

handicap because the Norwegian merchant fleet was well on its way to becoming, by 1880, the third largest in the world. Its far-flung crews wanted and needed a purely Norwegian diplomatic service.

Oslo once again

Karl Johan was adept at making a timely concession to court popularity, and the welcome he received on visiting Christiania in 1838 was probably sincere, as was the public grief when he died six years later. Although changing Christiania's name back to Oslo obliterated a Danish memory, the capital was, and is, content to leave its main street named after Karl Johan.

LEFT: Eidsvoll, where the Norwegian constitution was signed on 17 May 1814.
RIGHT: King Karl Johan XIV.

The Great Exodus

One thousand years after the first Norwegian Vikings turned their longships towards the west, pushing out as far as North America, a second wave of Norwegians began to cast their eyes in the same direction.

The motives of these new emigrants were similar – lack of opportunity and poverty – but they had none of the warlike excitement of the earlier exodus. These new "Vikings" sought a place where they could work and prosper in peace rather than a place for exploration and conquest.

Yet the first emigrant boat, the 16-metre (54-ft) sloop *Restauration*, crammed full with 52 crew and passengers, must have been scarcely more seaworthy than the superbly built longships. But these early "sloopers", which sailed from Stavanger in July 1825, were idealistic and highly motivated. The leader, Lars Larsen Geilane, was a Quaker and there were members of the religious Haugeans sect among the crew. Their intention to found a classless society where they could follow their own religion had been further encouraged when the previous year another Norwegian pioneer, Cleng Peerson, returned with reports of the promised land.

The *Restauration* reached New York in October of the same year and these farming people, mostly from Rogaland, lost no time in settling on land bought for them by Cleng Peerson at Kendall on the shores of Lake Ontario. This settlement became a staging post on the road to Illinois, where many Norwegians made their homes.

When the *Restauration* left in 1825, Norway's population was only 1 million, yet the next three generations sent 750,000 Norwegians to North America, reflecting a population increase at home rather than an emptying of the Norwegian countryside, though early industrialists began to campaign against such a dribbling away of potential labour.

The early "sloopers" had more in common with the Pilgrim Fathers who left Plymouth in the *Mayflower* two centuries earlier than with those emigrants who came after them. The main motive among the second and later waves of country people was good land and good farming prospects rather than religious or political repression. To be an *odelsbonde*, who owned his own land, was to be a free man and the goal of every Norwegian peasant. The American merchant fleets were also eager to make use of skilful Norwegian seamen.

The newcomers prospered and regular letters home, reports, and Norwegian visitors from the New World increased the fever. The letters were printed in newspapers all over the country and one or two mid-Western American states began to use agents to encourage emigration.

By the middle of the 1830s new emigrants and some of the original "sloopers" had moved on to Illinois. Forty years later, their numbers had increased to more than 12,500. The 1862 Homestead Law, which granted land to immigrants, turned the early trickle into a steady flow, and Cleng Peerson founded Norwegian settlements in Iowa.

For many patriotic Norwegians it became *de rigueur* to help the expansion. The great violinist Ole Bull had a well-intentioned but crashing failure with a planned settlement, "Oleana", in Pennsylvania. He was too far from his Norwegian farming roots. The soil was ungrateful, communications impossible, and Bull lost more than $40,000.

Later, Norwegians also settled in Canada; but by the 1930s emigration had dwindled to a trickle. Yet the Norwegian influence was strong in the places where they settled. Today, the overt "Norwegian-ness" may have gone, but anyone who doubts it still exists need only read Garrison Keillor's winsome tales of life around Lake Wobegon. ❏

LEFT: this boy, aged eight, crossed the Atlantic alone in 1907 after his mother died.

His successor, Oskar I, immediately tried to placate Norway through gestures such as his title which, locally, became King of Norway and Sweden, rather than vice versa. He also agreed to a new flag which gave equal prominence to the Swedish and Norwegian colours.

Norwegian politics in the 19th century were dominated at first by the Venstre party which carried the banner of separatism and rallied against the royal veto. Its leader, Johan Sverdrup, was a lawyer who worked at creating an alliance between urban radicals and wealthy farmers. Their interests were too divergent, however, and the party split, leaving room for

The farmers' grip on the national heart-strings, and purse, has never been relinquished.

Putting peasants on a pedestal, however, did not ameliorate the hard facts of life. Emigration to the United States began in 1825, although statistics reveal the irony that emigration was highest when the economic conditions at home were good, and lowest when they were bad. Perhaps it was a case of being too poor in the lean times to pay the fare. In 1882 a record 29,000 Norwegians left, and by 1910 there were more than 400,000 people of Norwegian birth in the United States, their numbers growing right the way through to World War I.

the strong labour movement which characterised most of the 20th century.

It dawned on poorer farmers and peasants who had previously let the land-owning and merchant classes get on with government, that their special interests, especially a reduction in taxes, could be advanced only if they too became involved in the political process. They were assisted by a general mood in the country of national romanticism, a Nordic adaptation of the French philosopher Rousseau's belief in the nobility of savages. The Norwegian peasant farmer was portrayed as the salt of the earth.

ABOVE: emigrants leave Stavanger for the New World.

The arts flourish

The rise of nationalism throughout Europe produced in Norway an unprecedented, and subsequently unequalled flowering of the arts. Henrik Ibsen (1828–1906) and Alexander Kielland (1849–1906), giants among an extraordinarily talented assortment of writers – not forgetting composers, such as Edvard Grieg (1843–1907), and the painter Edvard Munch (1863–1944) – presented the world with a clearer insight into Norway than was available from the bestselling romantic writers.

It may be worth summarising, for strong stomachs, the plot of one such work, *Thelma: A Norwegian Princess*, by Miss Marie Corelli, which ran to no fewer than 47 editions (but is now out of print). Sir Philip Bruce-Errington encounters a crazy dwarf who lives in a cavern illuminated by antique Etruscan lamps. Sir Philip and the dwarf converse comfortably in English but that does not prevent Sir Philip from being amazed by the dwarf's intellect, when he correctly guesses his nationality.

Sir Philip then makes the acquaintance of old Olaf Guldmar, Princess Thelma's father. He is a wretched peasant farmer who is also fluent in English. Sir Philip is understandably full of admiration and respect when he discovers Olaf's library. It contains, for example, the

which appeared in the *Spectator* magazine in 1872 about a previously unheard of Norwegian poet named Ibsen who had written "short songs of irregular measure after the manner of Heine". The poet wrote a note of thanks to the writer, Edmund Gosse, adding "I shall consider myself most fortunate if you decide to translate one or more of my books," a modest hint that he may have written more than poems.

Poet and playwright

At home Ibsen and others like Bjørnstjerne Bjørnson (1832–1910) were leading lights in agitation against Danish domination in the arts.

works of Shakespeare, Byron, Keats, Plutarch and Chapman's translation of Homer. It turns out that he is an accomplished Latin scholar, although in religious belief still a devout pagan, "by Valhalla!" being his favourite oath.

Not a moment too soon, Olaf feels death coming on and, following custom, is carried aboard his vessel which is set on fire and pushed out to sea. "He raised his arms as though in ecstasy: 'Glory! – joy! – victory!'" And, like a noble tree struck down by lightning, he fell – dead."

That the reality of Norway might be different from the picture conveyed above was first mooted, at least in England, by a short article

The campaign included, for example, that Danish actors should no longer be employed on the Norwegian stage.

Henrik Johan Ibsen was born in the small town of Skien in Telemark *(see page 207)*. His father's financial indiscretions plunged the family into poverty, and Ibsen was apprenticed at an early age to a chemist in the even smaller town of Grimstad. His first poems, with titles like *Resignation*, *Doubt* and *The Corpse's Ball*, give a clue to the majestic gloom – punctuated, nevertheless by delicious wit – of his later work.

After working in the theatre in Bergen, he joined the Christiania Norske Theater (in Oslo), which had been founded to promote specifically Norwegian theatre. He fared miserably with one failure after another, poor health and no money. In the depths of depression he began to question the deplorable position of the creative artist in Norwegian society and that, ironically, put him on the road to better things. *The Pretenders*, first performed in 1864, was a great success and helped him to a travelling scholarship. He went abroad, first to Italy, and did not live in Norway again for another 27 years.

> ### IBSEN ABROAD
>
> According to George Bernard Shaw, Ibsen's influence in England "is almost equal to the influence which three revolutions, six crusades, a couple of foreign invasions and an earthquake would produce."

The plays for which he is best remembered were produced from about 1877 onwards. The first of these, *Pillars of Society*, broke new ground in dealing with the untruth and humbug of a small provincial town. In creating any number of great female roles, Ibsen touched on subjects that audiences and critics were not ready for. If his work was controversial at home, it was considered outrageous when eventually it travelled abroad. According to *The Daily Telegraph* in London the first overseas production of *Ghosts* was "positively abominable... a dirty act done publicly, a (lavatory) with all its doors and windows open ... gross, almost putrid indecorum ... crapulous stuff".

There were other points of view, however, like that of the essayist Havelock Ellis and of George Bernard Shaw who summarised Ibsen's importance to the English theatre with: "The Norman Conquest was a mere nothing compared with the Norwegian Conquest."

While the Norwegian element in the work of the great playwright Ludvig Holberg in the previous century could hardly be told apart from the Danish, there was no ambiguity about Ibsen. As a curious footnote, however, Ibsen once wrote to a friend in England saying that "there are very strong traces in me of Scotch descent. But this is only a feeling – perhaps only a wish that it were so."

Battle of wills

Ibsen's strong sense of national identity was mirrored in the political events swirling around him. Problems within the union with Sweden came to a head in 1905 over the long-running dispute about diplomatic representation. The government wanted its own consular service; King Oskar II refused. The government then argued that, if it resigned and the king was unable to obtain an alternative government, his royal power would effectively have lapsed. It would then revert to the Storting, which would choose a new king. The Storting agreed to this plan.

Oskar was hurt and the Swedish Government outraged. Neither would have been placated

by a plebiscite which showed 368,208 in favour of breaking away from Sweden and only 184 against. The "compromise" reached in 1905 was in truth a surrender to Norwegian demands: Oskar's abdication and Norwegian independence. The king's parting shot was that no member of his house would be allowed to accept the vacated throne even if it were offered. This was only in part petulance. Oskar was privately convinced that an independent Norway was bound to collapse and whoever was then king would thus be discredited. When that happened, an unsullied member of his house would, of course, be standing by to answer the call. That call was never heard. ❏

LEFT: an early drawing of Oslo's Storting (Parliament).
RIGHT: King Oskar II.

AN INDEPENDENT, MODERN COUNTRY

Invaded by Germany, then caught up in the Cold War, Norway has passed through difficult times to emerge as an international peace-broker

The prime minister who led Norway to independence was Christian Michelsen, a Bergen solicitor who founded one of the biggest shipping companies in Norway and was by 1903 a member of the government. In the meantime, he had formed a breakaway group in Bergen of "liberals" from the radical left.

Michelsen's initial modest aim was to settle the issue of whether Norway should have its own consuls abroad, which would finally destroy the union with Sweden; but by 1904 he was warning the Swedes not to assume that if negotiations failed this time, they could be resumed.

Michelsen had recognised the way Norwegian public opinion was running and the support the cause was getting from such famous Norwegians as the explorer Fridtjof Nansen (who later became Norwegian Ambassador in London) and the writer Bjørnstjerne Bjørnson. Soon Michelsen was heading a cabinet that included ministers from a wide range of parties and of many shades of opinion.

With independence established in 1905 and King Haakon VII on the throne, Michelsen quickly left the stormy waters of politics for a calmer and more profitable life in his shipping business, though he remained an active elder statesman until his death in 1925.

No foreign policy

In the long years of struggle, Bjørnson had claimed that "the foreign policy of Norway should be to have no foreign policy," and immediately after independence, the aim of all parties was to avoid entanglement in the affairs of the Great Powers. But, despite its determined neutrality, World War I had the ironic effect of throwing Norway and Sweden back into one another's arms. "A new union, not of the old sort, but a union of heartfelt understanding," was the Swedish king's description, "to maintain the neutrality of the respective kingdoms in relation to all the belligerent powers."

Norway did well out of its neutrality, at least for the first two years of the war. Germany was willing to pay top prices for all the fish Norway could supply, which attracted British attention and led to a secret agreement, backed by the threat to cut off supplies of British oil and coal, under which Britain would buy most of the fish itself. Norway, in return, would not export vital copper pyrites to Germany, but otherwise it was free to trade with both sides.

Those lucky enough to get a share of this trade, and of the domestic black market, flaunted their overnight fortunes in such a way that workers on fixed wages, which were forever falling behind rampant inflation, became rebellious. Employers retaliated with lockouts, and the government was forced to introduce compulsory arbitration.

German submarine warfare put a damper on profiteering. Most of the Norwegian merchant fleet was under charter to Britain and by the end of the war half of it, together with 2,000 crew members, was lost. In absolute terms only Britain lost more of its shipping. The intervention of the United States also made matters worse. The Americans demanded big cuts in trade with Germany before agreeing to make supplies available to Norway.

At the end of the war the neutral countries had little say in deciding the terms of peace. Despite its heavy losses the Norwegian Merchant Navy received no compensation in the shape of ships from the confiscated German Navy, and it was 10 years before injured seamen and the families of those killed received any compensation from the German Government.

THE NANSEN PASSPORT

Devised by Fridtjof Nansen, this "passport" offered those people made stateless by World War I a means of official identification.

neutral countries just two months after the League was founded to seek membership.

Norway, temperamentally against alliances, was fiercely divided and it was not until 1920 that the Storting finally voted for membership of the League, Norway's first real move into internationalism. Nansen, who had been so influential in the struggle for Norwegian independence, now had international links to the US, the Soviet Union and elsewhere, and became active in the League, particularly in the slow repatriation of nearly

Nansen and the League

During the war the Scandinavian monarchs had met to discuss and set up committees to review the position of neutral countries when hostilities ceased. Under Fridtjof Nansen, Norway formed an Association for the League of Nations and drafted a potential constitution. But, as the war ended, the Great Powers were not inclined to take much notice of mere neutrals. They themselves laid down the rules and allowed the

PRECEDING PAGES: a factory in Christiania (Oslo) producing iron stairs (*circa* 1895).
LEFT: King Haakon VII.
ABOVE: the Royal Family with their ski instructor.

half a million prisoners-of-war from Russia. He later donated his own Nobel Peace Prize money for similar work for Russian and Armenian refugees. He was still working on this at the time of his death in 1930.

But in 1920, of the Storting's 20 votes against membership of the League of Nations, 16 came from the steadily growing Labour Party which, at the time, took most of its principles and goals from the ideas behind the Russian Revolution.

Briefly in credit

Although Norway was one of the creditor nations when the war ended, the cavalier business atmosphere of the war years carried over as financial recklessness, if not ignorance. In very short order the country was further into debt than it had so recently been in credit.

By 1921 conditions had deteriorated into a full-blown economic depression with more than a million tonnes of shipping laid up, free-spending local authorities in difficulty and, unthinkably to Norwegians, one of the biggest banks going bankrupt in spite of secret state support.

The rise of Labour

Storms and controversies over prohibition caused the downfall of three different cabinets. The steadily growing Labour Party became

A lockout at Norsk Hydro produced not only the most notorious incident in the history of Norwegian industrial relations (police and troops fighting demonstrators) but also the rise to prominence of a figure as shameful in Norwegian memory as anyone since Eirik Bloodaxe.

The defence minister who ordered the troops in was Vidkun Quisling, and he was soon accusing Labour of plotting an armed revolution. Quisling was largely discredited in his own country by 1939. At that time he was in Berlin for reasons that were soon to become very clear.

By 1933, the economic crisis was so bad that the unlikely alliance of the Labour Party with

more revolutionary in its beliefs, and passed a resolution reserving the right to use "revolutionary action in the struggle for the economic liberation of the working classes". The point having been made, militancy declined and by the end of the decade the party had turned its attention back to parliamentary rule. In the 1927 elections, in spite of fragmentation, it became the biggest party in the Storting.

The Wall Street crash of 1929 compounded the economic misery. A third of all trade unionists were already out of work when employers tried to reduce wages which, in spite of nearly a decade of economic turmoil, were still very high compared to most European countries.

the Agrarian (Farmers') Party put a Labour prime minister into power. He was Johan Nygaardsvold, with lengthy experience in the Storting. He was prime minister from 1935 with a direct responsibility for creating employment and, by 1939, the average day's wage had risen by 15 percent.

Precarious neutrality

When World War II broke out in September 1939 Norway proclaimed immediate neutrality, but had taken almost no precautions to defend herself. Perhaps Nygaardsvold was too immersed in his economic renaissance. He remained prime minister until 1945 but in the recriminations and resultant inquiry that followed the end of the war, he was deemed partly to blame for not making adequate preparations.

The first warning signs came from the Allied side, with Britain complaining that its ships were being sunk by Germany in Norwegian territorial waters. Also, German ships were being given free access to strategic iron ore from the port of Narvik. The ancient Norwegian fleet was in no position to keep territorial waters neutral, so the British suggested mining them.

The dilemma was highlighted by the well-

UNPREPARED

When World War II broke out, Norway called up just 7,000 men and its coastal defences were only half-manned.

Government asked why Norway had been unable to prevent German abuse of its neutral waters, and Germany posed the same question, but the other way round.

Invasion by sea

Britain unilaterally began laying mines along the Norwegian coastline and, on the very day Norway lodged a protest – 8 April 1940 – German forces were on the high seas bound for Norway. Once the invasion was under way, the German minister in Oslo sent a note to say that Germany was only occupying a

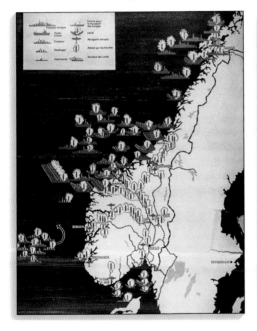

known *Altmark* affair. The *Altmark*, an auxiliary to the battleship *Graf Spee*, was on its way to Germany with 300 captured British seamen when it sought refuge in Norwegian waters near Egersund. The British Royal Navy was alerted to its presence and charged into the fjord to rescue the men while two small Norwegian vessels looked on, making vain protests. The Norwegian Government complained to Britain about violation of its neutrality. The British

LEFT: the meeting between Vidkun Quisling and Adolf Hitler prior to World War II.
ABOVE LEFT: strategic map from World War II.
ABOVE RIGHT: the struggle for Narvik, 1941.

few strategic points to keep the British out.

At last the Norwegian Government woke up to what was going on. The German heavy cruiser *Blücher* was sunk by the Oscarsborg fortress in the Oslo fjord near Drøbak, and two creaking Norwegian destroyers boldly took on a much larger German force at Narvik.

The Storting granted the government full powers "to take whatever decisions might be necessary to ensure the best interests of the country," the point on which many a debate would later hinge. On 10 April the Germans showed their hand. Quisling, whose National Unity Party commanded all of 1.8 percent of the electorate, was their choice as new prime

The Heroes of Telemark

The most celebrated act of resistance in Norway during World War II was the sabotage of the Vemork heavy-water plant at Rjukan, in Telemark, in February 1943. No visitor to Rjukan, dwarfed and darkened by mountains all round, could fail to be awed by the audacity of the saboteurs. More importantly, the production of heavy water in the plant, if it had not been stopped, could conceivably have aided the German development of

an atomic bomb. The operation was originally planned for a joint force of Norwegian volunteers and British commandos in two towed gliders. It ended disastrously when both gliders and one of the aircraft towing them crashed 160 km (100 miles) from Rjukan.

The next attempt was an all-Norwegian affair. "Gunnerside", the code name for six men who had been trained in Scotland, parachuted on to a frozen lake where they were supposed to join up with "Swallow", an advance party on the ground. The first person they bumped into was a reindeer hunter. He was later released with food and money on the promise that he would reveal nothing. Once the parties had linked up, they skied to the ridge

above Rjukan for the perilous descent on foot. They slithered down, up to their waists in snow. Just after midnight, the covering party took up positions while the six-man demolition team cut a chain on the gates and crept forward to the basement of the concrete building where the most vital equipment and the heavy-water storage tanks were located. All wore British uniforms and were agreed that no lights would be carried; weapons would be unloaded to avoid the accidental discharge of arms and anyone captured would take his own life.

As the basement was locked, the best way in appeared to be a funnel carrying cables and piping. Two of the men went through it. The solitary Norwegian guard was astonished, but agreed to lead them to vital components.

"I had placed half the charges in position when there was a crash of broken glass behind me," one of the pair wrote later. The other members of the team, not realising that their leaders had managed to get in, had decided to smash in through a window. With the rest of the charges laid, the six began a rapid withdrawal. They were nonplussed by the co-operative guard who, understandably getting out as well while the going was good, implored to be let in again. He had forgotten his glasses!

The request was granted, but the delay meant that the party had only gone a few yards when there was what members later variously described as "a cataclysmic explosion" and "a tiny, insignificant pop".

Five members of the parachute team reached Sweden after a 400-km (250-mile) journey on skis in indescribably difficult conditions; the sixth stayed on for another year. Of the Swallow party, an irrepressible character named Claus Helberg had the liveliest time. He was chased through the mountains by German soldiers whom he encountered, but escaped after an exchange of shots. Then he fell over a cliff and broke an arm. The next morning he walked into a German patrol but had a good enough story to be taken to a hotel to await treatment. Most of the hotel guests (but not the injured Norwegian) were turned out of their rooms to make way for Reichskommissar Joseph Terboven (the Nazi who ruled Norway) and his entourage. Later, and through no fault of his own, he was bundled along with the remaining guests "into a bus and sent off to the Grini concentration camp". Helberg jumped from the bus and escaped. In due course he turned up in Britain, reporting for further duties. ❑

LEFT: Kirk Douglas in the film *The Heroes of Telemark*.

minister. The government, which had moved itself from Oslo to Trysil, repeatedly refused to comply, and its defiance was repaid with a German bombing attack on the meeting place.

Norway's only hope against such lopsided odds lay in the Allies. From Britain's point of view, Narvik was the key because of the iron-ore traffic. The British Royal Navy went into action against German naval units in the area and destroyed them. A combined force of Norwegians, British, French and Poles fought to regain control of the city itself and on 28 May succeeded in doing so.

Earlier, on 14 and 15 April, other Allied troops had landed near Trondheim. They were joined by small Norwegian units. They put up a plucky fight but, practically without any air cover against the Luftwaffe, took a pasting from above. Towns where there was a British presence were bombed to ruin: Åndalsnes, Namsos, Steinkjer and Mosjøen.

The fight for Norway was overshadowed, however, by the German steamroller in western Europe and, with what were seen to be greater needs there, the Allied forces withdrew, leaving Norway alone.

The king and government, evacuated to the north and ready to fight on, decided that the best course of action was to decamp to Britain. On 7 June 1940 they boarded a British cruiser.

Reprisals begin

A Nazi, Josef Terboven, was despatched to Norway as Reichskommissar. Quisling was appalled; he had expected to be appointed Führer, in which capacity he would then conclude peace with Germany and mobilise Norwegian forces on its side. Terboven had little time for Quisling, but the latter had friends in Berlin who arranged to have him appointed "minister president". As such, Quisling ordered all children between the ages of 10 and 18 to join his version of the Hitler Youth. His plans for the Nazification of the civil service, courts, all professional bodies and trade unions were in every instance fiercely rejected.

Resistance met with grim reprisals. Two

RIGHT: Vidkun Quisling inspecting German troops in Berlin.

THE "SHETLAND BUS"

The old Viking character was alive in the small boats that regularly made the crossing between Shetland and Norway, keeping links open with the exiled king and government in Britain.

trade union leaders, Viggo Hansteen and Rolf Wickstrøm, were shot; the rector of Oslo University was arrested. A steady flow of prisoners, including 1,300 uncooperative teachers, arrived at Grini, the concentration camp established outside Oslo.

The most summary reprisals were meted out to members of the military underground, Milorg, a nucleus of survivors of the 1940 fighting augmented by volunteers and armed by clandestine shipments from Britain.

Telavåg, a village near Bergen, was razed to the ground when the Germans discovered it to be an assembly point for a clandestine ferry service, the "Shetland Bus", between Norway and Britain. The village men were deported to Germany, the women and children interned. A group of 18 men waiting in Ålesund for the trip to Britain were found and shot. The most famous of the resistance operations was conducted against the heavy-water factory at Rjukan in Telemark.

Celebration party

The final chapter of the Occupation was played out by German troops retreating from Finland through Finnmark in northern Norway. They adopted a scorched-earth policy which utterly destroyed many towns and villages. The inhabitants were herded into fishing boats to find their own way to the south.

The Germans were still very strong in Norway while their forces elsewhere capitulated – the army alone numbered 350,000. Fears that the whole country might be put to the torch were laid to rest only when they surrendered on 7 May 1945. The gates of Grini were thrown open and thousands streamed out to join what was undoubtedly the biggest street party ever held in Oslo. It was still going strong a week later when Crown Prince Olav returned, five

only now being replaced, and many of the small northern towns still have an austere anonymity.

Rising standards

Fast economic expansion and many crash programmes led to large investment and over-employment, but it provided a rising standard of living that climbed faster and further than most countries in Europe. By the early 1960s Norway used more electricity per head than any other country in the world and only three people in every thousand in remote areas had no supply. The merchant marine had made good its wartime shipping losses by 1949 and

years to the day after his reluctant departure.

Cleaning up after the war concentrated on Quisling's prosecution. Charges were brought against 50,000 people, many for petty crimes rather than full-scale collaboration. The courts were not unduly harsh, perhaps sensing that participation in Quisling's so-called "NS" would remain a stigma. Some 25 were executed, including Quisling and two of his ministers.

After that necessary purging, Norway's most pressing needs were to replace what had been destroyed during the war, and to modernise and expand industry and the economy. The whole of northern Norway had been so heavily devastated that in some cases areas of hasty rebuilding are

tonnage tripled within 15 years. By the 1970s Norway was almost overwhelmed by the riches it was receiving from the oil industry.

All this went along with over 20 years of socialist government, which introduced comprehensive social-welfare services, Scandinavian-style, and much state control of industry. But this was no far-left Labour Party in the style of its post-World War I predecessors, and many shared its belief in an equal society and care for all.

In keeping with similar parties in Sweden and Denmark, post-war Norwegian socialism had been middle-of-the-road, led first by Einar Gerhardsen, who had been a prominent Resistance worker, then Oscar Torp, and Trygve Bratteli. In recent years, the best-known Norwegian prime minister, ranking high in international esteem, has been Gro Harlem Brundtland. She was appointed prime minister for the first time in 1981. That tenure was short, lasting only until an historic conservative-led victory at the polls that autumn; but at 41 she was the youngest person ever to hold the office, and the first woman. In total, she held the post for more than 10 years before stepping down in 1996. In 1998 she became Director-General of

BRUNTLAND REPORT

Norway's Gro Harlem Brundtland was responsible for "Our Common Future", the United Nations' report on world environmental issues.

International links

In 1945 Norway was one of the founding signatories of the United Nations, and a former Norwegian foreign minister, Trygve Lie, became its first secretary-general. Lie held the office during the first hopeful years and continued to do so into the Korean War, in which United Nation troops took an active fighting role for the first and last time. Norway provided and staffed a field hospital in Korea. Since then some 32,000 Norwegians have worn a UN blue beret. Norway has continued its com-

the World Health Organization. In 2001, a new centre-right coalition won the national election, followed by a centre-left coalition in 2006.

The attitude of King Olav V, who reigned between 1957 and 1991, helped to keep Norway tranquil. King Olav took his father's motto of "All for Norway". When he died in 1991 his son Harald V succeeded him to the throne. Like his father, he is interested in sports and liked by his people.

LEFT: Crown Prince Olav (later King Olav V) returns to Norway at the end of the war.
ABOVE: for years Lenin's likeness looked across the border from Russia.

mitment to internationalism and peace, notably as broker in the 1993 Israeli-Palestinian peace proposals. Like the other Scandinavian nations, it has concentrated very much on human rights, humanitarian help and environmental issues. The important role played by this small country has not gone unrecognised: at the end of 2000, Norway was elected by the General Assembly to serve as a member of the Security Council for a two-year term commencing in 2001.

Joining NATO was more problematic. Norway saw its role as bridging the Cold War divide, and the country had no particular reason to fear Russia. Unlike Sweden, Norway had never been at war with Russia. The Russians had recently acted as liberators in Finnmark, and the two countries were, in fact, negotiating joint occupation of Spitsbergen.

Nevertheless, for most of the war years Trygve Lie had been advocating an alliance with the great Atlantic Powers for his "seafaring people", rather than with any power in Europe. The fate of Czechoslovakia, a country which also saw itself as a bridge-builder until the Iron Curtain came down behind it, convinced the doubters that Norway's security depended on more tangible Western links than would be afforded by Swedish-style neutrality. As NATO's most north-easterly outpost, with a short 196-km (122-mile)

border with Russia, Norway inevitably walked a tightrope between the superpowers. Soviet "merchant ships" visited the northern sea coast and unaccountably needed lengthy, unspecified repairs which kept them in harbour for months. Ships of the Soviet Northern Fleet, based on the Kola peninsula, were a common sight in the North Atlantic when crossing to Iceland.

There were never any major incidents, and, long before *glasnost*, Norway turned a philosophical face to its massive neighbour. Since the break-up of the Soviet Union, Norway has been more concerned about the environmental threat presented by outdated nickel works, nuclear power stations and nuclear waste from decommissioned submarines and other vessels of the former Soviet Northern Fleet.

Maintaining independence

The debate over whether to join the European Community aroused great passions, especially among farmers and fishermen who believed that membership would end their subsidies. The Storting was generally in favour of applying for membership along with Denmark and Britain, partners in the European Free Trade Association (EFTA), but the first approaches were rebuffed by an imperious General Charles de Gaulle.

A referendum was organised in 1972 to gauge public opinion on whether another attempt ought to be made. There was never any doubting where the farmers and rural Norway as a whole would stand. In the event, the country opposed joining by a vote of 52.5 percent.

In 1993 the anti-European Centre Party of farmers gained ground but not enough to stop Gro Harlem Brundtland taking the Labour Party back to power. Sweden and Finland having voted to join Denmark in the European Union, she felt confident enough to hold another referendum on membership in 1994, warning that, with oil and gas revenues declining at that point, Norway could no longer afford to stay out in the cold. But again the country voted no, by an even narrower margin than in 1972. Having been ruled by Denmark, Sweden and the Nazis, Norwegians seemed determined to hang on to every shred of their hard-won independence.

Although the opposite sides of the 1994 EU debate were unyielding, the situation normalised fairly quickly once the vote was over, but the issue continues to be hotly debated with polls indicating a swing towards a "yes" vote. Meanwhile, the Agreement on the European Economic Area (EEA), signed by the EU and EFTA countries in 1992, ensures Norwegian participation in the future of the EEA, gives it access to the EU market and opens the door to further co-operation.

In 2001, Norway signed the Schengen Agreement allowing citizens of other Schengen countries to travel without passports. The centre-right government elected in September 2001 had to relax the immigration laws in the face of labour shortages at home. Norway was gradually starting to become more outward looking. ❏

LEFT: Mother Teresa receiving the Nobel Peace Prize in 1979.

Norway and its Neighbours

If you walked into a room and met three Scandinavians, it would be hard to tell which was the Norwegian, which the Dane and which the Swede. They look alike, have similar interests, and seem to speak the same language, even if the accent is somewhat different.

The written languages, all based on Old Norse, are so similar they are generally understood by all, and SAS, the airline shared by the three countries, solves communication problems by allowing its crews to use their own language. This works well when a crew is Norwegian, but less well with Danes and Swedes who sometimes find each other incomprehensible.

This Scandinavian family is often taken to include Finland, though the Finns are of a different race with a language related to Hungarian – and that only marginally. In any event, all four countries are part of the Nordic group, which includes Iceland, the autonomous territories of the Faroes, Greenland and the Åland Islands in the Gulf of Bothnia.

Like all families, Scandinavians have the usual squabbles, jealousies, misunderstandings and false images of one another that come out of close proximity. To other Scandinavians, Norwegians are "blue-eyed" or naive, often the butt of innocuous jokes, yet both Swedes and Danes are astonished to learn that similar jokes are told by Norwegians against them. The family analogy continues in that the Danes tend to look on Norway as a younger brother, with all that that implies.

Sweden, with which Norway shares a 1,700-km (1,000-mile) border, is often looked on by Norway (and to a lesser extent by Denmark) as an elder brother, with allegations of arrogance and insensitivity from the smaller countries and a tendency for the larger to think it "knows best". But since Norway discovered oil in 1969, the big-brother attitude has taken a knock, and left Sweden looking at Norway with a degree of wonder and envy. The image of Norway as the junior partner is partly due to the fact that, after 500 years ruled first by Denmark then Sweden, the present Norwegian state is just over a century old, though Norway has been a nation for as long as any Scandinavian country.

RIGHT: conscripts undergoing winter training in the far north of the country.

Norway's only non-Nordic neighbour is Russia. The two countries co-exist without much friction on Spitsbergen (Svalbard), the remote northern islands, best known for coal, bird- and plant-life, and the sealers and whalers of former days.

In the days of the Soviet Union they were at odds over their joint border in the far northern Barents Sea, where the two countries are face to face on a dividing line more than 1,700 km (1,000 miles) long. Norway favours a border on the median line equidistant between the two countries, but their Russian neighbours have wanted to adopt a sector principle. The area under dispute is as big as Belgium, Switzerland and Austria com-

bined, and the Russian proposals would give Russia control of larger fish stocks and oil reserves.

During World War II, when only Sweden was neutral, the Scandinavian countries did their best to help one another, although neither Norway nor Sweden has yet managed to forget that Sweden allowed German troops to pass through its country on their way to attack Norway. Many Finnish children left for homes in Sweden, and that country also became an escape route from Norway. At the end of the war, Norway, Denmark and Iceland became members of NATO, Sweden continued to be non-aligned, and Finland (stuck in an uneasy position between the eastern and western blocs) declared itself neutral. ❑

WHO ARE THE NORWEGIANS?

Ask a visitor what defines a Norwegian and you might get a general description of a Scandinavian. While some of the stereotypes ring true, differences abound

One character in a Hans Christian Andersen story proclaims: "I'm a Norwegian. And when I say I'm Norwegian, I think I've said enough. I'm as firm in my foundations as the ancient mountains of old Norway... It thrills me to the marrow to think what I am, and let my thoughts ring out in words of granite."

Andersen was, of course, a Dane, and he was teasing the Norwegians, as their Scandinavian neighbours are apt to do. In much the same way as Italians are satirically reduced to being tearful opera- and ice-cream fiends, and Frenchmen become obtuse philosophers in onion necklaces, so the typical Norwegian is portrayed as a simple, stubborn peasant who from time to time needs a comforting pat on the head. The country's refusal, in 1972 and again in 1994, to join other Scandinavian countries in the European Union confirmed this view to many.

Naturally enough, Norwegians see themselves rather differently. A Gallup poll once asked 200 people from each of 12 countries to rank themselves in terms of culture, food, living standards, beauty, *joie de vivre*, and national pride. The Norwegians gave themselves top marks in virtually every category. This sweeping victory for the home side was surpassed only by the conceit of the American entry.

Generous hospitality

The Norwegian character is of course far more complex than Andersen would allow or Gallup could measure. It is sometimes said that Norwegians are xenophobic. While this may be an exaggeration, it is certainly the case that they do not accept outside criticism. Yet the hospitality shown towards foreign visitors far exceeds the demands of mere good manners. An English visitor arriving late was whisked off spontaneously to a wedding party in Oslo. As the only foreigner among 200 guests, he was disarmed when the bride's

father, advised of his surprise presence, gave away his daughter in English. Although the younger Norwegian guests were, as usual, fluent in English, some older ones were left in the dark, but they thoroughly approved of the gesture.

The same English visitor, immobilised by skis around his neck after capsizing on a narrow

cross-country ski trail, brought down a party of local skiers who descended on him too fast and too late to stop. The victims of this pile-up were disgruntled until they made sense of his choked apologies, in English of course, at which point they tried to make him feel that, in the circumstances, the violent introduction was an unexpected pleasure, not to say privilege.

Other signs of welcome are given without thinking. A visitor in the house is the signal for lighting candles, probably a throwback to the days when, compounded by the long hours of winter darkness, houses shuttered against the cold were rather gloomy. Until quite recently, most of Norway's population was thinly scattered across

---

PRECEDING PAGES: 17 May, National Day; fishermen at Verdens Ende; Royal Palace guards.
LEFT: a passion for sport.
RIGHT: shopping on Karl Johans Gate, Oslo.

a vast landscape in a patchwork of tiny communities, so visitors invariably arrived after a long and exhausting journey, sometimes on skis. The assumption was that they arrived hungry, and restorative food and drink still appear as if by magic. A planned meal for guests requires elaborate place-settings, and food bearing little resemblance to the low-calorie diet of everyday life.

Visitors will not be allowed to leave without a tour of the house and a look at the family album. The Norwegians are attentive hosts who expect very little in return – common courtesy, and some appreciative comments about their warm welcome as well as the tasteful interior decoration

The lesser-known Aksel Sandemose wrote Ten Commandments for village life, the essence being humility bordering on self-abasement. They included: "You must not think that you are worth anything; you must not think that you are better than anyone else; you must not think yourself capable of anything worthwhile; and you must not think that you are in any way exceptional."

Jingoistic chest pounding of the sort noted by Hans Christian Andersen is derived to some extent from Norway's peculiar position as both one of the oldest, if not the oldest, nation in Europe and at the same time one of the youngest.

of the house. Norway's vaunted standard of living is a relatively recent phenomenon, thanks mainly to a prosperous offshore oil industry.

The Ten Commandments

The more enigmatic aspects of the Norwegian psyche – including the Nordic gloom which descends after a drink too many – have been famously scrutinised by native Henrik Ibsen. He was brought up in small communities and, during a long exile, turned his critical eye on the experience. One of the themes running through his writings is the double-edged nature of life in such a community: mutual support in adversity weighed against a suffocating lack of privacy.

It is the oldest in the sense that the Norwegians can trace an unbroken line of descent from people who inhabited their territory in prehistoric times, a homogeneity whose origins predate the beginnings of Western civilisation in the Aegean.

Yet the present state of Norway was re-constituted only in 1905, which makes it younger than many of the junior members in the United Nations, themselves pasted together by the imperial powers in the 19th century. Having been relegated to a back seat in Scandinavian affairs for hundreds of years, these distant descendants of the illustrious Vikings need to pinch themselves – or blow a trumpet – as if they nervously expect to find that their independence was a cruel dream.

Norwegians enjoy amazing longevity. They manage to look remarkably healthy all their lives, and the octogenarian grandmother whizzing by on skis is not a myth. In any case, there are Norwegians alive who can remember, or have had drummed into them, the euphoria of liberation from their domineering Scandinavian partners.

Free to show the flag

Well-deserved national pride makes Norwegians ardent flag-wavers. This could be construed as a rude gesture to the Swedes who, under the union,

> **FLAG HAPPY**
>
> Many houses have flagpoles and every household possesses a flag which is hoisted on the slightest pretext, if only to indicate that the owner is in residence.

king who reluctantly oversaw Norway's independence predicted that bureaucratic incompetence would soon have Norwegians begging to be returned to the fold. The response, even now, is a reluctance to admit (to outsiders) that they are capable of making a mistake.

As long as authority was vested in foreigners, Norwegians did not regard it too highly. On assuming it themselves authority assumed the aura of divine right, before which loyal citizens should willingly prostrate themselves. Norwegian history is full of swings from

decided when, where and how the Norwegian colours were to be shown in foreign waters, relegating them to a mere patch on a much larger Swedish flag. The flag flown on Norwegian ships was, like separate consular representation and the establishment of a national bank, a perennial bone of contention before independence.

Norwegians would be distressed by their revered flag being desecrated as a pair of underpants or on shopping bags. Their dignity as a sovereign state is not to be trivialised. The Swedish

FAR LEFT: still cutting the grass by hand at 89.
LEFT: a great-grandmother with her 19th grandchild.
ABOVE: enjoying the September sun.

one extreme to another. Pagans who held out against Christianity until a surprisingly late date became, and in some cases remain, doggedly fundamentalist after seeing the light. And a nation once thought in danger of drinking itself to death has by no means buried the bottle even if alcohol consumption is now kept mainly for the weekend and Norwegians are adopting more continental customs – wine sales are up, hard liquor down.

Friendships worth forging

While drinking customs are becoming a little more moderate, there's no question that Norwegians become less reserved after a *skål* or two. Foreigners moving to Norway discover quickly that sober Norwegians aren't big on small talk. They rarely smile at or even acknowledge strangers in public, and don't count on assistants or cashiers greeting you in shops. They don't mean to be unfriendly, there's just no tradition of being gregarious. Many Norwegians would consider it superficial to tell a stranger to "Have a nice day."

In fact, Norwegians are very polite, even if the only equivalent to "please" in Norwegian is *vennligst*, which is formal and not frequently used. Nor do they say *takk* (thank you) as frequently as English-speaking people. The only thing

TRADITIONAL SPIRIT

Akevitt is a spirit concocted from potato and caraway seeds. It is similar in taste to Schnapps and is usually 40 percent proof or more.

a Thermos bottle, hard and cold on the outside, but nice and warm once you open them up." Society is very closely tied to family and long-term friends from school days. Many do not feel inclined to go much further to extend their relationships to outsiders and consequently, establishing friendships, even within a neighbourhood, could take time. But once formed, genuine friendship is taken very seriously indeed.

The Norwegians' penchant for sharing their wealth is also legendary, both at home and

remotely unruly in Norwegian manners occurs in the busy streets of Oslo. People jostle each other with impunity: don't be offended if you don't get an apology after someone bumps into you – as long as it's gentle. Of more concern are the mad darts people make across streets, without regard for traffic lights.

Although young people tend to be a lot less formal than their parents, Norwegians do still go about life with some surprisingly rigid rules of behaviour. Norwegians are great hand shakers. Strangers meeting will always shake hands and exchange full names. When meeting casual acquaintances, you usually shake hands as you arrive and leave.

A language instructor at the University of Oslo once claimed that "Norwegians are like

abroad. Many Norwegians say they pay their high taxes with pleasure, firmly believing that no one should be too rich or too poor, while their generosity in donating money to worthy causes and international relief efforts (as measured on a per-capita basis) leads all other countries.

The Norwegian language(s)

Norwegians can also be remarkably generous where they might be expected to be most possessive. There is little alarm about the predatory impact of, say, satellite television on a language which hardly exists outside Norway. Far from resenting visitors who presume to address them in a foreign tongue, Norwegians positively relish the challenge, usually responding with fluency.

Confidence in the hardiness of their language is curiously at odds with its historical background. Language was a burning issue in Norwegian politics until the 1950s, having forced a prime minister to resign in 1912. The long-running controversy started as a form of agitation against Danish rule, throughout which Danish was the language of the civil service, schools and the Church. For a long time after the Reformation the revised Bible was available only in Danish. Denmark got its first printing press in 1480 but Norway had to wait until 1643. Until then books were imported and in Danish.

the expense of the others, the language reformers concentrated on developing a composite.

The early language reformers included Ivar Aasen and Knut Knudsen, the latter a schoolmaster driven by his pupils' frustration in trying to work out Danish spelling. They worked on what became known as *landsmål* or *nynorsk*, but their efforts were not unreservedly welcomed. Danish was the language of society and the theatre, and if Norwegian had to be spoken, a "Danicised" pronunciation was fashionable. These tendencies eroded as intellectuals like Ibsen lent respectability to the campaign for the revival of a purely Norwegian language.

When reading aloud, Norwegians modified standard Danish through the use of their own pronunciation and intonation, eventually producing the hybrid known as *bokmål* (book language).

The search for a native language

However, the 19th-century nationalists still saw it as fundamentally Danish and wanted a national language which was authentically Norwegian. Unfortunately, there was no single Norwegian substitute as the language had developed many distinct dialects. Rather than choose one dialect at

---

LEFT: winter skiing in Nordmarka.
ABOVE: summer on a Telemark beach.

In 1929 *bokmål* and *nynorsk* were recognised as dual official languages, the hope being that they would drift towards a blend to be known as *samnorsk*. The names of cities and towns lost their Danish connotations. Christiania, for example, reverted to a Norwegian name, Oslo.

Progress towards *samnorsk* was given a nudge in the 1950s with a proposal to have school textbooks converted into it. There was such an outcry, however, that the government backed down. Subsequent policy has been to treat the two languages even-handedly, still hoping that they will one day converge. In spite of attempts to shore up *nynorsk* through radio and television, it looks as if it is losing ground.

Individualistic tongue

Educated speech is distinctly that of the south-east, although that does not prevent country dwellers on a visit to the capital, say, from laying on their regional accents thick for effect. The Bergensere, at the heart of the *nynorsk* area, are certainly proud of their individualistic tongue.

The regional fragmentation at the heart of the language debate extends to most facets of cultural and economic life. While Norway has since Viking times been a single nation, it has been a confederation of many parts. Norway can be divided north–south, east–west or a dozen different ways. Like the Renaissance, the Industrial

Revolution hardly intruded, so there was not the rapid urbanisation which occurred elsewhere. Trondheim, Bergen and Oslo were towns rather than cities. A later creation like Stavanger owed its existence to the arrival of vast shoals of herring, which were the basis of jobs, trade and other prerequisites of a cash economy. Most of Norway remained rooted in subsistence agriculture.

Preserving old necessities

Rural families tended to be isolated and self-sufficient. Their lives depended on agriculture, and the land was not good enough to support more than a family or two in a single valley. Separated from their neighbours by mountains which were

ironically easier to cross in winter (on skis) than in summer, they effectively lived in different worlds. There were hardly any villages where tradesmen could be found and paid in cash. The versatile family managed on its own, a resourcefulness which still runs in the blood. It is not unknown for young couples living in Oslo today to solicit the help of friends to build their first home with their own hands.

The modern Norwegian makes a virtue out of what used to be necessity. The ideal *hytte*, as a country cabin is known, is isolated. It will probably have electricity, but running water may be considered effete. Visitors who decide, sensibly, to rent a *hytte* will almost certainly come round to the view that water drawn from a stream is not just an exercise in rural nostalgia but also doubly delicious. In winter there is the added joy of first having to drill a hole through the ice to reach it.

Messing about in boats

The old necessities carry over to the passion for owning a boat. On summer evenings, Oslo fjord is alive with boats, a pattern repeated everywhere. Although Norwegians are said to grow up on skis, messing about in boats is equally ingrained. Both used to represent basic transport in a land where road and rail construction costs billions because of the mountainous terrain and deep fjords. Although the country is now well served in both departments, the boat was once both a tool of daily life as well as a source of recreation.

Modern Norway has the reputation of being an enlightened, progressive state on the Scandinavian model, but it does Norwegians no disservice to recognise the Viking beneath. A man found sitting in a hole on the snowbound Oslo golf course said with a twinkle that his ancestors had devised a system of digging holes which, taking into account the direction of the wind, provided an emergency – and actually quite comfortable – refuge in the event of snowstorms. He felt he was doing his bit, preserving some of his heritage for posterity. He put his palms to his temples and waggled his outstretched fingers.

That the Vikings wore horns is doubtful, if not an outright fallacy; but only the most churlish observer would wish to deny someone who saw sport in sitting in a snowbound hole a certain degree of historical licence. ❏

LEFT: at the end of a day on the fjord.
RIGHT: traditional *bunads* worn at church on Sunday.

EPIC EXPLORERS

Whether because of exile, scientific exploration, or wanting to be the first,

Norwegian explorers have travelled the world from North to South Pole

Although exploration is most often associated in modern times with rocket journeys into space, the names of at least two Norwegian explorers are as evocative now as at the time of their epic achievements: Roald Amundsen (1861–1930) is forever remembered as the man who beat Captain Scott to the South Pole; and Thor Heyerdahl (1914–2002) for the *Kon-Tiki* expedition.

Their fame steals some of the limelight which ought to be apportioned to a much larger cast of intrepid Norwegians, beginning with Bjarni Herjulfsson who, in 986, lost his way while sailing from Iceland to Greenland and ended up, according to an ancient saga, as the first European to sight the American continent. On Bjarni's return, Leiv Eiriksson borrowed his boat to investigate the mysterious sighting and became the first European to set foot on the American continent.

Early migrations

A 19th-century Norwegian explorer, Fridtjof Nansen (1861–1930), set the pattern for the investigation of human migration. He established his reputation in 1888 with a hazardous crossing of Greenland from east to west. A few years later he was excited by the discovery near the southern tip of Greenland of some wreckage whose origins were traced to the New Siberian Islands. How had it got there?

Nansen determined to find out. His vessel, *Fram*, was designed to lift herself under the crushing pressure of the drift ice in the Arctic Ocean. She was set adrift off the New Siberian Islands in September 1893 and, two years later, emerged near Spitsbergen – but without Nansen. He had left the ship in charge of his second-in-command in a heroic but vain attempt to reach the North Pole with dog-drawn sledges. He and his companion survived a win-

ter in Franz Josef Land, living in an ice hut and eating whatever they could shoot. They reached safety on practically the same day as *Fram*, and Nansen's six volumes of findings are the basis of the science of oceanography.

Such was Nansen's fame that, when war threatened between Norway and Sweden over

the dissolution of their union, he was sent to London and Copenhagen to win support for the Norwegian cause.

The purpose of the 1947 *Kon-Tiki* expedition was to test a theory about the origins of the Polynesian people and culture *(see page 162 for details on Kon-Tiki Museet)*. Heyerdahl demonstrated that a balsawood raft set adrift off the coast of Peru could eventually – it took him about four months – reach the Tuamotu archipelago 8,000 km (5,000 miles) to the west. In the 1960s he successfully conducted a similar experiment – the *Ra* expedition – to discover whether West African voyagers using their traditional rafts may have reached the West Indies before Columbus.

PRECEDING PAGES: the *Fram* stuck fast in the Arctic ice.
LEFT: Hanssen, one of Amundsen's expedition members to the South Pole, next to the flag.
RIGHT: Roald Amundsen.

Viking explorers

The father of Norwegian exploration, or at least the earliest recorded explorer, is Erik the Red, a man who seems to have had a liking for slaughter. In the 10th century he was banished from Norway to Iceland for murder, and then from Iceland as well for several more killings. Unwelcome anywhere, he sailed west with a shipload of livestock and discovered the world's largest island – a lump of ice, more than 3 kilometres (2 miles) thick in places.

Obviously a keen angler, Erik was so engrossed by the excellent catches to be had in summer that he neglected to collect enough ani-

and in every respect a temperate, fair-dealing man", which would seem to set him apart from his father. His 35-man expedition left Greenland about the year 1000. They landed first at "Markland", a wooded region on the coast of Labrador, and then continued south to "Vinland".

An inscription on a map probably drawn by a monk in Basel in 1440 – about half a century before Columbus sailed to the New World – describes Leiv Eiriksson's discovery of "a new land, extremely fertile, and even having vines… a truly vast and very rich land". Attempts to settle the land were defeated by the hostile natives.

mal fodder for the winter. His livestock starved to death. He resolved to risk violation of his ostracism to collect replacements from Iceland and to persuade others to join him on return. Erik trumpeted his new-found land with the zeal of an unprincipled estate agent. It was so wonderful, he told his audiences, that he had decided to call it Greenland. By 985 he had acquired animals and enticed enough colonisers to fill 25 ships, of which 14 reached the destination.

It was in one of the settlements founded by Erik the Red that his son, Leiv, having heard Bjarni Herjulfsson's strange tale, prepared to find out for himself what it was all about. He was "big and strong, of striking appearance,

American proof

Certainly the existence of "Vinland" was known to Adam of Bremen, a chronicler in the 1070s, and to writers of the sagas, but it was through a typically bizarre quirk of archaeology that Eiriksson's discovery of America is put virtually beyond doubt. Excavations on the site of a Greenland farm which belonged to a member of the "Vinland" expedition produced a lump of coal which proved to be anthracite, a material unobtainable in Greenland but plentiful on the surface in Rhode Island.

The case was strengthened in 1960 by Helge Ingstad, who thought about the likely landing place on the American continent of an expedition from Greenland. Working like a detective, he backed a hunch and at L'anse aux Meadows, on the northern tip of Newfoundland, discovered that six buildings had once stood on the site. Carbon dating proved they were medieval, and the archaeological remains left no doubt that the occupants had been Norsemen.

Race for the Pole

Roald Amundsen had served a rigorous apprenticeship for his famous assault on the South Pole, which came about as a last-minute change

NORTH TO SOUTH

Børge Ousland was the first man to reach both the North (1994) and South (1995) Poles alone on skis without the help of man or beast.

pipped him to the post, in 1910 he secretly went south instead in Nansen's old ship, *Fram*. But not until he reached Madeira did he let anyone know what his intentions were.

Amundsen decided to dispense with all scientific work in his sprint to the South Pole. Scott had a head start but discovered too late that his Siberian ponies were useless in the conditions. He and his team had to pull their sledges. Amundsen took a shorter, rougher route and had the benefit of dog teams. In the event, he beat Scott by a month.

of plan. Although he had taken part in a Belgian expedition to Antarctica his first interest was the Arctic. He was stuck for two years off King William Island in a seal-hunting boat, *Gjøa*, and applied his time to studying the Innuit inhabitants and making reckonings on the magnetic pole.

Amundsen knew about Captain Scott's ambitions to reach the South Pole but he himself was more concerned in reaching the North. Nevertheless, faced with the shattering disappointment of the news that Robert Peary had

LEFT: Thor Heyerdahl's *Ra* under construction in Egypt.
ABOVE: Monika Kristensen.

The dispirited English team perished on their return, and this unlucky fate took some of the lustre off Amundsen's feat. At last, though, the director of London's Royal Geographical Society, which had backed Scott, paid tribute to Amundsen's effort as "the most successful polar journey on record".

To the overwhelmingly male-dominated ranks of Norwegian "explorers" it is refreshing to add the names of Liv Arnesen (born 1953), who, in 1994, was the first woman to reach the South Pole alone, and Monika Kristensen (born 1950) who led a South Pole expedition in 1986–87, following in the footsteps of Roald Amundsen. ❏

FOLKLORE: SAGAS AND FOLKTALES

Among the treasures of Norwegian heritage are its legends and sagas. This form of popular story-telling is an important part of the national psyche

The Norwegian word for folktale, "*eventyr*", crops up as early as the 12th century in the form "*ævintyr*", borrowed from the Latin word "*adventura*", meaning event or strange occurrence. These folktales were imaginative stories passed from one storyteller to another, and depicted relationships expressed in fantastic and symbolic terms. Narrators were often clergymen who used folklore as a moralistic vehicle. The folktale style was, above all, objective: however fantastic the subject, the narrative was always realistic and believable.

COUNTRY LEGENDS

A constant topic in Norwegian legend is its landscape. Many of the stories connected with the sea involved mythical creatures, the best known of which are the Lake Mjøsa monster and Draugen, the personification of all who have died at sea. In lakes and rivers lives the sprite Nøkken (*Nixie*). Many mythical creatures inhabit the mountains and forests, and tales about landmarks created by trolls exist all over the country. Marks left by trolls show their size, such as the Giant Cut (Jutulhogget) in Østerdal.

▽ **PAGAN RELIGION**
Lom stave church in Gudbrandsdal, dating from around 1200, is decorated with carved dragons and fantasy creatures entwined with tendrils of vine.

◁ **TROLLS**
The immoral troll's ambition is to wield power over mortals, but they are stupid and easily duped.

△ **THE GOLDEN BIRD**
Theodor Kittelsen's illustration of a Norwegian folktale, *The Golden Bird*, is from the collection of legends and sagas by Asbjørnsen and Moe.

THE GOLDEN AGE OF LITERATURE

On 17 May 1814, after almost 300 years of Danish rule, Norway signed the constitution at Eidsvoll. This event heralded a revival of the Norwegian language. Per Christen Asbjørnsen (1812–55) and Jørgen Moe (1818–82) were part of this "golden age". Inspired by the German Brothers Grimm and Norwegian Andreas Faye, who published *Norske Sagn* (Norwegian Legends) in 1833, Asbjørnsen and Moe began compiling the first collection of Norwegian folktales as *Norske Huldre-Eventyr og Folkesagn* (Norwegian Ghost Stories and Folk Legends). Their first volume appeared in 1845, the second edition in 1852. Asbjørnsen went on to publish an illustrated version, commissioning some of the best Norwegian painters of the time, including Erik Werenskiold *(work seen above)* and Theodor Kittelsen. Asbjørnsen and Moe's collections have become classic Norwegian folktales; Kittelsen and Werenskiold's illustrations have given the troll its visual image.

△ **MYTHS AND MONSTERS**
Stories about fantastical beasts form the largest group of Norwegian folktales. They often lurk in bottomless lakes and terrorise the forest.

◁ **CHRISTMAS CHARACTER**
The Norwegian version of Santa Claus, *Julenissen*, is a mixture of the Nordic *nisse* (the mischievous gnome) and St Nicholas.

◁ **BRONZE AGE TOTEMS**
The Bronze Age rock carvings at Leirfall (Lerfald), near Hegra include totemic figures performing pagan rituals linked to hunting seasons.

▷ **ANCIENT GRAFFITI**
The prehistoric rock carvings (*c.* 4500 BC) on the Lista peninsula indicate early ship-building skills and a sea-faring culture.

OFF-THE-SHELF MONARCHY

Imported from Denmark in 1905, Norway's popular monarchy has passed through various trials on its way to the very heart of the nation

For the chronically under-employed off-shoots of European royalty, the rash of new states in the 19th and early 20th century brought blessed job opportunities. Their prospects were reduced by republican tendencies and other disappointments: Albania offered its throne to the England cricket cap-

tain, who declined, but in 1905 Norway's criteria were less capricious. The new state had a long royal pedigree, but it had died out during 400 years under Danish and Swedish rule. While Norwegians saw some advantages in a Scandinavian as king, there was the feeling that a Danish or Swedish monarch would amount to the despised *status ante quo*. In the event, the former considerations outweighed the latter, and an invitation went to Prince Carl, second son of the future King Christian IX of Denmark and grandson of Sweden's King Karl XV.

Prince Carl, then 33, was married to Maud, Princess of Wales and daughter of England's Edward VII. Carl insisted first on a plebiscite.

The result was favourable, so on 25 November 1905, having assumed the title Haakon VII, he stepped ashore in Norway sheltering his young son, born Alexander Edward Christian Frederick but quickly renamed Olav, from driving snow. Haakon himself continued to sign letters to friends and relatives in England as "Charles".

Republicanism survived in Norway. Politicians complained that the cost of the monarchy was too high. The royal apartments in the palace were scarcely habitable to begin with and the government would pay only half the repair costs. Frugality was paramount. By watching expenses as carefully as he observed constitutional niceties, Haakon gradually won over the sceptics. Left-wing doubts ceased in 1926 when he called on the Labour Party to form a government.

The king worked hard at not being a foreigner. He travelled widely and impressed his subjects with a dignified modesty. The crown prince needed no encouragement to make up the perceived deficiency in the family tree. Although born in England, he felt at home and proved it by winning prizes on the Holmenkollen ski jump, as daunting a test of Norwegian authenticity as there could be. He also represented Norway as an Olympic sailor, another huge plus to his sea-minded subjects.

Resistance in exile

World War II was the supreme challenge. Implacably opposed to Hitler, King Haakon had to contend with the local clamour for neutrality. "I must be careful... not to say too much," he wrote to Queen Mary, his sister-in-law in London, "so that my ministers cannot say I am more English than Norwegian." He would abdicate rather than bow to German demands for recognition of the Quisling government. Running the gauntlet of the Luftwaffe, he escaped to England. His work, and that of the crown prince, with the Norwegian exile movement, inspired dogged resistance at home and cemented a bond which gave the king a tumultuous reception on his eventual return to Oslo.

Haakon died in 1957 at the age of 85, and became known as Haakon the Good. His only child, who succeeded as Olav V, inherited the same unassuming manner, evident in his endearing discomfort while delivering the traditional New Year's Eve television broadcast, and the affection in which his father was held.

When he died in 1991, the people's grief was genuine. It was not just the passing of an old man, but personal sorrow at the loss of one so dear to many.

PERSONAL PROTECTION

When an American reporter found King Olav V travelling alone on the train and asked whether it wasn't a security risk, the king replied "not with four million bodyguards!".

Changing with the times

King Olav V was succeeded by his then 54-year-old son, who assumed the title of Harald V. Harald had been raised to carry out his royal duties, while maintaining strong personal ties with the people and his own time. King Olav's announcement in 1968 that Crown Prince Harald wished to marry a commoner triggered a heated debate on the future of the monarchy. The decision was made by King Olav himself after consultations with the government. The response was favourable and the majority of the population accepted Sonja Haraldsen as queen. She quickly became inseparably linked with the national unity symbolised by the royal family.

King Harald has made a name for himself as a competitive sailor. In 1987 he won the world championship with his new yacht *Fram X*, which was a gift from the Norwegian business community on his 50th birthday. Both King Harald and Queen Sonja are involved in various outdoor sports, as is their daughter, Princess Märtha Louise (born 1971), who has achieved considerable success in the equestrian field.

Public face, private lives

The king was less than amused when, in 1994, Princess Märtha Louise's interest in equestrian sports extended to being cited as co-respondent in a British divorce case as a result of an alleged affair with a married showjumper. Not that it caused much of a stir in the Norwegian press, which long had tacitly agreed not to encroach on the private lives of the members of the royal household. This privacy was tested with Crown Prince Haakon's choice of bride in 2001: unwed

mother and former waitress, Mette-Marit Tjessem Høiby. Like his father, Haakon has chosen to "marry the girl he loves rather than love the girl he marries". The partnership added fuel to the flames of republicanism, but in a country in which nearly 50 percent of babies are born out of wedlock, was not so remarkable. The couple has since had two children of their own.

Haakon and his sister were educated at state schools. The crown prince then embarked on naval training and later studied political science

at the University of California, Berkeley. His preparation as a future head of state has continued as a trainee at the Norwegian Ministry of Foreign Affairs in Oslo and at the London School of Economics. In 2002 Princess Märtha Louise also married a commoner, author Ari Behn.

All this fits in with the egalitarian outlook that pervades Norwegian society. Like the flag and the 17th of May celebrations, the Norwegian monarchy symbolises independence from the almost 400-year rule under first Denmark and then Sweden. What often appears to be fervent nationalism is in fact no more than national pride and a desire to hold on to a hard-earned self-determination. ❏

LEFT: King Harald and Queen Sonja with their son and daughter. **RIGHT:** King Harald at a skiing event.

THE SAMI: PEOPLE OF FOUR NATIONS

Behind the popular image of the Sami with their colourful costumes and large herds of reindeer lies a rich, complex culture that is an important part of modern Norway

The Sami (or Lapps, as they are sometimes called despite its derogatory overtones) have lived in Norway from time immemorial. Traces of their presence stretch back more than 8,000 years. The name Sami comes from the Sami *sápmi*, denoting both the people themselves and their traditional territory. Samiland extends from Idre in Sweden and adjacent areas in Norway south to Engerdal in Hedmark; to the north and east it stretches to Utsjoki in Finland, Varanger in Norway and on to the Kola peninsula in Russia. It covers a larger area than Norway and Denmark combined, and the population is cautiously estimated at 70,000, of which around 45,000 live in Norway, mainly in Finnmark.

Norwegian Sami divide roughly into three groups. The Mountain Sami are the most widespread, ranging from Varanger to Femunden. They live mainly by breeding reindeer. The River Sami live around the waterways in the interior of Finnmark and have turned increasingly to agriculture and animal husbandry, though hunting, fishing and berry-picking still add to their income. The third group, the Sea Sami, is the largest, making a living from fishing and farming in a lifestyle that differs little from that of other northern Norwegians.

Ancient culture

The Sami people have been very successful in conserving their rich cultural heritage and many unique traditions. Not the least important is the Sami language, which derives from the Finno-Ugric branch of the Uralic family and is closely related to the Baltic Sea-Finnish languages.

From ancient times, the sea has been of great importance as an abundant source of fish, and of seal to provide them with valuable hides. Walruses, with their precious tusks, were also highly prized, particularly by the Sami craftspeople who produced all sorts of tools and uten-

sils including needles, buttons, spoons, cups, and a variety of musical instruments.

Samiland is a mighty land, rich in lakes, rivers, small streams, grandiose mountains and boundless hills, which in some places reach as far as the Atlantic coast. Besides fishing, hunting also used to be important and there was much game, big and small. Squirrels, martens, foxes, even bears were all hunted, but the most important animal was – and to a certain extent still is – the reindeer. About 10 percent of Norway's landmass is used for reindeer grazing (mostly in Finnmark). While the economic value of this industry is minor on a national scale, it is important both financially and culturally to the Sami, with about 40 percent of the population living from herding reindeer.

Very few of the truly nomadic Sami people are left. Most Sami have settled down in the sense that they have a permanent address but move with their herds to the high ground in the summer. During late summer and in the autumn

PRECEDING PAGES: children in Kautokeino, Finnmark, ready for confirmation.
LEFT: traditionally Sami women love smoking pipes.
RIGHT: a Sami boy.

the reindeer are driven down to the woods near the foot of the summer mountain pastures where there is plenty of lichen. There they stay during winter, roaming in freedom until the spring when it is time once more to move up the mountain to the high slopes, now covered with succulent, nourishing vegetation.

Brilliant colours

Many visitors to Norway come north to Sami-land and to the beautiful *fjell* (mountains) in search of untouched nature. Mosses and lichens give a gentle splash of colour to the vast land, and grasses, especially sedges, are abundant here. At the beginning of summer the rare, pale pasque flower *(Pulsatilla vernalis)* is in bloom and the cinnamon rose *(Rosa majalis)* gives colour to the rocky hill side and the edges of the bog. Carpets of mountain avons *(Dryas octopetala)* are characteristic of soil that is rich in calcium, as are many other species, often with names that begin with *fjell*.

Perhaps the colours all around them have been a source of inspiration for the traditional Sami costume. In days gone by, this dress was for daily use; now it is kept for festivals, weddings, funerals and other important occasions. Easter is *the* big feast, particularly in Kautokeino, with

SINFUL SINGING

Of great importance when trying to get inside the world of the Sami people is to understand the importance of the *yoik*, a kind of primitive singing comparable with unac-companied humming or melodic scanning. To outsiders, it is particularly difficult to grasp since the words can be isolated or subordinated to melody and rhythm, followed by long sentences of meaningless syllables, such as *voia-voia, ala ala,* or *lu-lu-lu.*

The *yoik* probably originated as a way of keeping reindeer quiet and at the same time frightened wild animals away. But it is also used as entertainment, when people are gathered together. In Finnmark, *yoiking* has grown strong and each Sami has his own personal melody. Traditionally, a young Sami boy will compose his own *yoik* for the girl he is courting. However, today a suitable *yoik* can be composed to order for almost any occasion.

Like many other Sami traditions, the *yoik* was forbidden by the missionary Christians. At a time when the only decent song was a hymn, the *yoik* was seen as sinful. But a *yoik* could not be burnt like a troll-drum. Many of the old melodies are still alive, handed on from one generation to the next. With the current spread of world music, the Sami singer Mari Boine is known all over Europe, and her success has brought new life to Sami music and culture.

traditional reindeer racing and other events. Then the richly ribboned skirts and frocks, with red their most outstanding colour, are fetched from drawers and chests. These generous ribbons are used as wristbands or cuffs and as "stockings".

There are no bounds to this richness and colour, which makes a magnificent sight. With these lavish dresses go jewellery in silver, exquisitely worked into neckchains and elegant pendants. Another speciality is pewter embroidery, in which very thin threads of pewter are sewn in ingenious patterns on fine bracelets or on bags made of reindeer hide.

The old religion

Like many other people living in close contact with nature, the Sami had, and still have, a religion related to shamanism, in which nature and its forces are of the greatest importance. Beaive (the Sun) and Mannu (the Moon) were the supreme gods; next came Horagalles, the god of thunderstorms. Under these main gods there were many lesser gods and spirit beings, who ruled over fertility and over wild animals and the hunt, as well as over lakes and their fishes and other inhabitants. There were evil spirits as well. One was Rota or Ruta, the demon of illness and death; another was the Devil himself, Fuadno. In many areas Sami religion was related to Norse mythology: Horagalles corresponding to the Norse god of Thunder, Thor.

Christianity did its best to combat and extinguish this popular belief and Swedish Laestadianism did much to destroy the Sami religion. Many of the ceremonial "troll-drums", of great importance in Sami culture but anathema to the would-be missionaries, were burned.

The most effective Christian missionary was King Christian IV. He travelled to Finnmark around the turn of the 17th century and in 1609 introduced the death penalty for Sami who refused to give up their traditional faith. He followed this with an order to build the first Christian church in Varanger.

To go to church regularly was, nevertheless, impossible for many of the nomadic Sami, who had to travel over mountains and vast lakes. It was the great festivals which gathered the Sami

together and so it is today: New Year, Easter, Lady Day, and the spring and autumn equinoxes. In addition, the Sami people count eight seasons, all of them related to their reindeer and these too must be celebrated.

Language revival

Traditionally, Sami culture possessed an extensive oral "literature", including a vast number and variety of legends and fairytales, many of which were written down earlier last century by J.K. Ovigstad in his *Sami Fairytales and Legends*. This literature also includes a distinctive form of poetry designed to accompany

the traditional Sami "song" or *yoik (see box left)*.

In the first half of the 20th century, it was government policy to encourage the "Norwegianisation" of the Sami people and its language. This led to the irony that one of the greatest writers of Sami descent, Mario Aikio from Karasjok, wrote only in Norwegian, though today a number of younger writers are once again using the Sami language.

As has happened with many minority languages in recent times, Norway now has a policy of encouraging the Sami language. It is taught from the start of schooling and Sami people can pursue higher education in their

LEFT: a Sami woman at the reindeer round-up.
RIGHT: a character from the Sami theatre.

own language in various establishments such as the Universities of Oslo and Tromsø, and their their own Teachers' Training College in Alta.

Karasjok has the De Samiske Samlinger (Sami Museum, *see page 329*) while in Kautokeino, where the great Easter celebrations are held, there is the Kautokeino Kulturhuset (Culture Centre, *see page 325*).

When the Norwegian Broadcasting Corporation (NRK) planned a second radio channel in the early 1980s, it came up with the unusual idea of plac-

> **FALLOUT**
>
> Norway's Fisheries Minister wore her traditional Sami dress to a state dinner when she accompanied King Harald and Queen Sonja on their official visit to Ireland in 2006.

for reindeer grazing areas and recognition of the right to hunt and fish. Sami have also succeeded in curtailing some electricity development projects which would have flooded whole districts and jeopardised the local reindeer economy.

Today, the Sami people have their own Sameting (Parliament), based in Karasjok, which was opened in 1989 with great ceremony. Parliament is an elected body and to vote you must have a grandparent speaking the Sami language or "feel that you are a Sami". Further progress was made in 1990 when Norway ratified the ILO Convention, which dealt with the rights of indigenous and tribal peoples.

The Sameting deals with all matters pertinent to the Sami people and has gradually been given more autonomy. It has developed a plan of action for Sami coastal and fjord areas, an agricultural plan, and has participated in a Sami fisheries committee. In addition, it has conducted its own studies aimed at boosting local employment (in which tourism is playing an increasingly important role).

Nordic co-operation is also a central part of its activities. The Sami parliaments in Norway, Sweden and Finland decided in 1996 to collaborate through a special parliamentary council. There is now a political adviser for Sami issues at the Ministry of Local Government.

In the summer of 2006, the people of Finnmark finally won the right to administer their own lands. Crown Prince Haakon and several government ministers travelled north for celebrations marking a new law that shifts power from the state to the Sameting and local county councils.

ing the first station in the remote north of Norway and beginning broadcasts with the first Sami service, then gradually working its way south.

Towards home rule

The Norwegian Sami have also fought for political control over their own affairs and for the preservation of their way of life which has continued to be eroded by the opening up of the northern areas through improved roads and other forms of communication.

The establishment of national parks, for example, can lead to the protection of wild animals that prey on the reindeer herds and Sami people have been successful in gaining compensation

It was the biggest land transfer in Norway's history, encompassing an area the size of Denmark that is rich in natural resources. Local Sami, who long had made it clear they want their share of the area's potential wealth, also are keen on their share of offshore oil and gas riches from the Barents Sea. A poll conducted in September 2006 showed 75 percent of the residents of Finnmark support oil and gas exploration in the environmentally sensitive area. ❑

LEFT: the Sami singer Mari Boine is now known internationally.
RIGHT: an old Sami woman fixing her traditional *lavvu* (skin tent).

BOAT BUILDERS AND ENGINEERS

*Travelling around Norway has never been easy. However, Norwegian engineers
have come up with some spectacular solutions to speed you on your way*

Norway is 1,600 km (1,000 miles) long and has a coastline that resembles a set of jagged teeth and has a myriad of islands and more than its fair share of mountains. Added to such geographical difficulties are a harsh climate and a population of only 4.5 million people scattered the length and breadth of the country. In short, a nightmare for those whose job it is to plan and build a transport network.

In the 1980s offshore oil came to the rescue, generating wealth that was used partly to upgrade roads and improve the mountain and undersea tunnels that are so vital in this fierce terrain. Such spending produced some spectacular feats of engineering, but the North Sea bonanza is reaching its peak and so new solutions will have to be found.

In the wake of the Vikings

It is not surprising that Norway has traditionally relied on the sea (which had for so long concealed those oil riches) as its basic means of transport, or that most towns and villages lie along the coast and fjords and have harbours. When roads were still primitive tracks and railways in the early stages of construction, shipping routes for passengers and cargo were already well established. This was the main reason that early tours of Norway seldom penetrated inland but kept to the coast and fjords.

The backbone of the domestic sea transport system was, and still is, the famous Hurtigruten, the coastal express steamers which have linked the numerous communities along the coast for many years. These ships followed the route of the Vikings and were originally a series of unconnected independent services. Many operated only during the summer, anchored at dusk, and did not sail through the night.

It was the Vesteraalens Dampskibsselskab (Steamship Company) that established the first year-round express service in 1893, which

sailed between Trondheim and Hammerfest – without overnight stops. Later, other lines joined in and the Hurtigruten assumed a major role, carrying mail, cargo and passengers, including tourists, from Bergen in the southwest to Kirkenes in the northeast. Today, in spite of the development of other forms of

transport, coastal shipping continues to play an important part in the Norwegian communications network.

From *stolkjaerre* to the car

As new roads and bridges have been built and new tunnels bored, the number of smaller ferry services has steadily declined; but the ferries in the west and north of Norway have continued to play an important role into the millennium. National Route 1 in west Norway, for example, crosses no fewer than eight fjords between Stavanger and Ålesund.

Until a couple of decades ago, many quite important roads were still unsurfaced. Road

LEFT: Tjeldsund Bridge connecting the island of Hinnøya to the mainland.
RIGHT: landing on an Arctic airstrip.

building has never been an easy option in Norway and a lot of highways were narrow and rough, while those which crossed the mountains and *fjells* were closed in winter and regularly damaged by the harsh weather.

Before the car, the principal form of transport was the *stolkjaerre*, a two-wheeled horse-drawn cart without springs which seated two persons. An alternative, the *kalesjevogn*, seated a maximum of six passengers. When the car made its first appearance there was little to

engineers have risen to the challenge and created new highways with good surfaces, built superb bridges, and blasted numerous and lengthy tunnels.

The Norwegian skill at tunnelling through the solid rock that forms their mountains creates one of the biggest impressions on visitors. Norwegian tunnels are rarely flat or straight, but wind up and down the mountains with gradients, curves and spirals to make for adventurous underground driving. The more dramatic exam-

encourage it. However, gradually roads improved, although it was not until after World War II that the Norwegians took to motoring.

The Norwegian art of tunnelling

Since the 1980s a surge in road building has gained increasing momentum. But even today there are only a few short sections of motorway, and Norway has its own types of hazard, ranging from reindeer on the road to narrow bridges, blind corners and steep gradients.

Minor roads, particularly in the mountains, are frequently unsurfaced while some of those covered with asphalt – especially in the north – suffer from frost heave. But Norway's civil

ples can gain 300 metres (1,000 ft) in a few minutes, replacing roads that once clung to the mountain side in a succession of hairpin bends and steep gradients and which were closed by snow all winter long.

Nothing has deterred Norwegian engineers from tackling the incredibly difficult to the near impossible – such as the tunnel on the road between Skei and Fjærland which lies beneath an arm of the mighty Jostedal glacier. Previously Fjærland was isolated, reached only by ferry. The only hazards now are sheep, which have learned to appreciate the comfort of lying in tunnel entrances where it is cool in summer and warm in winter.

Underwater motoring

Having mastered the skill of tunnelling on land, Norwegian engineers have turned their attention to the seabed and undersea tunnels. One of the most spectacular burrows out from the mainland to Vardø, which lies on a small island off the north Finnmark coast. It is nearly 3 km (2 miles) long and descends 88 metres (288 ft) below the cold waters of the Arctic Ocean.

At Ålesund on the west coast two undersea tunnels, totalling nearly 8 km (5 miles) link the main town to the island of Vigra, where the airport is located, and have cut out the to the Oslo Gardermoen Airport travels 14 km (9 miles) underground from Oslo Sentralstasjon to Lillestrøm: the original budget was doubled when engineers struck a fault through which several lakes in Østmarka began to drain. Construction bores ahead nonetheless on new tunnels, including another under the Oslo Fjord, with plans for more.

Public transport

Public transport makes good use of Norway's road system to reach outlying towns and villages. The bus station in the centre of any town is busy from morning to night – a reve-

necessity of a ferry crossing. With an economical frame of mind, the Norwegians used the rock drilled out of the tunnels to extend the airport's runway.

The cost of these projects is enormous and the pace of the work has made it impossible for the government to contain them within its budget limits; increasingly, these improvements are paid for by tolls. Some complain that tunnel development has got out of hand, and, to a certain extent, this is true. The high-speed rail link

lation to those for whom a bus is almost an extinct species. What is more, Norwegian public transport has done a marvellous job of integrating road, rail, ferry and even airline timetables. The ferry often waits for the train, and the smaller planes owned by Wideroe and others hop neatly from small airfield to small airfield.

There are also reliable long-distance buses, which have become an increasingly popular mode of inter-city transport. A wide range of bus companies now offer services all over the country at relatively low fares, sometimes at the expense of the state railway since some train lines have been replaced by bus routes.

The slow train

A technical article published in 1850 came to the conclusion that because of the difficult terrain and inhospitable climate "the use of the locomotive is impossible or impracticable". But the engineers proved the writer wrong, although building a railway was slow going. The first line from Christiania (now Oslo) to Eidsvoll opened in 1854, principally for the transport of timber from the Lake Mjøsa region to the harbour at Christiania from where it was exported.

This was typical of how the railways developed piecemeal, with unconnected segments serving a particular industry. The tracks were

not even the same width and, although the question of the gauge was resolved in 1894, it was 1949 before the last line of importance converted to European standard gauge.

The most important rail route in Norway, from Oslo to Bergen, was also one of the most difficult to build and its 470 km (295 miles) did not open until 1909. Now electrified, the Oslo-Bergen line is regarded as one of the great railway journeys of the world. It climbs over the massif of the Hardangervidda, which was conquered by engineering audacity, sheer sweat and a state budget. To protect the line against snowdrifts, the engineers built snow fences, tunnels and snow sheds along the most

exposed stretches: from Utstaoset 100 km (60 miles) of track lies above the tree line. It includes 178 tunnels, and for many years the Gravhal tunnel was Norway's longest at 5,310 metres (5,800 yards).

At Myrdal there is a spectacular branch line to Flåm, on the Aurland fjord, which descends from 870 metres (2,845 ft) to just 2 metres (6 ft) above sea level in 20 km (12 miles). It is now one of the major tourist attractions of western Norway. The trains pause midway on the journey so that passengers can see and photograph the spectacular Kjosfossen waterfall. For safety reasons the engine has five independent braking systems.

All over Norway the many gradients and curves on virtually every line, plus the fact that much of the system is single track, mean that train speeds, even today, are not high. State railway NSB, however, remains a popular commuter alternative and hopes to cut travel time by improving service on some key lines, such as Oslo–Bergen.

Taking to the air

Just as Norway's natural conditions encouraged the development of coastal shipping, so the same conditions have proved to be made-to-measure for air transport. The thin spread of the population has not inhibited the development of an extensive domestic air network with 50 airports scattered all over the country. These services are used by 5 million passengers a year – a ratio of passengers to population which is claimed to be a world record. The domestic and international network is long established and the spur of daunting distances has meant that the Norwegians have brought to aviation much of the same spirit that they brought to the development of shipping.

The major international airline is Scandinavian Airlines System (SAS), a joint operation between Norway, Sweden and Denmark. SAS Norge, the main domestic carrier, is in competition with cut-price Norwegian Air, while Widerøe and some other small carriers operate on the "thinner" routes that serve many small communities, especially in the north of the country. Short-runway aircraft provide a regular service, even during the harsh winters, and most of the airports are tiny by international standards. ❏

LEFT: satellite communications in the Arctic.

Black Gold

It became clear in the 1970s that vast oil and gas riches lay beneath the ocean floor off the Norwegian coast, and yet the full extent of these resources is still being determined today. Current estimates predict that without major new oil discoveries oil production will gradually decline this century, but as a major gas exporter Norway can count on a longer perspective.

It all started in 1962 when, prompted by a gas find off Holland, the American Phillips oil company acquired the right to explore in Norwegian waters. Other companies soon followed. After clarification of legal problems and territorial rights with Denmark and Britain, drilling started in earnest in 1966. Four years later, Phillips announced the discovery of a giant oil field, Ekofisk. The 1970s saw a series of major discoveries: French Elf found Frigg; American Mobil found the world's largest offshore oil field, Statfjord; Shell confirmed the giant Troll gas field off Bergen. The Norwegians learned quickly and two Norwegian oil companies joined the fray. The state-owned Statoil discovered Gullfaks, and the semi-nationalised Norsk Hydro became the operator at Oseberg.

Oil production at the Ekofisk field started modestly from a floating rig in 1971. Permanent installations and a pipeline to Teesside in northeast England were commissioned in 1975. By the end of the 1970s Norway had built a gas processing plant at Kårstø, near Stavanger, and was exporting dry gas to the rest of continental Europe, and the Norwegian shipbuilding industry was entering a golden age as far as contracts were concerned.

Activities were for some time restricted to areas south of the 62nd parallel, in order to maintain a moderate tempo. Exploration off mid- and north Norway was not permitted until 1980, and even then it was strictly regulated. New finds were soon made at Haltenbanken off Trøndelag. Shell brought the Draugen oil reserves on stream in 1993. Further north, the Heidrun field started production in 1995. After several years of discussing production levels, the offshore industry was finally forced (by low oil prices and an inexperienced centre coalition government) into a 3-percent production cut, with the hope that this would help oil prices rise once again.

International terrorism and wars later sent oil prices skyrocketing, fuelling a new exploration boom that focused attention on the Barents Sea. Norwegian companies were keen to team up with Russian oil interests in the development of the Stockman field, while massive investment was also made in the Snow White field and its ground facilities at Hammerfest.

The Norwegian state has three sources of revenue from its offshore industry: taxes and duties levied on the oil companies; the state's direct economic involvement; and share dividends from its ownership stakes in Statoil and Norsk Hydro. Since the late 1990s, much of Norway's staggering level of oil revenue has been stashed into what initially was called the state's Oil Investment Fund.

The idea was to set aside oil revenues for future generations and prevent all the "petrokroner" from overheating Norway's economy. By 2006, its value equalled that of all the real estate on Manhattan, and it had become a serious player in international stock and bond markets. The money is earmarked for future pension demands, a key concern in a country that is among the most expensive in the world.

Despite Norway's supplies of oil and gas, much of it is exported and the country remains concerned about a looming energy crisis. Heavy investment is also being made in solar power and heat pumps, not least because hydroelectric plants often suffer from a lack of rain. Most Norwegians also continue to stock up on firewood every autumn. ❑

RIGHT: at work on an offshore oil platform.

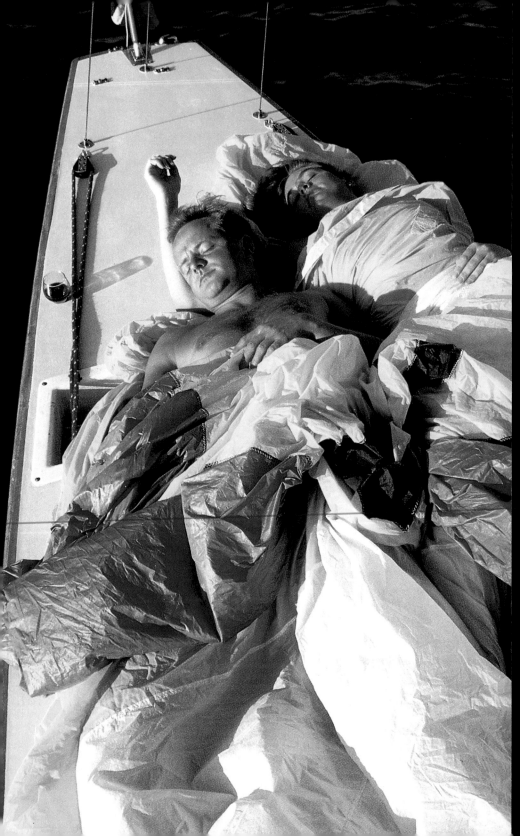

AN OUTDOOR LIFE

In Norway you are free to roam, through forest or over mountain; but wherever you end up, however remote, you can rely on the homely comforts of a hytte

As a race, Norwegians are quite at home in their wild, unspoilt country, and have a great feeling for its mountains. Composer Edvard Grieg, who did much to capture the Norwegian landscape in his music, wrote with passion of the Jotunheimen range in central Norway: "When I contemplate the possibility of a future visit to the mountains, I shudder with joy and expectation, as if it were a matter of hearing Beethoven's Tenth Symphony." There are higher, more remote, more exotically named countries with more photographically stunning landscapes, yet few can claim a population so attuned to its great outdoors.

One Norwegian in four counts outdoor recreation as a first pastime, and Norwegians excel at sports evolved from outdoor pursuits such as cross-country running or skiing, orienteering and cycling. Everyone, from all walks of life, takes part: urbanite and ruralist, commoner and king tramp the terrain, year round. Foreign visitors, unaware of this, often find the mass migration to the open air unnerving, especially if they arrive on business at Easter or during July, the prime times of the year for moor and mountain, sea and shore.

Free to roam

Centuries of that view evolved into one of the country's shortest laws – the 1957 *Lov om friluftslivet* (Outdoor Recreations Act) – which states succinctly that: "At any time of the year, outlying property may be crossed on foot, with consideration and due caution." The few restraints imposed are for environmental or safety reasons. Camping isn't permitted in the immediate watersheds of drinking-water reservoirs, and bonfires are forbidden during summer dry spells that can turn the taiga to tinder.

This liking for untethered roaming seems an integral part of the national character. Among the country's real-life heroes are Fridtjof

Nansen and Roald Amundsen, towering figures of polar exploration around the turn of the 20th century, and Thor Heyerdahl, probably the most widely known Norwegian abroad.

Though on a smaller scale, encounters with nature thread the fabric of everyday life. A family returning from an autumn hike to collect

wild mushrooms for the table will drop into a public mushroom check station to verify the edibility of their harvest. In the winter, city dwellers heading for a ski tour in a nearby forest dial the same snow report number as they dialled the previous summer for the water temperatures at local bathing areas.

Norwegian kindergartens and day-care centres are usually small buildings attached to extensive outdoor playgrounds, designed for day-long activity. Only in extreme weather, defined in most places as below −10°C (14°F), do the kids stay indoors or at home. Coddling in Norway does not include separation from the wrath of the elements. Yet Norwegians see no

---

PRECEDING PAGES: walking along a forest trail.
LEFT: at the end of a day's sailing.
RIGHT: climbing a glacier in the Jotunheimen.

valour in doing battle with nature. As the British polar exploration chronicler Roland Huntford pointed out, that's more the British psyche: Norwegians are much more likely to meet nature on its own terms and seek or make their own comfort wherever they go.

The *hytte*, a home from home

In a country where winter days are short and nasty weather can crop up any time of the year, comfort translates to secure shelter, often your own. Fully a quarter of the country's households also own a holiday home, or *hytte*. By an accident of etymology, *hytte* translates to "hut",

Following the red "T"

Supreme on that scale are the *hytter* run by Den Norske Turistforeningen (DNT), called "the Norwegian Trekking Association" in English (www.turistforeningen.no). Now well into its second century of housing and otherwise providing for walkers, skiers and climbers, DNT and its sibling local tourist associations own *hytter* throughout the Norwegian wilderness. Even the simplest put to rest any thought of a hut, while the larger make the title ludicrous.

Well-marked walking trails connect the lodges or cabins (two better translations of *hytter*) which stand at crossroads on networks so

but there the similarity stops. A *hytte* is by no means a rough structure; most are well-appointed small wooden houses, and many are larger than their owners' permanent homes.

Those without a *hytte* of their own are frequently related to, or are close friends of, *hytte* owners. Otherwise, there are many paths to the comforts of a *hytte*. Clubs and associations often own one, and one of the standard business perks is liberal use of the company *hytte*. Even though holiday flats and time-share apartments are on the increase, the *hytte* still reigns supreme in fulfilling its original intent: to supply comfort in remoter places where it is otherwise unavailable.

extensive that DNT's trail marker, a red painted letter "T" on cairns, has become synonymous with serious walking. When winter snows cover the cairns, poles in the snow serve the same purpose.

The bulk of the trails and lodges are conveniently in the middle of the triangle bounded by the cities of Oslo, Bergen and Trondheim. A central entry point is Finse, situated above the timber line at 1,200 metres (4,000 ft). Finse's main street is the station platform; there are no cars because there are no roads. When a train has gone and the last passengers have left, Finse returns to normal, a speck in a seemingly infinite expanse of rock, ice and snow.

A few hundred metres from Finse railway station is the DNT *hytte*, with its 114 bunk beds in two and four-person rooms, hot showers, a staffed dining room serving three meals a day, a snack bar and three lounges. Other DNT lodges are still larger: Gjendesheim in Jotunheimen has 129 bunks. The DNT also has unstaffed self-service accommodation. Here you can prepare your own food or purchase from a pantry. You pay upon leaving, by putting money in a box on the wall. The honour system works well.

FARAWAY SO NEAR

So ethereal yet so accessible is Finse that it was chosen as a location for the space adventure film *The Empire Strikes Back*, the sequel to *Star Wars*.

scale of noteworthy mountains where sheer altitude, not challenge, is the main criterion. Though this fact has led to relative anonymity – few Norwegian peaks appear in the classic mountaineering literature – it does mean that you can ascend the equivalent of the Matterhorn or Mont Blanc without having to cope with the problems of altitude.

Most Jotunheimen trails meander from 900–1,200 metres (3,000–4,000 ft) above sea level and there are few or no acclimatisation problems at that height.

Accessible mountaineering

To the north of Finse lie the Jotunheimen mountains, the range that took its name from Norse mythology, literally "Home of the Giants". The name is appropriate: peaks jut a kilometre and more skywards from lake-studded, moraine-strewn flats, all above the timber line. Nonetheless, even the loftiest of the Jotunheimen peaks, Galdhøpiggen and Glittertind, which are the highest in northern Europe with summits more than 2,400 metres (7,900 ft) high, rank low on the international

Some of the glaciers that hewed the Norwegian landscape left offspring. One, Jostedalsbreen (the Jostedal glacier), is the largest on the mainland of Europe. Jostedalsbreen and its siblings throughout the country are the places to see crampon-shod parties wielding ice axes from spring until autumn. Contact with the ice that shaped their land is currently the Norwegians' fastest-growing wilderness recreation and many centres now organise specialist courses.

Skiing

Skis have been a source of benefit and pleasure to Norwegians for thousands of years, with much of local community life in winter

LEFT: a typical *hytte*, in Ottadalen.
ABOVE: going for a quick dip in the fjord.

dependent on skis. In the 19th century skiing evolved into a mass sport, urged on by the Morgedal pioneer Sondre Norheim. The first skiing competitions were arranged in the mid 1880s – the term "slalom" originated in Morgedal from the Norwegian words *sla*, meaning slope or hill, and *låm*, depicting the track down it.

STONE-AGE SKIER

The Rodøy Man, a 4,000-year-old rock carving in Nordland, is evidence that skiing in Norway dates back to the Stone Age.

Norwegians have practically unlimited access to skiing and skating facilities. About 30,000 km (18,600 miles) – three times the distance between Norway and Australia – of

ing has again surged in popularity in recent years. There are some 600 ski-jumps in Norway *(see page 105)*. In the total absence of snow, there is always skating or ice hockey. In winter, municipalities up and down the country convert sports fields and playgrounds into ice rinks by getting the local fire brigade to spray them with water. These are then used for ice hockey and speed skating. When the fjords freeze over, whole families take Sunday "walks" on skates among the rocks and islets.

marked ski trails wind their way through unspoiled scenery. Cross-country skiing in the mountains may be enjoyed until well into May. The winter darkness is no obstacle with some 2,500 illuminated tracks providing for a bit of serious exercise after work.

Alpine skiing has gradually increased in popularity in Norway. Though by no means as universal as cross-country skiing, most communities have a locally prepared piste. Major ski resorts include Trysil in Hedmark, Hemsedal and Geilo in Buskerud, Voss in Hordaland (which is a year-round resort), and, of course, Lillehammer in Oppland, the location of the 1994 Winter Olympics. Ski-jump-

Outdoors in reach

In travelling time, even the remote wilderness areas are close to the bulk of the population: the wilderness itself is still closer. Oslo is bounded on its landward side by Øslomarka, a vast area of forests (larger than Greater London) set aside for outdoor recreation. Likewise, Bergen has its Vidden, Trondheim its Bymarka, Tromsø its Tromsdalen. No Norwegian city is without nearby natural surprises. But to Norwegians, who are as likely to shoulder rucksacks as to carry a briefcase, that's no surprise. ❏

ABOVE: one of the many small harbours along Norway's long coastline.

The Great Ski Jump

The Holmenkollen Ski Festival is the oldest in the world and 1 million people leave the centre of Oslo for Holmenkollen during the 11 days of the festival in March each year. At the climax on Holmenkollen Sunday, more than 50,000 people gather at this famous ski-jump hill to watch ski jumping in the country that invented it. But though the Nordic skiing competitions (cross-country and ski-jumping) and the newer events attract top competitors eager for World Cup points, Holmenkollen is much more than yet another international winter competition. This is very much a citizens' festival, a chance for ordinary Norwegians and visitors to take part in the events.

The idea of sitting or strolling as a spectator all day in the middle of a Norwegian winter might sound like the best way of catching a cold but the excitement is high. Wrapped in boots, anoraks, gloves and hat, with the necessary extra of a warm cushion to sit on, everything is happening and you need no more than a regular quick coffee, best laced with aquavit, to keep out the cold.

Norway was the first country to introduce ski competitions when Norwegian soldiers began to compete as early as 1767 and the first civilian event took place in 1843 at Tromsø. By the 1880s, the Norwegian Society for the Promotion of Skiing already held a winter competition and in 1892, this transferred to Holmenkollen. That year, the longest ski-jump was 22 metres (72 ft). Today, it is more than 126 metres (413 ft).

In the very first days the competitors were all Norwegian but even by 1903 Swedes had arrived, and were soon joined by French and German skiers. Since World War II, foreigners from most skiing countries have taken part – and won. Women first competed in 1947, when Alpine skiing events were introduced, but they weren't admitted to the cross-country race until 1954.

Norway's King Olav V, a first-class sportsman, made his debut on the Holmenkollen jump in 1922, and was a faithful spectator for nearly 70 years. His son, King Harald, has inherited this keen interest in the sport. As long as there is a jump at Holmenkollen, the royal family will watch the events from the royal box.

The fortnight begins with the Handicap Ski Race; next comes the Guards' Race, followed by the

RIGHT: Holmenkollen Sunday.

Norwegian Members of Parliament – fitter perhaps than their counterparts elsewhere – and local politicians, and cross-country skiing at all levels. On Children's Day more than 5,000 children swarm into the arena for events to mark the end of the season at the children's ski school, and the Holmenkollen March attracts around 7,000 to 8,000 people, many just ordinary skiers, to ski either 21 or 42 km (13 or 26 miles) through the Nordmarka forest finishing right under the jump.

The atmosphere of Holmenkollen Sunday is electric. They call it Norway's second national day, after Constitution Day on 17 May, and most spectators arrive early for a large breakfast-cum-brunch at one

of the local hotels to keep out the sub-zero cold, before making their way to their seats. First come the children's events and demonstrations of skills such as Telemark skiing and parachute jumping, leading up to the climax, the great ski jump.

The huge crowd packed into the arena hushes as the first skier appears. Up there on the top platform, he looks like a being from another world. The silence lasts until the tiny, bright figure takes off and, in a second, is flying through space with an ease that makes it look simple. Then as skier follows skier in graceful arcs, a roar loud enough to cause an avalanche fills Holmenkollen. A new ski jump will be built at the site in time for the Nordic World Championships in 2011. ❏

SPORTING PASSIONS

To Norwegians, sport is almost a religion, permeating every aspect of life, and there is room for everyone, from Olympic champions to Sunday goalkeepers

Put the question "Are you a skier?" at almost any social gathering anywhere in Europe, and you could expect a few positive responses and perhaps a lecture or two on the virtues of the sport. Put the same question to someone you meet of a Sunday afternoon at one of the ski-trail lodges in Norway, which you can only reach on skis, and the answers will be quite different: "No, I'm a bank clerk"; "Who me? Never dream of it!".

A way of life

Why the disparity? The answer lies in a tradition that has woven sport deeply into the fabric of Norwegian life. It is even reflected in the language. While English has just one word, "sport", Norwegian has two: *sport* and *idrett*. The Norwegian *sport* is the umbrella word that covers all sporting events, so that a sports journalist in Norway plies exactly the same trade as his or her foreign counterpart. The word *idrett* is reserved for events in which the limits in performance are determined by the capabilities of the human body. Horse riding is not *idrett*, while scuba diving is. There is a further nuance: *aktiv* (active) means a person currently competing in a sport classified as *idrett*.

This explains why, when you ask skiing Norwegians "are you a skier?", you have asked if they currently compete in the sport. Ask often enough, and you unearth the astonishing fact that one Norwegian in three is *aktiv*.

Mad about sport

This amazing statistic reflects the high priority Norwegians give to sport. Oslo has numerous statues of living Norwegians in sporting poses: a statue of King Olav V skiing, near the Holmenkollen ski jump, one of marathon runner Grete Waitz running, of course, at the marathon gate of Bislett Stadium, and statues of speed skater Oscar Mathisen and figure skater Sonja

Henie near the Frogner Park Stadium. All new high-rise flats are obliged by law to include "sports gear storage rooms". Within the Ministry of Church and Education there is a department for "Youth and *Idrett*". City newspapers vie with each other for sales on the strengths of their sports sections, and almost 14 percent

of the Norwegian Broadcasting Corporation's output is devoted to sports.

So pervasive is sport that visitors sometimes ask "Where is the flash, the excitement?" The answer is that the pinnacles are there, as high and sometimes higher than elsewhere, but the surrounding plateau of sporting achievement is so high that it makes the peaks less prominent.

Norges Idrettsforbund (NIF), the Norwegian Confederation of Sports, is the umbrella organisation for 53 separate sports federations with, in total, more than 1.7 million members. It spotlights this fact in its motto "Sport for All", and the pinnacles are grouped and designated "elite". So, for the Confederation and its

LEFT: on the cross-country trail.
RIGHT: a youthful Prince Haakon Magnus shows his skill as a water-skier.

Morgedal and Telemark Revival

For jazz fans, New Orleans is the ultimate magnet, just as Wimbledon is for tennis players. For skiers, the start of it all is Morgedal, in the southern county of Telemark, a hamlet that long remained an entry only found in history books pored over by scholars of the sport of skiing. Today, that has all changed because of a reawakening of interest in the style of skiing called Telemark, which evolved in Morgedal.

In the mid 19th century, there were even fewer people than the 200,000 who live in Telemark today – a hardy breed of woodsmen, small farmers, hunters and traders, who fashioned their own implements including the skis they needed to get about on winter snows. Morgedal is in the mountains, so the ski makers there sought designs that would perform well in the surrounding rugged terrain, both in everyday winter skiing and for impromptu sporting meetings. Among the best in the mid -1800s was Sondre Norheim, a young tenant farmer. He excelled not only in village ski meetings but also in ski-making skills.

Norheim devised bindings (devices that hold ski boots to skis) that were firm and were the first to give the feet control over the skis. He also gave the skis what is known as "sidecut", the slight hourglass profile of a ski seen from above. Sidecut is what enables skis to run true and turn easily, even to this day.

Norheim and his fellow Morgedal skiers used the new designs to perfect new skiing manoeuvres, including ways of turning and stopping on snow, and ways of landing from airborne flights off snow-covered rooftops and natural outcrops. Their fame spread and, by 1868, Norheim and his farmers from Telemark were ready to show off their new skills. He led them on skis for the 180-km (112-mile) journey from Morgedal to Christiania (now Oslo), where the city crowds turned out to greet and applaud the peasant skiers and their miraculous new techniques. This led to the start of the big ski-jumping contest at Husaby near Oslo in 1879, where 10,000 spectators led by the king cheered the skiing pioneers from Telemark. Around the same time, the Telemark skiers established the world's first ski school in Oslo.

In 1902, the first ski-jumping rules committee met to compile criteria for judging the style of competitors at the annual Holmenkollen ski-jump meetings. They honoured the origins of the two most skilful groups by affixing their names to the two turns then executed by ski jumpers to come to a stop after landing from flight. The turn in which the skis are held parallel throughout was named the Christiania, while the bent-knee stance with one ski trailing became the Telemark.

In modern Telemark skiing, the heel is free to lift up from the ski, and turns are steered, with one ski trailing and at an angle to the other. From the side, the manoeuvre looks like a genuflection in motion. Although competitive Telemark ski races are now held on packed slopes, as are Alpine ski races, true Telemark skiing is a throwback to the skiing of Sondre Norheim's time. The rebirth of the Telemark turn has revived another old skiing practice – skiathlon – in which competitors must ski-jump, ski through a slalom course, and run a cross-country ski race, all on the same pair of skis.

The name is new, but the combination of manoeuvres dates to the times when the men from Morgedal first mastered the ski-jumping meets in Christiania some 130 years ago. A ski–jumping performance required the competitor to jump through the air, come to a stop after landing, ski back uphill to the top of the ski jump, and jump again before finishing. ❑

LEFT: traditionally Telemark skiing uses one stick only.

member associations, competitive sport is both egalitarian and elitist.

International competition

From the broad base of people for whom sport is a major leisure-time activity come the elite, competitors who enter the many national championships and represent Norway in international sports meetings. The results speak for themselves. For a country with such a small population, Norway has always been disproportionately strong in sports.

Traditionally, Norwegian competitive prowess has been in winter sports and in sail-

of the profits of the state-run football pools and Lotto, the national lottery.

In addition, the 5,000-odd clubs use extra-curricular activities, such as bingo and local lotteries, to raise up to 40 percent of their income. Wherever you go, you are besieged by young people selling lottery tickets to support the local sports club.

However, recreation-type activities have been gaining in popularity at the expense of more strenuous sports. The Ski Association, Handball Federation and Athletics Federation are losing members while golf, billiards and amateur dancing federations are growing.

ABOVE: the Norwegian football team in action.

ing, but Norwegians have also won international medals in a wide range of events including marathon running, cycling, wrestling, handball, javelin, canoeing, rowing, shooting, weight-lifting, women's football and ballroom dancing.

Such pervasiveness and prowess have their price. The annual turnover in sports, excluding the sports equipment sector, is more than NOK1,400 million (£120 million), and sports are supported through many channels: the NIF receives a major chunk of its revenue from central government, and sport receives one-third

Football figures first

As elsewhere in Europe, football (soccer) is Norway's number one sport, with more than 1,800 clubs and a total of over 280,000 players. It is also the best supported, through funds from the football pools and from the sale of players to the major European leagues, in particular the English Premier League. As a result, a number of English clubs are well supported by Norwegian fans.

While Norwegian football struggles to drop its amateur status (the population is too thin, too self-engaged, and too busy to generate serious gate money), foreign coaches and eager agents find rich pickings among the home-grown talent.

Individual sports

Number two in the statistics and, its supporters contend, spiritually number one, is the country's traditional stalwart, skiing, with more than 1,500 clubs and a total membership of over 200,000. Together, the five skiing disciplines – cross-country, Alpine, ski jumping, biathlon (a cross-country skiing and rifle-shooting combination event), and combined (ski jumping followed by a cross-country competition) – receive as much funding as football.

Third in line is gymnastics, with more than 500 clubs and over 100,000 members. Then follow handball, track and field athletics, orienteering, shooting, swimming, sailing and volleyball. Of these top ten only three, football, handball and volleyball, are team sports. The balance is almost the complete reverse of most countries, where team sports dominate, a possible reflection of the Norwegian mentality.

Grass-roots support

The backbone of Norwegian sports is, of course, Norwegian involvement. A great deal of work on sports facilities is local and voluntary. Approximately half of the country's 1.4-million families with children are involved in sports in some way other than direct participation. Father is an official of the local club, and mother helps on the stalls at the annual club flea market. The older children sell club lottery tickets. In fact the whole family helps to run the annual club meets. Most families have one member who is either a certified coach or is training to become one.

One persistent reminder of this involvement is the seeming ubiquity of sports facilities and sports instruction. There are 10,000–12,000 sports centres in Norway, from the most modest local football field to major stadiums and indoor halls. In summer and autumn, they are hatcheries for future football and track-and-field athletic talents. In winter, their iced surfaces swarm with figure and speed skaters and serve as mini-arenas for ice hockey and *bandy*, a related sport played with a ball instead of a puck, to rules more closely resembling those of field hockey.

This high involvement has some drawbacks. In the more popular sports, competition has become so fierce that the criteria for doing well have been elevated to seemingly unattainable heights. Youngsters pushed into competition by overzealous parents can burn out prematurely, and this has become a recognised problem in almost all sports.

Such intense involvement, though, doesn't diminish the everyday enjoyment of sport. Internationally renowned violinist Arve Tellefsen's prime lament is that his infrequent sports ventures – his boyhood skills of ski-racing and football – invariably rate more media coverage than his violin virtuosity. But that doesn't prevent him from putting on a pair of skis or kicking a football at the weekend. ❑

WINTER OLYMPICS

Norway can claim more Winter Olympic medals than most other countries in the world, and winter sportsmen and women rank among the country's heroes. Its performance at the 1994 Olympics on the home turf of Lillehammer is legendary, and Norway came second only to Germany, and ahead of Russia, Canada and the United States, at the 2002 Salt Lake City Olympics. It didn't fare as well in Torino in 2006, but veteran downhill racer Kjetil André Aamodt overcame injuries to win yet another gold medal at the age of 35. Other medals went to freestyle queen Kari Traa and biathlon star Ole Einar Bjørndalen.

LEFT: kayaking in Arctic waters.
RIGHT: climbing a frozen waterfall.

FISHING: SPORT AND SUSTENANCE

Norway's fjords, rivers and coastline are a veritable anglers' paradise. And when it comes to eating fish, Norwegians have a dish for every occasion

To Norwegians, fish is the standby staple. Even in modest markets, the variety of fish and fish products is amazing, and Norwegians look on a proper wet fish shop as an asset to a community. Fish is both humble fare and holiday cuisine. Fish balls in white sauce are the Norwegian dining-table stalwart, and steamed

cod is a favourite for Sunday dinners. On festive occasions, herring in myriad forms takes its place with other delicacies such as *gravlaks* (cured salmon), *rakørret* (half-fermented trout), and *lutefisk* (dried codfish marinated in a lye solution, a dish few foreigners appreciate).

It is not surprising that Norway is a country of fishermen of all kinds. The language differentiates between them accordingly: *fisker* means "fisherman", one who lives by commercial fishing; while *sportsfisker* is the amateur variety, an "angler". But there the similarity stops. Angling in Norway is done both for the sport itself and as part of other outdoor pursuits. Fishing tackle is among the paraphernalia of camping trips, just as it is the prime equipment for avid anglers.

The long coastline is a mecca for saltwater angling, yet freshwater angling is the more popular pastime, and there are a quarter of a million fishable inland lakes and ponds. The most common of around 40 freshwater species are trout and char; in the northernmost parts, and in lakes and ponds at higher elevations, they are the only fish. Grayling and pike are more common in larger lakes and rivers in eastern and central areas. Local legends about lakes rich in pike hold that the fish are descended from stocks set out in the late 18th century by the ruling Danes.

Bream, whitefish, perch and carp are found in most lower lakes in the southern part of the country, as well as in eastern Finnmark in the far north. Reliable varieties in saltwater include cod, coalfish, haddock, whiting, halibut, herring and mackerel.

The stars on the angling scene are the Atlantic salmon and sea trout, related varieties which are both popular game and commercial fish. The commercial varieties now come largely from fish farms, but the game fish still swim the rivers until they are two to six years old, migrate to the sea, and then return to spawn in some 400 rivers. Norwegians argue about the best rivers, but five in the northern part of the country stand out – the Alta and Tana rivers in Finnmark, and the Gaula, Namsen and Orkla rivers in Trøndelag, all of which draw anglers from around the world. There, the sport is so popular that you have to apply for licences as much as a year in advance.

Gaining a licence

You need two types of angling licence to keep within the law. The first one is the annual *Fiskeravgift* (fishing fee) that helps to offset the costs of overseeing fishing and the aquatic environment (particularly adding lime to the water). The *Fiskeravgift* can be obtained at a post office and covers freshwater fish and crabs, but not salmon and sea trout. The latter two are, however, included in the annual fishing licence, which is usually twice the cost of the fishing fee. Fishing in sea water is free, whereas fishing in lakes and rivers requires a further local licence. Freshwater fishing licences come from the owners of the fishing rights, usually the property owners along the banks of a river or the shores of a lake, whether private persons or communities. These vary in price, and are valid for specific dates and periods, ranging from one day to several weeks. You can buy them from local hotels, sports shops or tourist offices.

Fly fishing is popular, so much so that Norwegians compete in the sport, including the annual world championships in fly casting.

Other countries do better in fly-casting competitions, but the Norwegians pride themselves on their versatility. Lure fishing leads, spoon-hook fishing and trolling are also widespread.

Baiting the hook

Even youngsters start fishing using artificial bait. Theories abound as to why this is so, but the most plausible ascribes it to Norway's location and topography. In the north, there are few insects large enough to use as bait, and worms are hard to find on rocky shores. Minnows and other live fish are prohibited as bait, primarily to curtail the spread of parasites and diseases.

MAXIMUMS AND MINIMUMS

The question of size, whether with a record in mind or to protect juvenile fish, is never far away. Norwegian angling records include 32.5 kg (71.6 lb) for freshwater salmon and 37.5 kg (82.6 lb) for cod caught in the sea. Although trout average 0.5 kg (1 lb), the freshwater trout record currently stands at 15.3 kg (33.7 lb). As for the minimum permissible sizes for keeping caught fish, they are 25 cm (9.8 inches) in length for salmon, sea trout and sea char, and 30 cm (11.8 inches) for all other fish.

LEFT: the strange fascination of ice fishing.
ABOVE: cleaning the catch outside the family *hytte*.

For the same reasons, the transfer of live fish, water, or wet fishing boats or other equipment, from one watercourse to another is prohibited.

Just as winter does not deter Norwegians from walking (they switch to cross-country skis), frozen lakes do not halt fishing. Ice fishing is a prime wintertime hobby, a simple and straightforward form of angling, which requires only a baited hand line or short pole and line, warm clothing, and lots of patience. Ice anglers must hew holes in the ice by hand as motorised augers are prohibited. It's a sport for the hardy, and ice-angling contests, such as the popular Ice Fishing Festival at Vangsvatnet in Voss, are for the very dedicated. ❏

THE TRADITIONAL ARTS

Tradition is strong in Norway, especially when it comes to the folk arts; but to an inquisitive eye, that tradition contains some unexpected influences

In AD 793 "dire portents appeared over Northumbria and sorely frightened the people. They consisted of immense whirlwinds and flashes of lightning, and fiery dragons were seen flying in the air. A great famine followed those signs, and a little after that in the same year, on 8 June, the ravages of heathen men miserably destroyed God's church on Lindisfarne, with plunder and slaughter."

So the *Anglo-Saxon Chronicle* documented the destruction of the monastery at Lindisfarne, now Holy Island, just south of Berwick-upon-Tweed in Northumberland in the northeast of England. It was the first major impact on Christendom by the Vikings, the pagan men of the north who were to make their mark on European culture for the next three centuries. But in the end, it was a reciprocal cultural exchange. An early Viking king, Olav Haraldson, converted to Christianity, was baptised in Normandy, and returned to his homeland to introduce the faith. By the year 1030, when he fell in battle, he had firmly rooted Christianity in most areas as Norway's future religion.

Today, the legacy of the Vikings is neither blurred nor buried, but still highly visible in a myriad of forms, collectively termed the folk arts. Woodcarving, rustic painting, colourful national costumes and decorative painting are the most obvious forms.

Woodcarving

The Viking Age owed its very being to superior sea power. The Viking craft, or longships as they became known, were at once extremely seaworthy and boldly beautiful. They were clinker built (overlapping planks held together with iron rivets) on long keel planks that swept up to a stem at either end. The Vikings carved elaborate decorations on the prows down to the waterline, often with dragon heads and figures.

PRECEDING PAGES: traditional rose painting.
LEFT: a detail from Tidemand's *The Grandmother's Bridal Crown.*
RIGHT: jewellery on a national costume.

They also carved elaborate designs on everyday items, from the handles of implements to the lever of the aft-right mounted *styrbord*, or steering board. On land, the details of buildings were similarly enhanced. Pillars were carved, not just at their capitals, but over their entire surfaces. There were ornate friezes, inte-

rior mouldings were decorated and gable ends became display points. Woodcarving was a highly developed art, executed primarily for, and partly by, the Viking aristocracy.

Stave churches

By the 12th century, Christianity had supplanted the aristocracy as the prime patron of the arts, and the wooden *stavkirke* (stave church) became the major outlet of woodcarving as an art form. About 750 of these magnificent structures were built, most in a 100-year period from 1150 to 1250, and 32 survive to this day, making them among the world's oldest wooden buildings. Their ornately carved portals serve the same purpose as old book illumination in England. They are one of the country's manuscripts. First, there are the animal heads of Nordic mythology, documenting the remnants of the Viking Age; then the classical tendril of Christian art appears, springing from the jaws of a beast. Finally, tendrils and flowers assert themselves, sometimes solo and sometimes interwoven with other motifs, partly but not completely replacing the beasts. Aside from the stave churches and their various artefacts, these early people decorated chairs, beds, tables, ladles, bowls and other household items with ornate carving. Some of the best-preserved

for peasant pieces of native spruce or pine, the more ornately carved the better.

"Collecting old houses is something of a family mania," says one shipowner (the nearest Norway comes to an aristocracy). "My father, brother and I have been combing the back country for 40 years for handcrafted dwellings and objects, homesteads, barns, cabins and huts complete with their country beds, chests, baskets and cupboards. Each must be unique to its own valley and period."

Typical of the national mania for folk art, this family's collection began simply by bartering with valley farmers for small items, such as

examples of the work of Norwegian medieval artisans are the carved portals, window surrounds and other details of farm buildings.

A passion for the past

The traditions survive to the present day. The timber *hytte* – even the ultra-modern *hytte* built in the 21st century – must have some exterior carving, and the Frognerseteren Restaurant, which was built in 1891 on a hill side overlooking Oslo and remodelled in 1909, is one of the best examples of the more modern dragon style of decorated wooden buildings. Today's nostalgia in home furnishings is not for the lavish designs of the courts of the past, but rather

handcrafted butter and porridge *tine*. These colourful, wooden caskets, often a first gift to a betrothed, form an unbroken tradition from Viking times to the present. Always highly decorated, the *tine* are still used by country lads to show off their carving and rose-painting skills.

Rose painting

Much as woodcarving evolved from the urge to decorate functional items, the art Norwegians call *rosemaling* or "rose painting" sprang from humble surroundings. The two were often used together: carved building details and household furnishings and implements were frequently painted, both as enhancement of, and in contrast to, the carved wood. The name misleads: roses appear only in a few of the traditional patterns; it would be more correct to term it "rustic painting", which denotes its agrarian roots, far removed from the cities. True *rosemaling* is not limited to flowery designs, although variations of the tendril motif are its strongest themes. It also includes geometric figures, portraits, and an occasional landscape.

The earliest decorations have survived less well than the carvings on which they were painted, so the beginnings of rose painting remain an enigma. The oldest surviving examples date from around 1700, centuries after the necessary paints were first available.

Theories on its origins abound. One school of thought holds that originally it was used to add colour to drab interiors. From medieval times on the typical rural dwelling was an *årestue* (hearth house), a windowless room with an opening in the roof to let the smoke from the open fire in the centre to escape. Rose painting could have been the peasants' reaction to their otherwise grey interior environments.

Another line of thought, with some substantiation in contemporary historical records, is that the peasants emulated the ornate decorations of churches, which were then also the major civic buildings in rural areas.

Imported styles

Whatever its origins, rose painting evolved and, in its own right, became a record of its times. The earlier rose paintings of interiors and household articles clearly show that the art of the Renaissance reached as far as the Norwegian countryside. The colours are the peasant stalwarts, blue, green, red and yellow, but the patterns are definitely imported.

The prosperity of the late 18th century brought more clerics and more functionaries to rural districts and with the new professionals came their belongings, decorated household furnishings and implements. What the peasants saw they replicated as best they could in their own style.

Most were untutored and the commonest way of learning the skills was either from travelling artists or from local practitioners. The

relative isolation of the valleys, cut off from their neighbours by the high mountain ranges, meant that every valley became its own art centre for a particular style of painting.

Too conservative to borrow directly from outsiders, Norwegian farmers carefully extracted only those aspects that fitted their own sense of colour and decoration. Hallingdal farmers were partial to delicate S-curves applied to everything from walls to spoons and bowls. In affluent Gudbrandsdal, the locals carved their decorations into built-in benches and box beds. The most isolated districts, such as Setesdal, have a very simplified *rosemaling* tradition. So indi-

vidual were the styles, today's experts can identify the age and origin of almost any item with uncanny accuracy. Their knowledge is currently much in demand as rose-painted period furniture commands the highest of prices for Norwegian antiques.

Rose painting survives today, like woodcarving, as a nostalgic link with the past and throughout the country amateur rose painters keep that link alive. For most it is a hobby with the occasional spin-off of small profits from sales to local handicraft shops. But for some it offered more. One of the antique business scandals of 1989 concerned cleverly faked, rose-painted "antique" furniture.

LEFT: rose painting used to decorate a set of shelves.
RIGHT: Einar Holte at work on one of his famous miniature wooden boats.

The national costume

Norway's *bunad* is as colourful as the national costumes of any country. It is not just worn by folk dancers or for fancy-dress parties, but is in regular use as formal attire at weddings, official ceremonies, and at gatherings on national holidays. Many claim that the *bunad* is Europe's most often worn national costume.

The *bunad* is a throwback to the everyday clothing of times past, and the word itself means simply "clothes". It has developed variations in style, cut, colouring and accessories according to locality and the skills and tastes of its makers. There were costumes for men,

women and children, everyday *bunads* and dress *bunads*. As with rose painting, every area of the country had its own style.

Despite these differences, the *bunad* has common characteristics that identify the dress as Norwegian. Women's costumes characteristically have skirts or dresses of double-shuttle woven wool and bodices or jackets of similar or contrasting material worn over blouses with scarves. Sashes, purses, beautiful silver accessories and traditional shoes and stockings complete the costume. Men's *bunads* are essentially three-piece knickerbocker suits, with matching or contrasting waistcoats, white shirts, long socks and traditional shoes.

Like woodcarving and *rosemaling*, the design of a *bunad* is in itself a historical record. For example, those from coastal areas often reveal a stronger continental influence than those from the remote valleys, where housewives spun, dyed and wove their own woollens to local patterns.

Folk revival

In the mid-19th century, factory-made cloth and garments began to replace homespun products. As people moved from farm to town, the *bunad* seemed to be heading for extinction. It was rescued single-handedly by Hulda Garborg, a prominent author who saw a need to preserve the rural traditions. Shortly before the turn of the 20th century, she founded a *leikarring*, or folk-dance group, in Oslo. Folk dances should, she maintained, be performed in folk costumes which led her to compile the first anthology of *bunads*, published in 1903. It was a bestseller and Garborg and one of her dancers, Klara Semb, succeeded in starting the folkdance movement and a *bunad* renaissance which continues to the present day.

Although *bunads* are no longer daily wear, the number of known types and varieties is greater than ever. Some, like those from Setesdal, date back 300 years or more. Others, such as the costume from Bærum, a suburb of Oslo, have been designed in the past 40-odd years.

Its current popularity is matched only by the range of opinions about how it should be worn. Traditionalists contend that a *bunad* from a particular district should be worn only by a person born and bred there. Moderates maintain that correct style outweighs the circumstances of the wearer's birth and upbringing, and the radicals view the *bunad* as a style to be copied piecemeal in modern clothes.

While the standard dark suit has, like in so many other countries, become the bastion of the Norwegian male wardrobe, women still face the dilemma of what to wear for formal occasions. In Norway, a *bunad* is always correct. It is timeless and may be passed on from generation to generation, while the traditional silver belt is often a gift from a father and mother to their son's wife. ❏

LEFT: Hulda Garborg *(left)* photographed in 1899 dressed in a traditional *bunad*.
RIGHT: the 13th-century Heddal stave church.

TRADITION, NOT HAUTE CULTURE

Norwegian artists, writers and musicians dug deep into the country's rural past in search of a new national identity

Culture in Norway? Well, certainly it exists, in its own fashion. Just take a look at your fellow travellers in the Oslo Central Station. Half of them trudge around in boots and a backpack; the other half have only the backpack. They are all heading for isolated cabins – Norway's holy *hytte* – far away from the city and its pleasures. The Munch Museum and National Theatre take second place to trekking the highlands, searching mountain valleys for *rosemaling*, the indigenous folk art.

That is all culture certainly, though not of the grand, *haute* sort. Although Norway does not foster glittering opera soirées, galas do, of course, occur, a notable example being the awarding of the Nobel Peace Prize. But such parties are just the icing on the cultural cake and ever so slightly foreign, imported glamour (Nobel, after all, was a Swede).

Home-grown culture

Real Norwegian culture is something far more fundamental – folksy, a reaction to foreign domination. As a political entity, Norway was established in 1905 after centuries of Danish and Swedish rule. All Norwegian "dialects" were forbidden by the Danes for official documents and communications. The national constitution, which was drawn up at Eidsvoll in 1814, was in Danish. Such cultural imperialism was crushing to Norwegian self-esteem and national identity.

Ordinary Norwegians were driven away from the centres of power to rural farms. Tradition, folk costume and the old ways became a cultural refuge and eventually the treasuries of Norway's national personality. Culture with a capital "C" was something the overlords brought with them from foreign capitals. And it was something they took away with them when they left. Norway today has no noble families excepting the king and his household.

LEFT: Henrik Ibsen.
RIGHT: murals by Per Krohg and Henrik Sørensen in the main hall of Oslo's Rådhus (City Hall).

While politicians could elect a king and Parliament, it fell to cultural workers, especially writers and painters, to revive the national identity. They turned for inspiration to the traditions of those isolated valleys with their ancient farmsteads and their equally ancient verbal traditions, telling heroic sagas about an expansive

Norway of earlier days and of the greatness of native Viking lords.

Henrik Wergeland (1808–45), a richly talented poet and prose writer, became an early and passionate propagandist of this sort of Norwegian nationalism. Following the same call, artist J.C. Dahl (1788–1857) left his studio for the wilds of Norway's hinterland. His shimmering, majestic views of the mountains are major attractions at the National Gallery, which he helped to found in 1836.

On the dark side, the epoch's fears of isolation and rampant anxiety of the future inspired the violent, emotionally charged style of painter Edvard Munch (1863–1944). Death and desolation are his recurring themes most strongly expressed in *The Scream* (1893), *The Kiss* and *The Vampire* (*below*, both 1895). Munch's fears of enslavement come so close to the national heart that his works have been enshrined in their own museum in Oslo as well as on an entire floor of the National Gallery.

Equally loud cries for freedom came from Henrik Ibsen (1828–1906) whose poetic drama *Brand* was a spirited indictment of Norwegian authority at home. It put Ibsen on the cultural map for the first time even outside Norway.

At the same time, the close of the 19th century, other authors turned homewards for inspi-

ration. Alexander Kielland (1849–1906) abandoned a promising international career to write about old Norway. Nobel laureate Knut Hamsun's (1859–1952) chilling novel *Hunger* (1890) is an exposé of the abuses of bourgeois Swedish rule. His masterpiece, *The Growth of the Soil* (1917), reflects a deep love of nature and concern for the effects of material conditions on the individual spirit, themes that still dominate Norwegian writing.

Even architects abandoned continental idioms to embrace a native "Viking Romanticism". They began building in heavy timber and turfed roofs. Eaves and gables sprouted carved and polychromed dragon heads. An

excellent example of the style is Troldhaugen, the last home of composer Edvard Grieg (1843–1907). Just outside Bergen, the house fits perfectly into Grieg's unabashed folkloric, wildly romantic style. He titled his creations after national heroes such as the much-loved *Peer Gynt Suite* (1876, words by Ibsen).

Over a century ago, new plays by national playwright Ibsen, works by major authors such as Amalie Skram (1847–1905) and Kielland were front-page news in Oslo, Bergen and Trondheim. Critics and politicians publicly debated new works; plays became issues, even national causes. Literature became the smithy where the nation's identity was being forged.

Dramatist Bjørnstjerne Bjørnson (1832–1910) championed the Norwegian cause, working his entire life to free the Norwegian theatre from Danish influence. While director of Bergen's Ole Bull Theatre (1857–59) and the Oslo Theatre a few years later, he commissioned new, saga-like dramas drawing on Norway's epic past, such as the *Sigurd Slembe Trilogy*. His efforts helped to revive Norwegian as a literary language. He became poet laureate and his poem, *Yes, We Love this Land of Ours,* became a rallying point in the struggle for political independence from Sweden. The poem is now the national anthem of Norway.

New Norse vs *bokmål*

The political and extremely didactic approach in Norwegian literature finally disappeared in the 1980s. But there are still many attempts to emancipate individual languages. Norway has three languages: Sami, used almost exclusively by the Sami (Lapps) in the north; then there are *bokmål* (book language) and *nynorsk* (new Norse), two variations on a theme that have developed since independence.

Bokmål grew out of the gradual exchange of Danish loan words for words discovered in native dialects, by the substitution of Danish syntax with Norwegian, and by turning soft Danish consonants into hard Norwegian ones. It became the official language, used today by about 80 percent of the towns and throughout the entire northern districts.

New Norse is only used by about 15 percent of Norwegian primary school children. It draws heavily on the archaic Old Norse of the central-western dialects. Since this is a language based on rural culture, *nynorsk* suffered because of

20th-century urbanisation, losing ground to *bokmål* – though to complicate matters, *nynorsk* literature is very popular.

New concerns

The 1980s produced a sort of realistic novel, written in sociology textbook style, directly opposed to the older, bourgeois psychology novels, "a die-hard heritage from Hamsun, Cora Sandel and Torborg Nedreaas". Most readable among these "revolution" works are Dag Solstad's (born 1941) trilogy about World War II, *Svik* (Betrayal), *Krig* (War) and *Brød og Våpen* (Bread and Arms). This revival of

problems using "street language" and spoken modes of expression. Løvied's lyrically erotic *Sug* (Suck) rocked the staid Oslo critics but has brought her international recognition. Liv Køltzow's (born 1945) third novel, *The Story of Eli*, explores sex roles in society.

The 1990s saw a general literature boom. Whodunnits by Gunnar Staalesen, Kim Småge, Ingvar Ambjørnsen and Anne Holt are well known and popular. The first prize, however, must go to a book on the history of philosophy written for adolescents: *Sophie's World* by Jostein Gaarder. He is quite easily the most famous Norwegian writer since Knut Hamsun.

social realism allowed an author such as Asbjørn Elden (1919–90) to produce essentially modern yet "back to our roots" sagas about the inconspicuous lives of ordinary people, such as his *Rundt Neste Sving* (Around the Next Bend).

Women have come to the fore of Norwegian writing. Cecilie Løveid (born 1951) and Kari Bøge (born 1950) crashed on to the literary scene in the late 1970s with audacious, even shocking works. Ignoring male-dominated social realism, they picked apart purely female

LEFT: detail from Edvard Munch's *The Vampire* (1895).
ABOVE: writer and nationalist Bjørnsterne Bjørnson at the dinner table.

Post-war art

As with other cultural forms, Norwegian art began to drop its nationalist style after World War II. Gone (but certainly not forgotten) were the fairytale illustrations of Theodor Kittelsen (1857–1914) and morbid subject matter of Edvard Munch and in came the modernists. Impressionism inspired such landscape artists as Gladys Nilssen Raknerud (1912–1997) and Thorbjørn Lie-Jørgensen (1900–61); expressionism found its place through the likes of Arne Ekeland (1908–1994) and Rolf Nesch (1893–1975); and abstract expressionism appeared in the early 1960s through the work of Sigurd Winge (1909–70) and Jakob Weidemann

(1923–2001). However, the old nationalist style continued well into the 1950s with such artists as Hjalmar Haalke (1892–1964) and Søren Steen Johnsen (1903–1979) and the team responsible for the Oslo Rådhus murals.

There was also the inevitable reaction to the modernists. When Odd Nerdrum (born 1944) applied for a place at the National Academy of Fine Arts he submitted three works; two of these had been long-term projects, but he was selected on the basis of his third work, an abstract image thrown together the night before. With his scepticism towards the establishment and doubts about abstract art reinforced, the

Leading the way

If there is one area where Norwegians have the edge it is in furniture: consider Peter Opsvik's classic TrippTrapp chair for kids or his sculpture-like Cylindra Objects; and architecture, which in recent years has responded to increasing demands for sustainable development. Probably the most internationally renowned Norwegian architect is the "concrete poet" Sverre Fehn (born 1924), whose main materials have been concrete, wood, glass, and the Nordic light. In 1997, Fehn became the first Nordic architect to win the American Pritzker Architecture Prize, the "Nobel Prize" of archi-

young Nerdrum turned to the great masters, in particular Rembrandt, in whom he saw "eternal tranquillity". However, his subject matter was always on the controversial side – *Amputation* (1974), *Hermaphrodite* (1976–81) – and it took until the late 1980s for the Norwegian public to catch on to his postmodern classicism.

There is growing interest in the moderns, which had hitherto been the domain of the avant-gardist Swedes. The focal point of the Norwegian art calendar is the Autumn Exhibition in Oslo, and in recent years the city has seen the opening of three new contemporary art galleries, all exhibiting the works of national and international artists.

tectural awards, and the award cited "a marvellous, lyrical and ingenious architectural form... both forceful and extremely rational." To see his work visit the Nòrsk Bremuseet (Glacier Museum) in Fjærland, or the Hedmarksmuseet (Museum) in Hamar.

There is also a wealth of talent to continue the traditions of the prolific sculpture Gustav Vigeland (1869–1943). There are more 20th-century sculptures/statues per capita in Norway than in any other country in Europe: see *inter alia* Joseph Grimeland's Sailors' Memorial, Bygdøy; Arnold Haukeland's "dynamic" structure, Strandpromenaden, Oslo; and Knut Steen's Whaling Monument, Sandefjord.

Norway's Paganini

Norway has a long tradition in music. The skaldic poems of the Viking Age provide a medieval link to the music traditions of central Europe; Gregorian chants used in the worship of St Olaf are very similar to the Parisian school of the 13th century.

While higher forms of music stagnated during the 450 years of Danish rule, folk music unfolded freely, encouraged by the ecclesiastical centres and travelling musicians of the time.

Norwegian music developed for the first time in the early 1800s, mainly as a result of the union with Sweden and the influence of the Royal Swedish Court, but also because of the international breakthrough made by violin virtuoso Ole Bull (1810–80) in 1834. "The Nordic Paganini", as he was called, became a model for musicians and writers such as Grieg, Bjørnson and Ibsen. The 1870s and 80s became know as the Golden Age of Norwegian music with such prominent composers as Halfdan Kierulf (1815–68), Edvard Grieg and Johan Svendsen (1849–1911). Music took on a national flavour, urged on by Ole Bull's promotion of the Hardanger fiddle and Ludvig Mathias Lindeman's collection of Norwegian folk tunes. Most of the composers of the second half of the 19th century incorporated some element of folk music in their works.

With the end of the union with Sweden in 1905, Norwegian composers found the need to define a national identity, which they achieved by reverting back to the music of the Norwegian Middle Ages. Seeking inspiration in medieval poetry, German romanticism and French impressionism, David Monrad Johansen (1888–1970) tried to create a monumental kind of music based on musical archaisms. This national romanticism continued until just after the war. Germany was out; a new generation of composers went to study in Paris or the United States, consciously aware of the need to internationalise their musical language.

Today, Oslo, Trondheim and Bergen all have philharmonic orchestras, and the latter hosts the Bergen International Music Festival each May.

FESTIVAL CULTURE

Norway has a festival for almost everything, from the midnight sun and trolls to emigration. Music, crafts and national dress abound.

The Norwegians' yearning for culture is most explicit, however, in the myriad of festivals, especially folk festivals, that are organised each year. If you wish to find the real soul of Norway visit the country in May. It's a month when little gets done, much to the chagrin of foreigners who arrive on business. But it's the prime time for observing the patriotic emotions that lie at the centre of Norwegian culture. The month starts with the May Day festivals; but the high point comes on the 17th, Norway's National Day. ❑

NORWEGIAN CINEMA

Based around a unique system of municipal cinemas and the state-run Norsk Film, Norwegian cinema has come a long way from its first feature *The Perils of the Fisherman*, made in 1907. It gained a considerable amount of international attention in the 1970s with such films as Anja Breiens' *Wives* (1974). The prevailing style of social realism was replaced for a while by a variety of approaches, including Roar Skolman's surrealist *Junior Heads* (1981) and the Oscar-nominated *Pathfinder*, made in 1988 by Nils Gaup. In 2002, the Pelter Næss film *Elling* was also nominated for an Oscar.

LEFT: Norsk Bremuseet (Glacier Centre), Fjærland, when first built. **RIGHT:** the novelist, Liv Køltzow.

NATURE'S LARDER

Wild nature and a mild climate are the main sources of the ingredients from which Norway's culinary traditions have evolved

Magnificent landscapes and climatic contrasts have helped to create a natural larder from which Norwegians have helped themselves for centuries. Norway's long, varied coastline has provided ample opportunity for harvesting both "wild" and farm-raised fish; the slow ripening process of everything that grows during the light summer imparts an extraordinary aroma to berries, fruits and vegetables; and the animals that graze on the verdant grass provide meat with a distinctive full flavour. Today Norwegian comestibles such as Chinese cabbage, apples, pears, cherries and strawberries are in demand the world over. Although eyebrows are raised when the nation's chefs win international awards, it is not the first time that foreigners have been impressed by Norway's fare.

PAPAL SURPRISE

When papal envoy Cardinal Wilhelm Sabina attended the coronation of King Håkon V in Bergen in 1247, he arrived with apprehension having been forewarned about the food. However, in his speech following the banquet he lavished praise on the meal he had been served. Sadly, the historical record of his speech makes no mention of the menu, but visitors to Norway in the 18th and 19th centuries speak highly of the salmon, fowl, game and strawberries with cream – treats which modern-day tourists may also experience.

▷ **MARKET TRADING**
The famous Bergen fish market was once the place where locals gossiped about the latest catch: now they come here to catch up on the latest gossip.

△ **WILD PASSION**
Cloudberries (or *multebær*) are found in mountain marshlands in late summer/early autumn. Rich in vitamin C, *multer* is used as a jam, a liqueur and in desserts.

◁ **GONE FISHING**
Fish of all shapes and sizes, including cod (*torsk*), haddock (*hyse*) and plaice (*flyndre*), are landed daily in the ports along the west coast.

△ **SUPERIOR BREAKFAST**
Probably the most important meal of the day in Norway is breakfast (*frokost*), with copious amounts of cold meats, cheeses, crispbreads and black coffee.

AKEVITT – THE WATER OF LIFE

Akevitt (aquavit or "water of life") is the national spirit of Norway. The most famous aquavit, Løiten Linie, is matured through a 150-year-old process which includes a sea voyage in oak casks across the equator and back (each bottle carries details of its voyage on its label). This story originates from 1840, when the Norwegian ship *Preciosa* rounded Cape Horn; on board was aquavit, which the crew swore had improved in flavour.

Distilled from Norwegian potatoes, this blend of spirit, caraway and other herbs and spices is matured for several months in sherry casks. The result is a smooth spirit of about 45 percent proof by volume. Norwegians regard Linie as an accompaniment to pork *(ribbe)*; it also goes well with seafood and the Christmas *lutefisk* dish.

▽ **LOFOTEN TRADITIONS**
Klippfisk (dried, salted split cod) is a major Norwegian export and *rorbuer* (fishermen's huts) now accommodate tourists in Lofoten.

▷ **PRAWN COCKTAIL**
Fresh prawns *(reker)* are a favourite among Norwegians, served with white bread *(loff)*, mayonnaise, lemon and an ice-cold pils.

▷ **WOODLAND MUSHROOMS**
Chanterelle mushrooms are found in the forests north of Trøndelag and are a delicious complement to reindeer and game.

WHY DOES EVERYTHING COST SO MUCH?

Norway's high standard of living has its price, but it is not as expensive as it was in days gone by

Let's get this straight right from the start: day-to-day living *used* to be exorbitantly expensive in Norway, about 30 years ago, but there has been a gradual levelling out of prices in comparison with other European

countries. Today, some food items are generally less expensive than elsewhere, such as coffee and butter, but these are the exception rather than the rule. Visitors are often surprised at the relatively high prices for meat and, amazingly enough, fish. Staple vegetables are reasonable; exotic types, for which there is less demand, are expensive. Fruit follows the same pattern. You can find imported apples or tomatoes at normal European Union (EU) prices. To reduce costs, it's worth looking out for "lavpris" (low price) shops.

Somewhat surprisingly Norway produces a reasonable tomato crop, less because of sunshine and high temperatures and more because

of encouragement from the Norwegian Ministry of Agriculture, which sees independence from other countries as its main aim. The tomatoes don't always have much taste though, and their price shoots up when imports are restricted.

"Made in Norway"

Norway's desire to be self-sufficient has blossomed in unusual areas. The farmers in some tiny valleys in the west of the country live in grand style because their tomatoes, cucumbers, Chinese cabbages or cattle are highly subsidised. Only 3 percent of the land is used for agriculture, so variety is essential.

Cattle farmers are proud of their beef and pork, vegetable farmers praise their organically grown produce. Around 95 percent of the grain consumed is harvested in the country and cattle is almost entirely reared for the domestic market.

As far as foodstuffs are concerned, the logo "Made in Norway" is more an expression of a political principle than of exceptionally high quality. Things are changing though. The higher standard of living has stimulated a demand for a richly laid table. Admittedly, prices in Norwegian hotels are high – but so is the standard of the breakfast buffet. Anyone sampling a fully laden breakfast table can only start the day in a good mood: fruit juice, smoked salmon, pickled herring, fresh bread, fruit and muesli. This meal can easily get light eaters through the day and save them the expense of lunch.

Taxed to the hilt?

Not so long ago, it was fashionable to blame rich farmers and a false subsidy policy for high taxes. In reality these subsidies are cut each year and more and more smallholdings have been given up.

Income is subject to 30–45 percent income tax. But that's it. Social security, health insurance and pension payments are all included, and even the Church is funded by the state.

Other state revenue comes from oil and gas sales as well as taxes on various luxury items – which explains the high prices for cars, alcohol and cigarettes. Luxury costs money and Norwegians aren't supposed to enjoy luxury items – or at least they should do it in a different way.

The debate on cigarette and alcohol prices is an inevitable item in the annual budget discussions and only two of the eight political parties in the Storting vote to reduce these taxes. The rest squeeze yet a little bit more out of them every year.

MONEY BACK

Often a deposit of NOK 1 is charged when purchasing bottles, either glass or plastic. The money is refunded on return of the bottles.

have stopped arguing about prices, and drink their beer in peace.

As the alcohol takes affect, and especially if there are visitors present, many Norwegians feel obliged to explain why they are drinking. It is, they will say, because they can't remember when they were last in such good company or, as the case may be, feeling lonely and neglected. Before a dark cloud of Nordic gloom settles on the proceedings the subject is likely to broaden to why Norwegians drink so much, or not much at all.

To drink or not to drink?

Beer and wine prices are consistently on the increase. As Norwegians resignedly comment: "That's as certain as Christmas comes in December." But what is the reasoning behind this policy? The government insists that the treatment of alcohol and cigarette-related illnesses costs billions. And the budget discussions are also enlivened by the Christian Democratic Party, which rallies against these vices. Norwegians, however, have long learned to live with the link between vice and illness,

LEFT: Torget, the fish market in Bergen.
ABOVE: weekend market at Youngstorget, Oslo.

The question of alcohol and its corollary, teetotalism, have long been burning issues in Norway and are discussed so keenly that visitors, who are bound to become involved, might like to familiarise themselves with the background.

The climate is often blamed for Norwegian drinking. There may be some truth in this, since long winters used to put a premium on the art of preserving and storing food. Salt was the key, and it was therefore consumed in such quantities that great thirst necessarily followed. At one time, the "normal" consumption of beer and mead was between six and 10 litres (10–18 pints) per day. The aristocracy drank wine from the earliest times.

The 19th century produced a rash of travel books about Norway, and all of them drew attention to a weakness for drink. Even boys of 12 and 14 years, according to the Reverend R. Everest, indulged in the "odious vice", drinking quantities of brandy "that would have astonished an English coalman". Pontoppidan, whose *Natural History of Norway* was published in 1755, admired the Norwegians: "so hospitable ... liberal ... willing to serve and oblige strangers."

Not, however, when they drank: "When a

peasant with his family was invited to a wedding, the wife generally took her husband's (funeral) shroud with her; on these occasions they seldom parted before they were intoxicated with liquor, the consequences of which was fighting, and those battles seldom ended without murder."

Home brew

Although the Norwegians are extremely hospitable they will only offer alcoholic beverages once proper friendship has been established. Those who like the odd tipple can normally present a well-stocked bar. Sometimes the offerings are home-made. Every large

town has shops selling winemaking equipment, but most now have a state liquor store as well.

One thing visitors should not expect is the Viking drink of mead. This tradition has nearly died out – because honey is expensive and it's difficult to make.

Statistics prove, it is said defensively, that Norwegians actually consume less alcohol than almost any other European nation. These statistics also reveal that beer and wine have supplanted harder spirits. But unreported numbers are a lot higher: Norwegians like to travel and certainly buy the complete quota of duty-free items.

Also not included in the statistics is "HB", home-made schnapps made from sugar and potatoes. Even in this high-tech age, there are still quite a few moonshine distillers at work, and *sprit* (96-percent raw alcohol) smuggling is big business.

It would be unrealistic to seek reliable information about smuggling along Norway's long coastline, although there may be a clue in the fact that when a strike closed down the state-run *Vinmonopol* shops for months on end in 1986, there were no apparent shortages and, as soon as the suppliers had geared up for the unexpected windfall, the price of alcohol dropped down to levels unknown before or since.

A history of prohibition

The first attempt to curb drinking in Norway, possibly in the world, was made by King Sverre in Bergen in the 12th century. He was the leader of a rapacious bunch of ruffians called the *Birkebeiner*, who might have won the Battle of Fimreite for him against the rival Magnus Erlingsson had it not been for the fact that they were too drunk to fight on his behalf. Sverre's attempt failed.

The strident minority in favour of total prohibition saw World War I, in which Norway remained neutral, as an opportunity to press their case further. The excuse was to conserve the raw materials that went into the making of beer and spirits.

When the war ended the restrictions were not lifted; on the contrary, they were extended to cover all alcoholic drinks except wines below a certain, modest strength.

THE GREAT DEBATE

Since Norway's independence in 1905, the prohibition issue has been responsible for the downfall of three governments.

Unfortunately for the prohibitionists, France, Spain and Portugal were among the largest customers for Norway's important fishing industry, and they paid for the fish with wine, none of which qualified under the new regulations for sale or consumption in Norway.

Under pressure from the fishing industry, the limit was lifted just enough to admit the French wine, but the country was also saddled with 400,000 litres (88,000 gallons) of French brandy for which it had no possible use, having given an undertaking not to re-export it. The government immediately declared prohibition permanent, a signal to both Spain and Portugal that it would not be hoodwinked in similar fashion again.

Two years later, they let it be known that 500,000 litres (110,000 gallons) of fortified Spanish wine were nevertheless on their way, shortly to be followed by 850,000 litres (185,000 gallons) of Portuguese. The government resigned rather than face a country awash in untouchable drink. The new government lifted the ban on wine, and in so doing put the skids under national prohibition.

State control

Since 1923 and until the late 1990s the import and sale of wines and spirits had been a state monopoly. Government buyers decided what was to be made available (and the price) in the chain of *Vinmonopolet* shops, as well as in most hotels and restaurants. It was said that by this act the Norwegian state had made itself the biggest single buyer of alcoholic drinks in the world, a painful irony for the numerous prohibitionists who were still beating the drum.

In 1997, however, the Norwegian Government made a major concession to the EU by deregulating the import, wholesale and distribution side of the market. The effect of this means that hotels, restaurants and bars may now do business with independent importers, and *Vinmonopol* has been forced to privatise its distribution function. Although maintaining their monopoly on retail sales (and prices), the *Vinmonopolet* shops have slowly revamped their image – they used to be as uninviting as a dentist's waiting room – and

the stigma attached to walking around with chinking wine bottles in a plain plastic bag has all but disappeared.

One of the results of this, as visitors find out, is that drinks are freely available in major cities, albeit at numbing prices. Today, it is easier to be served a drink in Oslo at 2am than it is, say, in London. Laws affecting the sale of alcohol, however, are decided at the *kommune* level (i.e. by town and rural councils), so outside the cities, and especially on the west-coast *bibelbeltet*, it is a matter of luck whether a particular place is completely dry and without a legal drink within 100 km (60 miles).

Paying for the roads

It's no exaggeration to claim that car drivers have financed their own infrastructure. Here, as with alcohol and tobacco, Norwegians believe in the principle of cause and effect, which is paid for through high car prices (Norway doesn't have its own car industry), a large tax on petrol and toll charges: if you want to drive through Oslo (and there are few ways to circumnavigate it), Bergen, Trondheim or Stavanger, you have to pay a toll.

The road system, on the other hand, has been considerably upgraded and now, with numerous bridges and tunnels (including under the sea), reaches the tiniest villages. ❏

LEFT: a *Vinmonopol* shop.
RIGHT: home brewing in the attic.

PLACES

*A detailed guide to the entire country, with principal sights
clearly cross-referenced by number to the maps*

Norway is a long narrow strip of a country, stretching north from mainland Europe far into the Arctic. In the ancient capital of Trondheim, you are 500 km (350 miles) from the modern capital of Oslo, yet only a quarter of the way up the country's jagged coast. Oslo is as far from Monaco as it is from Nordkapp (North Cape), with Norway's northernmost outpost, the islands of Svalbard (Spitsbergen), hundreds of kilometres further on. With a population of only 4.5 million, Norway has, above all else, space.

Yet travel is not difficult. From early times, the Norwegians (as Vikings) were magnificent sailors, and this old way of travel continues today through the Hurtigrute coastal steamers and other ferries that link coastal communities. On land, the Norwegians have achieved in 100 years the seemingly impossible, connecting even the most isolated settlements by building railways, roads and bridges across their fjords and by tunnelling deep into the mountains and under the sea.

This is one of Europe's most beautiful countries. The scenery is dramatic and the land changes constantly, from mountain to sea, fjord to forest. Oslo, Stavanger, Bergen, Trondheim and Tromsø are small manageable cities that make good use of the surrounding countryside. Neither the Norwegian climate nor the people are as chilly as the northern latitudes might suggest. The Gulf Stream warms the western coastline so that the seas are ice-free all the year round, and the great distances and long journeys between villages, towns and farms have encouraged an age-old tradition of hospitality.

In the 1970s, oil brought wealth to Norway and now these stubborn, self-sufficient and deeply patriotic people enjoy one of the highest standards of living in the world.

Norwegians are an outdoor people, and Norway a country where inhabitants and visitors alike can make the most of limitless space for walking, skiing, touring and just breathing in the clear air. As a visitor you are advised to "explore" the amenities on offer, but do not expect all the man-made attractions to be as monumental as the country itself. The relatively small domestic market and short summer season are unable to finance major Disney-like attractions, and many of the museums, especially those in rural areas, exist more because of local enthusiasm and voluntary effort than to any supreme tourist policy and national funding. When you see a national-heritage symbol our advice is to go and investigate – you'll probably be pleasantly surprised. ❑

PRECEDING PAGES: storm over Borgundfjorden; a "light circle" in the Arctic city of Tromsø; Gamlehaugen.
LEFT: drying fish in the Lofoten Islands.

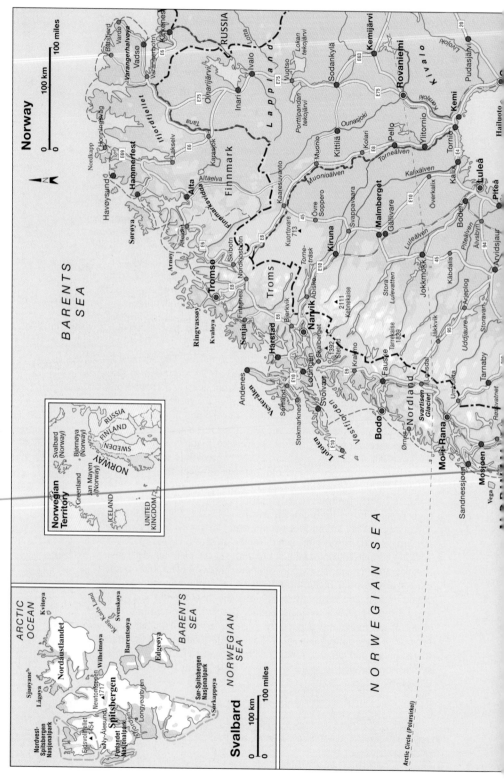

Norway

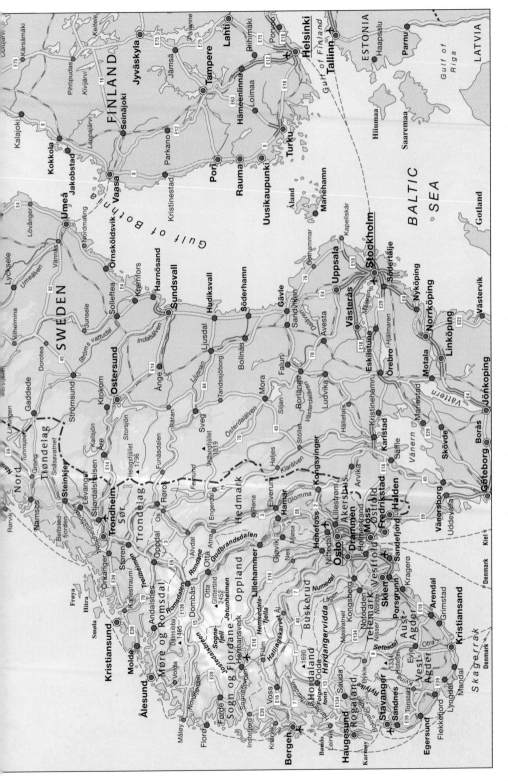

OSLO, NORDIC CITY OF LIGHT

Map on pages 148 & 156

Oslo has long since shaken off its dowdy image. Its compact centre is full of street life, with a multitude of galleries and museums. Oslo's fjord, hills, forests and a Viking ship are just a short ride away

I n the 1880s and 1890s, Edvard Munch drew and painted an Oslo seemingly inhabited by spectres. Men and women were dressed all in black, their hat brims pulled down low, their faces chalk. To him they were like "the living dead who wend their tortuous way down the road that leads to the grave."

This is the Oslo that was, a dour city lacking the vitality of Copenhagen or Stockholm; Munch left it to live in Berlin and Paris. Nearly 100 years later, until the mid-1980s, many of Oslo's cultural attractions were still imported, while native talent left for the brighter lights elsewhere. The only real cultural diversions were a few museums based around explorers and skiers.

Expensive and remote, Oslo also bore another black mark. Nights were meanly trimmed of their fun by laws that severely curbed drinking hours. And so travellers to Norway used to give Oslo no more than a passing nod as they steamed through on their way to Bergen and the more spectacular scenery of the west-coast fjords.

Coming alive

To call Oslo the Nordic City of Light may be too pat a way of saying that Oslo has come of age. However, in a fairly short space of time it has, and Oslo today – a city that celebrated its 1,000 birthday in the year 2000 – bears little resemblance to the dim place that Munch so hated, or even to the Oslo of the early 1980s. It still ranked as the world's most expensive city in 2006, but it has awakened to the attractions of city fun. The small capital by the fjord has developed into a metropolis with a revitalised cultural life and a diverse and lively nightlife.

Oslo's cultural rebirth in recent years has been in part conscious, in part a natural outcome of infusions of money in the right places. If the talent were to be lured back home, things would have to change dramatically. They did. On the back of the oil boom came more and more money for the arts. Suddenly there were sufficient goings-on at home to make artists curious enough to return. One famous Norwegian who stayed faithful to Oslo throughout her career was actress Liv Ullman, who frequently returned to perform here. Now, the building of a magnificent waterside National Opera House is underway, for completion in 2008.

Best by boat

Oslo is at the head of a fjord shaped like a swan's neck; it is surrounded by low hills. Your initial impression will depend on how you arrive. The ideal way is by boat, for then you get the most complete picture, though arriving by car from the south along the Mosseveien also offers some impressive views. There are a few tall buildings in Oslo, but your view from the fjord will still be dominated by the **Rådhus** ❶ (City

PRECEDING PAGES: outside Oslo's Parliament building on National Day. **LEFT:** Gustav Vigeland's great Monoliten. **BELOW:** Aker Brygge.

Hall; opening times vary; entrance charge May–Aug, otherwise free; guided tours Mon–Fri and of the clock tower in summer). It is a large, mud-coloured building topped by two square towers, called the "goat cheese" (*geitost*) by locals because of its resemblance to blocks of locally produced goat's cheese. The courtyard is adorned with fantastic figures and symbols from Norwegian mythology; note the **astronomical clock**, the **Yggdrasill frieze** by Dagfin Werenskiold and Dyre Vaas' **swan fountain**. The murals inside the main hall are based around more modern themes and this is where the Nobel Peace Prize is awarded every year on 10 December. The south-facing clock, at 8 metres (30 ft) in diameter, is one of the largest timepieces in Europe.

In defence

Walking south from the Rådhus, along the fjord, is the medieval **Akershus Slott og Festning ❷** (castle open May–Aug Mon–Sat 10am–4pm, Sun 12.30–4pm; guided tours on Thursday rest of the year; tel: 22 41 25 21; fortress open daily 6am–9pm; tel: 23 09 39 17; entrance charge). Built originally in 1299, it helped

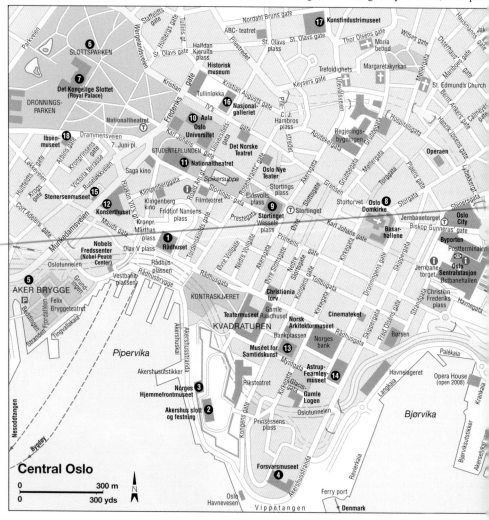

Central Oslo

0   300 m
0   300 yds

to protect Christiania (as Oslo was called until 1925) from marauders throughout the periods of Danish and Swedish rule. The Nazis took over Akershus during World War II and shot several resistance fighters by the old magazine. When the war was over, the traitorous Norwegian chancellor, Quisling, was shot on the same spot. The **Norges Hjemmefrontmuseum** ❸ (Resistance Museum; open Sept–May Mon–Fri 10am–4pm, Sat–Sun 11am–4pm; June–Aug Mon–Sat 10am–5pm, Sun 11am–5pm; entrance charge; tel: 23 09 31 38) in the grounds illustrates the intense story of occupied Norway, while the **Forsvarsmuseet** ❹ (Armed Forces Museum; open May–Aug Mon–Fri 10am–5pm, Sat–Sun 11am–5pm; Sept–Apr, Tues–Fri 10am–4pm, Sat–Sun 11am–5pm; tel: 23 09 35 82) covers Norwegian military and political history from the Vikings to the present day.

Thrusting up on the opposite side of the Pipervika inlet are the glass, chrome and neon buildings of **Aker Brygge** ❺. Centred around an open-air sculpture court, this renovated shipyard and harbour-side development is the setting for shopping arcades, bars, restaurants, food stalls, theatres and galleries, as well as outdoor summer festivals. Between Aker Brygge and City Hall is the new **Nobel Peace Center** (open daily; details at www.nobelpeacecenter.org; entrance charge; tel: 48 30 10 00), telling the history of the prize and offering exhibits on war, peace and conflict resolution. Housed in a renovated train station, it's an ultra-modern account of world affairs since the late 1800s.

In summer, greenery encroaches on Oslo from every side. From the fjord approach you'll see the tops of the trees of **Slottsparken** ❻ (Palace Gardens), and several parks stretching north beyond it to the wooded hills at Oslo's back. There your eye will inevitably be drawn to the Holmenkollen ski jump on one of the city's highest hills.

Map on page 148

TIP

Buy an Oslo Pass for free admission to the city's museums, free public transport and parking, plus discounts at shops, restaurants and on car hire. Passes are obtainable from tourist offices and hotels.

BELOW: the Rådhus (City Hall) at night.

A statue of Karl Johan XIV stands on the steps of Det Kongelige Slott, *the Royal Palace.*

Compact centre

Oslo city centre is large enough to be interesting yet compact enough to cover on foot. The main axis is **Karl Johans Gate**, originally designed in 1826 by the royal architect H.D.F. Linstow. It was widened some 30 years later to become Oslo's answer to the Champs Elysées. Its western end merges into the broad avenue leading to the doors of **Det Kongelige Slott** ❼ (Royal Palace, open for guided tours in the summer, tickets sold at local post offices), and the focal point of the National Day celebrations on 17 May. In the east it runs to Jernbanetorget, the location of **Oslo Sentralstasjon** (Oslo S station). To the south, the centre extends to the fjord.

Parallel to Karl Johans Gate to the north is **Grensen**, another busy, shop-lined street. The **Oslo Domkirke** ❽ (cathedral; closed for major renovation until 2009) dominates the Stortorvet (square) at the east end of Grensen. Completed in 1697, its exterior is of darkened brown brick, while inside artists of the 18th, 19th and 20th centuries have contributed to the cathedral's adornment, including stained-glass windows by Emmanuel Vigeland. Behind Domkirke is **Basarhallene** – a round, colonnaded market with food and handicraft stalls. Lille Grensen leads south to the **Storting** ❾ (Parliament; July–Aug guided tours) on **Karl Johans Gate**, from where **Eidsvollplass** spreads out in front of the Storting. Studenterlunden, the small park around the university, contains the main university building, **Aula** ❿, which is decorated with murals by Edvard Munch. **Nationaltheatret** ⓫ (National Theatre) is just opposite Studenterlunden, and Slottsparken is immediately west.

Artistic attractions

Norwegians, with their seagoing past, have always had a fine awareness of far-away cultures. But it has always been hard to entice foreign artists they admired,

BELOW: inside the Rådhus (City Hall), where the Nobel Peace Prize is awarded every December.

Map on page 148

to their own shores: Norway was too remote, the population too small. Riotously enthusiastic receptions can make up for a lot, however, and that's how Oslo now gets its favourites back year after year. The Oslo Philharmonic, whose home is the **Konserthuset** ⓬ (tel: 23 11 31 00) on Munkedamsveien, performs with a dazzling sequence of guest conductors and soloists. Away from the classical, the variety of music to be heard in Oslo's clubs and concert halls is vast, from South American folk music to indie rock; even international rock stars add Oslo to their world-tour calendar. In June, the Norwegian Wood rock festival is held at Frogner in Oslo, while every August there are international jazz and chamber music festivals.

Christian's town

The simple need for space to accommodate all these artistic ventures has also played a role in reviving neglected parts of Oslo. It has helped to breathe life back into **Christian IV's town**, "Kvadraturen", an historic area bounded to the north by Rådhusgata and to the south by Akershus Slott, and characterised by old customs and shipping houses and grand open plazas. At one time this area was frequented only by prostitutes and their pursuers. The town's history as a redoubtable part of Oslo is reflected in its former nickname, "Little Algerie" – see the painting in Engebret Café on Bankplassen, an artists' haunt since the early 1900s.

But **Gamle Logen** on Grev Wedels Plass is now a serious concert venue and there's also the **Cinemateket** (repertory film theatre) a few blocks away. The **Museet for Samtidskunst** ⓭ (Museum of Contemporary Art; open Tues–Fri 10am–6pm, Thur until 8pm, Sat–Sun 10am–5pm; entrance charge; tel: 22 86 22 10) is housed in the original Norges Bank (Central Bank) building, on Bankplassen, and

BELOW: Akershus Slott (Castle) og Festning (fortress).

has an extensive collection of 20th-century Norwegian art. Just around the corner is the **Astrup Fearnley Museum of Modern Art**  (open Tues, Wed and Fri 11am–5pm, Thur 11am–7pm, Sat–Sun noon–5pm; tel: 22 93 60 60), which focuses on international artists, although it too contains Scandinavian works. Galleries across the city are full of art in every medium, and established museums have opened their doors to the works of contemporary artists. Try the **Stenersenmuseet** ⑮ (Munkedamsveien 15; open Tues, Thur 11am–7pm, Wed, Fri–Sun 11am–5pm; entrance charge; tel: 22 49 36 00), which shows Norwegian art from 1850 to 1970.

A multitude of museums

Nasjonalgalleriet ⑯ (National Gallery, Universitetsgaten 13; open Mon, Wed and Fri 10am–6pm, Thur 10am–8pm, Sat–Sun 10am–5pm; tel: 22 20 03 41) is for anyone who has never heard of any Norwegian artist apart from Edvard Munch. The sheer size, if not the content, of the forest and fjord paintings of the Romantic artist J.C. Dahl (1788–1857) will impress you. You'll also see the work of his prolific contemporaries, Adolph Tidemand (1814–76) and Hans Frederik Gude (1825–1903). There is a wonderful series of etchings depicting barn dances, village scenes and festivities. The display of Impressionist works is excellent. And don't forget the Munch room.

A little further north is the **Kunstindustrimuseet** ⑰ (Museum of Applied Art, St Olav's Gate 1; open Tues, Wed and Fri 11am–5pm, Thur 11am–8pm, Sat–Sun noon–4pm; tel: 22 03 65 40). It is graced by two earthenware urns at its entrance and has superb displays of Norwegian textile, fashion and furniture design. The most famous tapestry it owns is the *Baldishol*, dating from 1180, and one of the most popular exhibits is of the royal costumes. On the uppermost floor is a collection of Scandinavian design for the home ranging from bent-wood chairs to streamlined kitchen gadgets.

West along Drammensveien from the National Gallery is the newly refurbished **Ibsen-museet** ⑱ (Arbins Gate 1; entrance charge; tel: 22 12 35 50; www.ibsenmuseet.no) with guided tours of Henrik Ibsen's apartment where he lived from 1895 until his death in 1906. For the technically minded there is the **Norsk Teknisk Museum** (Museum of Technology, Kjelsåsveien 143; 20 June–20 Aug daily 10am–6pm; rest of year Tues–Fri 9am–4pm, Sat–Sun 11am–6pm; suburban train, trams 12 or 15, buses 22, 25 and 37 to Kjelsås; entrance charge; tel: 22 79 60 00). This is a great day out for children, with lots of hands-on exhibitions about energy, industry, transport and telecommunications. Nearby is a water mill which feeds the Akerselva River.

Life on the streets

Along with an upturn in the arts, Oslo's streets are tangibly alive, especially in summer: festivals come fast and furious, and the crowds at restaurants and cafés brim over on to the pavement.

Oslo's growth in nightlife owes much to the extending of licensing hours to 3am in the 1990s. The number of **bars** and **clubs** that has sprung up in order to take advantage of late-night traffic is astounding. **Restaurants**, too, have flourished: the influx of immigrants

BELOW: in summer everything happens on the streets.

has resulted in a variety of kitchens being opened. Included among these restaurants are typical northwest Norwegian fish restaurants, which serve traditional dishes according to age-old recipes.

Norwegians are serious coffee drinkers. There are **cafés** that are simply cafés (*kafé*). Then there are *gjæstgiveris*, pubs, *kros*, *bistros*, *spiseris* and *kafeterias*, which all tend to be a bit more casual than restaurants; in other words, they are likely to serve smallish meals plus snacks all day and into the night. Seattle-style coffee shops are also popular.

Most eating and drinking places start to fill slowly after working hours and turn more boisterous after supper. Bars and clubs are spread throughout the city, and range from underground to upmarket – consult the *What's On* Oslo guide, ask someone who knows Oslo, or consult www.visitoslo.com. The "in" scene changes every year, but can normally be identified by the long queue in front of the building, which will certainly not disperse until after 1am. Hip places include Onkel Donald Kafe, Universitets Gate 26, and Smuget, Rosenkrantz Gate 22.

Evening entertainment

The Norwegians tend to divide their evenings into three different parts. Since eating and drinking in restaurants and bars is expensive, many people invite friends into their homes for a meal, or for "before" drinks (*vorspiel*). The richer crowds may opt for cinemas, theatres or restaurants, after which the real nightlife starts and the high price for a beer is no longer important. From 2am the pubs empty and act three is about to begin. Friends and neighbours (not necessarily the ones who were with you at the beginning of the evening) are invited in and offered the remaining contents of the house bar (*nachspiel*). Despite all the fun of enjoying

Map on page 148

The Fram, *Fridtjof Nansen's Arctic exploration boat, took Roald Amundsen to the South Pole in 1912.*

BELOW: enjoying a drink on Karl Johans Gate.

TIP

You can save on accommodation and sightseeing by booking an *Oslo Pakken* (Oslo Package) offered by travel agents. A room with breakfast at a choice of 42 hotels and the Oslo Pass *(see page 149)* are included.

Oslo until the last bars close, natives still pull on their boots and head for the hills the next day. Love of nature and folklore are inbred in today's Norwegians.

Come Sunday evening, it's a good idea to book tickets early if you want to see a film, since Sunday is Oslo's favourite time to go to the movies. The price of seats is reasonable and all cinemas show films in their original language with Norwegian subtitles.

There is no English-language theatre but Norwegians are devoted theatre-goers, and companies perform everything in Norwegian, from Eugene O'Neill to Andrew Lloyd Webber. You will find international drama festivals across Norway in summer, which is your only chance to see something in English. However, if there's an Ibsen play on that you know well, it might be worth seeing it in Norwegian – the emotiveness of Ibsen should break through any language barrier.

How to stay solvent

When it comes to budgeting for a stay in Oslo, there are a number of ways to save your kroner. Norwegian hotel breakfasts usually offer a large, help-yourself selection. The better assortments are likely to include toast and crispbreads, cheese, marinated and smoked salmon, herring, cereals, fruit, eggs, juice, tea and coffee. (The *koldtbord*, which is the lunch-time variation, will have some hot dishes added.) If you can have a hearty breakfast as your main meal of the day, and avoid eating a large evening meal in a restaurant, then you'll manage to keep to a reasonable budget. The most common street snack is the *pølse* – a long, skinny hot dog served either with *brød* (bread) or rolled in a *lompe* (potato pancake). But there are now a lot of cafés, brasseries and pizzerias where you can get small to medium-sized meals that won't break the bank.

BELOW: the rich pattern surrounding Vigeland's Monoliten.

Full meals can be reasonable, too, as long as you don't order a lot of alcohol.

Alas, the high cost of alcohol is near unbeatable, although beer can be purchased before 8pm at most supermarkets for a reasonable price. Bringing in your full duty-free allowance helps, but you can't really tote your own bottle around the streets or in restaurants, so that provides a limited solution. Drinking costs will be high even if you stick to beer, but if you choose wine or spirits, they'll rocket.

In summer, hotel rates are deeply discounted to make up for the lack of business and conference traffic. In winter, you can sometimes do fairly well with weekend rates, but watch out for school and ski holiday weeks when hotels are crowded and rates higher again. Pensions, mission churches and youth hostels are usually reasonably priced. Camping is another option in such an outdoor city as Oslo: the site at Ekebergsletta *(see Travel Tips page 369)* a hilly park suburb with wonderful views over Oslo and the fjord, is 3 km (2 miles) from town.

From Munch to minorities

Combining a museum visit with a stroll is a relaxing and usually a cheap way of spending part of a day or evening. Once you leave behind the bigger hotels and restaurants where businesspeople wine and dine, food and drink prices drop significantly. The exploring suggestions that follow focus on sights outside the very heart of Oslo.

One of Norway's best-known museums is **Munch-museet** ⑲ (Munch Museum, Tøyengata 53; open Sept–May Mon–Fri 10am–4pm, Sat–Sun 11am–5pm; June–Aug daily 10am–6pm; some closures, see www.munch.museum.no for updates; entrance charge; tel: 23 49 35 00; T-bane Tøyen/Munchmuséet). A tremendous collection of Munch's work is housed here, all donated by the artist himself. The

Map on pages 156–7

BELOW: sculpture and "echo" in the Vigeland-museet.

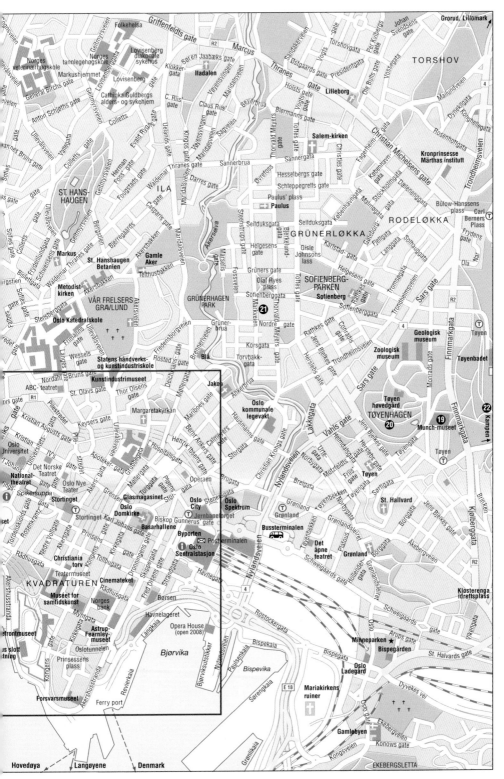

One of Oslo's many statues, overlooking the water in Eidsvollplass.

BELOW: enjoying a meal outside, down by the harbour at Aker Brygge.

life of Edvard Munch (1863–1944) was permeated by sickness – a theme reflected in his paintings. Himself a sickly child, both his mother and sister died at an early age from tuberculosis. Festive renderings of Gypsy families and blazing autumn landscapes counteract these gloomier works. The famous *Skrik (The Scream)* stolen in 2004 but recovered two years later, is darkly riveting, as is the *Marats død* series *(Death of Marat,* 1907) in which Munch portrays himself bleeding from gunshot wounds inflicted by an angry mistress. After a series of breakdowns, Munch returned to Norway, having spent most of his adult, artistic life in Paris and Berlin. He sought peace, but continued working, in his cottage at Åsgårdstrand in Vestfold.

The Munch museum is flanked by parks. The one to the east contains the **Tøyenbadet** (public swimming pools), including a lido, water slide and saunas. To the west is **Tøyenhagen** ⓴ (Tøyen Botanical Gardens) with the Zoological, Mineralogical, Geological and Palaeontological museums at its north end (open all year). In September and early spring this is the site of Norway's largest traditional circus.

A few streets northwest of Munch-museet, across Trondheimsveien, is the **Grünerløkka** district, a former working-class neighbourhood now densely populated with artists and writers. The most interesting street in Grünerløkka is **Markveien** ㉑, painted in muted pastel colours and lined with galleries and boutiques. In the courtyard near Markveien 42 a brick building houses various artists' studios. Parallel to Markveien is Thorvald Meyers Gate with many restaurants and bars open until 3am. On long warm summer nights you'd never believe you were so close to the Arctic. Continuing north on Markveien, you'll find a cross street called Grünersgate. From here up to Schleppergrells Gate are some magnificent residential courtyards: peer inside for a look at tranquil urban living in Oslo.

Just south of vibrant Grünerløkka is one of Oslo's biggest ethnic commercial neighbourhoods, **Grønland** (T-bane to Grønland station). It's largely Pakistani, but other cultures are evident in the shops, cafés and the dress of those out strolling. The recently opened **Grønland Basar**, at the corner of Tøyengata and Grønlandsleiret, offers everything from a halal butcher's shop to Middle-Eastern sweets, and Persian carpets. The old Grønland Police Station next door at Tøyenbekken 5 now houses the **International Cultural Center and Museum** (open Thur 10am–8pm, Tues, Wed and Fri 10am–4pm, Sat–Sun noon–4pm), with exhibits on immigration, a gallery and café.

Kampen ㉒, whose northern limit is Kampenparken (on the southeast side of Munch-museet), is a district of gorgeous wooden houses brilliantly painted in siennas, golds, pastels and vibrant blues. Some of the streets in lower Kampen are overhung by trees and are supremely quiet; look up, too, at the dormer windows above the street corners, hung with macramé and lace curtains.

Vigeland's vision

West of the city centre is **Frognerparken** (park) or **Vigelandsparken ㉓** (sculpture park; open all year). The park, containing the life's work of the famous Norwegian sculptor Gustav Vigeland (1869–1943), is a 40-minute walk from the centre. One way of getting there would be by continuing on north-west from the Royal Palace to Hegdehaugsveien, which becomes Bogstadsveien – a long, lively street of art galleries and enticing shops – or pick up a bus (Nos 20, 45 or 81) or tram (Nos 12) in the direction of Frogner. Any west-bound T-bane from the Nationaltheatret stops at Majorstuen, the end of Bogstadsveien, from where it is only a short walk to the beginning of the park.

Map on pages 156–7

Gustav Vigeland's brother, Emanuel (1875–1948), was a painter. It's worth visiting the Emanuel Vigeland Museum (Grimelundsveien 8; open Sun noon–4pm) to see Vita (Life), his alfresco decoration of the building.

BELOW: children on a day out in Oslo.

Nobel's Peace Prize

O
ne of the great ironies is that the Swedish armaments manufacturer Alfred Nobel should have been the founder of the world's most prestigious prize for peace. Was it the realisation that his invention of dynamite in 1866 could and had been easily turned from peaceful rock tunnelling to war that led him to include the peace category alongside prizes for physics, chemistry, medicine and literature? Or was his conscience troubled by the thought that his great riches were built on weapons of war? It may have been no more than a tribute to the Norwegian reputation as workers for peace.

Nobody knows what went on in the mind of this introspective, isolated man.

It is almost as strange that when he set up his trust fund, Nobel chose the Norwegian Storting (Parliament) to make the peace

award. It was a time when the near century-old union between Sweden and Norway was collapsing. Perhaps Nobel hoped that, by passing the Peace Prize into Norwegian jurisdiction, he might help keep the two nations together. If this was his aim, he failed. The union was dissolved five years after his death in 1901 and Norway was already a year-old sovereign state at the first ceremonies in 1906.

Except for the Peace Prize, the other categories are judged in Sweden and presented in Stockholm to those who, in Nobel's words, "shall have conferred the greatest benefit on mankind". The Nobel Peace Prize ceremony takes place in Oslo's City Hall (Rådhus).

Nobel's early instructions were that the Peace Prize should be used to award efforts to reduce the size of military forces and standing armies, but the prize broadened its remit to the promotion of peace in general. This vague brief can lead to controversy, as it did when the Israeli and Egyptian leaders, Menachem Begin and Anwar Sadat, received the Peace Prize jointly for their 1978 efforts to open up talks and communication between their two countries. Dr Henry Kissinger's award in 1972 also aroused controversy, particularly when his Vietnamese co-recipient, Le Duc Tho, turned down his own award for their joint efforts in ending the Vietnam war.

However, few begrudged Nelson Mandela and F.W. de Klerk their joint award in 1993. There were no dissenters when the Red Cross received the prize in 1917 for its work amid the battlefield carnage of World War I. The explorer Fridtjof Nansen regarded the Nobel Peace Prize as the greatest of the tributes to his years as internationalist, humanitarian and head of the Norwegian delegation at the League of Nations.

Among the many other recipients were Martin Luther King, Dr Albert Schweitzer, Amnesty International, the Dalai Lama and Kofi Annan. In 1979 Mother Teresa accepted her award in her customary habit and sandals despite the Norwegian winter. Even so her conservative views on abortion led to protests. ❏

LEFT: Alfred Nobel (1833–96).

Once inside the intricate wrought-iron gates, you'll come across **Vigelands-broen** (bridge), bedecked with 58 bronze figures of men, women and new-born infants, including the famous *Sinnataggen (Angry Boy)*. Next is *Fontenen (Fountain)*, six male figures raising a giant bowl. Vigeland was obsessed with the cycle of life which he depicts here in 20 reliefs around the edge of the fountain pool. Above the fountain on a raised plateau, and surrounded by 36 groups of granite figures, is **Monolitten ㉔**, a great spire 17 metres (55 ft) high and comprising 121 figures sculpted out of one solid block of a whitish granite. The last of the major sculptures, the *Livshjulet (Wheel of Life)* is a continuum of human figures in a kind of airborne ring dance. The **Vigeland-museet** (open Tues–Sun noon–4pm, summer 11am–5pm; entrance charge; tel: 23 49 37 00), containing the rest of his work, is at the southern end of the park. Vigeland spent 40 years of his life designing and constructing the park, all financed by the taxpayer, something which Munch found reprehensible; he made his own feelings clear by donating all his own work to the city.

Map on pages 156–7

A city in the making

Frogner Park also contains the **Oslo Bymuseum ㉕** (City Museum; open Tues–Sun 11am–4pm; entrance charge except Sat; tel: 23 28 41 70), which traces the city's history. Founded in 1050 by Harald Hardråde, Oslo was originally bounded by the (now subterranean) Bjørvika, Alna and Hovin rivers. It took another 250 years before it attained capital status during the reign of Håkon V (1299–1319). The town had just 3,000 inhabitants at the time.

A living exhibit in traditional dress in Oslo's Norsk Folkemuseum at Bygdøy.

BELOW: Norwegians are generous in a good cause.

Following a great fire in 1624, Christian IV decided to move the city settlements to where Akershus Festning (fortress) now stands, and the town became known as Christiania or "Kvadraturen". What was the centre is now called **Christiania torv**, where in 1997 a statue of Christian IV's index finger was erected to commemorate the historic event.

With its strict grid plan, Christiania had little in common with medieval Oslo. The greatest change, however, has happened over the past 150 years due to growth in its population. In 1880, Christiania had 120,000 inhabitants; by 1910 the population had doubled. By popular consensus the town reverted to its original name in 1925. From 1945 to 1955, Oslo went through a new period of growth, and surpassed the half million mark in 1997.

Norway's national jump

For **Holmenkollen ㉖** ski jump and **Skimuseet** (Ski Museum: open June–Aug 9am–8pm; Oct–May 10am–4pm, May–Sept 10am–5pm; entrance charge; tel: 22 92 32 00) take T-bane 1 to Holmenkollen. The jump is only used in February and March, and the crowning event of the ski-jump season is the competition on the second Sunday in March *(see page 105)*. Holmenkollen is a national symbol and a new jump will be built on its site for the Nordic World Championships in 2011. The adjoining Ski Museum is a monument to "One Thousand Years of Skiing". Very old skis and snowshoes are on display, as well as gear carried by such Norwegian explorers as Fridtjof Nansen,

Away from the city centre, the domestic architecture in some of Oslo's suburbs reflects the tranquil side of urban life.

BELOW: from the top of Tryvannstårnet, Oslo's radio tower, the view stretches to Sweden.

who crossed Greenland on skis. A simulator recreates the Holmenkollen jump.

The same metro line to Holmenkollen (T-bane) ends at Frognerseteren (with a restaurant of the same name, famous for its home-made apple pie). The area is thickly forested and popular for walking and skiing. If you choose to go back to Holmenkollen on foot, the walk is signposted and takes 15 to 20 minutes.

Other exploring possibilities are provided by the islands and peninsulas of Oslofjorden, most of which are accessible by ferry from Aker Brygge quay. **Nesoddtangen** is at the tip of a hilly, wooded peninsula jutting from the east side of the fjord. Local artists exhibit at **Hellviktangen Manor** ㉗ (open May–Sept; weekends out of season; entrance charge), where they serve coffee and waffles on Sundays. The house is surrounded by apple trees and gives directly on to the fjord. Several of the fjord's islands are popular for swimming and roaming, and accessible by ferries from **Vippetangen** on the Akershus Fortress-side of the inner harbour, adjacent to the DFDS and Stena cruise-ferry terminals to Denmark. The island called **Hovedøya** features the ruins of a cloister and myriad walking trails, while **Gressholmen** is best-known for its popular café. The ferries are run by the same public transit service that runs Oslo's bus and tram network, and the same tickets can be used.

Bygone days on Bygdøy

Oslo hugs the fjord, and the city limits extend quite far down its sides. Just west of the harbour is the **Bygdøy peninsula**, where the old Viking ships and the more recent explorer ships are kept, and where Norway's maritime past is commemorated (bus No. 30 or from May–Sept boat No. 91 from Rådhusbrygge).

It is home to the **Vikingskipshuset** ㉘ (Viking Ship Museum; open May–Sept daily 9am–6pm; Oct–Apr daily 11am– 4pm; entrance charge; tel: 22 13 52 80); the **Frammuseet** ㉙ (open June–Aug daily 9am–6pm; Sept–May daily hours vary; entrance charge; tel: 23 28 29 50), which houses Fridtjof Nansen's polar sailing ship *Fram;* and the **Kon-Tiki Museet** ㉚ (open June–Aug daily 9.30am–5.30pm; Sept–May daily hours vary; entrance charge; tel: 23 08 67 67), which contains, apart from the *Kon-Tiki* raft on which Thor Heyerdahl travelled from South America to Polynesia, *Ra II*, a fragile-looking reed barque on which he travelled from Morocco to Barbados. There is also a collection of his Easter Island artefacts.

The **Norsk Sjøfartsmuseum** ㉛ (Maritime Museum; open mid-May–Aug daily 10am–6pm; Sept–mid-May Fri–Wed 10.30am–4pm, Thur 10.30am–6pm; entrance charge; tel: 24 11 41 50) concentrates on the history of the craft of boat-building.

Also on Bygdøy is the **Norsk Folkemuseum** ㉜ (Norwegian Folk Museum; open mid-May–mid-Sept daily 10am–6pm; Oct–Apr daily times vary; entrance charge; tel: 22 12 37 00). The folk museum, established in 1894, is an indoor/outdoor museum devoted largely to Norwegian rural culture. The collection of outdoor buildings, including a stave church from Gudbrandsdalen, gives a good idea of what old villages and agricultural settlements looked like. Other exhibits include Sami ethnography, a pharmacy museum and a renovated

Oslo apartment building featuring flats as they have evolved since the 1800s.

The Holocaust Center (Huk Aveny 56, bus No. 30; open Tues–Fri 10am–4.30pm, Sat from 11am; entrance charge; tel: 22 84 21 00; www.hlsenteret.no) opened on Bygdøy in August 2006. Housed in the mansion occupied by traitor Vidkun Quisling during World War II, the centre offers a permanent exhibition on the Holocaust and the tragic fate of Norwegian Jews, while serving as a centre for studies of the Holocaust and religious minorities.

Map on pages 156–7

Weekends out of doors

A typical city dweller from Oslo spends huge amounts of time outdoors. On workdays, many take their *matpakke* from home (a basic lunch bag stuffed with sandwiches and fruit) and sit outside, weather allowing, between 11.30am and 12.30pm to eat it. (Lunch is eaten later in restaurants, from noon–2pm.) There is a large number of outdoor and pavement establishments, so those without *matpakke* can also lunch out of doors.

The Oslo area can get warm in summer and cold and snowy in the winter. So in summer, people are likely to plan outdoor activities after work, anything from swimming, berry-picking, walking, boating, or cycling at home in the suburbs in the light of the evening sun. Norwegians treasure their space and contact with nature, and many people who work in Oslo live a fair distance from the city; in winter, this means they can get quickly on to the floodlit slopes and cross-country ski trails after work.

Come the weekend, there is a widely followed pattern for the 48 hours. Friday night is usually a night out on the town. This may begin after dinner and a change of clothes at home, especially for younger people, who don't start to fill

BELOW: a statue of Camilla Collett, one of Norway's earliest female writers, in Slottsparken.

Maps, pages 148 & 156

the bars until well after 10pm. Saturday morning is given over to shopping, followed by gardening or watching football, and Saturday evening tends to be dinner or a party at someone's home. No matter how wild or calm the Saturday night, Sunday is *tur* day. The *tur* is a walk or ski tour, and a formidable tradition. Depending on a person's age, fitness, and the number of accompanying children, the *tur* can be anything from a one-to six-hour affair. The *matpakke* provides lunch in the forest. Some walks will include café stops in one of the 70-odd cabin lodges in the **Nordmarka** area of Oslo; if not, coffee and hot chocolate come along in a vacuum flask. Home then to change for an early dinner, then it's off to the cinema. And thereby hangs a weekend.

Oslomarka

Oslo is surrounded by hills and forests known as *marka*. Larch, birch, pine, aspen and several deciduous species dominate; the colour contrast in autumn is worth a special trip. Den Norske Turistforening (Trekking Association) at Storgate 3 has maps of most hiking and ski trails in these areas. Access to the trails from the centre is easy and cheap via public transport. For **Grorud** and the **Lillomarka** area (northeast of the city centre), take either T-bane 5 (destination Vestli) or bus No. 30 from Jernbanetorget. Trails begin just west of the Grorud T-bane. Due north is **Grefsen**, along a suburban train line (information from Trafikanten at Oslo Sentralstasjon), or via tram 11 and 12 (Grefsen/Kjelsås), or take the bus to Grefsenkollen.

For walks in the **Holmenkollen** area and northwest, part of Nordmarka, take T-bane 1 to Frognerseteren (not to be confused with Frognerparken) and stay on until the end of the line. You can even rent a sled *(archebrect)* there to take on a 3-km (2-mile) long downhill trail (the Corkscrew). The Trekking Association can recommend trails or, even better, ask a Norwegian to recommend a favourite *tur*. The trails are signposted, but if you get lost, seek help from other walkers. (See the *Oslo Guide* on www.visitoslo.com for other recommended routes.)

Many of the forest trails circumnavigate lakes, so a swimming break may be included if it's hot. Come winter, there's skiing (even at night on floodlit trails), skating and sledging to add to the general flurry of activity on a Sunday. If good snow cover has been established, walking trails double as cross-country skiing trails.

Something to take home

Handicrafts, textiles, woollens and pewter are favourites for visitors to Oslo. **Basarhallene**, one of the few older shopping areas at the back of the Domkirke, has a wonderful jeweller's, Elias Sollberg. Nearby are two big department stores, Glasmagasinet across the way (Stortorvet 9) and Steen & Strøm at Kongensgate 23.

Oslo City and **By Porten**, next to Oslo Sentralstasjon, and **Aker Brygge** on the waterfront are three major malls. Grensen is the street for bargains, while Lille Grensen has stalls selling everything from sausages to skateboards. A big art market takes place now and again, on Sundays, in the warehouses around the Blå concert hall off Nordregate. ❏

BELOW: out sailing on Oslofjorden.
RIGHT: a traditional "loft" house (food store) in the Folkemuseum at Bygdøy.

AROUND OSLO AND ITS FJORD

Map on page 170

The charms of the Oslofjord may need some searching out, for this is Norway's industrial heartland, but it is rich in natural beauty and Viking history, and the surrounding area echoes to its pulse

At dusk the islands of the fjord that leads to Oslo look like hunched pre-historic animals about to sink into a subaquatic sleep. In the colder months, the sky at sunset grows from lavender to purple while the islands turn slate-grey, then ominous and black. Summer sunsets bring twisted pink clouds underlit by a huge red sun that drops only briefly behind the fjord's western cliffs before rising again in the east.

Daytime along the 100-km (60-mile) long fjord reveals a high concentration of industry down both the eastern and western sides. With Oslo at its head, the fjord is the capital's workhorse, its roads travelled by juggernauts with cargoes of timber and oil, its ports and waterways busy with yachts and barges. Outside its working ports, Oslofjorden is a magnificent expanse of water stretching into the Skagerrak. Sprinkled liberally with islands, skerries, natural marinas and swimming beaches, the fjord is popular with Oslo residents in summer.

PRECEDING PAGES: old wooden houses on Oslofjorden. **LEFT:** a summer's evening on the fjord. **BELOW:** Moses with the Ten Commandments, Drøbak church.

The lungs of the city

Akershus, **Vestfold** and **Østfold** are the three main counties to touch Oslofjorden. Akershus county contains the Oslo metropolitan area, the national Gardermoen airport, plus a broad swathe of agricultural and forest land reaching to Sweden. At its northern reach lies the Mjøsa lake town of Eidsvoll, where the Norwegian constitution was signed and the modern state born in 1814. Østfold (east) and Vestfold (west) spread down from Oslo like a pair of lungs. Some of Scandinavia's oldest ruling families were found buried in Vestfold along with several sunken Viking ships loaded with booty, while Østfold is rich with ancient rock paintings and stone circles.

Both of these counties contain provincial cities of major historic significance: Fredrikstad in Østfold, a magnificent fortress town, and Tønsberg in Vestfold, the oldest extant Scandinavian city, founded in 872. Remains of **Kaupang**, the oldest Nordic town yet dis-covered, were found a couple of kilometres from Tønsberg and are now in Oslo's Historisk (Historical Museum). Corroboration of its early existence appeared in a world history by England's 9th-century monarch, King Alfred the Great. Larger towns usu-ally have an old section closely packed with superbly crafted wooden houses. Halden, near the Swedish bor-der in Østfold, and Larvik in Vestfold, are the south-ernmost points on the fjord, each accessible within a couple of hours from Oslo.

Despite its rich history and good travel links, the Oslofjord area doesn't get as many tourists as western Norway; the scenery isn't as dramatic. There are, however, more habitable islands than in any other fjord, many with sports centres and hotels offering

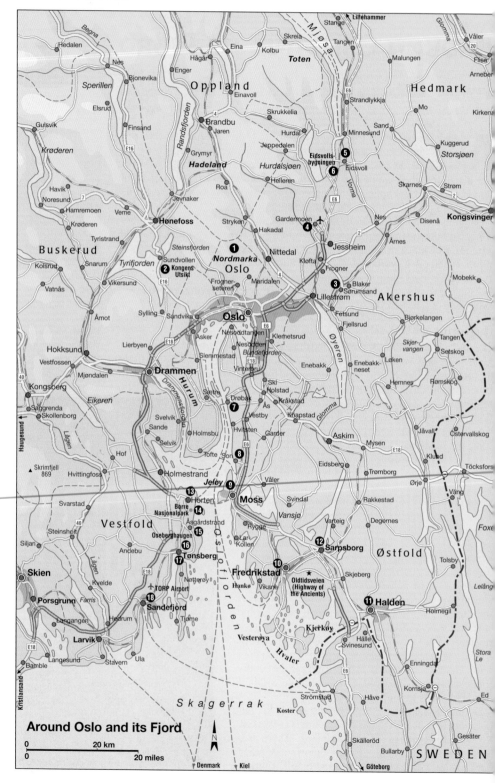

Around Oslo and its Fjord

0   20 km

0   20 miles

everything from tennis to windsurfing and swimming. Inland, the sloping countryside is punctuated by forests, orchards and tilled fields, and appeals to cyclists.

Walker's paradise

There are fantastic walks in **Oslomarka** (the forests surrounding Oslo) accessible by bus, train or tram. Much of **Nordmarka** ❶ (the area to the north of the city) is privately owned by timber barons who have kept it open to the public and, in any case, Norway's "Outdoor Recreations Act" permits everybody to cross outlying property on foot. Summer or winter maps covering the marka's network of cleared trails are available from Den Norske Turistforeningen (Storgata 3, Oslo; weekdays only; tel: 22 82 28 00). Around Grefsen, south of **Maridalsvannet**, is a luxuriant parkland (tram 11 and 12 or bus 37 to Grefsen, Grefsenkollen, Kjelsås). **Maridalsvannet** is a tremendous lake fed by a series of charming clear-water brooks. **Sognsvann**, the lake west of **Maridalsvannet**, is at the end of T-bane 5. The most heavily used trails start from Sognsvann and **Frognerseteren**.

By car you can explore further. If you're a fan of Norwegian rural architecture you'll have your fill in outer Akershus. Take route E16 in a westerly direction towards Tyrifjorden and Sundvollen into the **Krokkleiva** district. The paths cross wooded hills 400–500 metres (1,300–1,600 ft) high. **Kongens Utsikt** ❷ (The King's View) gives panoramic views across Steinsfjorden and Tyrifjorden.

Afterwards, rejoin the E16 northbound, direction Hønefoss. Leave it before Hønefoss, direction Jevnaker. There you can visit **Hadeland Glass Works** (open daily, all year) and the countryside of Hadeland. South of Highway 35 is a **wilderness** of pine marshland, secluded lakes, oak forests and stream-bordered fields (map: Oslo Nordmark – Nordre Del). Road 4 south returns you to Oslo and the junction with the E6; northbound it leads to Gjøvik on the western side of Lake Mjøsa.

Birthplace of the state

If you go east from the junction of Road 4 and the E6 along Road 170 you come to the small village of **Fetsund**, just past Lillestrøm, and the **Fetsund Lenser** (open June–Aug Tues–Fri 11am–4pm, Sat–Sun 11am–5pm; Sept–Dec Sat–Sun only 11am–4pm; Jan–May Sat–Sun only noon–4pm; entrance charge; tel: 63 88 75 50), a logging museum celebrating the industrial activity on the banks of the Glomma River. The museum includes a nature trail and boat trips to the North Øyeren Nature Reserve, a haven for migratory bird species. The café here specialises in serving grilled *gjedde* (pike) in burger form.

Heading northeast, a road to the left will bring you to **Sørumsand** ❸, where there is a narrow-gauge "Tertitten" railway (open Dec, July–mid-Sept Sun only 11am–3pm; tel: 63 86 81 50). From here, Road 171 will bring you back to the E6. Travelling north you come to the unusual landscape of **Raknehaugen** (burial site; open all year) at Jessheim near **Gardermoen** ❹. Continuing in a northerly direction, at the southern end of Lake Mjøsa is **Eidsvoll** ❺, about 80 km (50 miles) from Oslo. Eidsvoll is a lake town of old

Map on page 170

On the outskirts of the capital, Oslomarka (Oslo's fields) contain 2,500 km (1,550 miles) of ski trails, 110 km (68 miles) of which are illuminated at night. Trail use is free and there are lodges and cafés along the way.

BELOW: inscription at Skjeberg, Østfold.

The Norwegian Constitution was signed in 1814 in this wooden manor house near Eidsvoll, home of the Anker family.

wooden houses and churches, and nearby, on the other side of the E6 at Eidsvoll Verk, is a national landmark: the **Eidsvollsbygningen** ❻ (memorial building; open 1 May–30 Aug 10am–5pm; 1 Sept–30 Apr Tues–Fri 10am–2pm, Sat–Sun 10am–5pm; entrance charge; tel: 63 92 22 10), a mini-museum to the Norwegian Constitution which includes the room where the document was signed. The nearby **Eidsvoll Bygdetun** (Rural Museum; open June–Aug; entrance charge) consists of a collection of 26 old farm buildings and a World War II museum all set in beautiful countryside. Then tour Lake Mjøsa on the old paddle steamer *Skibladner* (tel: 61 14 40 80). The round trip takes 12 hours, with the halfway point at Lillehammer *(see page 183)*.

Tranquil countryside, sleepy shore

Heading south out of Oslo on the east side of the fjord, the quiet way to Fredrikstad is via the old **Mossveien**, which hugs the fjord as near as topography allows. Having taken the E6 or E18 out of the city, turn right off the main road at Vinterbru and head for the tip of Bundefjorden. Take the road signposted to Nesoddtangen and you will come across a signpost to **Drøbak** ❼.

The village of Drøbak was once a fishermen's settlement. Fishing vessels still arrive here and sell fresh prawns and fish on the quayside. Places of interest include the **Follo Museum** (Heritage Museum; open mid-May–mid-Sept Tues–Fri 11am–4pm, Sun noon–4pm; entrance charge; tel: 64 93 99 90) and **Oscarsborg Festning** (island fort; tours in summer; tel: 81 55 19 00; www.nasjonalefestningsverk.no/oscarsborg) out in the fjord from where gunfire sunk the German cruiser *Blücher* in 1940 (guided boat trips from Drøbak's harbour). Another point of pride is the cross-timbered **Drøbak Kirke** from 1776 (open all

BELOW: Drøbak, a fishing port on the Oslofjord.

year). The church has an elaborately carved model of a ship, a common piece of church decoration in seafaring towns. Rococo touches include wooden busts of Moses and Aaron. Gospel and jazz concerts are held here in summer.

Map on page 170

Artist centre

The road out of Drøbak takes off just before the ferry terminal, from where small car ferries run every half hour or so to the Hurum peninsula. Soon the road passes through fertile farmland and forest, first to Hvitsten and then to **Son ❽** (pronounced *soon*), a fetching artists' village hugging the edge of a sheltered sound. The surrounding countryside and shoreline here provided inspiration for the likes of Theodore Kittelsen and Edvard Munch.

The **Son Kystkultursenter** (Coastal Heritage Centre; open mid-May–mid-Sept Tues–Sun; tel: 64 95 82 13) explains how this one-time Dutch freeport (the original name was Zoon) has thrived variously on timber, ice and fishing. The unusual elevated building at the edge of the marina is the last remaining fishing-net-drying structure in the Oslo fjord. **Gallery X** and **Bakgården** are showrooms for local artists (open all year), while **La Riviera** next door is an excellent French restaurant with an authentic wood-burning oven. Son is a popular summer resort for boating enthusiasts and on a summer's evening, with a cold beer in hand, there is no better place to watch the sun set behind the billowing sails of a myriad of yachts.

Knut Hamsun, the Nobel prize-winning novelist, once lived in the Reenskaug Hotel in Drøbak, and the town became a rich source of material for his 1920 novel, Konene ved Vandposten (Women at the Pump).

South to Østfold

Østfold is a long funnel through which Norwegians drive on their way to cheaper shopping in Sweden. Despite its industrial towns such as Halden, Sarpsborg and Moss, Østfold buzzes with outdoor pursuits: canoeing and cycling are pop-

BELOW: the view over Halden from the fortress.

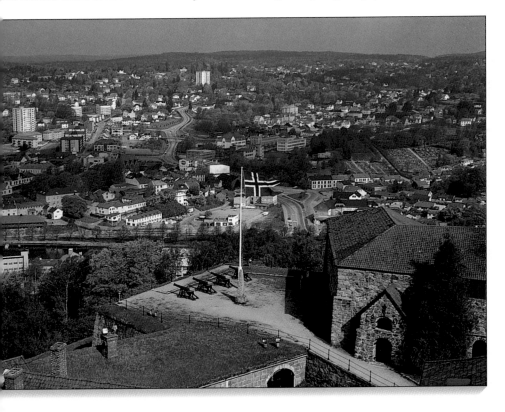

ular, and the area is dotted with hiking and skiing centres. There are also gol
courses, and the Mysen racetrack. Then there's the draw of the fjord. Jelø
peninsula is the site of **Galleri F15** (open all year; entrance charge) at **Jeløy**
which has fjord-side trails and stupendous lawns. Exhibitions are laid ou
through a light-filled house. Its cafeteria is a beloved coffee pit stop. Down th
coast is the royal enclave of **Hankø**, Norway's regatta centre. The summe
home of Princess Martha Louise's grandfather is located here.

Old centres

Fredrikstad ❿ is a gem among Østfold towns, and Scandinavia's only com
pletely preserved fortress town, dating from 1567. The cobbled streets of Gam
lebyen (old town) were laid by prisoners; wooden stocks face the former prison
now a bank (but with the prisoners' room preserved). And its restaurants and gal
leries keep their old facades. The stately Rådhus (Town Hall) was designed by
the architect who built Oslo's Stortinget. The old-style Victoria Hotel serve
fine meals; game is a speciality.

History and prehistory figure largely in Østfold's attractions. The
Oldtidsveien (Highway of the Ancients), between Fredrikstad and Skjeberg, ha
3,000 to 4,000-year-old rock paintings and burial sites like **Hunn**, covered with
stone circles. Another great drive is the road to the island community of **Hvaler**
which runs over the water at some points. It ends at **Kjerkøy**, with its charm
ing village centre.

Halden ⓫, situated south of Skjeberg and close by the Swedish border, is
dominated by **Fredriksten Festning** (fort; open daily; entrance charge; tel: 9
83 85 15), a largely intact ruin with many of its buildings serving as smal

Map
on page
170

hemed museums, including a historic pharmacy (1870), bakery and brewery. The streets below were laid out along the cannons' blast lines to give the fortress's defenders freedom to fire. In summer a passenger boat makes regular trips along the inland waterway system, navigating through the massive Brekke locks, which rise to 26 metres (85 ft).

Throughout Østfold, St Olav's Day (29 July) is celebrated with a great show of folk costume, music and dance. One of the best displays is at the **Borgarsyssel Museum** (open all year; entrance charge) in **Sarpsborg** ⑫, north of Skjeberg. Sarpsborg is the site of one of Østfold's two youth hostels, on Tune Lake (the other is at Moss), and it has brewery tours and trips on the jazz boat *Krabben*.

Across to Vestfold

The Moss-Horten car ferry connects Østfold and Vestfold in less than an hour. There is much shared history between Østfold and Vestfold. It was the fast action of troops on both sides of the fjord that led to the sinking of the *Blücher*, scuppering Hitler's plans for an easy invasion.

The **Marinemuseet** (Naval Museum; open May–Sept noon–4pm; Oct–Apr Sun noon–4pm; free; tel: 33 03 33 97) at **Horten** ⑬ documents this event and hundreds of others in displays bulging with weird and wonderful artefacts including a full-size submarine open to the public. There are also museums of photography and veteran cars in Horten (both open all year; entrance charge).

Heading southwards, tranquil **Løvøy** island has a solemn medieval stone church. This was Viking country, and **Borre Nasjonalpark** ⑭ (open all year; free access to grounds), en route to Tønsberg, contains enormous turf-covered humps con-

BELOW: in summer, berry-picking in the garden or forest is a popular activity.

Learning to sail on Oslofjorden.

cealing Viking kings' graves. Borre also has an extensive network of trails, and the largest collection of Iron Age burial sites in Scandinavia. Keeping to the coastline along Road 311, **Åsgårdstrand ⓲** is the site of **Munchs Lille Hus** (Munch's Little House; open May–Sept; entrance charge; tel: 33 08 21 31), where the artist lived when he returned to Norway from abroad. Munch painted *Three Girls on a Bridge* here. Åsgårdstrand Hotel is the town's only hotel. In summer a great gush of activity emanates from here: boat trips, barbecues, and the Åsgårdstrand Festival, when there are dance and piano concerts – and a great Wiener schnitzel barbecue. You can spurn these organised activities to cycle, swim in the fjord, fish in Borre's lake, or watch the fishermen come in each afternoon with the fresh catch.

Viking burial

Between Åsgårdstrand and Tønsberg is **Oseberghaugen ⓰** (burial mound), the most important Viking site yet discovered (open all year). Oslo's Vikingskips huset (Viking Ship Museum, *see page 162*) contains the finds, including the 20-metre (65-ft) arch-ended wooden ship. Only the mound itself, near Slagen church, remains, but as a symbol Oseberghaugen has a subtle, magnetic power.

Just south is history-rich **Tønsberg ⓱**, established in the 9th century and said to be Norway's oldest settlement. On the 65-metre (200-ft) high **Slottsfjellet** are the fortress remains and tower. The main street, Storgata, is flanked by Viking graves. These were excavated and incorporated, under glass, into the ground floor of the new library. Across the street are the walls of one of only two medieval round churches in Scandinavia. The most renowned king to hold court in Tønsberg was Håkon Håkonson IV (1240–63). The ruins of his court can be seen on Nordbyen, a street with old houses hunched along it. A more recent native son is Roald Amundsen, the polar explorer. Less known outside Norway is Svend Foyn, the Tønsberg whaling captain who invented the explosive-powered harpoon.

The steamship *Kysten I* (built 1909), moored on Byfjorden near the old customs house, does a three-hour islands tour. North of the *Kysten*, you can pick up Nordbyen which will bring you back into town.

To the south of Tønsberg, along the eastern side of the fjord, the islands of **Nøtterøy** and **Tjøme**, and the skerries, are fantastic summer hangouts. **Rica Havna** is on a gorgeous natural haven carved from rock. **Verdens Ende** (World's End) is, naturally, at the end – but for a few boulders – of the chain. Verdens Ende boasts a near 180-degree view of the sea. The old lighthouse here is a beautifully simple structure made of stone.

On the other side of Tønsbergfjorden lies **Sandefjord ⓲**, once the whaling capital of the world. The sea still dominates life here. One of the main industries is marine paint production. The town centre is compact, and the cosy old Kong Carl Hotel is one of its more handsome buildings. Near Badeparken are the former spa and the old town, along Thaulowsgate. Preståsen is the hilly park above it. Torp Airport, with flights to Europe every hour, is located here.

Just outside Sandefjord are **Gokstadhaugen** (burial site; open May–Sept; guided tours; entrance free to grounds), in which the Gokstad ship, now in the

BELOW: one of the many popular bathing sites around Oslo's fjord.

Map on page 170

Vikingskiphuset (Viking Ship Museum, *see page 162*) in Oslo, was discovered in 1880; and **Vesterøy** peninsula, a supremely peaceful place ideal for walking, cycling and boating. The film star Liv Ullman's summer house is in the vicinity.

Larvik ⑲ was home to two legendary boat lovers: Thor Heyerdahl, and Scotsman Colin Archer, designer of the polar ship *Fram*. Archer's first house was at Tollerodden, on the fjord. At Larvik's back is the huge Lake Farris.

There are many fine waterside spots around Larvik, such as **Mølland** beach, stacked with sea-rounded pebbles, and **Nevlunghavn**, an exquisite fishing cove tucked around the bay west of Stavern. The fish and shellfish festivals in the Larvik area are renowned. Hotels often host them; the Grand in Larvik has both excellent seafood and a superb "wild" menu including pheasant, ptarmigan (Arctic grouse) and elk in their seasons. Inner Vestfold's rivers run with salmon and trout. **Brufoss** is a favourite anglers' haunt (accommodation and day licences available, tel: 33 12 99 20). In winter, this is a popular downhill ski district. You will find a number of ceramic works which offer tours in outer and inner Vestfold and, in common with Østfold, every little hamlet seems to have an art gallery.

Knut Steen's Whaling Monument at Sandefjord.

Local pride

People who live around Oslofjorden have a strange modesty-pride complex. They are the first to point out the area's shortcomings – smallish mountains, the stink of some pulp and paper plants – but once these are out of the way, the superlatives begin to flow. The birthplaces of the most intrepid explorers are here, as are the best sailing races, the warmest summers, the finest archaeological discoveries, the best drinking water, summer resorts… the list goes on; for when it comes to this part of Norway neither the modesty nor the pride is false. ❑

BELOW: a refreshing beer in historic Tønsberg.

THE HEART OF NORWAY

Away from Mjøsa and its lake-side towns, central Norway extends east into the wilds around the old copper-mining town of Rorøs, and north towards the quintessentially Norwegian Dovre Mountains

Map, pages 182–3

Norway's heartland is centred on the counties of Oppland and Hedmark, and is characterised by three main features: Lake Mjøsa, the country's largest lake; the great massif of Dovrefjell to the north; and the long slanting valleys of Gudbrandsdalen and Østerdalen. In this widest part of Norway, these great valleys lie straight and narrow from southeast to northwest, their rivers like veins cutting between the mountain ranges. Alongside the rivers are fertile farms, which climb up the valley sides to forests. Then, above the tree-line come the bare slopes of tussocky grass and rocks, a playground for skiers and walkers. Despite Norway's busy network of rural buses, it can be difficult to get into some of the remoter corners; but this region makes wonderful country for touring by car. Each new vista is more magnificent than the last as the road climbs, dips and circles. Nevertheless, for some of the higher plateaux, it can be simpler and quicker to push further into the wilderness by train, which stops at many small stations along the main line between Oslo and Trondheim – almost as spectacular as the famous Oslo–Bergen route in the west.

PRECEDING PAGES: the opening ceremony of the 1994 Winter Olympics, Lillehammer. **LEFT:** a decorated *stabbur* (food store) from 1863. **BELOW:** Hafjell, near Lillehammer.

Mjøsa and Mjøsabyen

Lake Mjøsa ❶ also lies southeast to northwest some 160 km (100 miles) north of Oslo. One of the best ways to enjoy the lake and its surroundings is a trip on the old paddle steamer *SS Skibladner* (May–Sept; varying tours on alternate days excl. Sun; tel: 61 14 40 80). Built in 1856 as a continuation of Norway's first railway line between Oslo and Eidsvoll, she now plies the lake carrying tourists and is based in Gjøvik on the west side of the lake.

Around Mjøsa lies some of the most fertile agricultural land in Norway and throughout the gently undulating countryside are large farms, encircled by thickly forested hills. Where Lake Mjøsa is at its widest, some 17 km (10 miles) across, is the attractive island of **Helgøya**. At its southern tip, the island has a burial mound, part of the historic Hovinsholm, a royal estate from Viking times until 1723.

Three main towns lie along the lake: Hamar and Lillehammer are on the eastern shore and Gjøvik on the west. A bridge across the lake about half way between Hamar and Lillehammer links the municipalities and, in a commercial sense, has combined the area into what has been christened **Mjøsabyen**.

In the Middle Ages, **Hamar** ❷ was the centre of Roman Catholicism in Norway and the seat of the bishop. It enjoyed great prosperity and had an impressive cathedral. Hamar's downfall came in 1537 when the Danes carried off the bishop, and 30 years later when the Swedes burned the town to the ground. Now the cathedral ruins at Domkirkeodden (Cathedral Point)

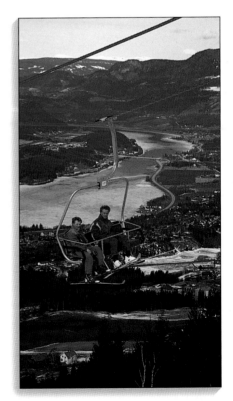

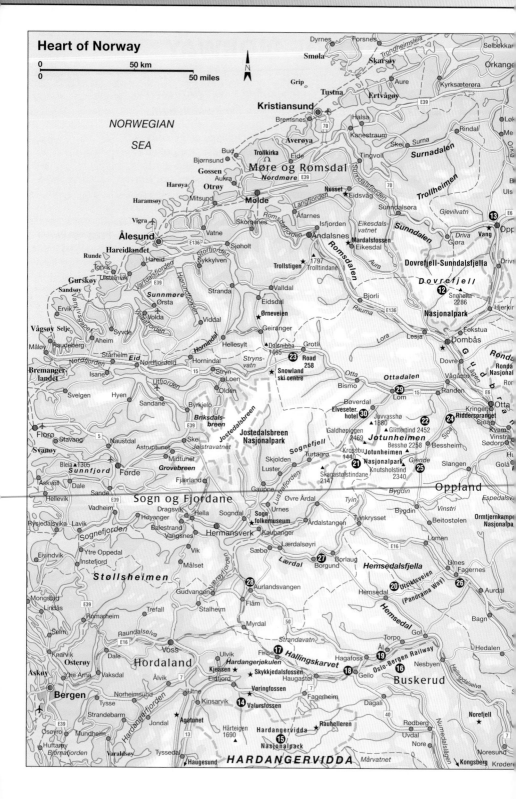

Heart of Norway

0	50 km
0	50 miles

NORWEGIAN
SEA

Dyrnes Forsnes Trondheimsleia Selbekkar

Smøla Skarsøy Orkange

Grip Tustna Aure Kyrksæterøra

Kristiansund Ertvågøy E39

Bremsnes Halsa Løk

Averøya Kanestraum Rindal Me

Bud Eide Tingvoll Skei Surna Orkla

Bjørnsund Trollkirka Surnadalen B

Gossen Nordmøre E39 Uls

Aukra Langfjorden 70 Trollheimen

Harøya Otrøy Nesset Eidsvåg Sunndalsøra

Haramsøy Mitsund Molde Gjevilvatn

Vigra Skorgenes Afarnes Isfjorden Eikesdals- Driva Vang 13

Ålesund Vatne Sjøholt Andalsnes vatnet Sunndalen Gjøra Opp

Hareidlandet E136 Mardalsfossen Vang

Runde Hareid Sykkylven Trollstigen 1797 Eikesdal Dovrefjell-Sunndalsfjella

Gurskøy Ulsteinvik Trolltindane Romsdalen Drivs

Sandsøy Sunnmøre Stranda Valldal Aura Dovrefjell 12 Nasjonalpark

Ervik Ørsta Eidsdal Bjorli Snøhetta 2286 Hjerkir

Volda Ørneveien Rauma E136

Vågsøy Selje Syvde Viddal Geiranger Lora Lesja Fokstua Dombås Ronda

Måløy Aheim Hellesylt Dalsnibba Grotli Dovre Rondå Nasjonal

Haudeberg Stårheim Eid Hornindal 1465 Road 258 Ottadalen Vågåmo Ror

Bremanger- Nordfjordeid Strynsvatn Snowland Otta 29 Lom 15 Randen E6

landet Isane Stryn ski centre Bismo Otta

Svelgen Hyen Loen Bøverdal Elveseter 30 Juvvasshø Kringen Riddersprangel

Sandane Byrkjelo Olden hotel 1880 22 24 Sjoa

Florø Stavang Briksdals- Jostedalsbreen Galdhøpiggen Glittertind 2452 Kvam Vinstra

Svanøy Naustdal breen Nasjonalpark 2469 Jotunheimen 2258 Bessheim Sødorp

Bleia 1305 Astruptunet Skei Sognefjell Krossbu Jotunheimen Slangen Golå Hu

Sunnfjord Førde Midtunet Jølstravatnet Turtagrø 1440 21 Nasjonalpark Gjende 25

Askvoll Grovebreen Luster Skjolden Skagastølstindane Knutsholstind 2340

Hellevik Dale Fjærland 2147 Bygdin Oppland

Sande E39 Sogn og Fjordane Gaupne Øvre Årdal Tyin Espedalsv

Rysjedalsvika Vadheim Dragsvik Sogndal Urnes Bygdin Vinstri

Lavik Høyanger Hella Sogn Ardalstangen Tvinkrysset Beitostølen Ormtjernkampe

Sognefjorden Balestrand folkemuseum Lomen Nasjonalpa

Eivindvik Vangsnes Hermansverk Kaupanger Lærdalsøyri E16

Ytre Oppedal Vik Sæbø Lærdal 27 Borlaug Ulnes Fagernes

Instefjord Målset Borgund Hemsedalsfjella Aurdal

Støllsheimen Gudvangen 28 Aurlandsvangen Hemsedal 20 26

Mongstad Flåm Ulsiktsveien Bagn

Lindås E39 Trefall Stalheim Hemsedal (Panorama Way)

Romarheim Myrdal 50 Torpo Gol Hedalen

Selm Raundalselva Strandavatn Ål Oslo-Bergen Railway Nesbyen

Knarvik E16 Voss Finse 17 Hagafoss 19 16 Buskerud

Osterøy Dale Ulvik Hallingskarvet 18 Geilo Nesbyen

Åskøy Ytre Arna Vaksdal Hordaland Hardangerjøkulen Haugastøl

Bergen Ålvik 7 Kjeåsen Skykkjedalsfossen Dagali

Tysse Norheimsund Eidfjord Vøringfossen Fagerheim

Strandebarm Utne Kinsarvik 14 Valursfossen Rødberg Norefjell

Osøyro Jondal Agatunet 40 Uvdal

Huftarøy Mundheim 13 Hårteigen Rauhelleren Nore Noresund

Bjørnafjorden 1690 Hardangervidda 15 Numedalslågen Kongsberg Krøderen

Varaldsøy Tyssedal Nasjonalpark Mårvatnet

Haugesund HARDANGERVIDDA

are part of the **Hedmarksmuseet** (open mid-May– mid-Sept; entrance charge; tel: 62 54 27 00). There's also an **Emigration Museum** in Hamar (www.museumdnett.no /emigrantmuseum) and the childhood home of opera star Kirsten Flagstad has opened to the public (tel: 62 54 27 00; www.kirsten-flagstad.no). Not until the 19th century and the coming of the railway did Hamar regain a measure of importance, as a railway junction with a locomotive building works. The works have gone, but the **Jernbanemuseet** (National Railway Museum; open 21 Aug–30 June daily 11am– 3pm; 1 July–20 Aug daily 10.30am–5pm; 1 Sept –31 May closed Mon; entrance charge; tel: 62 51 31 60), established in 1896, serves as a reminder. A highlight of this collection is the early steam engine, *Caroline*, built by George Stephenson in 1861. There are regular excursions on a narrow-gauge railway.

The landmark "Viking ship" Olympic **skating arena** (open all year; entrance charge) was built for the 1994 Winter Olympics, which were held in and around the Mjøsabyen towns. Seven of Norway's eight distilleries are located in the region. About 18 km (11 miles) east of Hamar towards Elverum is the **Løiten Brænderi** (guided tours; entrance charge; tel: 62 59 43 00), which is famous for Løiten aquavit. Løten is also the town where artist Edvard Munch was born.

Sandvig's collection

The largest of the three Mjøsabyen towns is **Lillehammer ❸**, situated at the northern end of the lake where it narrows to become the River Lågen and crosses Gudbrandsdalen. Lillehammer is known as the capital of Gudbrandsdalen and was the site of the 1994 Winter Olympics. A downhill ski area on nearby **Hafjell** and 500 km (300 miles) of cross-country skiing tracks were built for the occasion. Other facilities included an ice-hockey rink at Gjøvik, built inside a mountain.

For summer visitors, the biggest attraction is Norway's remarkable open-air museum, **Maihaugen** (open mid-May–Sept Tues–Sun 10am–5pm; Oct–May Tues–Sun 11am–4pm; entrance charge; tel 61 28 89 00). Some 120 buildings have

The old paddle steamer, Skibladner, on Lake Mjøsa travels between Hamar, Eidsvoll, Gjøvik and Lillehammer during the summer months.

BELOW: Odalen man's best friend, a *fjording* (Norwegian horse).

been brought into the 40-hectare (100-acre) site from all over Gudbrandsdalen, including a stave church and two farms. The museum was the life work of Anders Sandvig. A dentist by profession, he came to Lillehammer in 1885 suffering from tuberculosis and with a life expectancy of a mere two years. Whether or not it was the interest of the museum he founded in 1887 which kept him going, Sandvig lived for another 65 years and died in 1950. Sandvig is the town's only honorary citizen with his statue situated prominently in the marketplace. Apart from the buildings, which range from the medieval to the 19th century, Maihaugen has some 30,000 artefacts, all collected by Sandvig, and the many demonstrations of old skills and rural crafts give the museum a real sense of being alive.

For the motoring enthusiast, the **Norsk Veg Museum** (Museum of Vehicle History; open all year; entrance charge) at Fåberg, to the north of Lillehammer on the E6, has everything from horse-drawn sleighs, gigs and carioles to motor cars. There are some unusual examples, including steam and electric vehicles, a strange six-wheeled Mustad and a 1922 Bjering, which seated two people in tandem and could have its front wheels replaced by skis in winter. There is also the Troll, which ended its production run of 16 vehicles in 1956.

Artistic light

The quality of light in Lillehammer and its surroundings has attracted many artists to the area, including Fredrik Collett, Lars Jorde, Alf Lundeby, Einar Sandberg, Kirsten Holbø, Erik Werenskiold and Henrik Sørensen. As a result, the town has an impressive art gallery, the **Kunstmuseum** (Art Museum; open Tues–Sun 11am–4pm; tel: 61 05 44 60), which includes works by Jacob Weidemann and Norway's most famous artist, Edvard Munch.

One of Lillehammer's most revered names is Danish-born Sigrid Undset, winner of the 1928 Nobel Prize for Literature, who took up residence at nearby Bjerkebæk in 1921. Her home is also open to the public, through Maihaugen.

Aulestad ❹ (open May–Sept; entrance charge; tel: 61 22 41 10), about 11 km (7 miles) from Lillehammer, is the home of another notable Norwegian author and playwright, Bjørnsterne Bjørnson (1812–1910), one of the writers who inspired the nationalist movement in the 19th century. He wrote Norway's national anthem, *Ja,vi elsker dette landet (Yes, we love this land of ours)* in 1870, promoted Norwegian plays in the theatre in preference to Danish and won a Nobel Prize for Literature in 1903. His house is just as it was when he died.

Alongside these literary attractions, Lillehammer has not neglected its younger visitors. On the outskirts of the town, at Øyer, is **Lilleputhammer** (open May–Sept; entrance charge) with its quarter-scale version of the centre of Lillehammer as it was in 1900. You walk down the main street, peer in the shop windows and find some are open to the public. There is also the popular **Hunderfossen Familiepark** ❺ (open May–Sept; entrance charge; tel: 61 27 55 30) north of the town, which features the world's largest (fibreglass) troll. The park opens as Europe's first winter amusement park in 2007, with an ice cathedral and castle. Nearby is the **Huseskogen bob track**, built for the 1994 Winter Olympics and which offers dry runs for tourists during the summer. Many Olympic sites remain open for visitors (tel: 61 05 42 00).

Map,
pages
182–3

Østerdalen

To the east of Lake Mjøsa lies **Østerdalen**, which cuts through the mountains on a line roughly parallel to Gudbrandsdalen. At times the valley is narrow, with seemingly endless forests on either side, broken only occasionally by patches of farmland. The valley starts at **Elverum ❻** in the south and continues northwards for 250 km (150 miles) becoming broader and more open further north. Throughout its length flows Norway's longest river, the **Glomma**, kept company by the railway and the E3.

Elverum is one of the essential crossroads of Norway, and lies at the junction of many valleys, with routes to Hamar to the west, Kongsvinger to the south and Trysil to the northeast. It has the well-preserved **Terningen bastion** built in 1673, and a climb to the top of the water tower provides a good view. The town's most famous episode is commemorated in a monument to the fierce battle fought in April 1940, which delayed the German Army for long enough to allow the king and members of the government to escape further north before finally crossing to Britain to continue the fight in exile.

By far the most important of the town's attractions are two major museums. The **Glomdal Museum** (open late-Apr–Aug daily 10am–4pm; 1 Sept–31 Dec Sun–Fri 10am–4pm; tel: 62 41 91 00; entrance charge), opened in 1911 on a large natural site, has 88 old buildings of many kinds, brought in from Østerdalen and Solør. The indoor exhibition is divided into three sections – the farming year; transport and communication; and handwork and crafts – and it

Built for the 1994 Winter Olympics, Hamar's ice rink was designed along the lines of an upturned Viking ship.

BELOW: Lake Mjøsa at sunset.

shows what life was like in Østerdalen from 1870 to 1900. There is also a collection from the Neolithic age and Viking era, as well as an open-air theatre.

The **Norsk Skogsbrukmuseum** (Forestry Museum; open all year; entrance charge) encompasses forestry, hunting and fishing. The main building also has exhibits devoted to geology and wildlife, and children usually head for the aquarium. The outdoor collection is mainly situated on the small island of Prestøya in the middle of the Glomma River.

The town of Trysil is in the record books for being home to the world's oldest ski club, the Trysil Shooting and Skiing Club, founded in 1861.

Early skiing

To the northeast, **Trysil** ❼, in Hedmark near the Swedish border, is a popular winter sports area. In summer, Trysil is a centre for paragliding, rafting, canoe tours and mountain tours with pack dogs to carry the luggage. But it goes without saying that almost anywhere in the heart of Norway you only need to go a short way for the sort of outdoor recreation that mountain, river and lake can provide.

North from Elverum along the E3 there are few places of any size or importance, but the whole of this area is well off the tourist track and ideal for exploration. At **Koppang**, about halfway along the length of Østerdalen, you can take an alternative route north, along Road 30 past the long thin Storsjøen (lake), rejoining the E3 at **Tynset**. Northwest of Tynset you come to Kvikne and near it the rectory at Bjørgan, the birthplace of Bjørnsterne Bjørnson.

BELOW: as this selection shows, each area has its own design of *bunad*, Norway's traditional national costume.

Alternatively, try Road 219 which turns west at **Atna**, some 30 km (20 miles) north of Koppang, for a drive into the foothills of the wild and mountainous region of **Rondane**, where the peaks rise up to 1,800 metres (6,000 ft) high. At Enden, the road is joined by Road 27, which has taken the parallel route north from Ringebu. Called the **Rondevegen** ❽, the road climbs steeply from Gud-

Map,
pages
182–3

brandsdalen to some superb views of the Rondane Mountains. After coming this far, it is well worth continuing from Enden to Folldal, past the great peaks that include Rondeslottet at 2,178 metres (7,144 ft) high, with the **Rondane Nasjonalpark** to the west. Established in 1962, this was Norway's first national park and offers a wide range of trails of varying difficulty.

Road 27 ascends to nearly 915 metres (3,000 ft) before reaching **Folldal**, itself one of the highest permanently inhabited communities in Norway. The community's history begins from when copper was discovered in the area in the 18th century. Although the mine is no longer worked, the mining company is still based here to serve a new mine at Hjerkinn about 30 km (20 miles) away. The old Folldal mine, and some of its buildings, now form a **museum** (open all year; entrance charge) with guided tours in summer.

Along the copper road

From Folldal, if you head east you return to the Glomma River valley and the E3 at Alvdal, all connected to and part of the system of valleys and rivers that spreads out from Østerdalen. Along the way abandoned mine works indicate how important minerals were and, to some extent, still are to this area. North of Alvdal, rail, road and river head northeast, through Tolga and Os – which is the start of the **Kopperveien** (Copper Road) – before coming to the old copper-mining town of **Røros** ❾ *(see page 188* and www.worldheritageroros.no). Here, you can visit the old smelter in the **Rørosmuseet** (open all year; entrance charge), the impressive **church** (open June–Sept Mon–Sat; Oct–May Sun only; entrance charge), and a disused mine at **Olavsgruva** (open all year; entrance charge) out east along Road 31.

Røros is also a junction for roads which lead through an eastern wilderness

The unsung heroine of the Gudbrandsdalen valley is Anne Haav, the farm maiden who first made the uniquely Norwegian geitost (goat's cheese) in the 19th century.

BELOW: autumn colours come early on the fjords.

Røros and the Old Copper Country

Røros was the archetypal company town with life and society revolving around the mining of copper. Isolated, exposed, nearly 600 metres (2,000 ft) above sea level and surrounded by mountains and enduring winter cold, its existence was entirely due to the discovery of copper, which was first mined here over 300 years ago and was worked until 1972. The town was hardly beautiful, and slag heaps (slegghaugen) and the smelter (smelthytta) provided the backdrop to the miners' houses. These were usually small and overcrowded, but many workers also possessed a small patch of land and one or two animals as a source of food.

Further away from smelter and slag lived those higher up the company pecking order – in the executive area. By some miracle, Røros escaped the fires which so often laid waste to the wooden buildings of Norwegian towns.

Today, Røros has a unique townscape and almost the entire older part of the town is preserved by law. Doors, windows and colour schemes all have to conform, buildings have to be lived in and there is strict control of advertising signs and notices. As a result, Røros is in a time warp, retaining much of its mining-town atmosphere, and is on the UNESCO World Heritage list.

The most noticeable feature in Røros is the stone church – "the pride of the mining town" – which was dedicated in 1784 and replaced a wooden one built in 1650. The interior reflects the mining society, with paintings of clergymen and mining officials. Prayers were said every Sunday for the company and its directors.

The smelter was the heart of the copper-mining company and the focal point of the town. Its bell was rung at the start and end of each shift and is still there today. The smelter has been restored as a museum: the exterior still resembles the building as it was in 1889 but the interior is now given over to a series of exhibitions depicting life in the town, mining techniques in Europe in the 18th and 19th centuries, cultural features of the southern Lapp society and aspects of Røros society and its environs.

One of the most interesting elements in the museum is the series of working models to one-tenth scale which demonstrate the arduous methods called for when the only power available was water, horses and human muscle. In the past it was usual to make such scale models to see if a new technique or piece of equipment would work so today's replicas are following an old tradition.

Thirteen kilometres (8 miles) from Røros is Olavsgruva (the Olav mine), which was opened as a mining museum in 1979. A guided tour takes visitors 50 metres (165 ft) below ground. Up until 1880, when dynamite was introduced, the miners used the heat from wood fires stacked against the rock face to crack the rock. Back on the surface, the bare and bleak scenery surrounding the mine, even in the summer sun, is the most telling way to emphasise the wretched existence of those early miners. ❑

LEFT: both Rorøs church and the town's characteristic turf roofs are now preserved.

with little habitation: the first is Road 31 to the Swedish frontier, only 45 km (30 miles) away to the east, past several lakes, some artificial, dug to provide water for mining operations; another north to Ålen (Road 30) which has a small open-air museum, then through the fast-flowing gorge of the Gaula River until the valley broadens out near Støren; yet another is an alternative route to Femund Lake, Norway's third largest, which offers good fishing.

Peer Gynt country

After Østerdalen, **Gudbrandsdalen** is the second-longest valley in Norway. The Lågen River runs its full length and the valley stretches for 140 km (90 miles) northwest from Lillehammer to Dombås, the starting point for climbing trips into the Dovre rock formation. This huge plateau is very popular with walkers, not least because it is framed by impressive peaks such as the **Snøhetta** (2,286 metres/7,498 ft).

Perhaps because it was surrounded by mountains, which emphasised its sense of identity, the Gudbrandsdal valley has a long tradition of folk dancing and folk music; it is famous for its woodcarving and rose painting, and you can find good craftwork to take home. North of Lillehammer at **Ringebu ⑩**, you can visit the 13th-century **Ringebu Stavkirke** (stave church; open late May–Aug; entrance charge). Built of enormous upright timbers, it has a statue of St Laurentius, crucifixes and a baptismal font all from medieval times.

Vinstra ⑪ is the heart of what is known as "Peer Gynt country" after the legendary figure first written about by Peter Asbjørnsen in the 19th century. Asbjørnsen walked the country gathering material for a book of Norwegian folk tales, *Norske Folkeeventyr*, which he published with his friend, Bishop

Map, pages 182–3

Peer Gynt, as depicted by P.N. Arboe.

BELOW: low-lying farmland offers rich pastures.

Map, pages 182–3

Jørgen Moe, in 1844. Though Peer (or Per) Gynt is legendary, he is real enough to Norwegians as a marksman, ski-runner and something of a braggart who was often economical with the truth. Yet the character inspired the poet and dramatist Henrik Ibsen to write the play *Peer Gynt* (1867) and Edvard Grieg to compose his *Peer Gynt* Suite No. 1 (1888). Each summer the play is performed along with Greig's music in the outdoor amphitheatre at Golåvatnet southwest of Vinstra. One of the so-called Gynt cottages serves as the tourist information office in Vinstra (tel: 61 29 47 70). In the cemetery at **Sødorp**, 2 km (1 mile) away, is a monument to this curious icon of Norwegian folklore.

Today, Peer Gynt is a handy legend to use in the promotion of tourism, hence the creation of the **Peer Gyntveien**, a minor road which goes round in a huge semicircle through Golå and returns to the E6 at Tretten. It reaches an altitude of over 900 metres (3,000 ft) and presents a near continuous panorama of desolate mountains and lakes – stark but appealing. There are a number of mountain hotels in this area which are popular in both winter and summer.

Scottish visitors may want to stop at **Kringen** to see the memorial to a battle of 1612, when an army of Scottish mercenaries was defeated by local farmers. Despite their defeat, the Scots (said to be Sinclairs) have another memorial in the checked cloth used in one local costume, which looks remarkably like Sinclair tartan.

Solid as a rock

BELOW: Dovrefjell.
RIGHT: Maihaugen open-air museum, Lillehammer.

Travelling north from Vinstra, the E6 passes through Otta (where Road 15 heads west to the western fjords) on its way to Dombås. Here it turns northeast, accompanied by the railway, and climbs up and over **Dovrefjell ⓬**. To many Norwegians, the Dovre Mountains represent the strength of their country, something that brings their nation together. With admirable brevity, they sum it up in the old saying "*Enig og tro til Dovre faller*" ("United we stand until the Dovre Mountains fall").

The train stops at small stations such as Fokstua, Hjerkinn, Kongsvoll (with its historic, excellent lodge) and Drivstua to disgorge walkers with boots and backpacks. The summit of Dovrefjell is at Hjerkinn, reputed to be the driest place in Norway, and for the rest of the way it is all downhill across the **Dovre Nasjonalpark** en route to Oppdal. Dovrefjell is one of only three places in the world where you find musk ox in the wild.

Oppdal ⓭ looks up towards the Dovre plateau, and to Trollheimen (*see page 286*) to the northwest. In winter, it is a centre for skiing and in summer for walking, fishing, rafting and riding. The **cable car** takes walkers and skiers high above the village.

Not far from Oppdal, off Road 16, a small path leads to a peaceful place with trees and uneven mounds which are Viking graves. This is **Vang**, once the centre of the community until the railway brought Oppdal to life. There are 758 graves dating back to the early Iron Age. A track branches off to **Gjevilvassdalen** and its lake. It is here that Anders Rambech, an 18th-century country attorney and one of the negotiators of the 1814 Constitution, built **Tingstua**. Today the wooden building is a popular upland inn. Small and simple though it is, the inn has been favoured by Queen Sonja who made it her base for walking in Dovrefjell. ❑

PEAK AND PLATEAU

Whether on foot or by car, the peaks of Jotunheimen and the flat rocky expanse of the Hardanger plateau both mesmerise and stun the senses with their sheer size and magnificence

Map, pages 182–3

Jotunheimen ("Home of the Giants"), which includes Norway's mightiest mountain range, and Hardangervidda (*vidde* means "highland plateau") together form an extensive area of outstanding natural beauty. Centres of population are few, places of interest are also thin on the ground, but of superb scenery – mountains, glaciers, lakes and rivers – there is an excess.

The attraction of **Hardangervidda** resides in its wide open spaces. On average 900 metres (3,000 ft) above sea level, it lies south of Jotunheimen with three main valleys – Begnadalen, Hallingdalen and Numedalen – cutting across it. The centre of the plateau with its lakes and streams (a paradise for anglers) forms the source of the mighty Hallingdal and Numedal rivers. There are a number of magnificent waterfalls in the area, including **Vøringfossen** *(see page 238)* and **Valursfossen** , which drops 90 metres (300 ft) into Hjelmodalen. To the south, Hardangervidda broadens out from **Hallingskarvet**, a rocky wall rising to a height of 1,700 metres (5,700 ft).

Crossing the plateau

Hardangervidda is in many ways unique as Europe's largest mountain plateau, covering an area of 10,000 sq. km (3,860 sq. miles), nearly a third of which lies within the **Hardangervidda Nasjonalpark** ⑮. The flora and fauna of the plateau includes Arctic species and is hugely varied: several thousand reindeer roam freely, around 100 species of birds breed on these upland moors, and there are in excess of 500 different species of plants, an abundance due to the two distinct climates of Vidda – the gentle western coastal climate and the harsher inland climate of the east. There are tracks and trails galore and isolated cabins provide basic overnight accommodation.

The **Oslo–Bergen railway line** ⑯ cuts across Hardangervidda keeping Road 7 company as far as Haugastøl, where it goes north of the Hardangerjøkulen through **Finse** ⑰ *(see box, page 194)*, Myrdal and Mjølfjell. The road takes a different course, heading southwest across the wide, empty landscape with distant views of mountains, passing lakes and streams, before making a dizzy descent to sea level via a series of brilliantly engineered tunnels to Eidfjorden.

Travelling northeast from Haugastøl, both road and railway are initially dominated by Hallingskarvet. The immediate surroundings become somewhat softer as you reach **Geilo** ⑱, which has a good strategic position at the head of the Hallingdal valley and the gateway to Hardangervidda. Though it lies at a height of 800 metres (2,650 ft) above sea level, Geilo has grown into one of Norway's most popular winter sports resorts with 20 lifts, 34 well-groomed downhill runs

LEFT: view from the top, Jotunheimen.
BELOW: keeping traditional tunes alive.

and 220 km (135 miles) of cross-country tracks. With its range of hotels, Geilo has also become popular as a summer holiday centre and as a base for exploring the region by car (although the choice of roads is limited), on foot or horseback. In summer it still looks like a typical winter resort minus snow, with its spread out, slightly unfinished appearance.

From Geilo, Road 40 goes southeast past **Hol Bygdemuseum** (rural museum; open June–Aug; entrance charge) which takes the usual form of a collection of old buildings. In this case it includes the Mostugu from 1750, the Hågåstugu from 1806 and a mill from 1774. Road 40 continues along the eastern edge of Hardangervidda before it follows the Numedal valley to Kongsberg.

Road 7, meanwhile, continues northeast to Hagafoss where **Road 50** turns off it towards Lake Strandavatn. It leads along the north side of the long, clear lake dotted with small mountain huts. The landscape soon changes, however, allowing a magnificent view, and a summer skiing centre is located nearby. Suddenly the road begins to descend through a series of tunnels, including spirals, until the motorist is decanted into the Aurlands valley which continues to the village of Aurlandsvangen at the head of Aurlandsfjorden.

After being separated by Strandfjorden, Road 7 and the railway meet up at **Ål ⓳**, where the Norwegian-German artist Rolf Nesch (1893–1975) lived and worked for 25 years. The **Nesch Museum** (open all year; entrance charge) contains the largest exhibition of his work in the country. **Torpo** has no museum but a stave church (open June–Sept; entrance charge) which is the oldest building in Hallingdal. It dates back to the second half of the 12th century and has a splendid painted ceiling from the 13th century. The motifs include scenes from the life of St Margaret, to whom the church is dedicated.

TIP

Apart from Torpo Stavkirke, other stave churches worth visiting in Buskerud county are to be found further south at Uvdal, Nore, Rollag and Flesberg.

BELOW: summer skiing in Jotunheimen.

FINSE

To the south of the Jotunheimen lies the hamlet of Finse, the high point at 1,225 metres (4,000 ft) on the Oslo–Bergen railway line. Its high street is the station platform; trains are the local traffic, as there are neither cars nor roads. It's a small speck in a seemingly boundless expanse of snow and ice, and a gateway to some of Norway's most beautiful wilderness.

Finse has the country's largest *hytta* (holiday lodge) for hikers and skiers, and a hotel. It is the starting point for two giant trail networks, stretching as the crow flies 225 km (140 miles) north to the Jotunheimen and 100 km (60 miles) south to Hardangervidda. In summer the region offers more than 5,000 km (3,000 miles) of T-marked hiking trails. At Easter-time, 2,000 km (1,240 miles) of ski trails are marked by poles in the snow.

The *hytta* are one of the great secrets of Norwegian hiking and skiing. You need only carry a light sleeping bag, because they have comfortable bunk beds, and meals are provided in most. The majority of *hytta* are owned by Den Norske Turistforening (DNT; tel: 22 82 28 00). You need not be a member to stay in a DNT *hytta*, but the cost of membership is soon offset by the discounts offered on accommodation. Trail use is free.

Just past Gol, Road 7 turns south towards Nesbyen, site of Norway's oldest outdoor museum. Founded in 1899, the **Hallingdal Folkemuseum** (open Apr–Oct; entrance charge) has 29 buildings, the earliest – Staveloftet – dating from 1330. All come from different parts of Hallingdal. Some interiors are rose painted and the exhibition building houses collections of furniture, textiles and weapons.

The two other roads at Gol both lead the traveller through more attractive scenery. Road 52 goes northwest along the Hemsedal valley through **Hemsedal**, another winter sports centre with 22 lifts, 49 runs and 130 km (82 miles) of cross-country tracks. The church (open Mon) has an altarpiece from 1715 and a painting of *The Last Supper* from 1716. From the village a minor road goes past a small open-air museum near the village of Ulsåk and, further on, a private toll road winds its way across superb scenery to Ulnes on Road E16. This is the **Utsiktsveien** ⑳ (Panorama Way; summer only), a popular route which links the Hemsedal and Valdres valleys. Although narrow and rough in parts, it lives up to its name, threading its way between lakes and providing fine views of the Skogshorn, known as the "Queen of the Hemsedal".

Home of the Giants

Jotunheimen was, in Norwegian mythology, the home of trolls and giants and it is here that the mightiest mountains are to be found. In the east is the **Jotunheimen Nasjonalpark** ㉑, which includes the two highest mountains in the country: **Galdhøpiggen** at 2,469 metres (8,098 ft) and **Glittertind** ㉒ at 2,452 metres (8,043 ft). In west Jotunheimen is another range of crevassed mountains, the **Skagastølstindane**, which reach 2,000 metres (8,000 ft). The south-

Map, pages 182–3

BELOW: the mountain massif of the Jotunheimen.

ern part of the Jotunheimen has some major lakes, including Gjende, which is particularly beautiful with its greenish glacier water and flanked by impressive peaks. Other major lakes are Bygdin, Tyin and Vinstri, while glaciers add to the superb natural attractions.

Northern approaches

The northern border of Jotunheimen is the Otta River valley, which acts as a natural boundary. From **Otta** in the east the river and Road 15 wend through fertile countryside, with farms and forests, but beyond Lom the scenery gradually changes. The green and lush surroundings give way to forests and rocky outcrops and the river grows more turbulent. Eventually, at the tree line, the scenery becomes bare and inhospitable.

Grotli, which consists of little more than a large road-side hotel, cafeteria and souvenir shop, marks the beginning of Lake Breidalsvatnet. Shortly afterwards, at Langevatnet, Road 63 turns off and becomes a spectacular mountain road which skirts Djupvatnet and then descends steeply to Geiranger. Road 15 continues on its course through 15 tunnels until it reaches Stryn on Innvikfjorden. An alternative to Road 15 from Grotli is the old **Road 258 ㉓**. Some 26 km (16 miles) long, it climbs to a height of 1,139 metres (3,736 ft) and although narrow and unsurfaced in parts provides a thrilling journey. West of the summit it passes a summer ski centre and **Snowland**, a summer activity area for the family – with snow thrown in.

Between Otta and Grotli there are only two roads that go south, bold enough to penetrate the heart of Jotunheimen. Road 51, the most easterly, leaves the Otta–Grotli road at Randen and heads into the **Valdres** region. It starts by climb-

Ridderspranget (Knight's Leap) was so named after the Valdres knight Sigvat Kvier kidnapped Ivar of Sandbu's betrothed. Sigvat, hotly pursued by Ivar, and with the beautiful woman in his arms, escaped by jumping the River Sjoa at this spot.

BELOW: fish farming in Sunndalsfjorden.

ing into an area of upland pastures with a distant backdrop of mountains. A further climb to Darthus brings **Ridderspranget** ❷ (Knight's Leap) close at hand, where the River Sjoa is channelled into a narrow gorge.

Lakes lie scattered across to the west while beyond can be seen the peak of Glittertind. The most important stretch of water is **Lake Gjende** ❷, long and narrow and curving slightly to the southwest. Beyond Bessheim there are more inspiring views and this scenic feast continues for kilometre after kilometre.

Bygdin lies between two lakes: Lake Bygdin which stretches like a long finger pointing to more distant mountains in the west; eastwards is the major expanse of Lake Vinstri. There are boat trips on several of the lakes and Lake Bygdin has northern Europe's highest scheduled boat service, in waters 1,060 metres (3,477 ft) above sea level.

Map, pages 182–3

The River Sjoa is good for white-water rafting.

The heart of the Valdres

Between Bessheim and Bygdin the road reaches its highest point – 1,389 metres (4,557 ft). From here it descends, first to the tree line, then to more gentle scenery at **Beitostølen**. This winter sports resort got its first ski lift in 1964 and now has nine lifts, 12 runs and more than 325 km (200 miles) of cross-country tracks. It is a typical village of its kind with several hotels – very popular for cross-country skiing – and with a school for disabled and blind skiers, who plunge down the slopes with unbelievable confidence.

Fagernes ❷ is in the centre of the Valdres area. The focus of attention is the large **Valdres Folkemuseum** (open all year; entrance charge) which features some 95 buildings built between 1200 and 1900. Of particular interest are a 16th-century tapestry, medieval chests, a collection of antique silver, folk music

BELOW: the visitors stare at the goats, and the goats stare back.

Map,
pages
182–3

Mountain seter
(summer farms)
in autumn.

BELOW: summer
on Lustrafjorden.
RIGHT: Borgund
Stavkirke near
Flåm.

instruments and hunting weapons. On a modern note, Fagernes has one of Norway's newest airports, opened in 1987. This area is scattered with **stave churches** including at Hedalen, Reinli, Lomen, Høre, Øye, Hegge and Garmo.

In one direction the E16 heads southeast through the Begnadal valley and eventually to Hønefoss. In the opposite direction the road goes west through more exciting scenery on the southern edge of Jotunheimen. At Tyinkrysset a road goes off to Øvre Årdal on Årdalsfjorden while the E16 turns south, descending through forested scenery to **Borgund ㉗**. Apart from the stave church at Heddal in Telemark, the one at Borgund is regarded as the most typical and best preserved in Norway. Built in 1150, it is dedicated to St Andrew.

At **Sæbø** a **minor road** goes to **Aurlandsvangen ㉘**. It starts to climb almost immediately through lush scenery but this gradually changes as the narrow road ascends higher and higher, unfolding a series of stunning panoramas until the summit at 1,305 metres (4,284 ft). It then begins an increasingly steep descent to the village of Aurlandsvangen. "Breathtaking" is an over-used description but on this road it is justified, especially the view over Aurlandsfjorden from several thousand feet above it. Not for the fainthearted.

Across Sognefjell

The second route south from the Otta–Grotli road is Road 55 from Lom to Lustrafjorden, which is the part of Sognefjorden furthest from the sea. **Lom ㉙** is a typical Norwegian "junction" village with its two or three hotels, shops and garages, but it also has a fine stave church. The **Fossheim Steinsenter** (Stone Centre; open all year) in Lom contains stones, rocks and gems from all over Norway and it has a collection of minerals from Jotunheimen, while the associated **Norsk Fjellmuseum** (Mountain Museum; open all year; entrance charge) focuses on mountain life throughout Norway.

Starting out from Lom, you drive through the deceptively placid Bøverdal valley, passing small farms and villages, but the view gradually changes as it gains height and the mountains become more noticeable. At **Galdesand** there is a toll road to Juvashytta, which is the nearest point by car to the Galdhøpiggen mountain.

At 640 metres (2,100 ft) is **Elveseter ㉚** (open May–Sept), one of Norway's most unusual hotels. The Elveseter family has owned the property for five generations, gradually converting it into a hotel but retaining many of the old buildings. The oldest is from 1640 and has survived as a wooden building because of the dry mountain air. The first visitors arrived in the 1880s, but it was the opening of the Sognefjell road in 1938 that led to the expansion of tourism.

The road continues its upward ascent past the isolated Jotunheimen Fjellstue to the summit at **Krossbu** at a height of 1,400 metres (4,590 ft) amid superb mountain scenery. From there, make the steep descent to **Turtagrø** where the hotel (which is about all there is to Turtagrø) is a popular base for walkers and climbers; continue the downward course to softer surroundings at Fortun and, a few miles on, to sea level, at the end of **Lustrafjorden** at Skjolden. ❑

TELEMARK AND THE SOUTH

Map, pages 204–5

Norway's southern coastline is a magnet for summer visitors with its beaches and picturesque seaside towns. Inland, the scenery is starker and life in the mountain valleys lingers in the past

As they are proverbially advised to do "when in Rome", visitors to Oslo – or, equally, to Stavanger and Kristiansand – could usefully do what the locals do for recreation. The fundamental choice is either mountains and lakes, in which case they steer a course for **Telemark**, or the sea, which draws them to **Aust-Agder** and **Vest-Agder**, jointly known as Sørlandet (south land).

Locals would usually travel in their own cars, a definite advantage in trying to make the most out of Telemark but not so necessary on the coast, along which it is possible to leapfrog from port to port on ferries which are sufficiently frequent to permit an improvised itinerary.

Oslo, Kristiansand and Stavanger, the principal cities along the southern rim of Norway, have good connections, including flights, so they all serve as practical starting or finishing points for a tour, and you can combine Telemark and Sørlandet on one of several bus excursions. One from Oslo, for example, covers nearly 1,200 km (750 miles) by road and ferry and lasts five days.

Designed by a king

In 1639 King Christian IV of Denmark-Norway had the sort of whim which is the privilege of kings and very few others. He wanted to found a town and name it after himself. In the event, the choice of the site where **Kristiansand ❶** now stands was not entirely capricious. It was an admirable base from which to control the approaches to both the North Sea and the Baltic. The town had to be fortified, and much survives of the first of many forts to be built on the site, **Christiansholm Festning** (fortress; open May–Sept 9am–9pm; tel: 38 07 51 50). Through nearly three turbulent centuries, however, none of the forts ever fired a gun in anger (not until 9 April 1940), and gradually Kristiansand changed from being a military town to a trading and administrative centre.

Kristiansand has had its problems: with witches, one of whom confessed (in 1670) to having flown to Copenhagen to pour poison into the mayor's ear; fire (in 1734); syphilis (in 1782); and a "privateer" period (1807–14) marked by such wholesale swindling, bribery and corruption that it was said to have caused "violent upheavals in the economic life of the country".

Present-day Kristiansand has managed to put all that behind it. It is a pleasant city, laid out in a grid according to Christian IV's directive, and the sort of place which invites visitors simply to stroll about. The weather is more reliably sunny than anywhere else in Norway, the port and central market are always busy, the **Kvadraturen** is a picturesque quarter of old wooden houses, and one never has to look far for a spot to sit down and watch the world go by. "A total

PRECEDING PAGES: Norway's Sørlandet (south land) is rich farming country. **LEFT:** Brevik on the Telemark coast. **BELOW:** a farmer assesses his grain harvest.

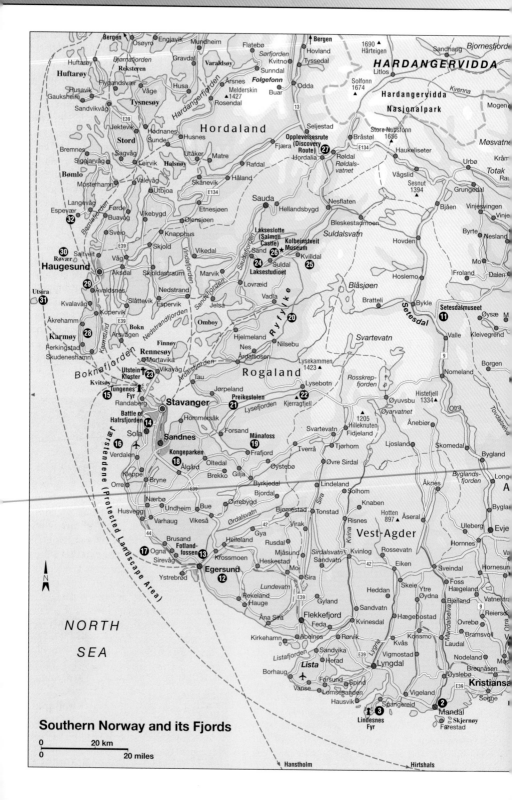

Southern Norway and its Fjords

0 _____ 20 km

0 _____ 20 miles

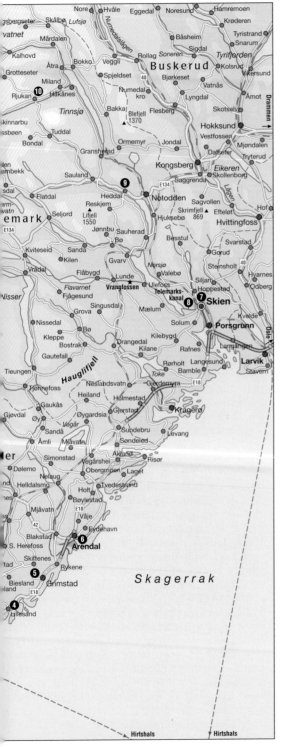

of more than 10,000 seats in cafés and restaurants" is the city's proud claim.

The city's zoo **Kristiansand Dyrepark** (open all year, times vary; entrance charge; tel: 38 04 97 00), which includes the miniature town of Kardemomme By, is the most visited family park in Norway. The fictional town is out of a popular children's story by Torbjørn Egner and besides the large zoo there are water chutes and other attractions. Just north of the centre the **Ravnedalen Park** is set in attractive, hilly grounds. The **Gimle Gård** (mansion; open mid-June–mid-Aug noon–6pm; May–June and mid-Aug–Oct Sun noon–5pm; entrance charge; tel: 38 10 26 80) across the River Otra is a magnificent symbol of 19th-century Norwegian capitalism. It was built by a shipping and trading tycoon, Bernt Holm, and passed down the family (with a five-year interruption while it was occupied by the German Army) until finally it was bequeathed to the town and opened to the public in 1985. The **Setesdalsbanen** (Railway Museum) with its narrow-gauge steam railway (summer departures, see www.setesdalsbanen.no; tel: 38 15 64 82) is a short way north of the city.

Dutch port

About 45 km (28 miles) west of Kristiansand is **Mandal ❷**. A busy port long before Christian IV felt the urge to build Kristiansand, it suffered from the competition afterwards. A 1799 traveller remarked that "the houses are jammed together so tightly that a careless pipe-smoker at any open window could spit into his neighbour's parlour." This is due to the nostalgia of foreign residents: Dutch who were there to trade, and Scots. The point known as **Kastellet** is where a wealthy Dane, who once reached into his pocket to make a personal loan to the notoriously empty-pocketed King Frederik IV, installed a cannon to keep pirates away from his estate.

The nearby lighthouse at **Lindesnes Fyr ❸** (open all year; entrance charge to museum) marks the southernmost point of Norway, and in bad weather is buffeted by ferocious winds. The small islands 5

A possible sighting of the Seljord Monster, as depicted here in an early illustration, draws many to the small Telemark village of Seljord.

km (3 miles) offshore are often mentioned in ancient Norse sagas as a refuge for Vikings ships waiting for better weather before turning the corner into or out of the Skaggerak. **Farsund**, a little further up the coast and once a privateer centre, has suffered the misfortune of being destroyed by fire so often that there is hardly a building left pre-dating the 20th century. Nevertheless, the relatively modern houses are painted white and present a pleasing spectacle.

The region is rich in rock carvings and ancient sites including, near **Vanse**, the remains of nine Iron Age homes surrounded by 350 burial mounds. **Lomsesanden**, a popular beach on the Lista peninsula, is all of 10 km (6 miles) of white sand. The last town before Vest Agder rises to meet Rogaland is the small port of **Flekkefjord**, known for its Hollenderbyen (Dutch Town), a historic area with Dutch-style white houses lining narrow streets. This is mountainous country which, apart from necessitating the construction of some of Norway's longest railway tunnels (there are 46 between Flekkefjord and Kristiansand), has created several waterfalls, especially around Kvinesdal.

Coastal journey

The principal centres along the coast east from Kristiansand are, in order, Lillesand, Grimstad, Arendal and Risør. **Lillesand ❹**, apart from being a pretty holiday town with a pleasant selection of cafés and restaurants around the harbour, has a special place in Norwegian history as the centre of an 18th-century revolt led by a farmer named Lofthus, a Robin Hood figure who travelled to Copenhagen to confront the crown prince with a long list of grievances. On his return he collected a force of 2,000 men and caused panic among the Danish "establishment" in the coastal towns. The house where he was finally arrested still stands; he spent the rest of his life in chains. The **Lillesand Bymuseum** (town museum; open mid-June–mid-Aug Mon–Fri 11am–3pm, Sat 11am–2pm, Sun noon–4pm or by appointment; entrance charge; tel: 99 23 23 28) tells the whole story.

Grimstad ❺ is indelibly associated with Ibsen. It was here that he served his apprenticeship to a chemist. Ibsen was an unhappy young man and Grimstad, though a pretty place, must have contributed (together with Skien, where he was born) to his searing exposure of goings-on in small Norwegian towns. His works caused a scandal at the time, but years have healed the wounds and he is commemorated in the **Ibsen House/Grimstad Bymuseum** (town museum; open in summer; entrance charge; tel: 37 04 46 53, tourist office tel: 37 25 01 68), which holds the largest collection of Ibsen memorabilia in Norway.

Arendal ❻ is full of character, every ounce of which was needed to thwart King Christian's plan to close it down and transfer the inhabitants to his pet project, Kristiansand. Arendal prospered in the 17th and 18th centuries as a conduit for timber shipments abroad, including much of the timber used for the rebuilding of London after the 1666 Great Fire. In 1863, Arendal itself was struck by fire, losing the houses on stilts which had earlier given it the nickname of "Little Venice" but, overflowing on to a number of small islands, it retains its lovely setting. An unusual and

BELOW: a statue of Henrik Ibsen in Skien.

recent addition to its attractions is a museum meticulously created by unpaid volunteers out of the contents of a pottery factory that went out of business a few years ago. Located in the Regency-style Kløcker's House (1826), the enthusiasm of the staff at the **Arendal Bymuseum** (town museum; open Tues–Fri 9am–3pm, Sat 10am–2pm; entrance charge; tel: 37 02 59 25) is infectious. The **Rådhus** (Town Hall), previously the home of a merchant, is said to be one of the largest wooden buildings ever constructed in Norway.

Risør, the most easterly town in Aust Agder, was also threatened by the creation of Kristiansand. Its traders were forced to maintain residencies in the new city but they kept their links with their home town. Mary Wollstonecraft, an English visitor in 1795, noted an addiction to tobacco. The men never took their pipes out of their mouths and absolutely refused to open a window. The women, she decided, dressed like "sailor girls in Hull or Portsmouth". Many of these women were probably Dutch since it was fashionable among young seamen to bring wives back from the Netherlands, the main trading partner. In Risør, as in other parts of Sørlandet, children may still be given distinctly Dutch names.

The ice canal

The capital of Telemark is **Skien** ❼, which was the birthplace, in 1828, of Norway's greatest playwright, Henrik Ibsen. His home, **Venstøp**, forms part of the **Telemark Museum** (Brekke Park; open mid-May–Aug 10am–6pm; entrance charge; tel: 35 54 45 00, www.telemark.museum.no) and has become a national shrine. Skien holds an Ibsen festival every August with concerts and plays, but originally came into existence producing stone projectiles for military slingshots, even stranger than another industry which prospered in the nearby

Map, pages 204–5

Ibsen completed his first play, Catalina, *in 1850 while still serving his apprenticeship to the chemist in Grimstad. Soon after, he left behind his provincial existence and headed for Oslo.*

BELOW: Kragerø, an earlier home of Edvard Munch.

Inside the silver mine at Saggrenda not far from Heddal.

village of Ulefoss until the close of the 19th century, namely the production of ice. Ice was easily transported along Telemark's natural waterways, which were later rationalised into a canal system.

The impressive **Telemarkskanal** ❽ (canal) stretches from the Telemarksjærgården, an unusual skerry formation that stretches out from Oslofjorden along the southern coast, to the foot of Hardangervidda. Eight sets of locks raise boats a total of 72 metres (225 ft) up to Flåvatn, which in turn runs into Kviteseidvatn and Bandak all the way to Dalen where travellers can check in at historic Dalen Hotel. Completed in 1892, the canal cuts 110 km (70 miles) into the interior and is now used by pleasure boats such as the **M/S Victoria** and **M/S Henrik Ibsen** (both operational May–Sept; tel: 35 90 00 30).

The canal is littered with attractions, including **Vrangfossen** (waterfall) above Ulefoss, and with places to stay. The best way to keep abreast of what's on is to visit www.visittelemark.com or telephone 35 90 55 20).

Interior isolation

Throughout Telemark one senses an older Norway lurking just beneath the surface. The upper districts were, until recently, impenetrable except on skis; travel in winter being easier than in summer. Isolated communities were not inclined to take orders from interfering outsiders, although a lot of water has passed under the bridge since the people were described (in 1580) as "shameless bodies of the Devil whose chief delight is to kill bishops, priests, bailiffs and superiors – and who possess a large share of all original sin".

A finger of Telemark reaches the sea at Kragerø, not far from the mouth of Oslofjorden, but the province is associated in most minds with the inland terrain,

BELOW: typical "Sørlandet houses" near Farsund, Vest Agder.

which inspired an eccentric farmer named Sondre Norheim to turn the pedestrian business of plodding about in snow on two planks into the sport of skiing. His discovery of the delights that could be achieved with planks that were properly shaped and had heel bindings made him overlook his domestic chores. It is apparently true that, when he ran out of firewood in winter, he simply hacked off another piece of his house and put that on the fire *(see "Morgedal and Telemark Revival, page 108)*.

Morgedal, where Norheim lived (he later emigrated to America) deserves to be called the cradle of skiing but it is now only one of dozens of skiing centres in the county, many of which have ski lifts to complement the traditional cross-country courses which do not need mechanical contraptions. Norheim's statue is a feature of the **Norsk Skieventyr** (Norwegian Skiing Adventure Centre; open mid-May–mid-June 11am–4pm; mid-June–mid-Aug 9am–7pm; late Aug 11am–4pm; entrance charge; tel: 35 05 42 50), located near to Kviteseidvatn and the canal.

Rural arts

Visitors with their own transport in Telemark can hardly go wrong: pick any of the winding roads that head inland and the scenery is bound to be breathtaking.

For those who do not have a car, the waterways are a wonderful alternative: Skien is on a main canal line from Oslo and a good place to pick up boats going north through Sauherad to Notodden (Road 36 then 360 covers the same route). Schedules change according to season – in some parts the boats press on with the help of a small ice-breaker – so it is advisable to check with the tourist office (tel: 35 90 00 20) in Skien. West of Notodden, along Road 11, lies **Heddal ❾** with its famous **Stavkirke** (open mid-May–mid-June 10am–5pm; mid-June–mid-Aug

BELOW: the popular bathing beach at Mandal.

Map, pages 204–5

9am–7pm; mid-Aug–mid-Sept 10am–5pm; entrance charge; tel: 47 35 02 04 00) the largest in Norway. Built between 1147 and 1242, it has a richly carved door way with animals and human faces. But Heddal is more than that. The Telemark ers are masters at expressing nature through art and nowhere is this more evident than in the rose paintings in the Ramberg room of the **Heddal Bygdetun** (farm houses: open mid-June–mid-Aug 10am–5pm; entrance charge; tel: 35 02 08 40)

Further on, Road 37 branches off to the north past Lake Tinnsjø toward **Rjukan** ❿. A breathtaking alternative route is to stay on E134 to Sauland and turn north, through Tuddal, to drive past Gausta Toppen, one of Norway's land mark peaks. The stretch between Rjukan and Rauland is also lovely and can be covered by public bus. Keep an eye open for highly decorative wooden houses and double-storey barns, sometimes bigger than the house itself, with a ramp leading to the upper floor.

The attraction of Rjukan and nearby Vemork is the heavy-water plant, now the **Norsk Industriarbeidermuseum** (Norwegian Industrial Workers Museum; open summer daily 10am–4pm, until 6pm in mid-June–mid-Aug; winter Tues–Fri noon–3pm, Sat–Sun 11am–4pm; entrance charge; tel: 35 09 90 00), but in 194 the target of a daring sabotage attack by the Norwegian resistance *(see "The Heroes of Telemark", page 54)*. Rjukan's library has a good collection of litera ture about the operation. Rjukan is generally rather gloomy because the sun is nearly always blocked off by surrounding mountains. On top of those mountains though, another world of vast vistas opens up, and it is said that on a good day it is possible to see one-sixth of Norway. You can take northern Europe's oldest cable car (open summer 10am–8pm; Sept 10am–6pm; Oct–June daily 10am–4pm entrance charge; tel: 99 51 31 71) from Krosso to the top of Gvepseborg at 860 metres (2,800 ft) for just such a view.

Medieval life in the 20th century

An alternative route inland is Road 9 from Kris tiansand, which climbs up the Otra valley and runs north along **Byglandsfjorden** to **Setesdal**. Until mod ern times this area was very remote. The inhabitants sent their timber down to Arendal by pushing it into a river, which plunged 700 metres (2,300 ft) over a dis tance of about 150 km (90 miles). They preserved their own almost medieval way of life, including a distinct dialect, dress and cuisine, into the 20th century.

Setesdal is a haven for those in search of rural cul ture. The most famous dwelling is **Rygnestadtunet**, a 16th-century windowless tower of three storeys with an amazing collection of relics, such as leather hang ings depicting St George's battle with the dragon. The tower was built about 400 years ago by Vond-Asmund who, on discovering that his fiancée was about to marry someone else, snatched her away from the wedding procession. From the upper floor of his fortress, he fired off arrows at anyone who approached and in so doing killed at least four people. His descendants still farm in the area. Rygnestadtunet is part of the **Setesdalsmuseet** ⓫ (Heritage Muesum; open all year; entrance charge tel: 37 93 63 03), which is 15 km (9 miles) to the south

You can also visit the Sommarland family park at **Bø** (open June–Aug; entrance charge; tel: 35 06 16 00). ☐

BELOW: collecting the honey in summer.
RIGHT: *Lindesnes fyr* (lighthouse) on the southernmost tip of Norway.

FJORDS

The Norwegian fjords are a defining feature of both country and culture – the difficulty is to decide on a favourite

To create a fjord, take a mountain and a river, and mix in an Ice Age many thousands of years ago. To describe the fjords is to find yourself running out of superlatives: the deepest water, the highest mountains, the narrowest, the most beautiful, the stillest, the most peaceful... each fjord has its own special characteristic, from the Sognefjord (the longest) to the Geiranger, which many people think the most beautiful. But who would argue? With so many fjords, everybody is entitled to their own opinion.

The fjords gave Norway its great seafaring tradition. From the early Vikings who found Scotland, Iceland and the rest of Europe easier to reach than the area around Oslo, to the modern traveller who chooses a ship as the most comfortable way to travel this magnificent coastline, the sea has provided the link.

The western fjords begin at Stavanger in the south, now Norway's oil capital, not far from Preikestolen (Pulpit Rock), the great slab of rock standing a dizzying 600 metres (2,000 ft) above Lysefjorden. They stretch north to the Hardanger, one of the largest in the country and an early favourite where the old traditions of music and storytelling influenced travellers such as the composer Edvard Grieg.

Further along the coast, they encompass Bergen, the fjord capital; Sognefjorden and Nordfjorden, in an area of glaciers, lakes and mountain massifs; Storfjorden, parts of which bite far into the land; and, finally, the calm of the Geiranger.

The famed Geiranger Fjord and its surrounding area were recently added to UNESCO's World Heritage List which came as no surprise to the locals. It's a magical place, narrow and far from the open sea, with waterfalls crashing down its steep mountain sides. Its popularity comes at a price, though, with heavy cruise ship traffic into the fjord causing air pollution concerns in the summer of 2006. Efforts are being made to protect the environmentally sensitive area so it won't be damaged by the thousands of visitors sailing and driving there every summer.

Norway's long coastline is punctuated by fjords all the way from Oslo in the southeast to the Arctic north. The most dramatic, though, are indeed found along the west coast, where small farms cling to every ledge and hectare of green. The fjords are beautiful, timeless, and everyone's idea of the soul of Norway. ❏

PRECEDING PAGES: passing through Trollfjorden, in the Lofoten Islands, is a delicate operation for the Hurtigruten ship.
LEFT: small coastal freighter at Femrissundet (sound) in the north.

ROGALAND

*This often overlooked corner of the country contains many delights,
from the picturesque fishing harbour of Egersund to an eagle's-eye
view over Lysefjorden from the top of Preikestolen*

Many people believe that Norway's fjord country begins at Hardangerfjorden and the city of Bergen, and stretches north. If so, they are
missing all the southern fjords and islands, where Norway first became
a nation. Today this area of Rogaland is centred on Stavanger, the centre of
Norway's international oil industry, and contains some of the fjord country's
most spectacular natural sights: what a pity to miss **Preikestolen** (Pulpit Rock),
a flat slab of rock swooping some 600 metres (2,000 ft) up from Lysefjorden,
which offers a 180-degree view over *fjell* (mountain) and fjord.

Rogaland has the mildest climate in Norway and the beauty of the coast is
unsurpassed. These coastal and outer fjord areas have the highest average temperature in the whole country, but pay the penalty for their closeness to the sea
in unexpected showers and a higher rainfall. In winter, thanks to the Gulf
Stream, there is little snow and the fertile fields are green for most of the year.

Starting in the south

By air, the way in is Stavanger's international airport at Sola, or you might
come by express boat from Bergen in just under three hours. From the south, the
main road is the E39, which crosses into Rogaland south of the old town of
Egersund ⑫, now Norway's largest fishing harbour.
There is also a coastal route (the scenic Road 44),
which hugs the coastline all the way north to Stavanger. At the southern corner of this route, small
fjords bite into a rough, rocky coast, which lead to
green valleys and a myriad of shining lakes.

LEFT: Preikestolen,
one of Rogaland's
best-known
landmarks.
BELOW: goat's
cheese made at
Egersund.

The best view of Egersund's sheltered harbour, with
its dozens of yachts both big and small, is from the top
of the lighthouse. The town itself has a fine **cruciform
church** (open June–Aug; entrance charge) from 1620
(renovated in the late 18th century) and the **Dalane
Folk Museum** (open June–Aug; entrance charge; tel:
51 46 14 10) which includes the **Egersund Fayance
Museum** (displaying painted earthenware crockery,
which was once the town's main industry).

Inland is the waterfall **Fotlandfossen** ⑬, and further north on the E39 you come to the southern end of
Ørsdalsvatn. From here, Rogaland's last remaining
inland waterway boat, *Ørsdølen*, sails the 20 km (13
miles) to Vassbø at the far end of the narrow lake. Near
there you can have a simple home-made meal before
the boat returns. A few miles further on is Vikeså,
where Road 503 to Byrkjedal runs past **Gloppedalsura**, where the boulders are as big as houses.

The flat and fertile country above Egersund is Norway's main area for the production of meat, dairy
products, poultry and eggs, but it was not always as
peaceful as it is today. In AD 872, it was the scene of

the **Battle of Hafrsfjord** , where King Harald Hårfagre (Fair Hair) won his final and most important battle to unite the warring Norwegian kingdoms. That battle is marked at the edge of Hafrsfjorden, the near circular fjord to the southwest of Stavanger, where three huge sculptured swords rise out of the ground.

In 1977, by royal decree, a narrow strip some 70 km (43 miles) long, from Raumen Island at the southern end to **Tungenes Fyr** (lighthouse; open June–Aug; entrance charge) northwest of Stavanger, became **Jærstendrene Landskapsvernområde** (the scenic Jæren beach's Protected Landscape Area), which includes offshore islands. Raumen itself is one of eight bird sanctuaries where, at different times of the year, you can find turnstones, ringed plovers and knots taking a brief rest on the long flight to or from southern Europe or Africa; offshore are wintering eider and long-tailed ducks, and the islands provide nesting places for seabirds, often in protected areas closed to visitors during the breeding season.

In the eight botanical reserves you can find such delights as the spear-leaved fat hen saltbush, and the rare marsh orchid growing in the reserve near **Ogna**. There are also four geological sites and no less than 150 monuments listed and protected. But this does not mean that Jærstrendene is given over solely to flora and fauna. **Beaches** with white-gold sand are popular picnic spots and, though the water can be chilly, this does not deter swimmers.

Bicycle land

Sandnes on Sandfjorden is Norway's "bicycle town", where the famous DBS bicycles are made and, whether this is the reason or not, where cycling is popular and you can hire bikes to explore the surrounding countryside. Another delight for youngsters is **Kongeparken** (open June–Aug daily 10am–6pm; May and Sept Sat–Sun only 10am–6pm; entrance charge; tel: 51 61 71 11), Norway's biggest amusement park, not far from Sandnes at the little town of Ålgård. At 80 metres (260 ft) long, Kongeparken's Gulliver is hard to miss. Inside, Gulliver's body is full of unusual playthings and the park has Scandinavia's longest bobsleigh ride.

In many of the mountain areas around the fjords, waterfalls cascade hundreds of metres below. One of the most famous is **Månafoss** on the Frafjord, the innermost finger of the Høgsfjord, reached by Road 45 south from Ålgård to Gilja. At Gilja, turn down the steep road to Frafjord, which gives a fantastic view of the fjord. There are directions to Månafoss in the car park at the foot of the mountain.

Fjords once more

The **Ryfylke area** northeast of Stavanger is true fjord country, one of the least-known parts of Norway despite the drama of its scenery. In the south, due east of Stavanger, Ryfylke starts with **Lysefjorden**, under Pulpit Rock, and stretches north past long narrow lakes that once were open fjords, until it reaches **Vindafjorden**, **Saudafjorden** and **Suldalsvatn**.

Although he never saw it, Victor Hugo described Lysefjorden in *The Toilers of the Sea* as "the most terrible of all the corridor rocks in the sea". Hugo probably

TIP

The walking trail to the top of Preikestolen (Pulpit Rock) starts from the Preikestolhytte and takes two hours each way. Sightseeing boats leave from Stavanger for the fjord under Pulpit Rock all year round.

BELOW: Månafoss waterfall.

meant "awesome" and that the fjord still is. Every visitor to Norway should try to walk out through heather moor and scrubland to stand on the top of **Preikestolen** ㉑, a rock platform high above the fjord. On the way you might see golden eagles, willow grouse, ptarmigan and other birds as well as reindeer and the angular shape of an elk. The great height of Preikestolen gives a view towards Stavanger and the fjords to the west, and upwards to the treeline and the rocky heights above. Everywhere there are lakes, waterfalls and rushing torrents.

From the village of Forsand at its mouth, Lysefjorden is 40 km (25 miles) long and, at its innermost end, has one of Europe's most remarkable feats of civil engineering: the road to the hydroelectric power station (open Tues–Sun; entrance charge) at **Lysebotn**, which is hidden hundreds of metres inside the mountain. This road, which seems to defy gravity, snakes up and down more than 750 metres (2,500 ft) with 27 hairpin bends and connects Lysebotn to Sirdal and Setesdal to the east along the Lyseveien. If you dare to keep your eyes open as the bus takes its near perpendicular route down, the view is magnificent.

Near the end of the fjord on the south side towers **Kjerragfjell** ㉒, an enormous granite mountain around 1,100 metres (3,550 ft) high. Lie on your front and look down through the wedge cut out of the mountain plateau to the fjord below. To get there takes about two hours' walking from several spots along the Lyseveien.

Inshore islands

The sheltered bay north of Stavanger, and the outer islands such as Karmøy, protect Ryfylke's inshore islands from the North Sea. Christianity flourished early here under the protection of the bishops of Stavanger and the islands have many churches. In summer, the 12th-century **Utstein Kloster** ㉓ (cloister; open

Map, pages 204–5

Wedged between two rocks, the famous Kjerragbolten offers a breathtaking vantage point from which to view Lysefjorden below.

BELOW: Gulliver at Kongeparken.

Sandvesanden beach on the island of Karmøy.

May–Sept Tues–Sun; entrance charge; tel: 51 72 47 05) on **Mosterøy** makes a beautiful setting for concerts which are mostly classical. It offers the traveller a refreshing break on the way from Stavanger to Boknafjorden. The cloister's setting, acoustics and the palpable sense of history give these concerts a very special atmosphere.

The many **lighthouses** are not only landmarks for islanders and seafarers but make excellent bird-watching sites, with the hunched outlines of cormorants and other seabirds on wave-washed rocks below. The waters around these peaceful islands are a sea kingdom for sailors of all kinds with enough coastline to give every boat a bay to itself and many yacht harbours. Most of the island grocers also provide boat services and it is easy to hire rowing boats and small craft with outboard engines.

Northeast highlands

Here fjords, lakes and rivers are rich in fish and fine for sailing and canoeing, and all these inland, eastern areas of Rogaland have good cross-country skiing tracks in winter as well as some fine Alpine slopes. Among the best holiday areas is the **Suldal district**, stretching from Sand on the Sandsfjorden, along the River Suldalslågen – where the rushing waters have produced huge salmon (the largest so far weighed almost 44 kg (75 lb) – to the long, narrow Suldalsvatn. At the Sand end of Suldalslågen is **Laksestudioet ㉔** (open daily mid-June–mid-Aug 10am–6pm; mid-Aug–mid Sept noon–4pm; entrance charge), an observation studio, built under a waterfall where visitors look through a large window at the salmon resting before their next leap up the fish ladder on the way to their spawning grounds. Where river meets lake is **Kolbeinstveit Museum** (rural museum;

BELOW: Utstein Kloster (cloister) on Mosterøy.

open June–Aug Tues–Sun 11am–5pm; entrance charge; tel: 52 79 93 04) with the old Guggedalsloftet Bygdetun (farm) which dates back to the 13th century.

From Sand, a bus follows the path of the river to the giant **Kvilldal** station, opened in 1982 by King Olav, who chiselled his signature into the mountain side, a popular royal tradition in Scandinavia. On the way to this cavernous power station the bus stops at the **Lakseslotte** (Salmon Castle) at Lindum, built by Lord Sibthorp in 1885, when the British "salmon lords" looked on a few weeks in Norway as part of the fishing season. River and lake still draw anglers from many countries and the castle is a popular guesthouse.

From Stavanger and Jæren, ferries and express boats reach this fjord country and its islands, and it is easy to combine bus and ferry. Vindafjord, Saudafjorden and Suldalsvatn look up to 1,500-metre (5,000-ft) peaks that lead the way to the great mountain massif of Hardangervidda, in the next county north, Hordaland. In summer you can take the exciting **old mountain road** north from Sauda to Røldal; the new road has tunnels to keep it open all year. At Røldal, where there's a stave church, you pick up the **Opplevelsesrute** (Discovery Route, E134), which has come over the Haukeli mountains from Telemark, and you can continue along until it becomes Road 13 towards Odda.

Back to the coast

The sea route north to Bergen is one of the most popular ways to see the northern coast. By taking an express boat (a cross between a catamaran and a hydrofoil) you can drop off at any of the harbour stops and stay a night or a week according to your whim. **Karmøy**, the island at the south of the outer islands chain, is big enough to merit its own boat service, which goes to **Skudeneshavn**

While on Karmøy, pay a visit to the Fisheries Museum at Vedvågen, with its saltwater aquarium. The building was designed by Norwegian firm of architects, Snøhetta, winners of the competition to design a National Opera House in Oslo.

BELOW: typical "seahouses" in Skudeneshavn.

Map,
pages
204–5

*Following claims by
the Norwegian film
critic Pål Bang-
Hansen that Marilyn
Monroe's father was
a Norwegian emigré
from Haugesund,
the town erected a
statue to the
Hollywood goddess
on the quayside.*

BELOW: young
buskers in
Haugesund during
the Film Festival.
RIGHT: fish market
on the island
of Utsira.

in the south, an idyllic old port with white, wooden houses along narrow streets (tours from **Mælandsgården Museum**; June–Aug). The north of the island is linked to the mainland just south of Haugesund, the first sizeable coastal town north of Stavanger, fast becoming prosperous through oil.

Karmøy's known history dates back to saga times, when it was the "North-way" shipping lane that gave Norway its name. Harald Hårfagre made his home at **Avaldsnes** ❷ after the battle at Hafrsfjord. Also here is **St Olaf Kirke** (church) which was built between 1248 and 1263 by King Håkon Håkonson and restored in 1922 as the parish church. Near its north walls stands St Mary's Sewing Needle, a strange 6.5-metre (21-ft) high stone pillar leaning towards the church wall. Legend tells that the Day of Judgement will come when the pillar touches the wall; many priests are said to have climbed the pillar at dead of night to pare away the top to make sure that the day is not yet nigh.

Roman connections

On the west coast at **Ferkingstad** are historic boathouses with walls made of stone blocks 1.5 metres (5 ft) thick. Further north on the west coast, outside the town hall at **Åkrehamn**, stand two stone pillars from the Iron Age. Crossing to the east coast, near the town of **Kopervik** are burial hills and mounds and stone pillars. The largest burial mound, Doøa Hill, was restored in 1978 and, though it has not yet been fully excavated, it dates back to the Bronze Age. Further north, on the mainland side of the bridge to Haugesund are **Dem Fem Dårlige Jomfruer** (Five Bad Virgins), stone monuments some 2.5 metres (8 ft) high, where excavations in 1901 revealed a Roman bowl dating from AD 300–400.

Haugesund has long been a centre for fishing, shipping and farming. Today its harbour is filled with pleasure boats; the town has also become a festival and congress centre and plays host to the International Trad Jazz Festival and the Norwegian Film Festival (both Aug; dates and prices vary).

Numerous fjords and lakes cut into the roughly shaped peninsula, like a piece of well-nibbled cheese, ideal for fishing, sailing, rowing, canoeing, diving and walking. A boat trip to the idyllic group of islands of **Røvær** ❸, around 10 km (6 miles) to the west, occupies a half or whole day and offers shore fishing, interesting flora and fauna and, in summer, a wharf-side café.

For the adventurous, *M/S Utsira* (tel: 52 72 50 55) provides a daily service to the island of the same name ❸, familiar from European shipping forecasts and Norway's western outpost. The 90-minute journey out makes a wonderful tour for bird-watchers, as does the island itself. Fishing is also excellent and Norwegian saltwater fishing is free to holders of a national licence (*see pages 112–13*). Day licences for lakes and rivers are available: contact Haugesund Tourist Office, tel 52 72 50 55.

To the north of Haugesund, the **Espevær** ❸, a fishing village situated at the mouth of Bømlafjorden River, is well endowed with its own heritage sites. The village itself is one of the best-preserved sites in Norway; there is a maritime and fisheries museum, as well as a bathing house. ❑

LAKE VIEW
BRAND
NET WEIGHT 3¾ OZ.
GHOICEST NORWEGIAN
BRISLING-SARDINES
IN PUREST OLIVE OIL
PACKED BY:
NORCANNERS LTD. STAVANGER·NORWAY.
MALLOTT JOHNSON CO.
DISTRIBUTORS. CHICAGO. ILL.

STAVANGER

Once the port from which thousands emigrated to the United States, today Stavanger attracts an international crowd – and cuisine – as the centre of Norway's thriving oil industry

Map on page 226

Strange though it may seem in a city which has devoted nearly 1,000 years to the sea, the best way to arrive in Stavanger is by overnight train from Oslo. As the dawn arrives, the train slips along the side of the fjord with black mountain peaks outlined on either side, past the huge latticework of oil rigs and drilling towers which have made Stavanger Norway's oil capital. Enormous though they are, somehow they do not intrude on the landscape because the size and grandeur of mountain and fjord dwarfs even these industrial giants.

Stavanger has been lucky because the sea has always been good to the city. As one source of prosperity disappeared, another arose. Shipping, fishing and trading have taken the city's ships and people all over the world, and brought seamen to Stavanger, to give it an easy-going relationship with other nations. Today, Norway's fourth-largest city is as international as ever: nearly a tenth of its 110,000 inhabitants are foreigners and it will be a European Capital of Culture in 2008.

International eating

This international community has demanded high standards and Stavanger has good restaurants, hotels, entertainment and a cosmopolitan atmosphere out of all proportion to its size. As well as the traditional **restaurants**, which specialise in good Norwegian food, there is a choice of Indian, Italian, Greek, Portuguese, Mexican and Japanese, and at least half a dozen Chinese restaurants. The city also has an annual food festival and a gastronomic institute.

Restaurants, and particularly alcohol, are expensive in Norway, but a great many cafés, bars and pubs have sprung up, sometimes with live music, plus a handful of youthful discos, which do not necessarily serve alcohol. In the **fish market** on the quayside, where fresh crabs eaten on the spot are the favourite buy, and at the **fruit and flower market** nearby you will hear many languages, and in the heart of Stavanger's shopping streets behind the market almost all the assistants speak English.

Apart from the oil prosperity, Stavanger is also the principal town and seat of government of Rogaland.

An American connection

In the 19th and early 20th centuries Stavanger was the exit port for Norway's extensive emigration programme to the United States *(see page 44)* – there are more Americans of Norwegian descent than there are Norwegians. Not surprisingly, therefore, the city is host to **Det Norske Utvandrersenteret** Ⓐ (Emigration Centre; open Mon–Fri 9am–3pm, Strandkaien 31; tel: 51 53 88 60), where Norway's emigration history is documented and commemorated. For a fee, genealogical researchers will help you to find your

LEFT: Stavanger's past prosperity was based on sardines.
BELOW: winter in Stavanger.

TIP

See Stavanger
Museum's five sites in
one day for the price
of a single ticket.
Stavanger Museum
itself, the Canning
Museum, the Maritime
Museum, the royal
residence of
Ledaal and the
19th-century manor
house, Breidablikk,
are all included.

Norwegian roots. In June the centre arranges the Emigration Festival with exhibitions, concerts, folk dancing, a crafts market, seminars, fjord cruises and city sightseeing. The highlight of the festival is the re-enactment of the 1825 sailing of the *Restauration*, the boat which carried the first emigrants across the Atlantic.

The smell of sardines

The *iddis* (the colloquial name, meaning sardine label, for a person from Stavanger) claims to be the oldest true Norwegian, dating from 872 and the Battle of Hafrsfjord, which took place just south of the city, and in which King Harald Hårfagre won his final battle to unite the kingdom.

When work began on the Domkirken (cathedral) in 1125, Stavanger was simply a cluster of small wooden houses at the end of the narrow inlet called **Vågen**. It was chosen as the heart of the bishopric, nevertheless, because it was the only recognisable settlement along this southwestern coast. From then on Stavanger was the most important town in the area. It grew slowly; the population was only 2,000 at the start of the 19th century, but had jumped to 30,000 by 1900.

In the 18th and 19th centuries, the city depended on fishing and maritime trade and faced the world with an unbroken row of wharves and warehouses dedicated to these industries. Around the 1870s, at a time when fishing and shipping were beginning to face decline, the fishermen turned their attention to brisling (small herring), which were cured and canned in the town and sent as Norwegian "sardines" all over the world.

At one time Stavanger had as many as 70 canneries and nearly three quarters of the population worked in the industry. In the first half of the 20th century, the smell of oily fish hung over the town, permeating every breath. But Stavanger

BELOW: an oil rig under contruction dwarfs the city.

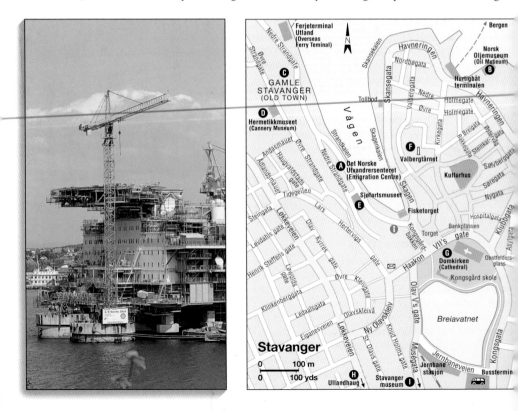

never doubted the value of that smell. When, on a particularly odiferous day, a cheeky youngster wrinkled a disdainful nose, a mother would say: "Don't scorn it, that's the smell of money." It was, and Stavanger thrived on sardines until, after World War II, that all-pervasive tang began to fade along with the demand for sardines. For nearly 20 years, Stavanger knew difficult times. Then, in the late 1960s, came oil – once again the sea had provided. Visit the modern, interactive **Norsk Oljemuseum B** (Norwegian Petroleum Museum, Kjeringholmen; open June–Aug daily 10am–7pm; Sept–May Mon–Sat 10am–4pm, Sun 10am–6pm; entrance charge; tel: 51 93 93 00) for an insight into this valuable source of energy.

Map on page 226

Present-day reminders

Many traces remain of these fluctuations in the city's fortunes. **Gamle Stavanger C** (Old Stavanger) is a preserved neighbourhood of more than 180 early 19th-century white wooden buildings looking down towards Vågen, with cobbled streets lit by old-fashioned streetlamps. But this is no museum. There may be a preservation order on the exteriors, and the owners take pride in keeping them in character, but the interiors have every comfort and gadget that modern Norwegians expect, and Gamle Stavanger is one of the most coveted areas in Norway in which to live.

Nor have the canning factories been lost. Many are converted into modern offices, without destroying their scale and shape, and buildings that once canned sardines may now be the headquarters of an international oil company. One factory at Øvre Strandgate, near the harbour, has been preserved in its original state as the **Hermetikkmuseet D** (Canning Museum; open June–Aug daily 11am–4pm; Sept–May Sun only 11am–4pm, closed Dec; entrance charge; tel: 51 84 27 00). In the big open room with its curing ovens, the guides describe

Artefacts from Stavanger's old canning industry are kept in the Hermetikkmuseet (Canning Museum).

BELOW: Gamle (Old) Stavanger is still a living community.

Stavanger waterfront at night.

the life of the people who worked long hours at the intricate process of threading the sardines on to long rods, smoking, then packing them, almost all of it being done by hand. On Tuesday and Thursday from mid-June to mid-August you can sample freshly smoked brisling for yourself, cooked in one of the original ovens.

Even nearer the harbour and the centre of the town is the **Sjøfartsmuseet** ❺ (Maritime Museum; open mid-June–mid-Aug daily 11am–4pm, closed Fri–Sat in early June and late Aug; 1 Sept–1 June 11am–4pm Sun only; entrance charge; tel: 51 84 27 00) in one of the old mercantile houses on Nedre Strandgate, with its warehouses towards the sea. It traces the history of Stavanger's maritime links over the past 200 years. Today, large windows have replaced the warehouse doors and you turn your head from the history behind you to the modern town outside. On the Nedre Strandgate side of the museum, away from the harbour, is a general store, full of the provisions and supplies that it would have held before World War II. Upstairs, where the owner lived, is an office just as it might have been when a crewman called in during the 1930s in search of a berth, or the skipper came to pay his respects. The flat shows the comfortable life of a shipowner in the late 19th century.

On the other side of the harbour facing the Maritime Museum is the site of the original Viking settlement. The **Valbergtårnet** ❻ (tower; open Mon–Sat all year; entrance charge; tel: 51 89 55 01), built in the 9th century as a fire lookout, is the best point from which to get a view over the whole city.

Centre of worship

BELOW: old wooden houses.
BELOW RIGHT: Stavanger Domkirke, the only remaining building from the city's medieval past.

The heart of modern Stavanger is the area around **Breiavatnet**, the small lake in the middle of the city, near the oldest and biggest building, the beautiful 12th-

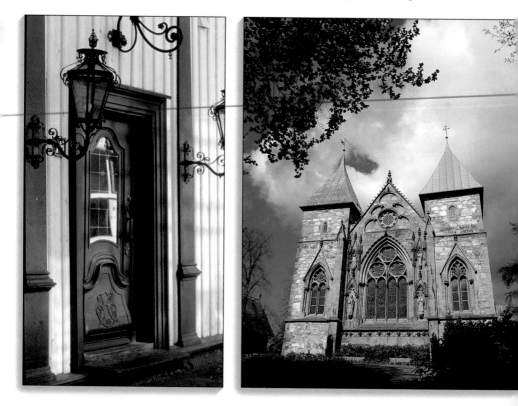

century **Domkirken** (open June–Aug Mon–Sun 11am–7pm; Sept–May Tues–Thur and Sat 11am–4pm; services every Sunday at 11am). Construction began in 1125 by Bishop Reinald of Winchester in the Anglo-Norman style. It can claim with justification to be among the best-preserved medieval cathedrals in Europe. Alongside is the **Cathedral School** built in 1758 on the 12th-century foundations of the Bishop's residence.

Inside, this stone cathedral has a feeling of austere strength in the massive pillars which contrast with the elegant arches of the chancel and a remarkable tapestry (made by Frida Hansen in 1927) in the vestibule. Both chancel and vestibule were rebuilt after 1272 in a style similar to the Scottish Gothic of the times, a reminder of Stavanger's international connections even in those early days.

Even earlier is **Jernaldergarden**, the Iron Age farm at **Ullandhaug** (open late May–early Sept Sun noon–4pm, late June–mid-Aug Sun–Fri 11am–4pm; entrance charge; tel: 51 84 60 15), about 2 km (1 mile) or so to the southwest of the centre. Here archaeologists unearthed and then reconstructed part of the farm to show three houses, parts of a cattle track and the original encircling stone wall from AD 350 and 550. This was a golden age in Norway, and the city's **Arkeologisk Museum** (Archaeological Museum; open June–Aug Tues–Sun 11am–5pm; Sept–May Tues 11am–8pm, Wed–Sun 11am–3pm; entrance charge; tel: 51 84 60 00) is gradually furnishing the houses to show how people lived then.

From Ullandhaug, it is worth visiting the nearby **Botanisk Hage** (Botanical Garden; open daily; entrance charge) which has a herb and perennial garden with more than 1,500 species from all over the world. Rogaland is rich in birds and fauna and the **Stavanger Museum** (open June–Aug daily 11am–4pm, Sept–May Sun only 11am–4pm; entrance charge; tel: 51 84 27 00) has an excellent exhibition, not only on Rogaland wildlife but on cultural history, and the history of fishing (covering the industry and its creatures, including whales and seals).

Chemical analysis has confirmed that the copper used to cover New York's Statue of Liberty came from one of the old Visnes copper mines on the island of Karmøy northwest of Stavanger.

Water buses

The inhabitants of the city jump on to a boat as unconcernedly as most of us jump on a bus. There are tours to the islands and fjords and fast ferries north to Bergen, where business travellers sit in their city garb alongside holidaymakers' picnic boxes and fishing gear. There are ferry lines between Newcastle (England), Stavanger and Bergen, and Sola International Airport has flight connections to several European capitals as well as a busy domestic service.

Outdoor activities

The city is right on the doorstep of the Jærstendene Landskapsvernområdet (Protected Landscape Area), which stretches 70 km (43 miles) down the southern coast and its offshore islands, with nature reserves and silver sand beaches, ideal for swimming and picnicking. Sport is good year-round: swimming, sub-aqua diving, sailing, windsurfing and fishing. There is an active hiking club plus tennis and horse riding in Jærstendene. In winter, you get the best of both worlds thanks to the Gulf Stream as the climate remains mild and the fields around the city are rarely covered with snow; yet the good ski slopes are not much more than an hour away. ❏

BELOW: much of Norway's food is grown in the area south of Stavanger.

HORDALAND

An inspiration to generations of Norwegian artists, the mighty Hardangerfjorden lies at the heart of this region, which mixes wild coasts with sheltered islands, and spring blossoms with fjord waters

Map on page 234

Nobody knows how many hundreds of islands lie off the coast of Hordaland. Deserted skerries, green islets, prosperous small harbours and busy communities stretch out along the coast like a knotted skein, from the southern island of Bømlo to the beautiful small island of Fedje not far from the mouth of Sognefjorden.

Many of the inner islands around the fjord capital, Bergen, are linked by bridges and causeways in a pattern of islands and sea that seems all of a piece with the many branched fjords, including the famous Hardangerfjorden. Inland, the further east, the higher the ground becomes until it reaches Hardangervidda, the great mountain plateau which stands 1,300 metres (4,500 ft) above sea level.

The beginning of Christianity

The southwest district of **Sunnhordland** has islands, skerries, sounds and straits, good harbours and sheltered bays. Though the North Sea is its neighbour, the climate is surprisingly mild. The main islands are **Bømlo, Stord** and **Tysnesøy**, and even so close to the sea they have a variety of scenery. An upland ridge on Stord reaches nearly 750 metres (2,500 ft) and the view stretches east to Hardangerfjorden and the white sheet of the Folgefonn Glacier, and south towards Haugesund. Everywhere are sails of all colours, the white wake of an express boat from Stavanger to Bergen and the smaller trails of pleasure craft.

Stord also makes a good paddling-off point for sea canoeing, either from island to island, or into the mouth of the Hardanger. It is an "oil island" too, where the gigantic outlines of oil platforms take shape, some rising nearly 380 metres (1,250 ft) out of the water.

The sagas tell that in 1024 St Olav first introduced Christianity to Norway in these islands. Today, an annual outdoor performance (late May or early June; tel: 53 42 66 20) of the historical play *Mostraspelet*, held at **Mosterhamn ①** on Bømlo dramatises this ancient saga. Nearby is a stone cross erected in 1924 on the 900th anniversary of the arrival of Christianity, and Mosterhamn has the **oldest stone church** in Norway (open May–Sept; entrance charge) built around 995–1100. The church bells bear images of St Olav.

Gateway to Hardangerfjorden

The mouth of the Hardanger fjord is as beautiful as anywhere in the fjord itself, but the irony is that Sunnhordaland as a whole tends to be overshadowed by the fame and drama of Hardangerfjorden. Too many visitors travel through quickly on their way to other places. The discriminating know it deserves a longer look. **Leirvik** on Stord is a good starting point with short ferry connections to most of the surrounding islands and to the

PRECEDING PAGES: a cruise ship in Eidfjorden. **LEFT:** sea wake. **BELOW:** blossom time below the Folgefonn Glacier.

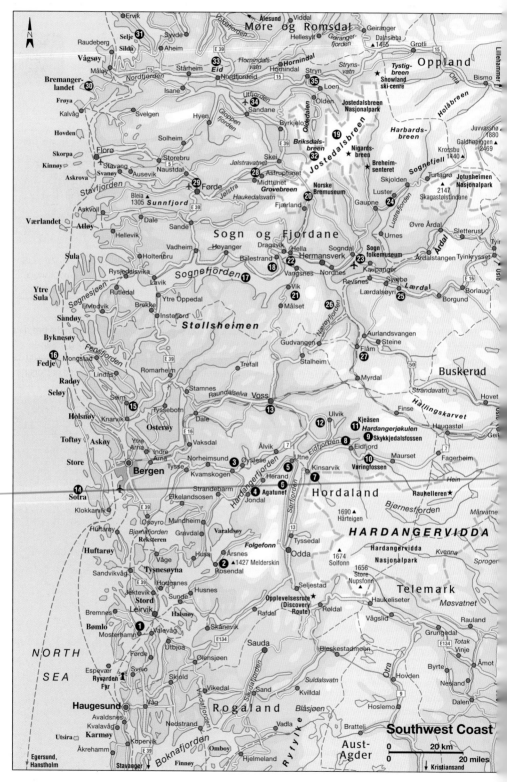

mainland. It is also the location of the **Sunnhordland Folkemuseum** (open all year; entrance charge) which was established in 1913 as the local history museum. To the south, the ferry to **Valevåg** puts you on the right track for **Ryvarden Fyr** (lighthouse; open Apr–Dec) at the mouth of Bømlafjorden, the home of the innovative composer Fartein Valen (1887–1952). There is also a museum, art gallery and café at nearby Møstrevåg.

To the east, a ferry to Sunde on the mainland brings you to where the cold waters of Hardangerfjorden begin to seep into the warmer tides from the west and the lovely 17th-century **Baroniet Rosendal** (Rosendal Barony; open May-Sept; entrance charge) in **Rosendal ❷**, the only one of its kind in Norway, which largely lost its aristocracy with the departure of the Danes. The manor house was built in 1665 by Ludvig Rosenkrantz. He is buried in the nearby medieval Kvinnherad Kirke (church), snuggled into the shelter of a rock face and once owned by the barony. The barony today has a peaceful park and a large carefully tended 300-year-old rose garden and is held in trust by Oslo University. Throughout the summer there are also art exhibitions, lunch-time concerts, and the **Rosendal Music Festival** during May and June.

A national inspiration

Hardangerfjorden is part of the Norwegian legend, the fjord that gave its name to Norway's national musical instrument, the eight-stringed Hardanger fiddle, and provided inspiration for the composer Edvard Grieg (1843–1907), the musician Ole Bull (1810–80) and, indirectly, for the 19th-century nationalist movement that eventually led to Norway's independence. Among these mountains and fjords, Grieg and Bull travelled on foot and horse, learning old melodies and dipping into centuries-old cultural traditions and customs.

Tourism came to the Hardanger district back in the 1830s when the poet Henrik Wergeland (1808–45) wrote about "wonderful Hardanger", and foreign as well as Norwegian artists, scientists and other travellers began to arrive; first in a trickle, then in a flood when, 30 years later, the steamers began to run from Bergen or Stavanger. Like the visitors of today, they came to Hardanger for its waterfalls, the smaller fjords that lead almost to the massif of Hardangervidda, and for glaciers and mountains that rarely lose their snowcaps, contrasted with orchards lining the fjord side. Nearly half a million fruit trees grow here, including plum, cherry, apple and pear, turning the fjord pink and white in spring as the blossom reflects in the deep, still water. At this time the waterfalls are in full spate, shooting over the sides of the mountains, and the Hardanger has two of Norway's highest and best known: Skykkjedalsfossen, which falls 300 metres (1,000 ft), and Vøringfossen, lower but famous for its beauty.

Crossing to the north side, Road 49 runs along the sunny side of Hardangerfjorden towards the fjord villages of **Norheimsund** and **Øystese ❸**. Alternatively, they can be reached through day or longer excursions from Bergen either by boat or road (E16 and then Road 11). Both of these villages offer excellent trips for exploring the fjords by car and ferry, and marked paths here and at **Kvamskogen** further inland make

Map on page 234

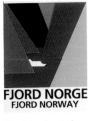

FJORD NORGE
FJORD NORWAY

Hordaland is at the heart of Norway's fjord country.

BELOW: the beautiful Vøringfossen (waterfall) lies at the end of Eidfjord.

for safe walking. But take time out to visit the **Ingebrigt Vik Museum** (open June–Aug; entrance charge) at Øystese, one of Norway's most distinctive museums containing virtually all the works by the sculptor of that name.

Not to be passed by is the **Hardanger Fartøyvernseter** (Hardanger Ship Conservation Centre; open all year) at Norheimsund where conservationists are patiently restoring the wooden craft that made Norwegian boat-building famous. They range from small rowing boats to the centre's most prestigious restoration, the *M/S Mathilde*, a 22-metre (73-ft) Hardanger yacht launched in 1884. This superb yacht has regained her former splendour under the guidance of Kristian Djupevåg (who also restored Roald Amundsen's polar vessel, *Gjøa)* and it has the world's largest authentic yacht rigging. The *Mathilde* sleeps 25 passengers in bunk benches or hammocks and is available for cruises and day excursions, when she can take 50 people to sail fjord and sea as they might have in bygone days.

Jondal ❹, on the other side of the fjord, is the entrance to the Folgefonn glacier, and the **Folgefonn Summer Ski-Centre**. The safe but exciting road to the new ski centre is clear from May to September. With snow for almost all of the year, there are three mobile ski lifts, Alpine and cross-country skiing tracks (you can hire all the equipment), a cafeteria and guided walks on the glacier.

Jondal itself has a country museum, in the old **Lensmannshuset** (Sheriff's House; open May–Sept; entrance charge), and Hardanger Cathedral (the largest church in the Hardanger region). Not far away at **Herand** you will find Bronze Age rock carvings and, at Herandsholmen, Hardanger's first guesthouse which opened in 1754. By now, into the inner fjords, the road suddenly turns sharply southeast along the short straight sides of Utnefjord to Utne village, part of Ullensvang *kommune*, which also includes both sides of Sørfjorden.

Edvard Grieg used to visit a small hytte *poised on the edge of Hardangerfjorden near to the village of Ullensvang where, with piano and writing desk at hand, he would compose surrounded by the beauty of the Norwegian fjords.*

BELOW: the old fjord village of Utne.

Map
on page
234

Five generations

When the fjords were west Norway's main "roads", **Utne** ❺ was an important junction between east and west and had the first post and telegraph offices in Hardanger, in 1836 and 1876 respectively.

Two establishments in Utne which sum up Hardanger life over the past centuries are the **Hardanger Folkemuseum** (open daily, closed winter weekends; entrance charge, for details *see below*), and the **Utne Hotel** (tel: 53 66 64 00), founded in 1722, the oldest hotel in Norway still in operation. Since 1787, five generations of the same family have owned the hotel. It first became famous internationally during the time of Torbjørg Utne (1812–1903), known with affection as Mor (Mother) Utne. Her picture hangs on the sitting-room wall. The family is represented today by her great granddaughter, Hildegun Aga Blokhus. It has always been a favourite spot for artists who have donated many paintings and the hotel also holds exhibitions of national costumes and characteristic embroidery.

Since it opened in 1911, the Hardanger Folkemuseum has collected old houses and farm buildings for its outdoor museum, formed into a "cluster farm" as it would have been before the Norwegian agricultural reforms in the middle of the 19th century. Along the shore are old boathouses and a merchant's shop, which was in use in Utne not all that long ago, and an orchard preserves many old varieties of fruit which have now disappeared from other parts of the Hardanger-fjord. Inside, the museum has a modern exhibition, other rooms showing old crafts, local folk costumes and folk art and the famous Hardanger fiddle along with a resident fiddle maker, and changing exhibitions on special fjord themes.

Past Utne, the fjord-side road turns due south into the **Sørfjorden**. Once you are used to the narrow road and would like to enjoy the magnificent view,

BELOW: traditional wedding at Voss led by a fiddler and toastmaster.

A traditional "children's wedding" at Voss.

you should stop at **Agatunet** ❻ (open May–Aug; entrance charge), the farm of a 13th-century local sheriff. From the Middle Ages to the recent past, Agatunet grew into a nine-family village with a cluster of some 30 buildings. Today, the families no longer live there but the buildings have been preserved.

On the eastern side of Sørfjord, a short ferry ride away, is the area's main amusement park, Ferieparken at **Kinsarvik** ❼. A favourite with children, it has a water chute, trampoline, a miniature zoo, a boating lake, and lends out surfboards, water mopeds and water skis. Kinsarvik was also part of the main east-west route and its marketplace attracted merchants from both sides of Hardangervidda to exchange bog iron and furs for sea salt. The **old stone church** is said to have been built by Scottish builders around 1160, and has a 17th-century pulpit painted by Peter Reimers. Until Utne Kirke (church) was consecrated in 1896, Kinsarvik had for centuries drawn its congregation from all around the fjords, and many worshippers arrived in church boats.

Falls, farm and forest

Heading northeast from Kinsarvik on the E13 and then Road 7 you will find one of the area's most beautiful stretches of water, **Eidfjorden** ❽. It cuts far into the dramatic landscape, which includes the **Hardangerjøkulen** and below it **Skykkjedalsfossen** ❾, Norway's highest waterfall, and **Vøringfossen** ❿, which falls 180 metres (590 ft) down into the wilds of Måbødalen. There is a path at the top overlooking the fall which is not for vertigo sufferers. Alternatively, you can walk down to view this great outpouring from below, and fitness fanatics might welcome the challenge of the age-old packhorse track up Måbøfjell, with 1,500 steps and 125 bends. From June to August look out for signs to the **Måbødalen Kulturlandskapsmuseum** (Cultural Landscape Museum; open June–Aug; guided tours available), which provides a network of trails all signposted and with information boards explaining the various points of interest. The public barbecue areas make fabulous picnic stops.

Above tiny Simadalsfjord is **Kjeåsen** ⓫, a mountain farm which claims to be the world's most isolated settlement. It lies like an eagle's nest 620 metres (2,000 ft) on near-vertical rock above the distant waters of the fjord. Those feeling strong and brave can tackle the old path to the top and marvel that this was how the villagers struggled up with their every need. For frailer spirits it is possible to reach Kjeåsen by car through a magnificent new tunnel. Inside the mountain is the **Sima Kraftverket** (Hydroelectric Power Station; open June–Aug; entrance charge), which arranges guided tours three times a day.

Crossing Eidfjorden at Brimnes you enter a farming and forestry district. Instead of taking the E13 take a right turn onto Road 572, which will bring you to **Ulvik** ⓬. Artists and other visitors have been coming here for longer than almost any other place in Hardanger and the village has permanent exhibitions by artists such as Tit Mohr (born 1917) and Sigurd Undeland (1903–1983). No one should miss the fine examples of **rose painting** in Ulvik's 19th-century church, painted in 1923 by Lars Osa (1860–1958).

BELOW: snowman outside Vangskyrkja (Voss Church).

Hang-gliding to skiing

Continuing on in a loop back to the E13 you come to **Voss** ⓭, which lies next to a lake, **Vangsvatnet**, in the middle of rich farmland. The Voss *kommune* (district) makes full use of its surroundings to attract visitors. In summer they come for touring, fjord excursions, mountain walking, parachuting, hang-gliding and paragliding from **Hangurfjell**, and fishing and water sports on Vangsvatnet. In winter, everything changes and Voss becomes one of the best centres for Alpine and cross-country skiing of the more energetic touring variety.

Voss is also a good place for mountain touring and sport fishing in the 500-or-so lakes and innumerable mountain rivers and streams, with the Vosso River famous for the size of its salmon. Even in summer the high mountains call for boots or very strong shoes and plenty of extra clothes – temperatures drop quickly; this applies in all upland areas.

The top station of the **cable car** up Hangurfjell gives one of the best prospects of Voss in its bowl-shaped valley. As the ground drops away below, the two gondolas, "Dinglo" and "Danglo", take only four minutes or so to lift you 570 metres (2,000 ft). On a sunny day, a coffee on the platform outside the cafeteria is magnificent, with the occasional excitement of a paraglider soaring into the sun and over Vagnsvatnet, spread out below.

At the beginning of World War II, Voss was badly damaged by German bombing and not much remains of the old town centre except the **Vangskyrkja** (church; open June–Aug daily), which dates back to 1277. The inside is certainly worth seeing with a colourfully painted ceiling liberally adorned with flying angels. Outside, a great stone cross stands in a field south of the church which, according to legend, was raised two centuries before the church was built by the

Apart from its artistic associations, the village of Ulvik has the unlikely privilege of being where the first potatoes were grown in Norway, back in 1765.

BELOW: moonrise over the island of Fedje.

proselytising King Olav Haraldson. The church walls are 2 metres (7 ft) thick and the wooden octagonal steeple is unique in Norway.

Below Hangurfjell, about half an hour's walk above the town, is **Voss Folkemuseum** (open all year; tel: 56 51 15 11), a collection of 16 old wooden buildings standing in traditional form around a central courtyard. The houses date from 1500 to 1870 and contain implements and furniture in use until 1927, incredible though it may seem. Yet somehow, despite the heavy farm work and meagre evening light, farm people like these managed to produce some beautiful embroidery, wood and other craft work. One of the most delightful is a traditional woodcarving of a Voss bridal party riding to church, with the bride's horse led firmly by her father as though he feared she might gallop away. The carving is by a local sculptor, and is based on a bronze relief in the little park below Voss station in which the main figure, the bridal fiddler, is the legendary Ola Mosafinn who died in 1912.

Artistic tradition

Voss has long been a centre for artists and musicians, and their monuments are scattered around. The 1957 Sivle monument marks the centenary of the birth of the author and poet Per Sivle (1857–1904), who grew up on the mountain farm of Sivle, in the great Stalheim Skleive (gorge); the monument behind Voss church commemorates three Bergslien artist brothers, Brynjulf, Nils and Knut; near Voss Fine Arts Society is a memorial to actor Lars Tvinde, born and bred on the farm of Tvinde, which lies below the Tvindefossen (a waterfall to the north of Voss); and on the same road the 1958 Sjur Helgeland Memorial commemorates another local fiddler and composer.

This artistic tradition continues and Voss is one of the best places to hear the Hardanger fiddle and see the old dances performed in beautiful costumes. On the main street is a shop where you can see, or even buy, the ornate silver belts and jewellery that go with the traditional Norwegian costume. An international jazz festival is held in the town every April.

BELOW: midday snack at the Hangur ski centre.

Around Bergen and north

From Voss the E16 is the quickest way to Bergen. Back in the city, Bergen's islands are linked so closely together that sometimes it is hard to realise that you have crossed water, but islands such as **Askøy** and **Osterøy** to the north of Bergen have their own character, and the area round the **Bjørnafjorden** (the Bear fjord) to the south is particularly mild and green, and full of boats of all sorts.

After an hour's drive to the long narrow island of **Sotra** ⓮, which shelters the city from the North Sea, there is no doubt that this is a different world. Sotra is a good base for sea canoeing in and out of its small offshore islands and rocks and, in good weather, as far as the open sea to combine canoeing with ocean fishing. In any case, shelter is never far away.

North of Bergen is a second island district, **Nordhordland**, that stretches as far north as Sognefjordenen and includes the islands of Holsnøy, Radøy and Sandøy. At weekends, it is a favourite area for Bergensere who go sailing, swimming and fishing. Although this region depended on ferries for a long

Map on page 234

time, today taking the car is no problem: most of its fjords and sounds can be crossed via modern suspension and pontoon bridges.

In Nordhordland the sea can be at its wildest, smashing against the western coast, yet the area has been inhabited for some 8,000 years. Håkon den Gode (the Good) is buried at **Seim ⓖ**, near Knarvik (around half an hour from Bergen by express boat). Another rare reminder of the Vikings is a beech wood, also at Seim, 1,000 years old and the northernmost beech wood in Europe.

Today, fish farming is important to Nordhordland, which exports vast quantities of salmon and trout all round the world, and the fish farmers are now attempting to rear cod, halibut and other species. Some fish farms are open to the public. There is good sea fishing for cod and coalfish, and special rosy-coloured trout inhabit many of the lakes. Diving and sub-aqua fishing, as well as treasure hunting, are easy in these transparent waters. Oil is a modern, though not conflicting industry in this widespread area with the night gleam of the light from Mongstad one of the few reminders of this large refinery.

Dangerous waters

Most remote of all, and a target for both sailing picnics and holidays, is the island of **Fedje ⓰**, an important navigation point for many centuries with two 19th-century lighthouses still in use today. In these ever-changing waters, Norwegian sea laws insist that all ships must carry a Norwegian pilot, and all tankers destined for Mongstad refinery are navigated from here through the unreliable waters. Stay overnight on Fedje in one of the guesthouses in Kræmmerholmen or in the Pensjonat or lighthouse there and enjoy some time in the idyllic bird and flower habitat. ❑

BELOW: the Stalheimskleive (gorge), near Voss, was the scene of fierce fighting during World War II.

NORWAY IN A NUTSHELL

If you have only a day to spare in this region, this tour which, but for the lack of an island or two, might well be called "Hordaland in a Nutshell", covers many of the sights. Organised by Norwegian State Railways and Fjord Tours, it runs throughout the year and combines bus, ferry and train *(see page 350)*.

The tour starts with a train journey from either Oslo or Bergen to Myrdal and can be done in a day in the summer months (in winter an overnight stop is necessary). From Myrdal it sets off on one of the steepest train journeys in the world, the 50-minute panoramic trip down 850 metres (2,800 ft) of mountain gorge to the pretty village of Flåm, stopping – thanks to one of the five separate sets of brakes – to photograph the torrent of Kjosfossen and to pick up passengers at one or two of the tiny stations.

The next leg is by ferry, which travels through Aurlands-fjorden and Norway's narrowest fjord, Nærøyfjorden, its rocky sides twice as high as the water is wide and now included on UNESCO's World Heritage list, to Gudvangen. From here the journey continues by bus to Voss, skirting Oppheim Lake. In summer the bus makes the hairpin ascent to the Stalheim Hotel. The hotel parapet looks down over the depths of the Stalheimskleive (gorge). A tortuous descent leads to the fjord.

BIODIVERSITY AND SUSTAINABILITY

About 20,000 years ago Norway was covered in ice and barren tundra. But, as the climate changed and ice melted, flora and fauna began to thrive

The first species to arrive in Norway, following the melting of the glaciers, were the Arctic animals such as reindeer, fox, wolf and wolverine. Trees came later, accompanied by a rich flora and fauna including bears, lynx, moose, marten, hare, beaver and otter, and small rodents including the lemming. The forests were filled with grouse, owls and woodpeckers. The lakes provided a habitat for geese, grebes, ducks and cranes; shadowed closely by birds of prey. The coastline teemed with kittiwakes, guillemots, auks, puffins, cormorants and gulls. The coastal waters were awash with arctic fish such as cod, haddock and halibut, and the rivers offered spawning ground for salmon, trout and char. Perch, powan, pike and grayling joined the ecosystem via the freshwater Baltic. Mankind entered the scene about 10,000 BC, with a strong hunting instinct. Whales, seals, lynx, bear and wolf almost became extinct, replaced by sheep and about 200,000 domesticated reindeer.

FROM PREDATOR TO PROTECTOR

Today large areas of Norway have been designated as national parks to protect special habitats and support biodiversity. Hunting is strictly controlled: wolves are regularly sighted in east Norway and the last of Europe's wild reindeer, about 15,000 in total, are now found on the Hardangervidda. Norway promotes sustainable management of ocean resources and has resumed commercial whaling based on studied whale counts. The moose, on the other hand, has benefited from commercial deforestation and numbers have grown.

▽ **WATER BIRDS**
The clownish-looking puffin *(Fratercula arctica)*, with its parrot-like bill, is an expert diver and adroit fisherman.

▷ **WORKING MAMMALS**
Reindeer often serve as a substitute to cattle or horses and are used to draw sledges and logs. They thrive on lichen moss.

▷ **WILD CATS**
The Eurasian, or northern lynx *(Felis lynx)*, is an agile climber and often hides in trees ready to pounce on small animals and birds. Lynx are also highly valued for their fur.

◁ **BEAR NECESSITIES**
Brown bears *(Ursus arctos)* are a protected species. There are about 55 in the country with numbers increasing annually.

◁ **KING OF THE FOREST**
The moose may stand up to 2.4 m (8 ft) high. The males' flattened, broad antlers are shed each year after the mating season.

COMMERCIAL WHALING

Norway was once a great whaling nation and, before electric lighting, benefited from a prosperous whale-oil industry. Today it has a whaling quota of 1,052 minke whales but only around 500 will be caught as long-distance hunting is not commercially viable and consumers have turned away from whale meat. Still, Norway continues to hunt in order to maintain its coastal communities and has recently introduced a DNA registry for all whale meat sold, to prove it was caught legally. The hunt is held in summer when fishing activities are low and much effort goes into teaching and pursuing correct hunting methods.

◁ **GREAT WHALES**
Although Norway still pursues commercial whaling, the species has recovered. Sightings are common in the west, with almost daily minke or beluga appearances.

△ **ARCTIC KING**
The polar bear *(Ursus maritimus)* is Europe's largest predator and chooses his habitat where there is an abundance of seals.

▷ **MOUNTAIN GIANT**
The musk ox *(Ovibos moschatus)*, once close to extinction, is found in Arctic regions and feeds on grass, moss and sedge.

BERGEN

*With its relaxed atmosphere, stunning setting and vibrant
cultural life, Bergen is an appealing mix of the cosmopolitan
and the outdoors, with easy access to the western fjords*

Map
on page
248

Thaving's always a sense of symmetry and order about a city built on hills. If
it also stands on a peninsula and has a harbour at its heart, it is bound to be
beautiful. Bergen, the capital of west Norway, has all these things. Built on
even hills, the city grew outwards from the coast and harbour in the quaintly
amed Puddefjorden and spread across the steep slopes and over the bridges that
ink islands and headlands.

The best place to get a feel of this natural shape is to take the newly mod-
rnised funicular, **Fløibanen Ⓐ** (every half hour, May–Aug 7.30am–midnight;
ept–Apr until 11pm; charge), that climbs more than 300 metres (1,000 ft) in
ist eight minutes from the centre to **Fløyen**, high above Bergen. On the down-
vard journey, you seem to be tipping headfirst into the city.

At the top is the lovely old-fashioned building that houses Fløyen Restaurant,
wilt in 1925, and the start of eight marked walking routes, the longest no more than
round 4 km (2½ miles), though this does not mean they do not contain steep hills
hrough woods and open moor. There are several huts for shelter along the way.

A leisurely coffee or lunch on the verandah of the restaurant gives a chance
lso to drink in the superb view over hundreds of islands, many with small
ytter (wooden cabins) and a couple of boats tied up to a landing stage that
ums up a Norwegian's ideal summer. All around are
nountains and hills that cradle the city – Fløifjellet,
Damsgårdfjellet, Løvstakken, Sandviksfjellet, Run-
lemånnen, Blåmannen, and the highest of them all,
Jlriken at around 640 metres (2,100 ft) reached by a
able car (every seven minutes, summer 9am–9pm,
vinter 10am–5pm, May and Sept 9am–7pm; charge).
The Ulriken mountain café is open when the cable
ar is running. There is a double-decker bus connec-
ion with the cable car from Torget, the site of the
amous Bergen fish market.

A long tradition of international trade has made this
ity the most outgoing in Norway and given the
3ergensere a jauntiness in their walk that hints at
enerations of sailors, quick wits, worldliness and a
ense of their own worth. Bergensere are certain they
re the best, secure in the knowledge that, although
Dlso may now be the capital, it is historically a mere
oddler compared with Bergen.

Olav Kyrre's city

King Olav Kyrre is credited with founding Bergen in
1070 at Torget. But it would be naive to believe that,
ong before, the perfect natural harbour and sheltered
jords were not a home for people who depended on the
ea. During the 13th century, Bergen became the first
apital of a united Norway, and a great ecclesiastical
entre, with a cathedral, 20 churches and chapels, five

PRECEDING PAGES:
Bergen harbour.
LEFT: "Jacob",
the street sign for
Jacobsgården.
BELOW: Fløibanen
on its way up
Fløyen, one of
Bergen's seven hills.

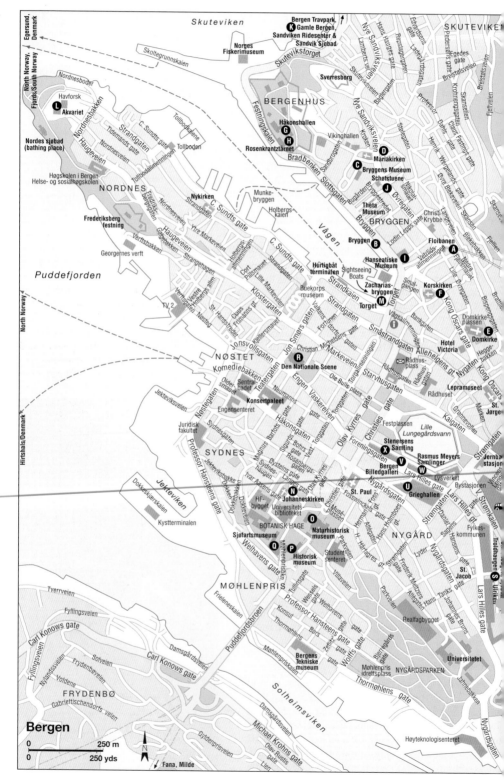

Skuteviken

Bergen Travpark,
K Gamle Bergen,
Sandviken Ridesenter &
Sandvik Sjøbad

SKUTEVIKEN

Norges
Fiskerimuseum

Skoltegrunnskaien

Skutevikstorget

Sverresborg

BERGENHUS

Håkonshallen
G
Vikinghallen
H
Rosenkrantztårnet
Bradbenken
D
Mariakirken
C
Bryggens Museum
Schøtstuene
J
Théta
Museum
BRYGGEN

Nordnesboder
Havforsk
L Akvariet
Nordes sjøbad
(bathing place)

C. Sundts gate
Tollbodkaiene
Tollboden
Tollbodalmenningen

Høgskolen i Bergen
Helse- og sosialhøgskolen
NORDNES

Nykirken
C. Sundts gate

Munke-
bryggen
Holbergs-
kaien

Frederiksberg
festning

Georgernes verft

Vågen

Bryggen
B

Floibanen
A

Hanseatiske
Museum
I

Puddefjorden

TV 2

Hurtigbåt
terminalen
Sightseeing
Boats

Buekorps
museum

Zacharias-
bryggen
M Torget

Korskirken
F

Smal-
gangen

NØSTET

Komediebakken

Den Nationale Scene
R

Rådhus-
plass

Hotel
Victoria
E Domkirke

Lepramuseet
Rådhuset

Konsertpaleet

Juridisk
fakultet

SYDNES

Festplassen
Lille
Lungegårdsvann

Stenersens
Samling
X
Rasmus Meyers
Samlinger
Bergen
Billedgalleri
V
W

St. Paul
N Johanneskirken
O

HF-
bygget
Universitets-
biblioteket

BOTANISK HAGE
Sjøfartsmuseum
Q P
Naturhistorisk
museum

Historisk
museum

NYGÅRD

U
Grieghallen

St.
Jacob
S Ulriken

MØHLENPRIS

Bergens
Tekniske
museum

Universitetet
NYGÅRDSPARKEN

FRYDENBØ

Bergen

0 _____ 250 m
0 _____ 250 yds

N

Fana, Milde

Høyteknologisenteret

monasteries and two hospitals for the poor. Bergen lost its capital status to Oslo during the Middle Ages, but still dwarfed the new capital. In medieval times, it was the biggest city in the Nordic countries and, until 1830, the largest in Norway. Today, with a population of around 240,000, it is roughly half the size of Oslo.

Much of this early size and success came when Bergen was chosen as the hub of the medieval German Hanseatic League in the north. Their trading base on the north side of **Vågen** became the powerhouse of all trade on the northwest Norwegian coast. But the Hansa began to grow too powerful all over Scandinavia and, at last, Norway broke the tie that kept the west in thraldom.

BERGEN

The perils of fire and war

As in all wooden cities, fire has swept through Bergen on many occasions, often devastating it. The result is that the oldest surviving buildings are noticeably built of stone, and the present streets, following the last fire in 1916 when a gale fanned the flames to an inferno, are wide and designed as fire breaks.

During World War II, Bergen was a centre of the resistance movement and many young people from the town took the perilous route out through the islands to Shetland. One group, with members aged 19–22, escaped to Scotland and returned with radio equipment to establish contact with exiled Norwegian authorities in England. The actions of the movement are commemorated by the **Theta Museum** in Bryggen (open mid-May–mid-Sept Tues, Sat, Sun 2–4pm; entrance charge; tel: 55 32 29 95). Yet the major disaster of this unhappy period came not directly from war but through accident caused by war. In 1944 a Dutch ammunition ship in the harbour blew up, damaging many of the oldest buildings on the northern promontory, including Håkonshallen and Rosenkrantztårnet. Anti-German feelings ran high at that time. The famous Tyskebryggen (quay named after Hansa merchants) has been tactfully renamed **Bryggen ❸**.

Serving as the starting point for numerous tours and cruises, Bergen is known as the "gateway to the fjords".

BELOW: trolls guard the entrance to a souvenir shop.

Starting with the past

The earliest archaeological remains are in **Bryggens Museum ❹** (open May–Aug daily 10am–5pm; Sept–Apr Mon–Fri 11am–3pm, Sat noon–3pm, Sun noon–4pm; entrance charge; tel: 55 58 80 10), past the Hansa houses on the north side of the harbour. The museum contains the medieval remains uncovered during archaeological digs between 1955 and 1972. There are also many artefacts and re-creations of medieval rooms. Together it gives a picture of the time when Bergen was a small fishing and sailing community that clung to the shallow slopes above the shore.

Nearby is the oldest building still in use, **Mariakirken ❹** (St Mary's Church; open June–Aug Mon–Fri 9.30am–4pm, Sept–May Tues–Fri 11am–12.30pm; entrance charge in summer; tel: 55 31 59 60), built in the early years of the 12th century and justly proud of its rich baroque pulpit. The only other medieval churches to survive periodic fires are the present **Domkirke ❺** (cathedral; open June–Aug Mon–Fri 11am–4pm, Sept–May Tues–Fri 11am–12.30pm; tel: 55 31 04 70), once dedicated to St Olav – the church has been rebuilt five times owing to fire, and **Korskirken ❻** (Church of the Holy Cross; open

National Day celebrations in Bergen.

Mon–Sat 11am–3pm), most of it now in the Renaissance style of the 17th century. The latter two are relatively close to the harbour and all three merit a visit.

Holmen was the site of **Bergenhus**, the old timber-built royal palace used when Bergen first became a capital. At a time of much building in the 13th century, it was converted to a fortified stronghold of stone, and the restored remains are close to where the original cathedral and bishop's residence stood. There are two particularly notable buildings: **Håkonshallen** (open mid-May–Aug 10am–4pm; Sept–mid-May daily noon–3pm, Thur 3–5pm; entrance charge; tel: 55 58 80 10), built by King Håkon Håkonsson between 1247 and 1261, which was used for the wedding of King Magnus Lagabøte (the Lawmaker), who was Håkon's son and co-ruler; and **Rosenkrantztårnet** (open May–Aug 10am–4pm; Sept–May Sun only noon–3pm; entrance charge), which was the work of a Danish governor of Bergenhus, Erik Rosenkrantz, who grafted it on to Håkon's original "Keep of the Sea" in the 1560s.

Håkonshallen is the largest secular medieval building still standing in Norway. When both it and Rosenkrantztårnet were badly damaged in the 1944 explosion, Norwegian historians took the opportunity to reconstruct them as closely to the originals as possible. Today, Håkonshallen makes a magnificent concert hall. Rosenkrantztårnet is now a museum, with both permanent and special exhibitions.

The power of the Hansa

In summer, guides from Bryggens Museum also conduct tours through the row of **Hansa houses** that line Bryggen. These Hansa homes and warehouses were all built after the great fire of 1702, which destroyed many buildings, and they are on the UNESCO World Heritage list. One key to understanding the Hansa way of life is a visit to the **Hanseatiske Museum** (open mid-May–mid-Sept 9am–5pm; mid-

BELOW: Bergen's sheltered harbour.

Sept–mid-May Tues–Sat 11am–2pm, Sun 11am–4pm; entrance charge; tel: 55 54 46 90), furnished in the style of the time when the merchant had his accounting room within the main office on the first floor. This small room enabled him to keep an eye on the liquor room next door. The adjoining room, decorated with a "royal cod", distinguished by a bump on its head and said to bring luck, served as dining and sitting room for merchants and apprentices. On the floor above are the apprentices' tiny box beds, one above the other. The sleeping quarters were tiny, but importantly retained heat. Although apprentices were merchants' sons, sent to learn their business with a colleague, they were locked into their "prisons" at night.

As a fire precaution – all too often in vain – no heating was allowed in these Hansa houses and the Germans must have suffered torments of cold in the biting damp of a Bergen winter. No wonder that **Schøtstuene ❶** (open mid-May–mid-Sept daily 10am–5pm, mid-Sept–mid-May Sun 11am–2pm; entrance charge; tel: 55 54 46 90), the assembly rooms nearby, were so popular during winter when trade was slack and few ships were in the harbour. The long central table held both beer jugs and the Bible, exemplifying the two religions of the Hansa. In a drawer was the cane used to discipline the apprentices who had their schooling there. The "rules of the club" adorn one wall, written in Low German (old northern dialect).

At Elsesro, further out along the coast road, past Bergenshus and the North Sea quay, is **Gamle Bergen ❻** (Old Bergen; open May–Sept 9.30am–4.30pm; guided tours only, every hour; entrance charge; tel: 55 39 43 00), the obligatory open-air museum beloved of Scandinavia. Here there is a collection of 40 wooden buildings from the 18th and 19th centuries, the interiors decorated to show different styles. Along the cobbled streets, guides in traditional red calf-length costumes and black shawls lead tours which range from the French

Map
on page
248

Historic wooden sign in Gamle (Old) Bergen.

BELOW: Torget, the city's famous fish market.

Empire splendour of the official's drawing room to the tiny house where the seamstress plied her diligent needle in the 1860s. Nearby is the popular **Sandvik Sjøbad** (bathing area) which looks out over Byfjorden to the city.

Back along Vågen, a short ferry trip from below Rosenkrantztårnet to the Nordnes peninsula gives a good opportunity to view the beautiful lines of the sailing ship *Lehmkuhl*, which trains youngsters in sailing techniques and gleams with polished brass. A short walk towards Nordnes point reveals another castle, **Fredriksberg** (no visitors) and further north is **Nordnes sjøbad**, which includes a heated outdoor pool. Here, too, is **Bergen Akvariet** ◐ (aquarium; open May–Aug 9am–7pm, Sept–Apr 10am–6pm; feeding times 11am, 1pm and 2pm all year; entrance charge; tel: 55 55 71 71).

Morning market

Early each weekday morning, **Torget** ◍ is the site of Bergen's fish, fruit and flower market. Customers engage the fishermen in serious conversation about the day's catch, watched by an interested circle, and the stalls sell *gravlaks* (cured salmon), lobster and *klippfisk* (dried cod). This busy scene is the heart of Bergen, where there is always something going on and where people linger to watch the transactions or peer into the boats tied up at the quay after a night's fishing.

Just south of the fish market is another square where people like to linger, **Torgalmenningen**, housing many of the city's best shops. The square also holds the **Sailors' Monument**. Carved figures march round the base of this memorial dedicated to all Norwegian sailors who lost their lives at sea. Alternatively, just up the hill from the fish market in another old section of the city is the **Gamle Rådhuset** (Old Town Hall). Originally built as a private house in 1558, it was presented to the town in 1562 and served the city for several centuries until, in 1974, the city administration moved to an inelegant high-rise modern block. Another attractive old building in the area is the **Hotel Victoria**.

Museum cluster

Bergen is a good walking city and, if you fix your eye on the tall steeple of **Johanneskirken** ◑ (St John's Church; open Tues–Fri 10am–2pm), a short walk up Vest Torggate from Torgalmenningen takes you to the top of **Sydneshaugen**, near the university area and the site of a clutch of museums: the **Naturhistorisk Museum** ◐ (Natural History Museum; open June–Aug Tues–Sun 10am–4pm, Sept–May Tues–Fri 10am–3pm, Sat, Sun 11am–4pm; entrance charge; tel: 55 58 29 20) standing in the fine **Botanisk Hage** (botanic garden), the **Historisk Museum** ◐ (Cultural History Museum), and the **Sjøfartsmuseum** ◐ (Maritime Museum; open June–Aug daily 11am–3pm; Sept–May Sun–Fri 11am–2pm; entrance charge; tel: 55 54 96 00) which traces the history of this seafaring area from the Old Norse period to the present day.

The university area consists of beautiful merchants' villas from the turn of the 20th century, and is where the Arctic explorer Fridtjof Nansen spent the early years of his career. It was also a base for the father of weather forecasting, Vilhelm Bjerknes.

BELOW: underwater at the Bergen Aquarium.

Famous names

It is not surprising that this lively city, with its close European links, should have been the birthplace of many famous people. It was also a strong base for 19th-century nationalism which culminated in 1905 in Norway gaining its independence from Sweden. The prime minister at the time was Christian Michelsen, whose home **Gamlehaugen** (house open June–Aug Tues–Sun noon–3pm, rest of the year weekends noon–3pm, English tour at noon; gardens open all year; entrance charge; tel: 55 11 29 00) at Fjøsanger is now the residence of the king when he is in Bergen.

Nationalism had strong roots in the 19th-century revival of Norwegian culture, led by the playwright Henrik Ibsen, the violinist Ole Bull, the composer Edvard Grieg, and writers such as Bjørnstjerne Bjørnson. Though Ibsen and Bjørnson were not natives of west Norway, Bjørnson was for a time director of Bergen's **Den Nationale Scene ⓡ** (National Theatre) founded by Ole Bull in 1850, and Bjørnson's statue stands on the steps in front.

The virtuoso violinist Ole Bull's contribution to Norwegian culture came through his wanderings in the villages of west Norway and the great Jotunheim mountain plateau east of the fjord country. Here he collected many old folk melodies which were played on the Hardanger fiddle, the area's traditional instrument. Later, Grieg transcribed some of these folk tunes for piano, saving them from being lost. He also founded Norway's National Theatre and hired a young Henrik Ibsen as a writer.

Every year, thousands of visitors come to look round Grieg's summer home at **Troldhaugen ⓢ** (open May–Sept daily 9am–6pm; Oct, Nov and Apr Mon–Fri 10am–2pm, Sat–Sun noon–4pm; mid-Jan–Mar Mon–Fri only; entrance charge; tel: 55 92 29 92) some 8 km (5 miles) south of Bergen on a high point above

Map on page 248

Edvard Grieg (1843–1907).

BELOW: a dragon boat procession along Bryggen.

*Fantoft stavkirke
(stave church), in the
Paradis district
of Bergen, was
brought from its
original home on
Sognefjorden in 1879.
It burnt down in 1992
and has since been
meticulously rebuilt
(open May–Sept).*

BELOW: view from
the top of Fløyen.

the fjord. Here Grieg found the peace to compose in his *hytte* (holiday lodge).

The house is just as Grieg left it; his manuscripts are scattered around and even his piano is in working order in the comfortable drawing room. In the past, this room was the venue for many musical evenings; today, if you are lucky, the curator will play some of Grieg's music for you. The size of the room inevitably limited the size of the audience and in 1985 Troldhaugen opened a special **Chamber Music Hall** seating 200, with a turf roof and built into the hill side so that it is barely visible among the tall trees. The floor-to-ceiling windows behind the stage provide the audience with a lovely view of the composer's *hytte* and Lake Nordås. The latest addition is the **Edvard Grieg Museum** close to the concert hall and villa.

Troldhaugen is a wonderful setting for a concert and a continuation of the summer evening tradition when Grieg and his wife, Nina Hagerup, a Danish singer, would entertain their friends in the quiet garden outside the drawing room. Any bus for the Fana district goes to Hopsbroen, then a 15-minute walk leads to Troldhaugen; many city excursions also include Troldhaugen.

Ole Bull built his home on the island of **Lysøen** ❶ (open mid-May–Aug Mon–Sat noon–4pm; Sun 11–5pm; Sept Sun only noon–4pm; entrance charge; tel: 56 30 90 77) in 1873, when his fame had long spread throughout and beyond Norway. Bull turned the island into a park with woodland and walking routes and the house itself is unlike any other in the country. Made of traditional Norwegian wood, the decorated and screened balcony and the pointed arches of the windows on the front of the building have an almost Moorish flavour, and the tower topped by a minaret is reminiscent of St Basil's in Moscow's Red Square. To get there, take the bus marked "Lysefjordruta" from bus station gate 19 or 20. The ride takes 50 minutes and stops at Beuna Kai. Then take the Ole Bull ferry,

which leaves at noon, 1pm, 2pm and 3pm. By car, take road 553 and head south in the direction of Fana. It's a good idea to combine the visit to Lysøen with a stop on the way at **Lysekloster**, the ruins of a 12th-century Cistercian abbey, a daughter monastery of Fountains Abbey in Yorkshire, England.

Map on page 248

Artistic legacy

Whether as a result of the fame of people such as Bull and Grieg, Bergen has a lively artistic and cultural life – hence it was honoured as one of the European Cities of Culture 2000. The **Bergen International Festival of Music**, held each May and early June, attracts international artists and thousands of visitors. At the end of the 1970s, the festival led to the building of a new concert hall, **Grieghallen Ⓤ**, with marvellous acoustics. The outside of the building looks remarkably like that of a concert grand piano, perhaps as a tribute to the composer whose name it bears. This is the heart of the 12-day festival but the whole city is involved, with events in Håkonshallen, Troldhaugen, Lysøen and Mariakirken.

Bergen also has several strong art collections, mostly centred on **Lille Lungegårdsvann**, the octagonal lake in the middle of the park, not far from the statues of Edvard Grieg and of Ole Bull playing his violin, and near Grieghallen. Here are the **Bergen Kunstmuseum Ⓥ** (Bergen Art Museum; open June–Aug daily 11am–5pm, Sept–May closed Mon; entrance charge; tel: 55 56 80 00), with a large collection of Norwegian painting from the past 150 years; **The Rasmus Meyers Samlinger Collection Ⓦ**, also specialising in Norwegian paintings with many by Edvard Munch; and the **Stenersens Samling Ⓧ**, with works by Munch, Picasso and Klee amongst others (all part of the Bergen Art Museum). Bergen is also strong in private galleries, many of which specialise in modern painting.

BELOW: a concert in the ornate music hall of Ole Bull's house on Lysøen.

Map on page 248

Shops often offer opportunities to see traditional crafts. Best known is **Husfliden** (on Vågsalm), which has richly decorated Norwegian costumes, textiles and woodwork, including the famous *rosemaling* (rose painting). For Norwegian glass try **Irgens** in Markeveien and Bergen's **Glasmagasin**.

Tradition in action

During the summer (mid-June to late August) the open-air stages at Lille Lungegårdsvann and Torgalmenningen are used almost daily for music and dance performances. Folk dancing and music from rural Norway are particularly popular with the Bergensere and visitors alike. Nearest to the real thing is **Fana Folklore** (summer, tel: 55 91 52 40), in the district of Fana to the south. This is designed as a country wedding with typical Norwegian food, such as *rømmegraut*, a rich celebration "porridge" which bears little resemblance to the breakfast variety, alongside cured mutton and sausage, flat bread and other traditional dishes.

To experience Fana Folklore, travel by bus from Festplassen to **Fana Kirken**, the 800-year-old church, for a recital of hymns and melodies by the organist; then on to **Rambergstunet**, and a welcome by the *lur*, an instrument similar in sound to a coaching horn, and then to the long trestle tables for the wedding fare, accompanied by folk dancers weaving and jumping in the prescribed steps that almost died out during the 19th century. There are also displays by children and songs accompanied by one of Norway's *langleik*, a seven-string zither.

Outdoor city

The most popular pastime is **sailing**. Not far behind are sea fishing and swimming. Or you could simply take a fjord cruise. Try the Norway-in-a-Nutshell bus, train and boat tour for a great overview of the area *(see page 241)*. The hills above Bergen, just 10 minutes away from the centre, are ideal for walking, and **Sandviken Ridesenter**, not far from the Gamle Bergen Museum, organises horse-riding tours.

For something different, try a night at **Travpark** (Fri, from 6pm; tel: 55 39 68 00) at Åsane, around 16 km (10 miles) from the city (bus 285). This is a peculiarly Scandinavian sport. The atmosphere is electric as the "trotting" horses and their drivers race round the track.

Apart from the gardens at Troldhaugen and Lysøen, the Norwegian Arboretum at **Milde** (open daily; tel: 55 98 72 50), founded in 1971, has with gusto planted up shrubs and trees from many parts of the world, and this pretty area along the shore has rocky gorges, hills and a small lake. The Fanafjord also provides good swimming. To get there take bus 525 to Mildevågen, and then a 15-minute walk to the arboretum.

Too many people make the mistake of allowing only a day or even half a day for Bergen at the start and end of a visit to the western fjords, which doesn't give the city a chance. It is much better to use it as a base for a fjord holiday, combining the cosmopolitan delights of the city with the splendid scenery of the fjords. Bergen has plenty to do and see, or you can simply spend some time just soaking up the atmosphere down by the busy harbour. But take an umbrella: on average it rains 219 days per year. ❑

BELOW: Ole Bull nicknamed his house "the Little Alhambra".
RIGHT: old houses in the maze of narrow lanes behind Bryggen.

Map
on page
262

THE MOST BEAUTIFUL VOYAGE

This is one of the great sea journeys of the world: from Bergen to the end of Norway and back again, the vessels plying the Hurtigruten are mail boats, freight ships and passenger liners in one

The ship slips out of **Bergen**'s hill-ringed harbour at 10.30pm, day in, day out, all year round. In winter, it has been dark for hours and passengers linger no longer than to wave goodbye to the lights of the city before scuttling below to the warmth of saloon and cabin. In summer, it is a different matter: the deck is crowded as the big steamer sweeps out towards the fjord, leaving behind the small houses where the Hansa merchants once lived.

The coastal express heads north through Byfjorden and Hjeltefjorden, past the islands of **Askøy** and **Holsnøy** for the open sea, at the start of a trip of 1,250 nautical miles round Nordkapp (North Cape) and then to Kirkenes near the Russian border, crossing the Arctic Circle en route.

Nowadays, this coastal voyage has become one of the most popular journeys for visitors, but it is much more to the Norwegians themselves. From earliest times, this long and beautiful coast has been the main link in Norway for communication and trade, connecting communities hundreds of kilometres apart; the western and northern Norwegians once regarded Scotland and Iceland as being easier to reach than the region around present-day Oslo. In winter, it was the only way to travel because the Gulf Stream kept, and still keeps, the seaways open all year round.

The swift route

The first steamship, the *Prinds Gustav*, set out from Trondheim to Tromsø in 1838. In time, other steamers also began to journey between the coastal towns and in 1893 a local steamship company, Vesteraalens Dampskibsselskab, opened the Hurtigruten (literally "swift route") between Trondheim and Hammerfest, in the far northwest. As the line extended to Bergen and Kirkenes, several shipowners became involved. Following various mergers, the last two companies running the fleet merged to form Hurtington Group in 2006. The group also operates 54 ferry and fast-ferry routes, two vessels in the Antartic and Svalbard, and bus lines, hotels and the cargo carrier Nor Lines. A round trip from Bergen to Kirkenes on its modern ship takes 11 days. Shorter trips are available.

The Hurtigruten makes 34 ports-of-call along this ever-changing coast, some at places no bigger than a handful of houses around the harbour, with local people waiting on the quayside to collect a car or a container or to greet friends who have hopped a short distance between small towns where the alternative is a long, difficult drive. Part of the charm is watching a working ship going about its business: the efficient mooring as the crew shout down to the dockers, the

PRECEDING PAGES: sunset at sea. **LEFT:** resting on the aft deck. **BELOW:** the view from on board *M/S Nordlys* between Rørvik and Brønnøysund.

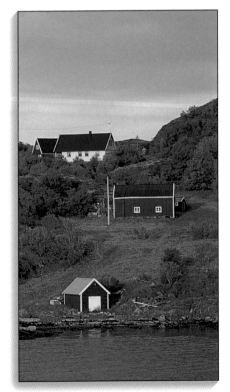

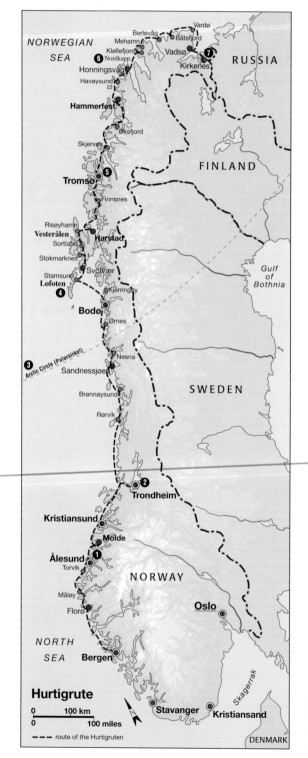

crane winching over a tractor which has been chained fast to the deck during the voyage, and the nervous face of its owner as a car is winched up.

From October to May the first stop for going ashore is Ålesund **❶**, one of the three Møre towns. It has all the natural design of a town built round a harbour and, because of a disastrous fire in 1904, it was rebuilt all of a piece, with the wooden houses in an Art Nouveau style, carefully preserved and painted in brilliant colours. From June to September, the vessel heads north to **Molde** instead of Ålesund. The high point of the tour is descending Trollstigen's (Troll Road's) 11 hairpin bends.

The next main stop is **Trondheim ❷**, further up a magnificent coast with 87 peaks, snowcapped for much of the year. When it was the ancient capital of Norway, Trondheim was called Nidaros, and **Nidaros Domen** (cathedral) is a national shrine; it contains a memorial to King Olav Haraldson, who became St Olav the Holy after his death at the Battle of Stiklestad. The Trondheim stop is long enough for a morning tour of this historic city, with its busy harbours and bays, and wide streets lined with small wooden houses and old warehouses. From May to September, the tour also visits the Museum of Musical History at Ringve.

Early next morning, as the ship steams north again, it crosses the **Polarsirkel ❸** (Arctic Circle) and sails into "the land of the Midnight Sun". From April to September passengers can board a smaller vessel at Grønøy to navigate the narrow Hollandsfjord inland. The tour then alights at the foot of the spectacular Svartisen, Norway's second-largest glacier. At the Arctic Circle crossing, "King Neptune" joins the celebrations on board to award Arctic Circle certificates.

Hamsun's Nordland

Into the spectacular **Lofoten Islands ❹**, the ship is now in Nordland, the territory of one of Norway's most famous writers, Knut Hamsun. Hamsun named the old trading centre of **Kjerringøy**

"Sirilund" in his novels, which describe the surprisingly outward-looking lives of these northern fishing and trading families around the turn of the 20th century. A Hamsun novel, particularly *The Wayfarers*, is a good accompaniment to a voyage that illuminates his own characters and their thinking, and gives an insight into life in these northern lands today.

On deck, as the steamer weaves in and out of the islands, bird-watchers find it difficult to go below even to eat or sleep, in case they miss one of the numerous seabird colonies, the congregations of colourful exotic ducks in winter harbours and, particularly, the comical little puffins in their hundreds of thousands.

Between **Svolvær** and **Stokmarknes**, the ship makes a brief detour (weather permitting) into **Trollfjorden**, something no big cruise liner could do because the sheer faces of rock and scree press close in this narrow fjord. This, too, calls for a celebration and the ship's chef serves a special Trollfjorden soup to the accompaniment of Grieg's most troll-like music and the arrival of a troll to delight the passengers. In winter, ice makes entry impossible, but instead there is the endless fascination of the **Aurora Borealis** (Northern Lights) – sometimes white spears, at others a brilliant blue-green aura across the sky, or a multicoloured spectacular that gleams and sparkles. The high mountains of the fjord country further south have disappeared by now but, during the brief light of a winter day, the low slanting sun picks out the white cones of snow-covered hills.

Watching the seasons go by

In spring and autumn, the 11-day journey feels like a voyage through the seasons. Leave Bergen in May, when the fjord valleys are brilliant with blossom, and the hills and mountains of the north will still be white as snow flurries

Map on page 262

On the Hurtigruten there is time to see the Norwegian Crown Jewels on display in Trondheim's Nidaros Domkirke (cathedral).

BELOW: a steamer dwarfs the dock side at Øksfjord.

Map
on page
262

Arriving at Sortland.

BELOW: heading
north near Skjervøy.
RIGHT: late evening,
during the midnight
sun, north of Bodø.

scurry across the fjords and mountains. The return journey is the reverse: just as the north is beginning to slip out of its winter grip, the swift Norwegian summer marches north and will have already reached Bergen and the mountains around it, and it could be warm enough to lie out in a sheltered corner of the deck as the ship nears the end of its long journey.

The northern city of **Tromsø ❺**, set on an island in a rugged landscape, has a relaxed cosmopolitan atmosphere that fits with its nickname "Paris of the North" and can be enjoyed in its numerous restaurants and street cafés. It has the most bars per capita in Norway, with a bustling nightlife. Among the stops are **Tromsø Museum** and the **Ishavs** (Arctic) **Cathedral**, which has the largest stained-glass window in Europe. Returning south to Tromsø in summer, there is time for a midnight excursion by cable car to the summit of **Mount Storsteinen**. At 410 metres (1,350 ft) above the sea, there is a wonderful sunlit view of coast and country.

Into Finnmark the ship sails past a coast of scoured hills and watercourses with forests along the valleys, to **Hammerfest**, Norway's most northerly town. In summer, the steamer, working ship or not, makes a concession here and slips through the Margerøy Sound to Honningsvåg and the start of an excursion by bus to **Nordkapp ❻** (North Cape) – a highlight of any visit to Norway.

North Cape also marks a change of direction to the east across the very top of Norway on the way to **Kirkenes ❼**, 5 km (3 miles) from the **Russian border**, a coast where the place names begin to show Sami (Lapp) and Finnish origins. Kirkenes itself is a mining town in a strange no-man's land between East and West, which is also influenced by the local Sami culture. Another bus then passes through Kirkenes and heads for Storskog and the Russian border.

Nowhere missed

Heading south, after visiting Tromsø, the vessel takes in a brief sightseeing tour at Harstad before moving on to **Trondenes Church**, the world's northernmost medieval church and, at 750 years old, the historical centrepiece of Trondenes. After a visit to Trondheim, passengers take in a short tour of the beautiful coastal fishing town of Kristiansund then arrive at Molde to experience the panoramic views of the Romsdal fjord and the Romsdal alps. On the way south again, the ship stops by day at the places it visited when northbound passengers were fast asleep below decks, so nowhere is missed. Nor is it generally a rough voyage: the Hurtigruten hugs the coast or weaves in and out of islands that shelter the ship from the excesses of the Atlantic Ocean and the Norwegian Sea, even in the far north.

Although the network of small aircraft linking scattered communities has done much to reduce its traffic, the coastal steamer is still there when airports are closed and roads blocked. For supplies and deliveries to distant industries and traders, ships are invaluable and can carry things too big for a plane. Even so, with the ever-increasing tourist traffic this emphasis is changing. Hurtigruten is increasingly offering cruise-orientated packages and even side trips into Geiranger Fjord. For booking information visit www.hurtigruten.com or tel: 76 96 76 00/81 03 00 00. ❑

FROM SOGN TO NORDFJORD

The presence of the last Ice Age is felt strongly here, in the shape of the great Jostedal glacier; but humans have also left their mark, in the form of ancient rock carvings and a plethora of stave churches

Map on page 234

Frrom a seat in one of the small planes that somehow contrive to land on the narrow strips along the fjords or the tiny green patches between the mountains, it looks an impossible territory. Yet the land that runs from Sognefjord in the south to Nordfjord to the north has all the features that made Norway famous: the world's longest and deepest fjord, Europe's largest glacier and Jotunheimen, Scandinavia's greatest mountain massif.

The large *fylke* (county) of Sogn og Fjordane lies between a zigzag coastline drawn by the waters of the North Sea and the start of Jotunheimen's heights. Narrow fingers of water push inland from the main fjords to reach far into the mountains, and waterfalls tumble hundreds of metres into the fjord below. The force of all this water feeds powerful hydroelectric power stations tucked away inside the mountains. Aluminium plants also make use of the spouting waterfalls to generate power and, among other things, produce the road barriers for many of Europe's mountain roads.

In the past, fjord, mountain and valley could be near impassable in winter. Today, though journeys often take longer than elsewhere, travel is made easier thanks to the network of ferries, tunnels and bridges. From Bergen, an express boat (a catamaran with water-jet engines) reaches deep inland as far as Sogndal on Sognefjorden, almost halfway to Sweden.

Deepest and longest

At 205 km (120 miles) long and 1,300 metres (4,260 ft) deep, **Sognefjord ⑰** is unmatched anywhere in the world. After British visitors discovered it in the 19th century, royalty too endorsed the fjord's delights. As crown prince, Edward VII came over from Britain as early as 1898, and Kaiser Wilhelm II was on holiday in Sogn when he learned of the assassination of the Archduke at Sarajevo which triggered World War I.

In spring, the fjord's scenery is pink and white when this apparently ungrateful soil puts up umbrellas of fruit blossom in orchards and gardens. In the warm summer days, far above the fjord, cattle and sheep cling to the small grass plateaux around the mountain farms or *seter* where once women and young girls spent the summer making cheese. The majority of the 106,000 people in the county still make their living by farming or fishing, forestry or fruit growing.

On both sides of the fjord small villages cling to every square metre of land, each with its own atmosphere. **Balestrand ⑱** has been a favourite since the 19th century and has an English church, St Olav's, founded by one of those fearless Victorian Englishwomen who travelled the world. German artists from the Düsseldorf Academy were also quick to appreciate the beauty of Sognefjorden and built Swiss-style houses, decorated

LEFT: Flåm village.
BELOW: St Olav's Kirke in Balestrand.

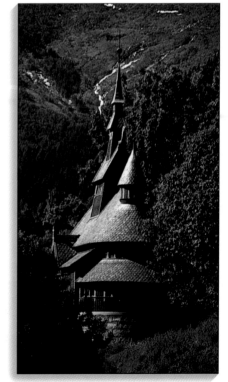

TIP

In summer, guides
from the Jostedals-
breen National Park
Centre, 20 km (12
miles) east of Stryn,
lead tours and glacier
explorations to differ-
ent offshoots of the
great Jostedal (details
tel: 57 87 68 00).

with dragon heads in deference to their hosts' Viking past, to add to the charm of this picturesque village. The area is renowned for having a particularly mild climate and lush vegetation; across a small neck of water at **Dragsvik**, a local pastor-botanist planted exotic trees which thrive in the sheltered bay.

Ice spectacle

A narrow side fjord leads to the little community of **Fjærland** (road connections here were not completed until 1986), a dairy-farming centre near the two southernmost offshoots of the great **Jostedalsbreen** (Europe's largest glacier). Nestling at its base on a large, flat esker deposited thousands of years ago is the **Norsk Bremuseum** ❷⓪ (Norwegian Glacier Museum; open June–Aug 9am–7pm, Apr–May and Sept–Oct 10am–4pm; entrance charge; tel: 57 69 32 88). In 2007 the museum will include a new wing devoted to natural and artificial climate change.

Tourists come to Fjærland every year to climb (or merely gaze at) the awesome glacier. From a distance, the concrete and glass building designed by Norwegian architect Sverre Fehn looks like part of the glacier itself. The museum includes a special cinema for viewing panoramic shots of Norwegian glaciers.

The ferry from Dragsvik runs to **Vangsnes** on the south side. From there, it is only a few kilometres to **Vik** ❷① and the 12th-century **Hopperstad Stavkirke** (open May–Sept; entrance charge), with dragon heads on the outside and rich decorations within. Vik also has a stone church, **Hove Kirke** (open mid-June–July Wed–Sun 10am–4pm; entrance charge) only 20 years younger than Hopperstad. On the way back, stop at the statue of the heroic Norwegian Viking figure Fritjof den Frøkne (Fritjof the Courageous), a gift from Kaiser Wilhelm II in 1913.

Going east from Balestrand, a short crossing takes you to **Hella** ❷② and past the

BELOW:
a solitary boat
on Sognefjord.

glistening arc of **Kvinnafoss** (Lady's Waterfall) close to the main road. At the head of the fjord, **Sogndal** is the centre for trade and administration in an area of forestry and farming. The pretty little town swells considerably during term time because it is also a centre for education, with university colleges and Norway's oldest folk high school. To the north, farms are dotted along Sognadalen's narrow lake. This is a popular spot for walking in summer and skiing in winter. Sogndal's airport is located at Haukåsen, next to Kaupanger.

Map
on page
234

Kaupanger Stavkirke (open June–Aug; entrance charge), a little further along Road 5, was built in the 12th century; its plain dark wood exterior has been restored, and it is a lovely place to listen to the organist's summer recitals. **Sogn folkemuseum** ㉓ (open May and Sept 10am–3pm, June–Aug 10am–5pm; entrance charge; tel: 57 67 82 06) was set up in 1909 as a living museum with animals, including 35 houses and farm buildings, to show how people lived in Sogn from around 1500 up to the present. The museum is used as a setting for folk music and dancing. Standing tall beside the fjord at **Nordnes** is a stone to mark the Battle of Fimreite in June 1184. That was when King Sverre and his peasant Birkebeiner (so-called because of their birch-bark leggings) defeated King Magnus Erlingsson and the nobility, a turning point in Norwegian history.

Taking a break on the Flåm to Myrdal mountain railway.

Cool, green waters

In **Luster** ㉔, to the northeast of Sogndal, is **Urnes Stavkirke** (UNESCO World Heritage Site; open June–Aug 10.30am–5.30pm and by appointment; entrance charge; www.lustertourist.com), thought to be the oldest stave church in Norway and linked with the coming of Christianity. Also within easy reach is yet another icy tongue from Josterdal glacier, called **Nigardsbreen**, where one of the delights is a boat trip over the ice-cold, green waters of a glacier lake.

BELOW: Urnes Stavkirke (stave church), high above Lustrafjorden.

South of Sogndal, Sognefjorden ends in the two most easterly fjords leading to Årdal and Lærdalsøyri, lovely valleys with mountain farms, plenty of opportunities for walking, climbing, or fishing in upland lakes and streams. The **Norsk Villakssenter** (Wild Salmon Centre; open May–Sept, hours vary; entrance charge) at **Lærdalsøyri** ㉕ provides an observation pool for wild salmon. Lærdal's one-time importance as an east–west trading route is evident at Gamle (Old) Lærdalsøyri, an area of beautifully restored 18th- and 19th-century listed building (open June–Sept; entrance charge).

Aurlandvangen, Flåm and Gudvangen lie along the innermost recesses of the fjord, which stretch south from the main fjord like an upside-down "Y". **Nærøyfjorden** ㉖ to the west is the narrowest in Europe and now a World Heritage Site. Both provide the most dramatic fjord cruise in west Norway, the mountains pressing so close that you wonder if the boat will squeeze through. Also not to be missed is the **mountain railway** ㉗ from Flåm to Myrdal, which spirals up the steep mountain gorge *(see page 241)*.

Life on the lake

If from Balestrand instead of heading inland you turn northwest, along Road 5/13 towards Førde and the coast, you come to one of the region's many lakes –

The replica Viking knarr (freighter) Saga Siglar in Sognefjorden before leaving for a two-year, round-the-world voyage.

BELOW: sunset lights up the slopes of Sognefjell.

Jølstravatnet – that penetrate the foothills of the high tops in the east and feed into the fjords in the west. On the south side lies the farm **Astruptunet** ㉘ (open May–Sept; entrance charge; tel: 57 72 67 82), home of the artist Nikolai Astrup (1880–1928) who found themes for his art in his own surroundings. Astruptunet is just as it was during the painter's life, though the barn has been replaced by a new art gallery with a permanent exhibition.

From Jølstravatnet, it is easy to reach **Grovebreen** (glacier), some 1,600 metres (5,250 ft) high, and Haukedalsvatn to the south is quite close to the far side of the glacier. Walkers can reach the great icefields of Josterdalsbreen. A series of valleys, lakes and fjords links these high plateaux into the Nordfjord system to the north.

After leaving Jølstravatnet the Jølstra, said to be one of the best salmon rivers in the area, drops hundreds of metres by the time it reaches **Førde** ㉙ on Førdefjord. Here you find the main **Sunnfjord Museum** (open June–Aug Mon–Fri 10am–6pm, Sat–Sun noon–5pm; Sept–May daily 10am–3pm; entrance charge; tel: 57 72 12 20), a collection of 25 restored buildings, 17 of which are reconstructed as a farmstead from around 1850.

Along the coast

The best view of Sunnfjord's hundreds of islands is from the high peaks in the east, though the coast itself is by no means flat. **Bleia** rises straight from the north side of Førdefjord to more than 1,300 metres (4,300 ft), the summit of the Sunnfjord Alps, and many of the islands have high peaks. These islands stretch the length of the coast, from Fensfjord and the island of Sandøy, north to Vestkapp (West Cape) where the Hurtigrute (coastal steamer) turns northeast to its next stop at Ålesund.

It's an odd thought that **Florø**, the only community in this large county big

enough to be called a town, should lie on the remote edge of the sea, but not so strange when you remember that Norway has always depended on the sea for food, trade and transport. The **Sogn og Fjordane Kystmuseet** (Coastal Museum; mid-June–Aug Mon–Fri 11am–6pm, Sat–Sun noon–4pm; Sept–mid-June until 3pm; entrance charge; tel: 57 74 22 33) in Florø has a fine collection of old boats. This most westerly town had its birth in the herring industry which flourished in the middle of the 19th century. Today, it still depends on the sea for fish, while oil and gas fields away to the west have, nevertheless, turned Florø into an oil centre.

Map on page 234

Offshore sights

There are many places to see: rock carvings at **Ausevik**, southeast of Florø; the nearby island of **Svanøy** with the ancient stone cross of St Olav, covered in runic inscriptions, a manor with an old garden and magnificent trees; a Romanesque medieval church on **Kinnøy**, where the Kinna Play, *Songen ved det store djup (The Song of the Great Deep)*, is performed by the county theatre group and local people, and draws thousands to the island each June.

To the north of Fløro, at the mouth of Nordfjorden, is the island of **Bremangerlandet** ⑳ with its **Vingen carvings,** which are even older than Ausevik's and show the lives of the fishing-settlers of Nordfjorden. Further north, the village of **Måløy** on **Vågsøy** is one of Norway's largest fishing and trading ports, and at Raudeberg fish of all kinds are salted and dried. But size is relative, and industry does nothing to detract from the rural quietness of this hilly island. Måløy features the Allied Monument, a 6-metre (20-ft) high granite obelisk raised in memory of 52 Allied soldiers who died during the Måløy raid in 1941.

North of Vågsøy and Raudeberg is **Silda**, a tiny island for sea-anglers, divers

In summer, it is possible to see sea eagles along the coast of Sogn og Fjordane. This is the furthest south that this magnificent bird of prey builds its nest.

BELOW: the sturdy *fjording* (fjord horse), typical of the region.

and bird-watchers. It has fewer than 30 inhabitants, no cars and, on an islet in the middle of the harbour, a restored fish-salting works serves a feast of seafoods. On the nearby island of **Selje** ❸ are the medieval ruins of **St Sunneva Kloster** (monastery). On the northernmost tip is **Vestkapp** where winds blow fiercely. Its closest neigbouring land is the Shetland Isles off the north of Scotland.

Inland along Nordfjorden

Hornindalsvatnet is Europe's deepest freshwater lake. Following the melting of the ice at the end of the last Ice Age, the Hornindal valley flooded to a depth of 514 metres (1,686 ft).

Nordfjorden is 100 km (60 miles) shorter than Sognefjord. With so many side-fjords, lakes and valleys it is easy to get into the mountains or make the journey up **Briksdalsbreen** ❷, one of the most beautiful glaciers in the fjord country. Even better is that you can climb up to the base of the glacier in the two-wheeled farm carriages, *stolkjærrer*, pulled by small, sturdy, cream-coloured *fjording* (fjord horses; details: Briksdalsbreen Tourist Information, tel: 57 87 68 00).

The traditional home of the *fjording* is the Eid district, centred around **Nordfjordeid**, where Nordfjorden proper has already divided itself into Eidsfjorden and Isefjorden. **Eid** ❸, which is also connected to the coast by Road 15, is famous for **Firdariket**, the seat of the last Viking chief, and the town has traditional white-painted buildings. The church, which dates from 1824, is decorated with beautiful **rose paintings**.

To the south of Eid, Road 1 crosses Utfjorden and then runs along Gloppenfjorden, which ends at **Sandane** ❹, the main town of Gloppen, the biggest farming district in the whole county and also a large fur-breeding centre. The **Nordfjord Folkmuseum** (open mid–May–mid-Sept daily 9am–4pm, mid-Sept–mid-May Sun 1–4pm; entrance charge) started in 1920 with five turf-roofed houses but now has more than 40 historic buildings, including a mountain *seter*.

BELOW: summer swimming in the cold fjord waters.

At the fjord side is a 100-year-old **sailing barge**, *Holvikjekta*, the last of the traditional freighters that served coast and fjord. There is also a fine adventure
centre, **Glopen Camping og Fritidssenter** (tel: 57 86 62 14), which offers a
week's programme of riding, canoeing, windsurfing, mountain and glacier walking, mountain cycling and sightseeing to various beauty spots.

Continuing east along Road 15 from Eid you come to Hornindalsvatnet, which
leads to Grodås, sited where the ground begins to climb. Hornindal valley has traditions in handicrafts and folk music, and musicians wear the black breeches, or the
long black skirt and green bodice of the area. The most famous artist here was
Anders Svor (1864–1929), first a woodcarver and then, after a time at the Copenhagen Academy of Art, a sculptor. The **Anders Svor Museum** (open May–Sept,
times vary; entrance charge; tel: 57 87 97 76) contains more than 400 sculptures.

Fjord end

Further east you reach the Inner Nordfjorden, where the fjord system ends at **Stryn
㊴**, **Loen** and **Olden**, the start of three spectacular valleys stretching up to the
northwest edges of the Jostedalsbreen. Nowadays, three tunnels out of the Stryn valley cut right through the mountain to the renowned Geirangerfjord to the north.
Stryn is famous for summer skiing on the northeast of Strynsvatn, where the ground
rises to Tystigbreen. Oldedalen is the route to Briksdalsbreen (glacier) from the
Briksdalsbreen Fjellstove; go by horse and carriage or on foot, and then a half-hour
walk leads to the great cascade of ice which hangs above the ice floes and the
green waters of the glacier lake. Small birds flutter over the water and, in past
times, farmers from eastern Norway drove their cattle over these great icefields
down into the kindlier valleys of the west.   ❑

Map
on page
234

*The town of Loen
suffers from severe
rockfalls. In 1905, a
piece of the
Ramnefjellet
mountain fell into the
lake and caused a
flood wave 50 metres
(164 ft) high that
killed 63 people.*

BELOW: the
Briksdals glacier,
part of the great
Jostedalsbreen.

MØRE AND ROMSDAL

Map on page 278

The county of Møre og Romsdal has a bit of everything: a jewel of a fjord, Geirangerfjorden; the Art Nouveau Ålesund; the peaks of Trollheimen, Home of the Trolls; and delightful islands to spare

For nearly a century the coastal steamers of the Hurtigrute have called at Ålesund, Molde and Kristiansund along the sea route that leads to Trondheim and the north. This part of Norway's jagged coastline is 6,000 km (3,730 miles) long; more than 10 percent of the county's population lives on islands. It's scarcely surprising then to learn that, even today, the sea is still the great provider for Møre og Romsdal. Prospecting and providing for the oil industry are the most important activities, and North Sea oil and gas are likely to become even more significant as Norway seeks new fields.

Looking at the jumble of coastline, islands and fjord mouths on a map, it is sometimes hard to distinguish where sea and islands end and fjord and mainland begin. Yet move inland and half the area lies above 600 metres (2,000 ft). In the southeast, the highest peaks reach more than 1,800 metres (6,000 ft). The county is divided into three municipalities: **Sunnmøre**, **Romsdal** and **Nordmøre**, of which the main centres are Ålesund, Molde and Kristiansund.

Sea trade has always been important and, from the Middle Ages, the accolade for a settlement was to be given *kaupang* (market) status. At that time there were just two: Borgundkaupangen, 5 km (3 miles) from the centre of Ålesund, in Sunnmøre; and Veøykaupangen, in Romsdal. Both were centres for north–south and east–west trade routes on sea and land. Today buses 3, 14, 24 and others marked Møre from Ålesund will take you to the **Sunnmøre Museum** (Open Air Museum and Coastal Heritage Site, Borgundkaupangen and Medieval Age Museum; varying opening hours; common entrance charge; tel: 70 17 40 00).

Rare harmony

Ålesund ❶ is Norway's largest fishing town but best known for its Art Nouveau architecture, built in 1904 after a great fire which destroyed the centre and which gave rise to the Norwegian saying: "I've never heard anything like it since Ålesund burnt down."

First to the rescue came the Norvegophile, Kaiser Wilhelm II of Germany, who sent four ships laden with supplies and building materials (the stained-glass windows in the gable end of the **church** were an inauguration gift from the kaiser) and German architecture students. With help and donations from all over Europe, the people of Ålesund and the students completed the rebuilding of the town by 1907 in the now carefully preserved Art Nouveau style. **Ålesund Museum** (open all year; entrance charge; tel: 70 12 31 70) features exhibitions on the 1904 fire and subsequent rebuilding.

Towers, turrets and medieval-romantic frontages, often with more than a trace of Nordic mythology, give the town a harmony which extends to the painted wooden warehouses along **Brosundet**, the deep inlet

PRECEDING PAGES: around Olden. **LEFT:** looking down into Geirangerfjorden. **BELOW:** Art Nouveau detail on a door in Ålesund.

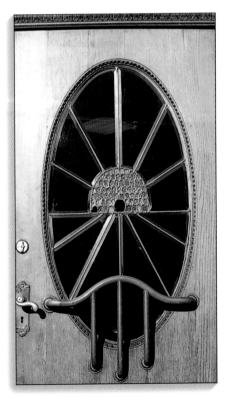

of the inner harbour. Until the 1950s, Ålesund was a veritable gold mine for fish, fishermen and their boats, and *klippfisk* (traditional Norwegian split, dried cod). But as fishing changed so did Ålesund, which added fish processing and fish farming. Many former warehouses are now offices and restaurants, pleasant places to try out one of the more unlikely local specialities. These include *bacalao*, a dish created in Portugal from Kristiansund's export of *klippfisk*, and the more traditional *brennsnute*, a potato and meat stew.

From the top of the 418 steps up **Aksla** hill in the centre of the town – if the climb doesn't leave you breathless, the view certainly will – you can see over several islands, now all linked by 12 km (8 miles) of deep underground tunnels. With great practicality, the builders used the rock from the tunnels to extend the airport on the nearby island of **Vigra**.

Every book and brochure that describes the county's thousands of islands shows similar happy pictures of people in, on or under the sea, and anglers with magnificent catches. There are sea caves, tunnels and bird cliffs, little harbours, camp sites, clean, white beaches and *hytter* (holiday lodges) to rent. Some have relics of the Vikings, many have summer festivals. What these sea islands have to offer is almost unlimited: the difficulty is which to choose.

Bird island

The island of **Runde** ❷, 67 km (42 miles) southwest of Ålesund, is not to be missed. Runde attracts professional and amateur naturalists from all over the world. More than 200 bird species have been recorded but this small island is best known for breeding birds, which line the cliffs in their hundreds of thousands. When they fly, it looks as if a gigantic swarm of insects has darkened the sky. One of the

Hauling the catch aboard just off the island of Rundøy.

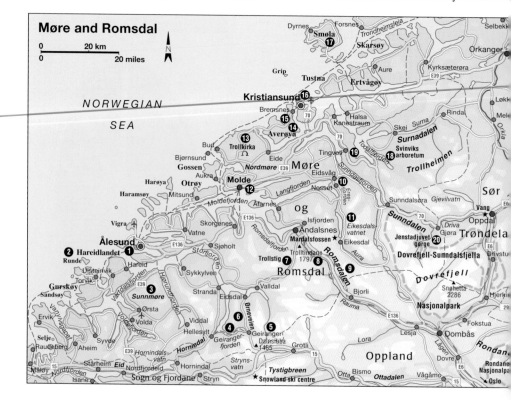

est ways of seeing the island is by taking a four-hour tour on board the *Charming Ruth*, which departs from Ulsteinvik harbour daily from mid-June to mid-August. As a bonus, in the waters round the island are interesting wrecks; not so long ago divers found a cache of gold from a Dutch ship, *Ackerendam*. An express boat/bus connection that takes 2½ hours leaves from Ålesund at 8.30am weekdays.

Map on page 278

Gateway to the Geirangerfjord

South from Ålesund between the Vartdalsfjorden and the Hjørundfjorden, the **Sunnmøre mountains ❸** plunge straight into the fjord near Ørsta, one of the early targets for the many British climbers who first made Norway's mountains known to the world.

Ålesund is also the main entrance to **Storfjorden**, where the cruise ships turn in to reach their goal of **Geirangerfjorden ❹**, claimed by many to be Norway's most beautiful fjord. One road (No. 60) to Geiranger goes through Stranda, main town of inner Storfjorden, another (No. 1) via Ørsta, both ending at **Hellesylt**. From there you can travel to the inner end of Geirangerfjorden by boat or, in summer, there is a path along the fjord's high southern wall.

In this most secret of fjords far from the sea, great waterfalls tumble in such delicate cascades that they are given feminine names – **De Syv Søstre** (The Seven Sisters) and the **Brudesløret** (Bridal Veil). Lofty mountains are reflected in the mirror-still water and, in some places, farms cling to unlikely pockets of green.

The spectacle is much too beautiful to miss and everyone stays on deck until the boat reaches **Geiranger ❺**, which huddles under the half circle of mountains. Halfway up the winding road behind the village is the appropriately named **Hotel Utsikten Bellevue**, which has one of the best views in Norway, and further on the

One way of sampling the full range of Norwegian cuisine is to visit Ålesund in August, when it plays host to the annual Den Norske Matfestivalen (Food Festival; late August; tel: 70 15 76 25).

BELOW: the coastal town of Ålesund seems to float on the water.

road passes by **Dalsnibba**, the highest peak in Sunnmøre. To reach the wild valley of **Norangsdalen**, drive from Hellesylt to **Øye**, where you'll find the classic wooden Hotell Union Øye, a car ferry over the fjord and more stunning views.

Along the troll road

Heading north once more (along Road 63) towards Åndalsnes, the first stretch to Eidsdal on the Norddalsfjord is known as the **Ørneveien** ❻ (Eagle's Road), and it is not difficult to see why as it winds ahead to **Ørnesvingen**, another vantage point. Over the fjord is the start of an even more spectacular road across the **Gudbrandsjuvet** gorge. Mountains rise into the distance to the west, until you reach the top of **Trollstigen** ❼ (the Trolls' Ladder or Trolls' Causeway). This is the heart of inner Romsdal. To the east is Trolltindane, around 1,800 metres (6,000 ft), and this fascinating mountain range can be admired before or after the journey on Trollstigen. From vast amounts of snow up here (even in July) it is only a short but exciting 15-minute journey down through 11 gigantic bends hewn out of solid rock into the green valley towards Åndalsnes.

Åndalsnes is known as "the village between fjell and fjord". It sits on a promontory in a circle of fjord and mountain, looking up to tops that challenge climbers of every nationality. They arrive by the score to tackle **Trollveggen** (Troll Wall), part of craggy **Trolltindane** ❽, which rises almost vertically from Romsdalen in the east, to its summit bowl of permanent snow. Trollveggen itself has more than 1,000 metres (3,300 ft) of vertical and overhanging rock, first climbed in 1965. New routes are still being discovered. By less hazardous paths, the climb up Trolltindane takes around four hours and requires boots and strong clothing.

Åndalsnes is the terminus for the train from Oslo through **Romsdalen** ❾ to Trondheim, which brings enough visitors each year to double or treble the population. A 19th-century British traveller, Lady Beauclerk, described Romsdalen as "precipitous, grey rocks ending in points apparently as sharp as needles… emerging into the sunniest, and the most lovely little spot… sheltered from every wind by the snowcapped mountains that surrounded it, while a most tempting river ran through the dale". It is as true today as it was then.

Famous climbers

The pleasant valley was the base camp for early climbers such as William Slingsby and Johannes Vigdal who, in 1881, made the first ascent of **Store Vengetind**. In the same year, another early Danish pioneer, Carl Hall, made the second ascent with two local climbers to the sharp point of **Romdalshornet**. It had first been conquered 50 years before by two local farmers.

To cater for all this early interest, a local police sergeant, Anders Landmark, opened a simple wooden inn at **Aak**, regarded as Norway's first tourist hotel, and many of Europe's mountain addicts stayed there. Some 5 km (3 miles) into the valley from Åndalsnes, it has recently reopened as a mountain sports centre, with summer courses in climbing and scrambling and, in winter, instruction in ice climbing and mountain (or Telemark) skiing. Rafting and canoeing are also good possibilities on the Rauma River, one of Norway's well-known fishing rivers, which runs through the valley. But it is not necessary to be a rock climber to get high into these mountains. Most have easy alternative routes, and roads reach more than 850 metres (2,800 ft).

Map on page 278

Back to the coast

Proceeding back towards the coast and Molde along Road 64, it is worth taking a detour into Langfjorden until you reach **Nesset** ⑩ on Eresfjorden, deep into the mountains. Norway's prominent 19th-century writer and patriot Bjørnstjerne Bjørnson, who had a summer home in the area, described the Nesset mountains: "some standing white, others standing blue, with jagged, competing, agitating peaks, some marching along in ranking row."

The view today from the ferry along the **Eikesdalsvatnet** ⑪ shows you what he meant. The mountain peaks rise abruptly out of the fjord sides, and you get a glimpse of **Mardalsfossen**, northern Europe's highest waterfall at over 650 metres (2,000 ft) high. In the 1970s, hundreds of people chained themselves together near the waterfall, to prevent the building of a hydroelectric power station. It became a hot political issue and, though they did not win the final battle, the protesters ensured that the summer falls still exist. The struggle also brought the unexpected gift of making Nesset famous and encouraging climbers and other visitors.

Molde ⑫ is part of an archipelago sheltered from the Norwegian Sea; its mild climate, green vegetation and rose gardens earn it the title "Town of Roses". The statue of the Little Rose Seller stands in the marketplace. Stalls sell everything from fruit and vegetables to clothes and, of course, roses. This modern and easygoing town was almost entirely rebuilt after German bombing in World War II. It is an excellent base for touring the fjords by boat or car. From **Varden**, Molde's

BELOW: transporting hay the traditional way on a mountain farm in Romsdal.

When rough weather comes in from the west, the coastal Atlanterhavsveien (Atlantic Road) lives up to its name.

best vantage point, you look over fjord and island to the snowcaps of the Sunnmøre mountains – townspeople claim you can see 87 peaks – and half an hour away to the north are small fishing villages which brave the worst of the west winds.

Molde has the inevitable outdoor museum, the **Romsdalsmuseet** (open mid-June–mid-Aug, hours vary; entrance charge; tel: 71 20 24 60), which includes the Hjertøya Fishery Museum – in a particularly beautiful spot where the timber houses, national costumes and folk dancing seem to fit in with the landscape. The museum's collection of *bunads* (national costumes), showing the fine details of shawl, head-dress, bodice, jewellery and embroidered purse, is one of the most appealing. The Fishery Museum (open mid-June–mid-Aug; tel: 71 20 24 60), 10 minutes by boat from the marketplace, is in the form of a small fishing village from the 1850s.

Yet there is little that is traditional about Molde's entertainment. The modern stadium is well used, with an all-year football ground located, spectacularly, by the sea, and the streets are often full of musicians, particularly during the famous **Molde International Jazz Festival** (mid-July; tel: 71 20 31 50).

Another fine route is to take roads 64 and 664 from Molde to the 16th-century village of **Bud**, right on the west coast. Here a boat trip goes to the old fishing station of **Bjørnsund**, now only inhabited in the summer. Before Bud, a walk from Road 64 reveals **Trollkirka** ⓭ (Troll Church) – a cave, some 70 metres (230 ft) long, divided into three sections, with a great waterfall tumbling down from the upper opening into a white marble basin in the mountains.

Travelling the Atlantic Road

BELOW: the harbour at Torvik on the island of Averøya.

From Bud a small coastal road leads back to Road 64 and the **Atlanter-havsveien** (Atlantic Road) to Kristiansund, over **Averøya** ⓮, the biggest island

in the area. As this road heads north across the rim of the ocean, it's a bit like driving on the sea itself. Averøya deserves more than the view from a car window.

Archaeologists believe that this was one of the first places to be settled after the last Ice Age, and their finds in 1909 are remnants of the early **Fosna Culture** that existed around 7000 BC during the Stone Age. ("Fosna" was the original name of Kristiansund.) One of the best ways to get around is a 50-km (30-mile) tour which varies from seaward skerries and small islands linked by bridge or causeway, to hills around 500 metres (1,600 ft) high. There is a fine stave church at **Kvernes** (open July–Aug 10am–5pm; entrance charge) with an unusually richly decorated mid-17th century interior in homage to shipping.

Near **Bremsnes** **⑮**, on the northeastern tip of Averøya, is the Viking **Horgsteinen** (Stone of Horg), where the victor of Hafrsfjord, Harald Hårfagre, had his famous hair cut and washed, having fulfilled his vow not to touch it until Norway was united. It is just 15 minutes by ferry from Bremnes to Kristiansund.

The *klippfisk* capital

Unlike Ålesund and Molde, **Kristiansund** **⑯** has little protection from the worst the North Atlantic can do. It is right on the coast, with weather-beaten rocks pounded by the sea, yet not far inland are grassy areas and small woods. This is the *klippfisk* town, for long the biggest exporter of Norwegian dried cod. There are only 17,000 inhabitants but, because of the centuries-old links with other countries thanks to its sailors and fishermen, and the foreign merchants who settled here, the atmosphere is quite cosmopolitan.

Like most Norwegian towns with "Kristian" in their title, Kristiansund was named after a Danish King, Christian VI, who gave it town status in 1742. A

Map on page 278

BELOW: the Vågen Kystkultur Museum (Coastal Culture Centre) on the waterfront at Vågen, Kristiansund.

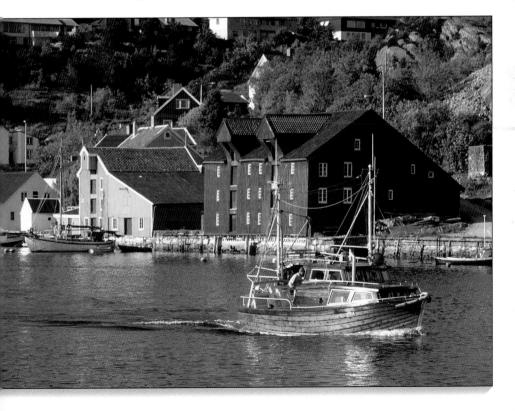

A Country Afloat

To the world, Norway and seafaring are synonymous; the very word Viking means "Men of the Bays". From the age of sail until after World War II, the Norwegian merchant fleet was one of the world's largest, and Norwegian could be heard in ports worldwide.

Among the country's most popular museums by far are the Sjøfartsmuseum (Maritime Museum) on the Bygdøy peninsula in Oslo, along with the Vikingskipshuset (Viking Ship Museum), with magnificently preserved long ships, the Kon-Tiki Museum, with the rafts used by ethnographic explorer Thor Heyerdahl, and the Frammuseet (Fram Museum), built around the sturdy vessel that carried Fridtjof Nansen and Roald Amundsen on their heroic polar explorations.

Norwegians seem happiest when they are in, on or around the sea. Each year, over a third of the population spend their summer holidays partly or completely in craft that range from small dinghies to large motor launches and ocean-going yachts. Even the most conservative estimates place the number of pleasure craft in Norway at 650,000, about one for every seven Norwegians. The sea is a natural part of life.

Geography and topography are the deciding factors. There are thousands upon thousands of islands, and the fjords and coastal archipelagos are a paradise for competitive and recreational sailors, king and commoner alike.

King Olav V, the father of the present King Harald, was, in his day, the country's foremost sailor in more than name only. He won a gold medal in sailing in the 1928 Olympics, making him the world's only Olympic medallist monarch. He also won medals in the Sailing World Championships in 1971 and 1976.

In founding its first sailing club in 1868 in Tønsberg, then a major merchant fleet port, Norway triggered a long latent urge. In 1883 the Royal Norwegian Sailing Association was formed in the capital, and in 1900 sailing became an Olympic sport. Norwegians were a major force in Olympic and championship sailing and in regattas worldwide.

By chance, Norway's leading position in international sailing coincides approximately with the country's yacht production. In the days of wooden yachts, Norwegian shipyards and naval architects were among the world's best, and one in particular stands out: born in the port of Larvik, Colin Archer (1832–1921) grew up with boats and at an early age started building craft to his own design. Among his best known are the stable, sturdy rescue schooners that bear his name and the three-masted Arctic exploration vessel *Fram*, built in 1892. The tradition of boat building continues to this day, albeit somewhat altered: fibreglass hulls and masts changed the picture completely. Nowadays, Norway exports motor cruisers and imports yachts.

Wherever there's water, there are all manner of motor and sailing craft. Small boat harbours in and near major cities, particularly Oslo, Kristiansand, Ålesund, Stavanger and Bergen, never fail to impress visitors by the numbers and types of crafts lying there. From windsurfing in fjords to major regattas, Norwegians love being on the water. ❑

LEFT: relaxing after a day's sailing.

good introduction is by *sundbåtene*, the harbour boats which for more than 100 years have linked the town's islands. **Mellemverftet** (open Mon–Fri 8am–7pm; tel: 71 58 70 00), once one of four shipyards in **Vågen**, is working again as a centre for preserving the craft of shipbuilding, carefully restoring the beautiful lines of traditional Norwegian boats.

Kristiansund consists of three islands. One of them is **Innlandet**, the oldest preserved part of the town with its first customs house (1660–1748), hospital, school and other buildings which are being restored. Walk to the **Sjursvika** on the east side for a look at the old warehouses. These interesting parts of the harbour are being amalgamated into a coastal culture centre, to tell the history of the maritime people of old, alongside harbour life that continues today.

The **Nordmøre Museum** (open Tues–Fri 10am–2pm, Sun noon–3pm; entrance charge; tel: 71 58 70 00) includes archaeological finds from the Fosna culture and the history of *klippfisk* processing. But the town's oddest monuments are the tall pointed natural stones, tributes to town dignitaries: Bäckstrøm, who built the reservoirs, Brinchman, the provider of the water supply, Bræin, the musical founder of a musical family, which gave birth to an annual Opera Festival, and Hanson, the polar explorer.

Kristiansund's main church was destroyed by bombing in 1940. The architect responsible for its replacement named his creation "Rock Crystal in Roses", and whether you love it or loathe it, you cannot ignore this stark, white building. Inside **Atlanterhavskatedralen** (Atlantic Ocean's Cathedral; open all year), the choir wall is a 30-metre (100-ft) sweep of 320 stained-glass panels which at the foot symbolise the heavy, dark colours of the earth soaring up to eternal light.

Island excursions

An entirely different church stands on the island of **Grip**, northwest from Kristiansund. The island has a long and eventful history of flood and storm, and the islanders often took refuge in the small church. In 1796, a nor'wester tore down and washed away 100 houses and, when the same thing happened seven years later, the pastor recorded the piteous prayer: "Almighty God, spare us further destruction and misery." Whether it was that plea or not, the ancient little red stave church survived, only 8 metres (25 ft) above the sea. Once 400 souls lived on Grip, scraping a living from fish: today people live there only in summer when it metamorphoses into a holiday island and makes a popular excursion from the town. A wedding in the 15th-century church is a very special occasion.

To the north and northeast of Kristiansund, the last big island is **Smøla** ⑰, at the mouth of the Trondheimfjord, where the county ends in a gaggle of islands which retain something of the life of the old farmer-fishermen.

Sanden is one of several buildings that form Smøla's scattered museum, with the main 18th-century building, warehouses, barn and a storehouse on wooden pillars, just as it was when the last owners left a few years ago. A number of these old fishing grounds where cod was split, salted and dried on the rocks are now marinas with simple accommodation,

Map on page 278

"Fishwife", next to the harbour in Kristiansund.

BELOW: fishing for trout or salmon is a popular pastime in the country.

Map on page 278

seafood menus, and the atmosphere of earlier days. The idyllic island of **Kuli** off Smøla is rich in relics, the most famous being the Kuli stone. On this stone the name Norway is mentioned for the first time in an inscription which dates to the first years after the coming of Christianity.

Land of the trolls

Inland, the northern part of the county ends in a crisscross of fjords eating into the islands and peninsulas which lead to **Trollheimen**, the "Home of the Trolls", where the mountains reach nearly 1,600 metres (5,000 ft). This haunt of climbers and skiers is bounded by two important valleys, **Surnadalen** and **Sunndalen**, with between them the tiny **Todalfjorden**. Beside the last is the surprise of the **Svinviks Arboret ⓲** (arboretum; open mid-May–mid-Aug; entrance charge; tel: 71 66 35 80), beautiful gardens with thousands of plants, including rhododendrons and conifers. Despite the northern latitude, plants from all over the world grow at Svinvik, owned and run today by the University of Trondheim.

On the way to Sunndalen along Road 70 from Kristiansund, you come to **Tingvoll ⓳**, which has Nordmøre's oldest church, popularly known as the **Nordmøresdomen** (Nordmøre Cathedral; open June–Aug; entrance charge), in an area with a large selection of churches from different centuries and styles. The Tingvoll church is believed to date from the 12th century; it's a well-preserved granite and brick structure surrounded by a stone wall with an arched entrance way.

Sunndalen is deep in the Nordmøre wilderness, with narrow valleys between the mountain ranges forming sheltered farming country which supplies grain for most of the county. At the end of the fjord lies the industrial town of Sunndalsøra, once a mecca for the British "salmon lords": the **Leikvin Kulturminnepark** (heritage park; open mid-June–Aug; entrance charge) at Grøa records their privileged position in society up to the end of the 19th century. The River Driva debouches into the fjord and the surrounding mountains are of breathtaking beauty – a magnificent area for walking and skiing as well as fishing.

Road 70 follows the course of the valley to Oppdal on the third side of Trollheimen. On foot, there are more energetic routes over the mountains, with a mountain centre in Innerdalen and ski lifts as well. The **River Driva** is one of the most famous in a country of good salmon and trout rivers. Between the head of Sunndalen and Grødalen, next door at Åmotan, the spectacular **Jenstadjuvet ⓴** (gorge) is the place where five valleys and their watercourses meet in two furious waterfalls. Grødalen has an oddity in **Alfheim**, a small hunting lodge from 1876 built in Scottish Highland style by a Scot, Lady Arbuthnott, who became something of the "laird" of the valley. Her old farm at Elverhøy is now the **Sunndal Museum** (open June–Aug; entrance charge; tel: 71 69 61 80).

To the north, Surnadal has another good salmon river, the **Surna**; side valleys lead up to the heart of Trollheimen, and to signposted trails from mountain hut to mountain hut, in what seems like the top of the world. At valley level, the road through Surnadal is the inland route out of west Norway, straight on to the city of Trondheim, the gateway to the north. ❑

BELOW: in autumn, mountains and forests are bright with berries.
RIGHT: De Syv Søstre (Seven Sisters), Geirangerfjorden.

TRONDHEIM

Although the city has lost its political role, to many Norwegians it remains the country's historical, cultural and religious capital, and is host to the annual celebrations of its patron saint, St Olav

Map on page 292

A thousand years ago, Trondheim, then Nidaros, was the capital of Norway, and the resting place of King Olav Haraldson. Founded in 997 by King Olav Tryggvason, a reminder of Trondheim's early days and of the old harbour is provided by the **wharves** and the narrow streets *(veitene)* which run between the wooden buildings. Though they date back only to the 18th century, these coloured warehouses echo the architecture of medieval times, and it is not too difficult to feel what the atmosphere must have been like around that busy harbour when fish and timber dominated the city.

Today, Trondheim is the home of SINTEF, Scandinavia's largest foundation for scientific and industrial research, and is at the forefront of Norwegian education and church affairs. Not far from SINTEF is the Norwegian University of Science and Technology (NTNU), the country's second-largest university. The city has been a scientific centre since the 18th century – the **university museum**, from 1760, is Norway's oldest scientific institution – and today both SINTEF and the university attract high-tech businesses to Trondheim, with the advantage of being able to turn to the research establishments for help.

Modern though it may be, Trondheim has retained much of the charm of the past, with the heart of the old city lying on what is virtually an island between the **Nidelva River** and **Trondheimsfjorden**, joined only by a narrow neck of land to the west, once the western fort. One building that unites past and present is the **Nordenfjeldske Kunstindustrimuseum** **B** (National Museum of Applied Art; open all year; entrance charge; tel: 73 80 89 50) on Munkegata.

Saint and martyr

Though King Olav Tryggvason had attempted to introduce Christianity to Norway in the late 10th century, many Norwegians still clung to their pagan gods, and it was only after the death of his successor, Olav Haraldson, at the Battle of Stiklestad some 30 years later *(see page 297)* that Christianity acquired a focal point in Norway. Olav's men buried him in sandy ground near the river but when miracles began to happen he was moved to the town's only church. Then, according to the sagas, a spring began to flow near his first grave and "men were healed of their ills by the waters". The king was declared a saint and martyr in 1164. His nephew, Olav Kyrre, built the great stone church over the place where the saint's body had lain; which is now **Nidarosdomen** **C** (cathedral; open all year; to book tours tel: 73 53 91 60; entrance charge includes entrance to Archbishop's Palace), which is Trondheim's finest building. Once again, the saint's body was moved and the cathedral became a place of pilgrimage. For centuries, pilgrims came from the south

PRECEDING PAGES: Trøndelag countryside in autumn.
LEFT: gutting the catch.
BELOW: looking out over the city to Trondheimsfjorden.

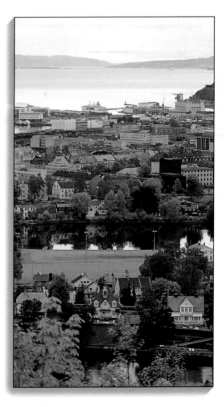

of Norway, from Sweden and Finland, and from Iceland, the Faroe Islands and Greenland to pay homage to St Olav. When the Reformation came to Norway in 1537, the cult of the ancient relic was abolished and pilgrimages ceased. From mid-June to mid-August, a special musical evening mass is held for visitors.

Royal tradition

Until the Reformation, Nidaros Cathedral was the seat of the archbishop, and the setting for the coronation of Norwegian monarchs, a tradition revived after 1814, when Norway shrugged off its 400 years of Danish rule and united with Sweden. In 1991 King Harald V was crowned in Nidaros Cathedral. The **crown jewels** are on display in a side chapel (open June–Aug Mon–Fri 10am–4pm, Sat 10am–2pm, Sun 1–4pm; Aug–June times vary).

The **great arched nave** is in a Gothic style and, looking back to the west end, the most striking feature is the brilliant stained-glass **rose window** above the main entrance, the work of Gabriel Kjelland in 1930. Both inside and out there are many statues of saints and monarchs; but the beautiful interior lines of the cathedral, built in a green-grey soapstone, are its finest feature.

Next door to the cathedral is Scandinavia's oldest secular building, once the **Erkebispegården** ❷ (Archbishop's Palace; open mid-June–mid-Aug Mon–Fri 10am–5pm, Sat 10am–3pm, Sun noon–5pm; mid-Aug–mid-June times vary; entrance charge). In 1222, Archbishop Guttorm was empowered by King Håkon Håkonsson to mint and circulate coins, a privilege which his successors exercised until 1537 and the Reformation. Their mint was uncovered in the 1990s when the museum was rebuilt after fire and is a highlight. A new Crown Regalia Exhibition also features royal crowns, sceptres and details of the monarchy. The building was

Trondheim is the site of the world's first bicycle lift, "Trampe", built on Brubakken hill in 1995. It operates like a ski tow. Cyclists pay using keycards at the bottom and are pulled 130 metres (430 ft) to the top.

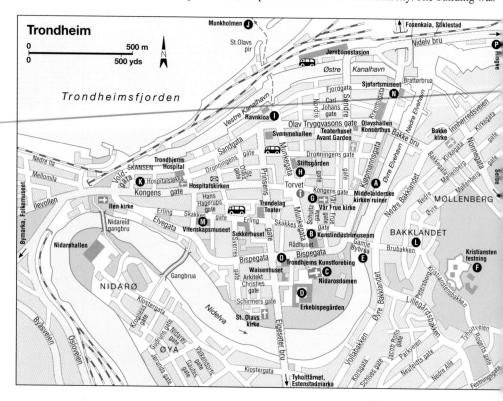

at one time a military establishment, and the **Rustkammeret** (Army Museum; open June–Aug Mon–Fri 9am–3pm, Sat–Sun 11am–4pm; entrance charge) includes exhibits on World War II and the resistance movement. Nearby is **Waisenhuset**, a beautiful timber building dating from 1772, originally an orphanage.

All around the original medieval city are the remains of fortifications, which were reinforced or built in the late 17th century by a military architect from Luxembourg, General Johan Caspar de Cicignon, after the great fire of 1681 devastated most of medieval Trondheim.

From the cathedral area it is just a short walk to **Gamle Bybrua** ⓔ (Old Town Bridge), also erected after 1681 when de Cicignon was constructing **Kristiansten festning** ⓕ (Kristiansten Fort) on a hill to the east, at that time outside the city proper. The first bridge had a sentry box and excise house at either end and the western building still remains, now used as a kindergarten. The present bridge and gates were built in 1861. The local tourist office (tel: 73 80 76 60) organises guided tours to these sites.

Map on page 292

Gamle Bybrua (Old Town Bridge) offers good views of the warehouses along Kjøpmannsgate.

View over the city

Kristiansten Fort, now part of the city, provides one of the best views of Trondheim. From here you can see the old stone walls of the 13th-century **Vår Frues Kirke** ⓖ (Church of Our Lady; open Wed 11am–2pm, concerts held Sat 2pm from Aug–May) and **Stiftsgården** ⓗ (open June–Aug Mon–Sat 10am–5pm, Sun noon–5pm; entrance charge), Scandinavia's largest timber mansion, on **Munkegata**. Stiftsgården was built as a private house in the 1770s and today serves as the official residence of the Norwegian royal family when visiting the city.

Northeast from the bustling harbour of the **Ravnkloa** ⓘ at the northern end

BELOW: colourful old buildings along Trondheim's waterfront.

of Munkegata, and past the ornate railway station, is **Fosenkaia**, where sightseeing and other boats tie up. At midday, the Hurtigrute coastal express *(see page 261)* will be lying at one of the two main quays, with a half-day to spend in Trondheim before it heads north. Returning south on a summer evening, the ship is outlined against the light as its passengers make an excursion to see the midnight sun from the summit of **Mount Storsteinen**. The remains of Trondheim's old defences, **Skansen**, lie to the west where the city gate once stood. Skansen is now a park. Also near the harbour is a curious warehouse built out on iron stilts over the sea; its shape is explained by the fact that it was a World War II U-boat bunker when German forces occupied the city.

Well out into the fjord is the islet of **Munkholmen ❶** (hourly ferry from Ravnkloa; open late May–Aug; entrance charge) where Benedictine monks built a monastery very early in the 11th century, one of the first two monasteries in Norway. Even earlier this had been Trondheim's execution ground and in 1658 it became a prison fort. You can make a tour of the fort and the island offers good sea bathing and a restaurant.

St Olav, who introduced Christianity to the Vikings.

BELOW: a good way to get around the city in the snow is by *sparkstotting* (kick-sledge).

Walking around

Trondheim is an easy walking city where many people still live in the centre. Two places best toured on foot are **Hospitalsløkka ❸**, the area around the old Trondheim Hospital, and **Bakklandet ❹**, on the eastern side of the Nidelva, not far from the old town bridge and opposite the river-side warehouses.

In the grounds of the hospital, which was founded in 1277 and is Scandinavia's oldest surviving hospital, lies the first **octagonal timber church** (1705) to be built in Norway. The surrounding area *(løkka)* is full of old timber houses, lovingly restored by their present owners. Bakklandet is another area of old wooden houses, and was originally the working-class section of the town. It and the Mollenberg and Rosenborg districts have been restored to form complete communities of houses and shops.

Looking into the past

For an understanding of the past of this ancient area of Trøndelag, two museums are invaluable. At the **Vitenskapsmuseet ⓜ** (Museum of Natural History and Archaeology; open May–Sept Mon–Fri 9am–4pm, Sat–Sun 11am–4pm; Sept–Apr Tues–Fri 9am–2pm, Sat–Sun noon–4pm; entrance charge) the main exhibits trace the history of the area up to the Middle Ages, and the development of church furnishings from the 13th to the 18th century. There is also a display covering Trøndelag flora and fauna. **Sjøfartsmuseet ⓝ** (Maritime Museum; open June–Aug 10am–4pm; entrance charge), situated in an old penitentiary from 1725, covers shipping, fishing and whaling.

Trøndelag Folkemuseet (bus 8 or 9 from Dronningensgate; open June–Aug daily 11am–6pm; Sept–May Mon–Fri 11am–3pm, Sat–Sun noon–4pm; entrance charge) in Sverresborg, on the west side of the city, looks at life in days gone by. Here, more than 60 reconstructed buildings from the Trondheim area are centred round a market square, including a post office and dentist's surgery. There is a stave church dating from 1170 and exhibits of old trades and crafts, such as *passementerie* (the making of trimmings and lace for women's Sunday best). Within the museum are the remains of King Sverre's palace, **Zion**, from around 1180, and the 18th-century tavern has a good restaurant. There is also a Sami Museum.

Trondheim also has Norway's oldest theatre building, **Trøndelag Teater**, in the centre of the old town, as well as **Teaterhuset Avant Garden**. Other arts are represented by galleries and institutions such as the **Trondhjems Kunstforening** ⭕ (Academy of Art; open June–Aug Mon–Fri 10am–4pm, Sept–May times vary; entrance charge; tel: 73 52 66 71), showing and selling contemporary paintings.

Of great interest is the **Ringve Museum** ❶ (Museum of Musical History, Ringve; buses 3 and 4 from Munkegaten; opening hours vary; entrance charge; tel: 73 87 02 80). The museum is in an ancient manor. A permanent exhibition opened in 1999 in the former barn. Here, light and sound guides you through various historic stations, such as "the invention of the piano" or "pop and rock". Since the late 19th century, it belonged to the Bachke family. In 1946, the last representative, Christian Anker Bachke, died and his widow, Russian-born "Madame Victoria", worked steadily to build up the couple's collection of musical instruments from all over the world. Her persuasiveness in prising relics from many countries is legendary and when the museum opened in 1952 the collection had grown magnificently. A selection of the instruments are played by the music-student guides during the tour. In addition to the more formal, classical instruments, there are examples of music boxes, old folk instruments such as the *langeleik*, a sort of Norwegian zither, and clay flutes shaped like birds and soldiers.

Just before her death in 1962, Madame Victoria opened the museum's concert hall, which seats 270; it was built into the old cow sheds and is used for formal

Map on page 292

The Ravnkloa clock by the fish market.

BELOW: Trondheim is a major stop for the Hurtigruten coastal steamers.

Map
on page
292

TIP

For a bird's-eye view of the city from the 124-metre (406-ft) telecommunications Tyholttårnet (tower; open all year; entrance charge) take buses 20 or 60. There is also Norway's only revolving restaurant.

BELOW: an old view of Stiklestad by Johannes Flintoe for an 1839 edition of the *Norse Sagas*.

musical occasions. After the museum, stroll around the **Ringve Botaniske Hage** (Botanic Gardens; open daily), just next door, one of the most northerly botanical gardens in the world (Trømso being the most northerly, *see page 323*).

Outdoor life

Trondheim's back garden is **Bymarka** to the west, where Gråkallen (Old Man) at some 520 metres (1,700 ft) is the city's favourite skiing area. In summer, it is a good spot for walking. Its counterpart to the east is **Estenstadmarka**.

Fishing is good in the River Nidelva, which is renowned for the size of its salmon. The Gaula to the south is another fine fishing river, while the fjord itself is ideal for sea fishing from boat or shore.

As well as the hourly boats to Munksholmen, in summer the tourist office runs 1½-hour tours of Trondheim from the sea, which leave from Ravnkloa at 2pm; there is also a two-hour tour of Trondheim, which takes in a number of sites and museums, departing daily at noon next to the tourist information office. You can also visit the ancient manor of **Austråtborgen** (open May–Aug; entrance charge) at Ørland on Trondheimsfjorden. Another idea is to take a short leg of the Hurtigrute and return by bus or train. Alternatively, you can travel southeast to the **Strikkemuseum** (Knitting Museum; open all year; entrance charge) at Selbu, which shows the history of the famous Selbu knitwear from 1853. Road 705 to Selbu features a particularly scenic route marketed as **Ferieveien** ("holiday road").

For most people Trondheim means history and culture. Like the pilgrims of old, visitors come to see the cathedral, the Archbishop's Palace and de Cicignon's 17th-century city, and for historical events such as the annual 10-day **St Olav festival** at the end of July *(see opposite page)*. ❑

Stiklestad

Stiklestad is a name that is revered by Norwegians. A momentous battle on this site in 1030, at which King Olav - Haraldson died at the hands of King Canute, was a turning point in Norwegian history. For Stiklestad, 100 km (60 miles) north of Trondheim, saw the foundation of Norwegian national unity and the adoption of the Christian faith. A church marks the spot where Olav died.

In the 11th century Norway was a country constantly disrupted by disputes between rival chieftains, and Olav's ambition was a united Norway. He also aimed to create a Christian country with Christian laws and churches and clergy.

He was not the first to attempt this. In the previous century Olav Tryggvason (a descendant of Harald Hårfagre) had been converted to Christianity in England and confirmed by the Bishop of Winchester. He returned to his native land in 995 with the express purpose of crushing the chieftains and imposing his new-found faith. But Olav Tryggvason's conversion had not swept away all his Viking instincts and in his religious zeal he used great cruelty to convert the populace. As a result, he fell in the Battle of Svolder in the year 1000, due to the defection of some disenchanted Norwegian chieftains.

Olav Haraldson was also a descendant of Harald Hårfagre and he ascended the throne in 1015. But, like his predecessor, Olav foolishly made too great a use of the sword to establish Christianity. The result was the same: with his eye on the Norwegian throne, King Canute of Denmark and England gave support to discontented factions within the country and in 1028 invaded Norway, forcing King Olav to flee to Russia.

Undaunted, King Olav returned with a few followers, but whatever loyalty he had once inspired had been lost through his ruthless methods. He died on 29 July 1030 at the Battle of Stiklestad. Olav's corpse was taken to the then capital, Nidaros (Trondheim) and buried on the banks of the River Nidelva. When the body was disinterred a year later by the bishop, it showed no signs of decay: his face was unchanged and his nails and hair had grown, at that time taken as a sign of sanctity.

Following this revelation, Olav was proclaimed a saint and his body placed in a silver shrine in Nidaros Cathedral. Faith in the holiness of King Olav – or St Olav as he now was – spread and, until the Reformation, his shrine became a goal of Christian pilgrims.

Canute's triumph at the Battle of Stiklestad was brief. He ceded the reins of power to his son Sweyn but, as the rumours of Olav's sanctity grew, support for Canute evaporated and Sweyn was exiled to Denmark in 1035. All the while, St Olav's son, Magnus, had also been in exile, in Russia. Norway now invited Magnus to return and accept the crown.

Stiklestad has been a place of pilgrimage ever since. People still come at the end of July to commemorate the battle. Stiklestad has a beautiful open-air theatre, and on the anniversary of the battle, a cast of more than 300 actors, choristers, dancers and musicians re-enact the events of July 1030. ❑

RIGHT: a statue of St Olav in front of the Stiklestad open-air theatre.

NORTH, INTO THE ARCTIC

North of Trondheim lies a beautiful but often harsh landscape,
caught between the warm sea and the mountains inland, and cutting
across it an imaginary border into the vast expanse of the Arctic

Map on page 302

T he city of Trondheim is the gateway to the north. But anyone who looks for an immediate change in scenery will be disappointed. The first county north of Trondheim, Nord Trøndelag, has wide areas of rich agricultural land and with prosperous-looking farms. Running right up the middle of the county is Norway's north to south jugular, the E6 highway, which lures drivers ever further north. But this is also rail country, and the Nordland railway follows much the same route. Just north of Trondheim, a branch line (with a companion road) reaches over the border into Sweden. It veers off at the small village of **Hell**, whose station must be one of the most photographed in the country and whose tickets are collectors' items. In June, Hell hosts an annual Blues Festival, which attracts international stars to this otherwise quiet settlement.

From a motorist's point of view, there is not a great deal of interest along this section of the E6 and the inclination is to keep going north; but make time for **Værnes ❶**, which has an interesting church from the Middle Ages with a fine baroque pulpit. Adjoining that is the **Stjørdal Open-air Museum** (open mid-June–mid-Aug Mon–Wed and Fri 11am–4pm, Sun noon–4pm; entrance charge; tel: 74 82 70 21). The **Frostatinghaugen rock carvings** at Frosta are the site of the first Norwegian legislative assembly (AD 600–1000) with rock carvings going back a further 3,500 years.

Some 6 km (4 miles) east of Stjørdalshalsen on the E14 is the **Falstad Museum** (open Jan–Nov; entrance charge; tel: 74 02 80 40) at Levanger. Located in the main building of Norway's only SS concentration camp, the memorial includes two execution sites and a cenotaph in the Falstad forest. About 4 km (2½ miles) further on lies **Hegra Festning** (fort; open June–Aug 11am–5pm; entrance charge). Built following independence, it was the site of several battles during World War II as well as a 25-day German siege. The fort has been restored and includes a Resistance museum.

St Olav's battleground

Just north of Verdalsøra is the road to **Stiklestad ❷**, the battleground where King Olav Haraldson was killed in 1030, and revered by Norwegians as the birthplace of Norwegian national unity *(see page 297)*. The **Nasjonale Kultursenter** (National Arts Centre; open all year; entrance charge; tel: 74 04 42 00) in Verdal produces an annual open-air play about St Olav (end of July), a spectacular dramatisation of the battle and Olav's death. The centre also has exhibitions about local natural and cultural history, and includes a Resistance museum, a folk museum with 30 buildings and Stiklestad Church from 1180.

The first town of any size north of Trondheim is **Steinkjer**, which has been a centre of commerce for

PRECEDING PAGES:
Arctic reflections.
LEFT: the turbulent waters of the giant maelstrom south of Bodø.
BELOW: a favourite subject for English-speaking photographers.

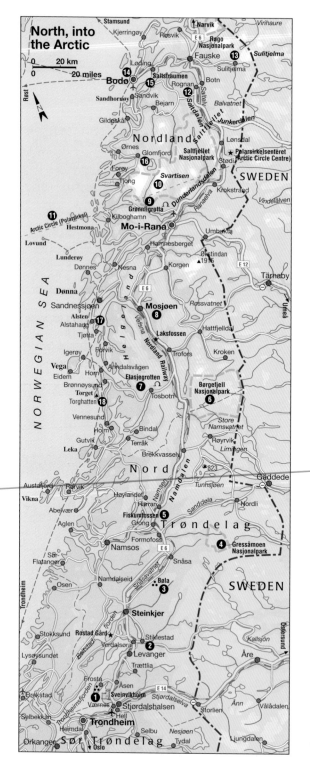

North, into the Arctic

more than 1,000 years. Like so many northern Norwegian towns, Steinkjer was destroyed in World War II. After the German invasion in 1940, the king and government moved north, eventually to Tromsø, before they left to continue the government in exile from London. This meant that these sparsely populated northern areas suffered dreadful destruction through the bombing which followed the German invasion

The Nord Trøndelag county museum has two branches near the town, one of which is sited in the former factory of **Dampsaga** (open all year; entrance charge) and features some works by the Norwegian painter Jacob Weidemann (born 1923), who also decorated Steinkjer's church with murals and a beautiful stained-glass window.

North of Steinkjer it is worth branching off the E6 onto Road 763, which runs along the eastern side of Snåsavatnet (lake), to take a look at the impressive rock carvings near **Bøla** ❸ (open May–Oct). Of these, the best is the 6,000-year-old Bøla reindeer. The scenery around the lake is remarkably soft and gentle for a latitude between 63- and 64-degrees north, and at its northern end is **Snåsa**, the centre of south Sami (Lapp) culture. It has a Sami school and cultural centre which includes a museum (open June–Aug; entrance charge; tel: 74 15 15 90).

To the east, about 50 km (30 miles) away and close to Sweden, the **Gressåmoen Nasjonalpark** ❹ contains an area of typically thick Trøndelag forest and mountain landscape.

Dotted throughout Norway – and particularly in the north – are small towns or villages which are essentially crossroads for many forms of transport. Typical is Grong, where the E6 runs north to south and the road and railway to Namsos, on the coast, goes off to the west, while just south of the town the secondary road, No. 74, runs east through wild countryside to the Swedish frontier at Gaddede. It is also the junction of two rivers, the Namsen and the Sanddøla, both popular with anglers. Each river has an impressive waterfall not far from Grong: to the north, **Fiskumfossen ❺** on the Namsen and to the south, **Formofossen** on the Sandøla. You can learn all there is to know about salmon at the **Namsen Laks-akvarium** (aquarium; open June–Aug; entrance charge) at Fiskumfossen.

Map on page 302

Touched by the Gulf Stream

This is the beginning of the long valley of **Namdalen**, while to the northeast is **Røyrvik**, a huge mountainous area which stretches to the Swedish frontier. Half this region is above the tree line and there are three major lakes: Tunnsjøen, Limingen and Store Namsvatnet. The first has an island peak soaring to 812 metres (2,660 ft), and was once a Sami place of sacrifice to their gods.

Here the contrast between the east and west of Nord Trøndelag is very marked. The frontier mountains to the east, which bulge into Sweden, have a harsh beauty but much of the land is desolate and empty. To the west, the coastal scenery is a pleasant surprise, green and fertile. All year round, the Gulf Stream warms the western coast to the very north of Norway, making the climate much gentler at the same latitude than it is further inland and allowing the Hurtigruten (coastal steamers) to continue working even in the depths of winter.

The north end of Namdalen valley marks the border with the county of **Nordland**, the beginning of the real north. This border is straddled by the **Børgefjell Nasjonalpark ❻**, a district of high mountains, lakes and numerous watercourses – a backpacker's idyll for walking and to see nature.

Nordland stretches 500 km (300 miles) north to Narvik. The Polarsirkel (Arctic Circle) runs through the middle and the county includes the long, narrow islands of Vesterålen, and the grey peaks of the Lofoten Islands *(see The Far*

The Bøla reindeer.

BELOW: a picnic on the coast by the light of the midnight sun.

North, pages 315–18). Nordland has immense variety. If you take in all the fjords and islands, it contains a quarter of Norway's coastline, as well as mountains more than 1,900 metres (6,200 ft) high, countless islands and skerries, the second-largest glacier in Norway, Svartisen, and the largest inland lake, Røssvatnet.

Near the Helgeland coast is **Bindalen** (valley), green with forests. At one time, the discovery of gold turned it into a mini-Klondike. Today, it has gone back to sleep. Close to Bindal is the mountain massif of **Tosenfjellet**, a favourite haunt of potholers and cavers. The biggest cave is **Etasjegrotten** 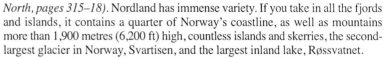, which is 1,400 metres (4,600 ft) long, where cavers have discovered an underground lake.

Between Trofors and Mosjøen on the E6 is the wide but shallow **Laksfossen** (waterfall) which has a 16-metre (50-ft) drop. At **Mosjøen** 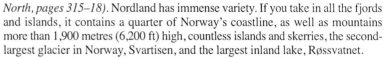, an industrial town where a splendid location fights for domination with a large aluminium works, there is **Dolstad** church, built in 1735 and the oldest octagonal church in north Norway. Look closely at the traces of the old ornamental decor and at a wooden angel in the ceiling which is lowered for use as a baptismal font. Near the church is the **Vefsn Open-air Museum** (open July Mon–Fri 10am–3.30pm, Sun 11am–4pm; Aug–June Mon–Fri 10am–3.30pm; entrance charge; tel: 75 11 25 30). Founded in 1909, it brings together 12 buildings from the surrounding district and a collection of some 5,000 objects from the old days of farming, fishing, hunting and domestic life.

Last stop before the Arctic

Beyond the town the scenery changes as farmland gives way to bare mountains (*fjells*). There are camping sites with tents and cabins on both sides of the road north to cater for the outdoor holidaymakers who especially love these northern regions. **Mo i Rana** is also on a fjord and, like Mosjøen, is dominated by industry – in this case, former steelworks of Norsk Jernverk, now privatised. These industries in small remote towns may displease the casual visitor but they illustrate a Norwegian determination to minimise the pull of the more populated south and to help people to find work locally.

Though Mo i Rana itself may be too modern for a visitor's taste, it is within reasonable distance of several "must sees" – caves, a glacier and the Polarsirkel (Arctic Circle). The **Grønnligrotten** 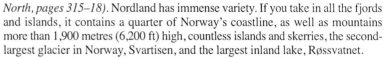 (caves; open June–Aug; entrance charge; tel: 75 13 92 00) lie about 20 km (12 miles) north of the town and guides shepherd parties 40 minutes through a glittering underground world of stalactite-hung caverns. At **Setergrotta** the cave calls for care and is more suitable for enthusiasts, with unexplored caves, crevices and passages, and interiors of marble and limestone.

From Mo i Rana, it is easy to reach Norway's second-largest glacier, **Svartisen** 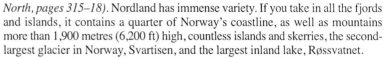 (The Black Ice), which covers 370 sq. km (140 sq. miles) over two separate glaciers, east and west side. It is also one of the lowest-lying glaciers on the European mainland, reaching down to within 170 metres (560 ft) of sea level. The route lies off the E6 32 km (20 miles) north of Mo i Rana, which heads northwest to Svartis Lake. You then cross the water by boat, and walk about 3 km (2 miles) to the glacier.

TIP

The best time to see Norwegian waterfalls is in late May, or even June this far north, when summer creeps northwards melting the snow and ice to swell the rivers.

BELOW: on the edge of the glacier.

Crossing the line

Many try but few have managed to explain why it is so exciting to cross a line you cannot see. But most people experience an inexplicable thrill and sense of achievement as they cross the **Polarsirkel ⓫** (Arctic Circle). It seems to mark the end of modern comforts and the beginning of the wild north, and nowhere is that sense of entering the unknown stronger than on highway E6 on its long trek north.

Map on page 302

From Mo i Rana, the road makes its way through the temperate landscape of Dunderlandsdalen, past Storsforshei iron-ore mine. Then, beyond Krokstrand, the scenery begins to change as the road approaches **Saltfjellet**, a wild and majestic mountain valley flanked by bare, brooding mountains. Apart from the road, railway line and river, there is nothing else until you come to the monuments that mark the Arctic Circle. Alongside the official markers are numerous small stone cairns erected by visitors who felt a common need to mark the event. A short visit to the architecturally pleasing **Polarsirkelsenteret** (Arctic Circle Centre; open May–June and Aug 9am–8pm; July 8am–10pm; Sept 10am–6pm; tel: 75 69 02 40) is a good way of celebrating the moment. The centre provides information on the flora and fauna, the climate and Sami culture – and also sells souvenirs. Nature, it would seem, cannot be left to its own devices.

There is a darker and sadder side to this area, which dates back to World War II when thousands of prisoners of war, mainly Yugoslavs and Russians, were used to build the railway. Many perished in the bitter winter conditions, and their memorial stands in the wild mountains where they worked and died.

The summit of the Saltfjell road, at **Stødi**, is 700 metres (2,300 ft) high; these mountains mark the limit for most temperate flora and fauna, though a few brave exceptions survive. As the road begins to descend, first the trees re-appear

BELOW: reindeer have right of way on the roads.

at Lønsdal and then, as it races down towards sea level at Rognan, the vegetation becomes lush and abundant but flanked by impressive mountains on either side. About halfway down, a detour to the right and a steep climb to **Junkerdalen** takes you to the "silver road", a historic route from Skellefteå on the Gulf of Bothnia in Sweden, to Bodø. This dramatic mountain scenery also leads to a remarkable botanical phenomenon. A bedrock of mica, which provides exceptional growing conditions, has led to a profusion of rare plants such as cyclamens, usually found only in lowland or more temperate regions. Nowhere else can you find similar growth at this height and nearly 67 degrees north.

At **Rognan ⑫**, the **Saltdal Museum** (open mid-June–Aug daily 11am–5pm; entrance charge) includes the ominously named **Blodveimuseet** (Blood Road Museum; open mid-June–Aug daily 11am–5pm; tel: 75 50 35 00), the only museum in Norway dedicated to prisoners of war. The 1,657 Yugoslav, Russian and Polish prisoners who died here in World War II are buried in a cemetery a little further north at **Botn**. Though these prisoners slaved to build a road and not a railway, the result was the same and the stretch between Rognan to Fauske earned the name of the "blood road". In another cemetery nearby 2,700 German soldiers are buried and a plaque commemorates the 1,932 who died on the battle cruiser *Scharnhorst*, sunk off Nordkapp (North Cape) in 1943.

Copper, silver and gold

Fauske, on the Skjerstadfjorden, is another crossroads town. The ever-present E6 goes north to south, while another road (No. 830) disappears east towards the mountains. It stops at **Sulitjelma ⑬**, which owes its existence to the discovery of copper by a Sami in 1858. The mines go down to 400 metres (1,300 ft) and

The area around Fauske provides the unique reddish marble known as Norwegian Rose, which has been used to decorate major buildings all over the world, including the United Nations building in New York.

BELOW: landscape in Nord Trøndelag.

produced half a million tonnes of ore a year. Copper pyrites, sphalerite and iron pyrites were extracted from the ore, plus a useful haul of silver and gold.

For many years, a railway was the only link between Sulitjelma and the outside world, but when that closed the road was built over the former track-bed. The wild and desolate mountain scenery of this remote area is dominated by the **Sulitjelma glacier**. Scenery like this and the mining museum (open June–Aug; entrance charge; tel: 75 64 02 40) at Sulitjelma make a detour worthwhile, and there is tourist accommodation and a camping site.

In this narrow part of Norway – and even more so as the road heads north – you are never far from either the sea or the Swedish border. At Fauske, midway between both, Road 80 and the railway turn west and run along the north of the fjord to Bodø, on the west coast.

End of the line

Bodø ⓮ is another marker along the way to the far north. Like many of the coastal towns, it began as a small community, a safe place for boats and fishermen, and stayed small until the 1860s, when three changes brought prosperity: the herring fisheries developed fast, the Sulitjelma mines started production, and the first coastal steamer service began to link the towns of the west coast. It, too, was largely laid waste in attacks by German forces in May 1940 and today it is a spacious modern town with a population of around 45,000.

Bodø is the commercial and administrative centre of the area. It is also a staging post for summer visitors, the end of the Nordland railway line, where the backpackers get down and continue north by coastal steamer or bus. The midnight sun can be seen in Bodø from 2 June to 10 July. The town is home to the **Norsk Luft-**

Map on page 302

The winter colours of the Arctic fox stand out against the summer landscape.

BELOW: sunset over the Sulitjelma mountains.

Aeroplanes on display at Bodø's Norsk Luftfartssenter (Norwegian Aviation Centre).

fartsmuseum (Norwegian Aviation Centre; open all year; entrance charge), which includes U2s, Spitfires, Mosquitos, a flight simulator and even an old traffic control tower. Forty km (25 miles) to the north on the coast is the old trading centre at **Kjerringøy** (open late May–Aug; entrance charge). Long overtaken by Bodø, Kjerringøy was one of the richest trading settlements in northern Norway in the 19th century. It has 15 preserved buildings, all with their furnishings, and some typical Nordland boats.

South, away from the E6

If you are travelling north on the E6, largely an inland route, when you reach Bodø again on your return journey, take another route south even though it takes in innumerable ferry crossings. Road 17 starts by bridging the **Saltstraumen ⑮**, where the combination of powerful currents and a narrow channel twice a day creates a vast rush of water, and violent "kettles" or whirlpools. This is the most powerful maelstrom in Scandinavia, some 370 million cubic metres (480 million cubic yards) of water pour through the sound which is less than 15 metres (50 ft) wide, at a rate of up to 28 knots. Saltstraumen is a joy to anglers and seabirds alike, as the current brings an abundance of fish. Nearby is the **Saltstraumen Opplevelsessenter** (Experience Centre; open May–Sept; entrance charge) which explains the phenomenon in depth.

The road follows coast and fjord on its way south, and passes **Våg** on the island of Sandhornøy, and **Blixgård** (manor house; open June–Aug; entrance charge) which has a memorial to the poet Elias Blix.

At **Glomfjord ⑯** a chairlift gives wonderful views and you can also reach an arm of the Svartisen glacier (Norway's second largest). However, it is better to keep to Road 17, which goes through a major tunnel under the outer edge of the glacier and comes out alongside Nordfjorden, cross the Holandsfjorden and then walk to the base of the glacier.

BELOW: puffins are very common on the northern coasts.

Four ferries later, the road reaches **Sandnessjøen**, on the northern tip of the island of **Alsten**, a trading centre for more than 300 years. **Alstahaug ⑰** on the southern point has a 12th-century church and memorial stone to the parson-poet Petter Dass who lived there from 1689 until his death in 1707. Dass was so well known that, after his death, most Norwegian ships carried a black patch on their sails as a badge of mourning, a practice that continued for more than 100 years. Today, his life and work are commemorated by a biennial event organised by the **Petter Dass Museum** (open June–Aug daily 10am–5pm; entrance charge; tel: 75 07 50 91) at Alstahaug.

A short ferry crossing takes you to the island of **Dønna**, where **Dønna Manor** has been an estate from saga times until the present day. The 13th-century stone church has secret passages cut into the walls which revealed a hoard of coins, some dating back to the time of King Håkon Håkonsson (1204–63).

On the eastern side of Alsten is a mountain range with seven peaks known as **De Syv Søstre** (The Seven Sisters). South of Sandnessjøen is **Tjøtta** which was the home of Hårek, one of the chieftains who killed King Olav at Stiklestad. This entire area is full of burial

Map
on page
302

mounds and monoliths. There is a cemetery for 7,500 Russian prisoners of war, and equally heart-rending is the **Riegel Cemetery**, which has the graves of more than 1,000 of nearly 3,000 Russians, Germans, Poles, Czechs and Norwegians who died when *Riegel* was sunk in 1945 outside Tjøtta, destroyed by Allied aircraft unaware of its human cargo.

Old hat

Further south near Brønnøysund, and after two more ferry crossings, is another strange natural phenomenon. The high hat-shaped peak of **Torghatten** is pierced 160 metres (520 ft) up by a great hole more than 40 metres (130 ft) high. Legend has it that the hole was made by a horseman, thwarted in love, who shot an arrow at his lady, the Maid of Leka. Just in time, the mountain king of Sømnafjellet saw what was happening and threw his hat in the air to intercept the arrow.

At that very moment the sun rose and all were transformed into stone. The Maid of Leka stands petrified on the island of **Leka**; Torghatten has its hole; and to the north is the island of Hestmona to represent the horseman. A more prosaic explanation lies in the action of frost and sea towards the end of the last Ice Age when the island was much lower than it is today. A small road takes you to Torghatten, from which it is a 30-minute scramble up to the hole.

The Brønnøysund area has some of the most fertile land and the largest farms in northern Norway. The island museum of Leka has many curiosities, including boats and fishing equipment. South of Leka is **Vikna**, linked to the mainland by a bridge over the Nærøysund, which, so the old legends relate, was the battleground of giants and trolls. After one more ferry, Road 17 deserts the coast and moves inland through Namsos until it joins the E6 just north of Steinkjer. ❏

BELOW: Bodø lit by the midnight sun.

LAND OF THE MIDNIGHT SUN

Some of Norway's most stunning natural wonders lie within the Arctic Circle and are a prime target for tourists visiting the north in summer

The phrase "Land of the Midnight Sun" was originally coined by the French American explorer Paul Belloni Du Chaillu (*c.* 1831–1903), who published a travelogue by the same title in 1881 after travelling extensively in northern Europe. The name caught on: more than 100 years later, tourists still flock to the North Cape every summer to experience this natural spectacle.

The midnight sun is the appearance of the sun above the horizon at midnight. The phenomenon is due to the inclination of the Earth's axis, and to the fact that the axis points in the same direction during the whole period of the Earth's yearly revolution around the sun. It may be witnessed at any point on the Arctic Circle on 21 June or on the Antarctic Circle on 21 December. Within these circles the length of time the sun is in the sky without setting gradually increases, being 76 days at latitude 70° and 134 days at latitude 80°. For six months, the sun never sets at the poles.

WINTER DARKNESS

Of course, the down side to the phenomenon is that during the winter the sun never appears above the horizon and thus all regions within the polar circles are plunged into darkness as they experience a long polar night. In Tromsø this period of darkness lasts from 26 November to 15 January, while the midnight sun can be seen from 20 May to 22 July. For the people of the north, the midnight sun is not so much a phenomenon as a way of life.

▷ **AURLANDSFJORD**
At the head of enchanting Aurlandsfjord is Flåm and the start of the 10-km (6-mile) mountain railway up to Myrdal.

◁ **PREIKESTOLEN**
Preikestolen (the Pulpit Rock) soars 280 metres (920 ft) above Lysefjord. The view stretches towards Stavanger and the fjords.

▽ **GLACIER WANDERING**
The Jostedal glacier is the largest glacier on the European continent. The ice can be up to 230 metres (750 ft) thick in parts.

THE NORTHERN LIGHTS

▷ **BRIKSDAL GLACIER**
One of Jostedal's more famous sidearms is the Briksdal glacier, accessible from April to October. The glacier lies at the end of the beautiful Olden valley.

▽ **FOLGEFONNA GLACIER**
Near Sorfjord (below) is the Folgefonna glacier, Norway's third largest, which offers magnificent views of the surrounding fjords and mountains.

The northern lights, or *aurora borealis*, are a huge natural light show, filling the winter sky with patterns of light and colour.

In medieval Europe this remarkable phenomenon was thought to be reflections of heavenly warriors; we now know that it originates from electric particles sent out into space by the sun. These are drawn into the Earth's magnetic field where they collide with other particles in our atmosphere. The resulting electric charges give rise to the greenish patterns of light which dance across the night sky.

The sun has a number of holes in its corona from which high-energy particles stream out. These particles are ejected into the solar system as solar wind, which meets the Earth's magnetosphere, compressing it on the daylight side, while drawing out the tail at night.

The solar wind particles accelerate to Earth along the open magnetic fields of the polar regions. When the particles collide with air molecules their energy is transferred into light. These processes occurring simultaneously result in the northern lights.

◁ **WATER POWER**
Norway's rapids and waterfalls are very important commercially: Norway is self-sufficient in electricity from hydropower. They also provide recreation opportunities for fishing, kayaking and white-water rafting.

THE FAR NORTH

For many, the aim of travelling this far north is to visit Nordkapp, Norway's northernmost tip; along the way you can go island-hopping in the Lofotens or cross the expanse of the Finnmarksvidda

Viewed from the mainland across the broad expanse of Vestfjorden, the **Lofoten Islands** present an imposing wall of jagged peaks rising up sheer from the sea. On the west these mountains form a mighty breakwater from the onslaught of the Arctic Ocean, a 112-km (70-mile) archipelago which stretches from the tiny island of Røst in the south to the waters of the narrow Raftsundet in the north. In winter the coast is one of the stormiest in Europe, while the unsurpassed summer beauty of the islands makes them one of Norway's major tourist attractions. The midnight sun is visible from 27 May until 17 July.

Between the mountains, which are composed of some of the oldest rocks in the world, are stretches of fertile farmland, fjords and deep ravines while the coastline is sprinkled with fishing villages and one or two small towns.

A phenomenon peculiar to the Lofotens is the annual cod fishing which in the past involved up to 6,000 boats and 30,000 fishermen. Between January and March these migrant fishermen lived in simple waterside wooden cabins called *rorbuer*. By 1947 the number of fishermen was declining and today it is down to 2,000, and this seasonal event has been replaced by a year-round fishing fleet. In the summer, the cod is left to dry on traditional wooden racks by the harbour.

Svolvær ❶, the main town on the island of Austvågøy, has been a trading centre since the 17th century. Surrounded by water, and confusing to the visitor on that account, it is flanked by sharp, pointed rocky peaks. Some of these rise almost straight up from the gardens and the town has its own special mountain, the Svolværgeita ("Svolvær goat").

Svolvær is connected to the mainland by ferry to Skutvik, and by coastal steamer and air to Bodø. It, like the Lofotens as a whole, has attracted many artists and craftsmen and is now the site of the **Nordnorsk Kunstnersentrum** (North Norwegian Artists' Centre; open all year; entrance charge). Scenes like those described above are captured on canvas by local artist Dagfinn Bakke who owns and runs a gallery here (open May–Aug), while at nearby **Kabelvåg ❷** there is an art school and an impressive wooden church which looks old but was in fact built in 1898.

Payment in fish

On the outskirts of Kabelvåg is the **Lofotmuseet** (Lofotens Museum; opening times vary; entrance charge; tel: 76 06 97 90), sited where Vågar, the first town north of the Polarsirkel (Arctic Circle), existed in the Middle Ages. In the 14th century, 80 percent of Norway's national export was stockfish, allowing Vågar a broad market and cultural exchange with Europe. The main museum building was originally in the centre of the thriving fishing community and one room is furnished as a fish station owner's office from the 1880s.

PRECEDING PAGES: Røst in the Lofoten. **LEFT:** small boats and *rorbuer* (old fishing cottages) in Stamsund. **BELOW:** island fisherman.

Many of the old rorbuer on the Lofotens have been restored and fitted with modern conveniences and are rented out to summer visitors.

He would own all the *rorbuer* and the fishermen who rented them would pay in fish from their catches. There is a typical *rorbuer* from 1797, with its primitive and crowded living conditions, and a boathouse with three traditional boats of various sizes. Another building is devoted to the development of the Lofoten fishing industry, which in its modernised form plays a vital role in the economy of the islands.

Kabelvåg gained a new attraction in 1989 with the opening of the **Lofotakveriet** (aquarium; open Feb–Nov; entrance charge), which is designed as a small fishing village, and includes both salt- and freshwater fish and a seal tank.

Island hopping, Norwegian-style

To journey south on the E10 means going from island to island, all of which, bar one, have gradually been linked by impressive bridges. The one remaining ferry connection was replaced by an undersea road tunnel in 1990. This route must rank as one of the most outstanding in Norway. At every turn the traveller is confronted with another seemingly haphazard series of jagged peaks possessing a stark beauty which contrasts with the green scenery at sea level.

On the southern tip of Austvågøy is **Henningsvær**, one of numerous Lofoten fishing villages and home to the Karl Erik Harr Gallery. The imposing bridge over Gimsøystraumen, 840 metres (2,760 ft) long, provides access to the small island of Gimsøya. From here a second bridge takes the road across Sundklakkstraumen to Vestvågøy. **Stamsund**, on a secondary road, is a coastal village and a port of call for the coastal steamer.

The **Vestvågøy Museum** (open June–Aug Mon–Fri; entrance charge; tel: 76 08 49 00) is at Fygle, near Leknes, and has exhibits showing how the fisherman-farmer's life has changed over the years. **Leknes** is the main centre of population

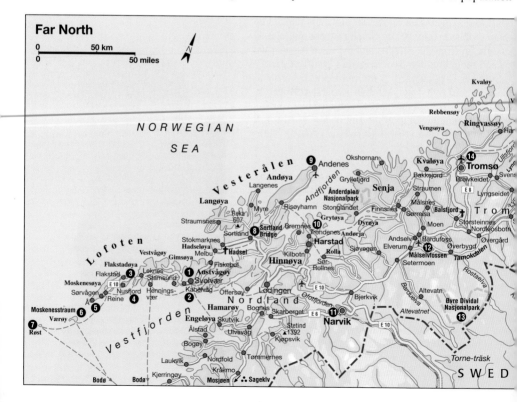

Far North

0   50 km
0   50 miles

NORWEGIAN SEA

on the island and a typical small Norwegian town with a long straggling main street. A few miles south at Lilleeidet was the ferry to **Flakstadøya**, which was replaced by a tunnel that goes 50 metres (165 ft) below the surface of Nappstraumen.

The west coast of Flakstadøya provides the surprise of wide **sandy beaches**. On a sunny summer's day, the sight of children paddling belies the fact that it is in the Arctic. The hamlet of **Flakstad ❸** has a pretty 18th-century church with an onion dome, while nearby are monuments to those who died in World War II and fishermen whose lives were lost at sea. **Nusfjord ❹** and Sund are two other fishing villages on the island. The former is on UNESCO's list of preservation-worthy environments while Sund has a small fisheries museum (open June–Aug; entrance charge). One section is devoted to early marine engines while the adjoining smithy is used by Petra Gjertsen, whose husband Hans was noted for his stylishly crafted steel cormorants. Also on the island is **Storbåthallaren**, the oldest known Stone Age settlement in northern Norway, populated 6,000 years ago.

The last bridge takes the road across to the island of Moskenesøya. This also has its quota of fishing villages of which the most picturesque is **Reine**. The road clings close to the coast and looks across the Vestfjorden.

Ending at Å

The E10 finally runs out at **Å ❺** – aptly named, as "Å" is the last letter of the Norwegian alphabet – which marks the end of the line of peaks that make up the **Lofotenveggen** (Lofoten "wall"). It has one of the few trading posts to be preserved in its original condition. There is the small **Fiskevaersmuseum** (Fishing Village Musuem: open all year, closed weekends Sept–June; entrance charge) in a 19th-century barn, and a café opposite offers coffee and home-made cakes.

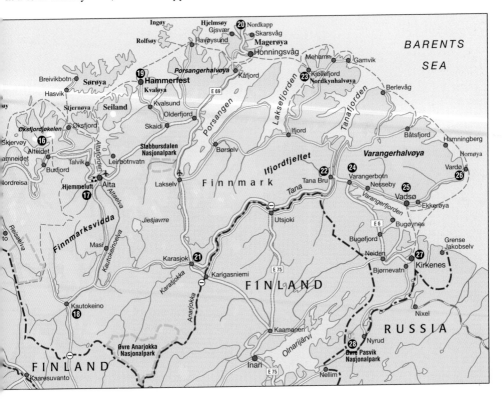

TIP

Whale safaris are very
popular, so it is worth
booking in advance.
Trips leave from
Andenes, Stø and
Nyksund and last 3–5
hours. If you don't spot
a whale first time
around, repeat the
journey for free.
Details from the tourist
information office
in Svolvær, tel:
76 06 98 00 or visit:
www.whalesafari.no.

BELOW: a statue
looks out to sea
from Leknes on the
Lofoten island of
Vestvågøy.

Beyond the tip of Moskenesøya is the **Moskenesstraumen** ❻, a maelstrom which may not match the Saltstraumen near Bodø but which was once greatly feared by sailors. Even in calm weather it seethes and boils and was made famous through the works of Jules Verne, in *20,000 Leagues Under the Sea*, and Edgar Allan Poe. The maelstrom separates Moskenesøya from the small island of **Værøy**, beyond which is the even smaller island of **Røst** ❼. These are the "bird islands", which attract thousands of different species including puffin, auk, eider, guillemot, kittiwake and cormorant. Both islands have small airfields with scheduled flights to Bodø, obviating a sea trip which, because of the rapidly changing sea conditions, can be unpleasant. Thanks to the Gulf Stream, Røst or Værøy do not have severe winters and sheep can graze on the meadows.

Vesterålen: home of the Hurtigruten

North of Svolvær the views may be splendid but they do not quite measure up to those in the south. The road keeps close to the Austnesfjord, beyond which, to the northeast, is Raftsundet and the narrow **Trollfjorden**, which is used by the coastal steamer in summer. At Fiskebøl the ferry takes the visitor away from the Lofotens to **Melbu** on the first of the Vesterålen Islands, **Hadseløya**. As if to emphasise that you have left the Lofotens behind, Melbu has the **Vesterålen Museum** (open all year; entrance charge; tel: 76 15 75 56), housed in an Empire-style manor house.

Between Melbu and Stokmarknes on the northern side of the island is **Hadsel Kirke** (church; 1824), distinctive in style and with an altarpiece from 1520. **Stokmarknes** is the headquarters of the Vesteraalen Steamship Company, founded by Richard With, sometimes called the father of the coastal steamer. At the **Hurtigruten Museum** (open mid-June–mid-Aug daily 10am–6pm; mid-

Aug–mid-June Sat noon–4pm, Sun–Fri 2–4pm; entrance charge), you may buy special Hurtigruten tickets for return trips to Svolvær.

Map, pages 316–7

From whaling to whale safaris

The Hadsel bridge carries the main road to the island of **Langøya**. Here the principal town is **Sortland**, a commercial centre with a fishing harbour that has a busy and pleasant atmosphere. The western side of the island has imposing mountains, the most unusual being the sway-backed **Reka** at 620 metres (2,000 ft), which is popular with climbers.

The **Sortland Bridge ❽**, 950 metres (3,150 ft) long, is the link to **Hinnøya**, Norway's largest island, which hosts a popular festival every June in Harstad. Away to the northwest is the long island of **Andøya**, which is also connected by bridge and, unlike most other Vesterålen islands, is flat. Much of the land is peat, renowned for its cloudberries. **Andenes ❾**, at the northwestern extremity, is a large fishing village with the **Polarmuseet** (Polar Museum; open late-June–mid-Aug; entrance charge; tel: 76 11 54 32). It was a fishing village in the Middle Ages and then a Dutch whaling base in the 17th century. Today, it is one of the starting points of the famous **whale safaris** (see "Tip" opposite).

Hinnøya's varied scenery includes farmland along the coastal fringe, green valleys, rugged mountains and fjords. Following the E10 southeast from the Sortland Bridge you come to Lødingen on the eastern coast, with a ferry service to **Bognes** on the mainland and the E6. A little further to the north is **Trondenes ❿**, which has a 13th-century stone church (open all year). In the bay below there are Viking burial mounds. Also here are the **Adolfkanonen** (Adolf Cannons; open June–Aug, or call Harstad Tourist Office; tel: 77 01 89 89),

The Sortland Bridge, one of the many stunning bridges between islands in the Lofoten and Vesterålen archipelagos.

BELOW: morning service at Hadsel Kirke (church), Vesterålen.

massive long-range guns installed by the Germans during World War II to protect the approaches to Narvik.

A final lengthy bridge carries the E10 over **Tjeldsundet** and on to the mainland, with the road skirting Ofotfjorden, which provides deep-water access to Narvik.

If the Lofoten and Vesterålen islands are ignored the only alternative way north is by the E6. From Fauske it clings to the side of fjords, going through a succession of tunnels, with the **Rago Nasjonalpark** away to the east. This is a vast mountainous area with no roads, judged to be the most magnificent but least accessible of all Norway's national parks.

A superb section of highway has been built from Sommarset, where formerly there was a ferry, which cuts across exciting mountainous country. There are several tunnels, the longest being below the Sildhopfjell. North of Kråkmo, at **Sagelv**, there are 5,000-year-old rock carvings of reindeer. At Ulvsvåg a road goes off west to **Skutvik** for the ferry to Svolvær. The road continues on to Engeløya island which was a seat of power many centuries ago and there are numerous graves and burial mounds, the biggest being at **Sigarshaugen**.

Back on the E6, a little north of **Bognes**, are more rock carvings depicting 40 different subjects. To the east of Tysfjorden is a mountainous section popular with climbers, especially **Stetind**, 1,392 metres (4,567 ft) high, which is called the "world's greatest obelisk". There are many caves for those who prefer to go down rather than up, the best known being **Råggejavie**, 620 metres (2,000 ft) deep.

Narvik

The deep, ice-free waters of the Ofotfjord allowed **Narvik** to become a major centre for exporting iron ore mined in northern Sweden. A railway was com-

BELOW: Rus students celebrate their graduation from the gymnasium in Sortland, Vesterålen.

pleted from the mining town of Kiruna to the port in 1883. Narvik is now the end of the Ofotbanen line, the Norwegian railway connecting with the northern Swedish line. In World War II Narvik was the scene of bitter fighting and German forces occupied it for over five years – portrayed in the **Krigsminnemuseum** (War Museum; open all year, times vary; entrance charge). For an overview of Narvik take the cable car (in summer) 650 metres (2,132 ft), to the top of Fagernes. At ground level Narvik is uninteresting, which is maybe why the local tourist office sells tickets for the "tourist train" (June–Aug), a three-hour guided tour between Narvik and the Swedish border, with photo opportunities and a chance to buy Sami souvenirs.

Troms, a county of contrasts

North of Narvik the E6 crosses Rombakfjorden over another major bridge, passes the junction with the road to Sweden, and joins with the E10 at Bjerkvik. Then follows a climb up Gratangseidet county boundary into Troms. Troms has widely contrasting scenery, all typically north Norwegian: rugged mountains with sharp peaks, countless islands and skerries, a softer landscape at sea level and fast-flowing rivers and numerous lakes. The county is split up by a number of major fjords and is also notable for its extensively forested valleys.

Setermoen, just north of Narvik, lies in the heart of a military area and has a large garrison. The military presence is also apparent further north at Bardufoss, with its major airbase. From Bardufoss the E6 follows the Målselv River until it turns abruptly east past Takvatnet where a new turn-off provides some stunning views of distant mountains. Near **Balsfjord Kirke** (church) about 10 km (6 miles) from Storsteinnes are rock carvings which are 2,500 to 4,000 years old. The area around Balsfjord has some of the richest farming land in Troms and goat farming is a major activity.

Alternatively, before you get to Bardufoss turn eastwards at Elverum onto Road 857 from which you can reach **Målselvfossen** ⑫ (waterfall). It may only have a drop of 15 metres (50 ft), but it extends over 600 metres (2,000 ft). There are salmon ladders and the Målselv River, which is renowned for its salmon, was discovered by English anglers in the 1840s. At Rundhaug a secondary road follows the Målselv River to Øverbygd, then continues along **Tamokdalen** until it rejoins the E6 near Øvergård. To the south, adjacent to the border with Sweden, lies the **Øvre Dividal Nasjonalpark** ⑬, where all four of Norway's major predators – bear, wolf, lynx and wolverine – have their habitat.

City of the Arctic

Tromsø ⑭ occupies most of the island of Tromsøya and overflows on to the adjoining island of Kvaløya. With a population of 63,500, it is the largest city in northern Norway and, until the opening of the bridge in 1960, everything had to be ferried across from the mainland. Today, there is a second bridge and an amazing network of road tunnels under the city, including subterranean car parks and roundabouts that appear to be formed around giant stalactites. The tunnel system links the city centre with Tromsø Langnes international airport: if you arrive by air and take a taxi the driver

Map,
pages
316–7

TIP

The rock carvings near Balsfjord Kirke (church) are part of the Tennes Heritage Trail, which is one of the many trails included in *Fotefar mot Nord* (Trails to the North) available from tourist offices.

BELOW: *rallar* (railwaymen's) statue in Narvik.

will gladly take you via the tunnel system (at the extra cost of the toll). The town has variously been called the Gateway to the Arctic, the Arctic Ocean City and the Paris of the North.

Archaeological finds indicate settlements dating back 9,000 years. Tromsø became an ecclesiastical centre in 1252 and much of the subsequent development from 1300 to the 1700s was influenced by the Hanseatic League. Trade restrictions led to strong dependence on Bergen throughout the Middle Ages. In 1794, the town was granted *kaupang* (market town) privileges and the right to independent trade, and became a focal point for the Pomor trade, with Russian ships bringing timber, rape, flour and other items from the White Sea in exchange for fish and goods brought by the Hanseatic traders.

In the early 19th century Tromsø was the natural starting point for trapping expeditions to the pack ice both to the north and the east to Svalbard (Spitsbergen). It has also been the site of a number of sea battles, including the sinking of the German battleship *Tirpitz*, pride of the German fleet, which was destroyed by British bombers while guarding the entrance to Tromsø in 1944.

Tromsø has one of the greatest amounts of Northern Light activity in the world, but in midsummer the skies are too light for this phenomenon.

Heavenly winds

Though fishing (for shrimps, herring and other fish) is of prime importance, Tromsø University and a regional teaching hospital are also major employers here. **Tromsø University Museum** (open all year, hours vary; entrance charge; tel: 77 64 50 00) focuses on the cultural and natural history of the north, and the Sami, and contains a reconstructed Viking longhouse. Polar explorers are the

Tromsø's nickname, Paris of the North, stems from the 18th century when traders brought the latest fashions from the French capital to sell to the wives of rich, local merchants.

BELOW LEFT: racks of drying fish have their own "guards" to deter hungry birds.
BELOW RIGHT: Tromsø Domkirke (cathedral) in winter.

Map, pages 316–7

centre of attention at the **Polarmuseet** (Polar Museum; open all year, hours vary; entrance charge; tel: 77 68 43 73) in the historic harbour area.

The **Nordnorsk Kunstmuseum** (Art Museum of Northern Norway; open all year Tues, Wed and Fri 10am–5pm, Thur 10am–7pm, Sat–Sun noon–3pm; entrance charge) has been going from strength to strength since moving in 2001 to its first permanent home facing Roald Amundsens Square. Sami and northern Norwegian art is well represented in the permanent collection.

In the centre of the town is the **Domkirke** (cathedral; open June–Aug, Tues–Sun) dating from 1861, one of the country's largest wooden churches. On the mainland is the striking **Ishavskatedralen** (Arctic Ocean Cathedral; open June–mid-Aug daily 9am–7pm, mid-Aug–May 4–6pm; entrance charge), designed by Jan Inge Hovig and completed in 1965. The cathedral features a huge stained-glass window by Victor Sparre covering the entire east wall, 23 metres (75 ft) high, depicting the Second Coming. Nearby is the cable car to the top of the **Storsteinen** (420 metres/1,380 ft), from where there are magnificent views over the town and the surrounding area. Tromsø also contains botanical gardens, and Europe's northernmost brewery, Mack, established in 1877 and famous for its Arctic Ale. The brewery is a short walk from the centre and there is a beer hall on the premises.

Where glacier and sea meet

To the northwest of Tromsø a number of islands stand guard where the lengthy Ullsfjorden and **Lyngenfjorden** reach the sea. Between these is a long wide peninsula. On its eastern side lie the range of mountains known as the **Lyngsalpene ⑮** (Lyngen Alps). The full majesty of these snowcapped peaks and glaciers is best seen from the eastern side of Lyngenfjorden. There is a short cut that avoids the main

BELOW: the Ishavskatedralen represents the shape of a Sami tent and the iciness of a glacier (Arctic Ocean Cathedral), Tromsø.

road and affords fine views of the mountains. Take Road 91 just south of Tromsø through the Breivik valley, a ferry across Ullsfjord to Svensby then drive to Lyngseidet and a second ferry across Lyngenfjorden to Olderdalen and the E6.

The more obvious route is south along the E8 to where it joins the E6 at Nord-kjosbotn and then northeast through Skibotn, keeping along the shore of the Lyn-genfjord with its views of the mountains across the water. After continuing east along the side of the Rotsundet, opposite the island of Uløya, the road swings inland before meeting Reisafjorden. There are fine views to the west, which are even better after climbing over the summit of **Kvænangsfjellet**. There is an impressive panorama of islands and mountains before descending to Burfjorden.

Just past Alteidet, a minor road goes north to the Jøkelfjord where the **Øksfjordjøkelen** ⓰ (glacier) calves into the sea, the only one in Norway to do so. To the east is the boundary into Norway's most remote county, Finnmark.

Finnmark

No-one describes Finnmark without a combination of superlatives and impressive statistics. It is Norway's most northerly county and the largest, covering 48,000 sq. km (18,500 sq. miles), equal to 15 percent of the entire country, and yet it has only 75,000 inhabitants, 1.7 percent of the population.

Finnmark lies along the same latitude as Alaska and Siberia, but the Gulf Stream ensures that the harbours do not freeze even in the depths of winter. Inland, the temperature can drop to a chilling –50°C (–70°F); while during the short summer it may hit 32°C (90°F). Between mid-May and the end of July the sun never sets – you can read a newspaper outside at midnight – while in winter the sun stays snug below the horizon from the end of November to the end of January.

BELOW: contrasting styles at the Sami market in Hammerfest.

The scenery is spectacular, with the highest areas in the northwest and a vast mountain plateau, the **Finn-marksvidda**, to the south and southeast. The bare grey rocks of the coast take the full force of the winter storms. It is the vastness of the uninhabited areas that make the greatest impression: ranges of mountains and *fjells* stretch away to the horizon, seemingly without end, silent and awe-inspiring.

Much of this wonderful county is now easily accessible by car or public transport on well-surfaced main roads, while there is an extensive network of air services which land at tiny airports dotted all over the area, and the ubiquitous coastal steamer serves towns and villages along the coast.

The people of Finnmark are greatly attached to their part of Norway, which has been inhabited for 10,000 years. They include not only Norwegians and Sami (Lapps) but also many Finns. The Norwegians settled the coast in the 14th century, but major changes in the 18th and 19th centuries brought in people from the south of the country. At the same time came a large migration from Finland and Sweden.

Scorched earth

World War II was a nightmare for the county when, as Soviet liberators crossed the northern border in the autumn of 1944, the German occupation forces began a "scorched earth" policy as they retreated south, burning towns and villages and even individual farms as they went. Signs of this can be seen in **Alta**, the first town across the county border from Troms and the biggest in the county, where some of the architecture is undistinguished, often the case in north Norwegian towns which had to rebuild rapidly after World War II.

On the southern outskirts is an outstanding collection of prehistoric rock carvings at **Hjemmeluft** ⑰ (signs from Alta; open all year, times vary; entrance charge; tel: 78 45 63 30). Discovered in 1972 and on UNESCO's World Heritage List, there are about 5,000 carvings on four different sites. The biggest concentration is at Hjemmeluft itself. These "stories in pictures" are about 2,500 to 6,000 years old and depict people, animals (particularly reindeer), boats and weapons. Traces of these early inhabitants, the Komsa people, were discovered in 1925 on Komsafjell, which bulges out into Altafjorden. The dwelling sites go back some 10,000 years – a sobering reminder of how long humans have lived in this inhospitable region.

One of the prehistoric carvings at Hjemmeluft.

Sami culture

Finnmark has few roads, so it's easy to find your way. Going south from Alta is Road 93 to **Kautokeino** ⑱ and the Finnish frontier. Kautokeino is the largest Sami community in the country, the centre of Sami education with a reindeer-herding school, and possibly the coldest town in Norway. The **Kulturhuset** has the only Sami theatre in Norway, and the **Samisk Museum** (open all year; entrance charge) has exhibits showing life in old Kautokeino. Northwards from Leirbotnvatn (around the fjord from Alta) to the village of **Skaidi** is 45 km (28 miles) of sheer emptiness. The E6 takes a lonely course through the wild countryside. Almost the only building is the small **Sami chapel**, dwarfed by its sur-

BELOW LEFT: selling skins and other Sami goods.
BELOW RIGHT: an early print of a Sami woman and child.

Watch out for moose crossing.

roundings. The only signs of life away from the road are the herds of reindeer. You are constantly aware of how little human activity has impinged on the grandeur of these great empty spaces.

History of disasters

Skaidi is a popular base for anglers, hunters and winter-sports enthusiasts. It is also the junction of the E6 and Road 94 to **Hammerfest** ⑲, 56 km (35 miles) away on the island of Kvaløya. Hammerfest, on its bare rocky island, is the world's most northerly town. Founded in 1789, for centuries it was the best ice-free harbour in northern waters, although storms and hurricanes plus many man-made disasters have repeatedly wrought havoc on the town. In 1825, a hurricane destroyed houses and boats, and an even more ferocious storm in 1882 moved the German kaiser, Queen Victoria and the tsar of Russia to donate money to repair the damage. In 1890, the town had ambitious plans for a hydroelectric power station but, only a month after work started, fire again destroyed two-thirds of the town. In the following year, nevertheless, Hammerfest became the first European town to have electric lighting when it purchased a generator from Thomas Edison in 1891.

The harbour has always been of importance both commercially and strategically and ships have long called there. For more than 100 years it was also the principal Norwegian base for hunting and fishing. When Norway was invaded in 1940, it was a growing and flourishing community. The retreating Germans burned down the entire town and by 10 February 1945 it had been wiped out except for the **chapel** in the graveyard. Today, it is Norway's main trawler port and an increasingly important base for offshore oil and gas activity tied to the Snow White field.

BELOW: boats and warehouses in Hammerfest harbour.

Measuring the planet

Hammerfest clings to the shoreline which is backed by a steep escarpment. Its most notable monument is the **Meridianstøtta** (Meridian Column), which was erected by King Oskar II in the late 19th century to mark the first international measurement of the Earth (1815–52), a joint enterprise by Russia, Norway and Sweden.

On the highest point of a walk from the town up the escarpment is the Midday Pole, topped by a cannonball. When the shadow from the pole points directly to the Meridian Column, the time is 12 noon precisely.

In 1809, after Norway entered the Napoleonic wars, two British warships attacked Hammerfest. The town fell and the British stayed for a week of plunder and destruction. The cannonball on top of the Midday Pole is the permanent reminder of this unhappy event. To prevent further attack the military built a redoubt or **Skansen** in 1810 with eight guns, which Hammerfest folk are happy to report never fired in anger. This walk also passes a beacon built by the town's young people in 1882–83 "as they had no other amusements".

More noticeable today is the circular **Isbjørnhallen** (Polar Bear Hall) used for sporting events and exhibitions. At the other end of town is the equally striking **church** (open June–Aug), its form inspired by traditional fish-drying racks. Its altarpiece, a glass mosaic dating from 1632, comes from the town's first church. In a shrewd move in 1963, Hammerfest created the **Isbjørnklubben** (Royal and Ancient Polar Bear Society), which offers one of the more attractive souvenirs of its kind. To get a certificate of membership, you must apply in person to the society's **museum** (open June–Aug daily 9am–5pm; Sept–June daily 10.30am–1.30pm; entrance charge; tel: 78 41 31 00) in the town hall.

Map, pages 316–7

BELOW: Nordkapp (North Cape) in winter.

En route to China

From Skaidi the E6 goes northeast across wild, uninhabited territory before the road descends to the sea at Olderfjorden. Here most visitors turn north for **Nordkapp ⑳** (North Cape). This is for many the Holy Grail, the end of their pilgrimage by car, motor home, motorbike, bus or even bicycle. The alternative is to fly to Honningsvåg or sail there by coastal steamer or cruise liner.

The road hugs the edge of Porsangenfjorden, with rugged country to the landward side, and ends at Kåfjord, where a ferry and tunnel connects to **Honningsvåg** on the island of Magerøya. Between Honningsvåg and Nordkapp lie 35 km (21 miles) of the only genuine Arctic scenery in Europe. It may be bare and treeless but there is an unusual beauty about the island which, on a sunny day, is emphasised by the clarity of the atmosphere; too often, alas, it is misty.

The name North Cape was given to this imposing headland by an Englishman, Captain Richard Chancellor. In 1553, as master of the *Edward Bonaventure*, he was seeking a new route to China when he rounded Europe's most dramatic northern point; but it was not until the 19th century that Nordkapp began to attract visitors. In 1845, passengers from the *Prinds Gustav* were rowed ashore and then had to struggle up 300 metres (1,000 ft) to the plateau at the top. After a visit by the intrepid King Oskar II in 1873, Thomas Cook arranged the first organised tour for 24 Englishmen in 1875. By 1880, a path with primitive railings from Horn Bay to the top had appeared and you can still see the remains of the quay by taking the 11-km (7-mile) walk from the plateau. The coastal steamers have provided the biggest impetus to tourist traffic and by 1920, the wild grandeur of the headland had learned to live with the incongruity of its first building. The road from Honningsvåg opened in 1956, as did a centre with the

Following Richard Chancellor's attempt in 1553 to find the Northwest Passage to China, it was to be more than 300 years before Nils Nordenskjøld finally succeeded in travelling from the Atlantic to the Pacific via the north in 1879.

BELOW: the children's statues at Nordkapp (North Cape).

Map, pages 316–7

usual souvenir shop, cafeteria and post office. In 1989, this earlier building gave way to the **Nordkapphallen** (North Cape Hall; open all year, times vary; entrance charge; tel: 78 47 68 60), with its circular Compass Restaurant and, below, the Supervideograph, a 225-degree screen with wraparound sound which brings the four seasons of Finnmark to the visitor, whatever the time of year. It also has a chapel for marriage ceremonies. Nordkapp illustrates the seasonal extremes in this area: 24-hour darkness occurs from November to the end of January, while the midnight sun lasts from mid-May to the end of July.

An underground tunnel leads from the new hall and champagne bar, which is like an amphitheatre cut out of the rock and overlooks the Arctic Ocean. Even if you suffer from vertigo, look briefly from the balcony which provides a spectacular view straight down to the sea far below. Along the tunnel are tableaux depicting historical events at Nordkapp. On what is in danger of becoming a crowded plateau are seven circular, wheel-like sculptures. They are monuments to the children of the world, sculpted in 1988 by seven children from seven lands as monuments to "joy, friendship, and working together".

The comical puffin can be found all along the northern coasts.

"Haddock" English

Apart from the main road to Nordkapp itself, there is only one other road on the island, which leads to the village of **Gjesvær** on the west coast. On the eastern side of Magerøya is the little fishing community of Skarsvåg. Honningsvåg, where the ferry arrives, has been a fishing harbour for many years and an important pilot station. In the old days, trawlers were the most frequent visitors, and up to 4,000 called each year. Most were British and, through their visits, Honningsvåg developed "haddock English", a mixture of sign language and occasional English words. Like other centres in the north, Honningsvåg was burned down during World War II, and by the end of the war, the 1884 church was the only building left standing. There is a small local museum, the **Nordkappmuseet** (North Cape Museum; open June–mid-Sept Mon–Sat 10am–7pm, Sun noon–7pm; mid-Sept–June Mon–Fri noon–4pm; entrance charge).

Most villages and towns in Finnmark sit along the coast but the two main Sami communities are the exception: Kautokeino and **Karasjok ㉑** are deep inland. Returning from Nordkapp, continue south through Lakselv at the end of Porsangenfjorden to get to Karasjok. The town's 1807 **Gamle Kirke** is the oldest church in Finnmark, having survived the war, and **De Samiske Samlinger** (the Sami Museum and Library; open all year, times vary; entrance charge) has a notable collection of Sami literature. Karasjok is the seat of the Sami Parliament and Samiland's capital. Since 2002, **Sápmi** (Sami theme park; open Sept–May 9am–4pm, June–Aug 9am–7pm; entrance charge) depicts Sami culture and history through dwellings, food and handicrafts.

At Karasjok the E6 makes a massive U-turn and heads north again, keeping company with the **River Tana** through its every twist and turn, all the way to **Tana Bru ㉒**, which is at the first bridge across the river and is the meeting place of four roads. One is the alternative route east from Lakselv (Road 888), which

BELOW: the Midday Pole in Nordkapp (North Cape).

Mending fishing nets on the quayside.

BELOW: a good catch: Atlantic salmon at Honningsvåg.

veers away from the E6 at the head of the Porsanger fjord. This long road has few communities but an abundance of beautiful scenery and it rolls ahead across two magnificent inland stretches – from **Børselv** to **Laksefjorden** and across the **Ifjordfjellet**. At Ifjord the road pushes further north to the Nordkyn peninsula and **Kjøllefjord** ㉓, Mehamn and Gamvik, across the very top of the country. About 15 km (9 miles) from Kjøllefjord, including a 30-minute ramble along a well-prepared trail, is the remains of the **Oksevåg whaling station**, which was used during the Finnmark whaling season from 1864–1905. Further walks are marked through the **Slettnes Nature and Heritage Reserve** at Gamvik (open all year).

Over the bridge at Tana Bru, the road divides; the E6 winds a long route east towards **Kirkenes**, only 5 km (3 miles) from the Russian border, while Road 890 heads north to **Berlevåg** and **Båtsfjord**, crossing the highest pass in Finnmark, the **Oarddojokke** at 400 metres (1,300 ft) above sea level. Berlevåg and Båtsfjord are fishing villages, both on the far coast of the Varanger peninsula. Places of interest include the **Løkvika Fiskehytte og Partisanhule** (Fishing Cabin and Partisan Cave; open all year), where locals fought off the Germans in World War II.

Continuing east on the E6, you come to **Varangerbotn** ㉔. In this part of Norway, where the fjords bite deep into the land, you are rarely far from water. Varangerbotn has a small but interesting Sami museum, the **Samiske Museum** (open mid-June–mid-Aug 10am–6pm, mid-Aug–mid-June weekdays 10am–3pm; entrance charge), and it is worth making a detour along the north coast of the Varangerfjord on Road 98 to **Vadsø** ㉕, the administrative centre of Finnmark. At **Nesseby**, you will find a wooden church (1858) and Varanger's oldest log cabin (1700). This remote area is rich in archaeological finds, with graves and places of sacrifice to indicate human occupation as early as 9000 BC.

Finnish migration

A monument in Vadsø explains why many inhabitants are of Finnish origin and Finnish-speaking (Kvens), and the local **Ruija Kven Museum** (open mid-June–mid-Aug, times vary; entrance charge; tel: 78 94 28 90) is housed in two buildings, one a Finnish-style dwelling, Tuomaingården, and the other, Esbensen-gården, a patrician house from 1840. Vadsø's **church**, built in 1958, is of striking appearance. In front, the King Stone bears the signatures of King Olav V of Norway, President Kekkonen of Finland and King Carl Gustav of Sweden, who all visited the town in 1977 to unveil the **Innvandrermonumentet** (Immigrant Monument) to the Finns who came to find food and work in Finnmark in the 1800s. Another landmark is the **Luftskipsmasta** (mooring mast) used by Amundsen's airship, *Norge*, in 1926 and Nobile's airship *Italia*, two years later.

Beyond Vadsø there is only the town of **Vardø** ㉖, Norway's easternmost town and the only one situated in the Arctic climate zone. There have been fortifications at Vardø since around 1300, but the present octagonal star-shaped redoubt was built in 1738. The only remnant of the original fortress is a beam which bears the signature of King Christian IV and is dated 1599, while later monarchs have added their names: King Oskar II (in 1873), King Håkon VII (in 1907) and King Olav V (in 1959); the beam is in the **Vardøhus Museum** and **Festning** (fortress; open June–Aug Mon–Fri 8am–6pm, Sat–Sun noon–6pm; Sept–May Mon–Fri 8am–3.30pm; entrance charge).

Along the coast west of Vardø is the abandoned fishing village of **Hamningberg** with its old architecture and church – one of the few not destroyed in World War II. As you return south again, you come to **Ekkerøya**, Finnmark's only bird rock accessible by car. Beyond Varangerbotn, the E6 follows the coast

Map, pages 316–7

After two months of winter darkness, Vardø celebrates the return of the sun, usually around 20 January, with a gun salute on the first day that the entire disc is visible above the horizon.

BELOW: the harbour at Vadsø.

Map,
pages
316–7

through another huge, uninhabited area to the southeast and some beautiful views across the waters of the Varanger fjord. **Bugøynes** is an old fishing village on the coast which, like Hamingborg, escaped destruction in the war. Further east, **Bugøyfjord** is an old trading centre and birthplace of the Sami artist John Savio.

Only 8 km (5 miles) from the Finnish border to the southwest, the little town of **Neiden** has the only Greek Orthodox church in Norway, where the Skollé Lapps worship. Each year since 1965, the church has held a service to bless the waters of the River Neiden to ensure that their reputed healing powers continue. The restored Labahå farm at Neiden, built by Finnish immigrants, is part of the **Sør-Varanger Museum** (open all year daily 10am–3.30pm; entrance charge) at Svanvik.

This easternmost wedge of Norwegian territory became important with the discovery of iron ore, at Bjørnevatn, which from 1906 until 1996 was mined and shipped from the port of **Kirkenes** ㉗. The region is also a centre for fishing, farming, forestry and reindeer husbandry. Kirkenes is dominated by the deserted installations of the Sydvaranger Iron Ore Company. Although it has acquired a luxury hotel, the Rica Arctic, the town's somewhat rough and ready appearance is explained and easily forgiven when you learn that the 20th century brought no less than four wars fought in or near it. Apart from Malta, Kirkenes acquired the unsolicited honour of being the most bombed centre in Europe in World War II. It was liberated by the Russians in 1944, which engendered a rare lack of nervousness of, and sympathy for, the "Russian Bear". Subterranean tunnels used to shelter residents during the war can be visited. Kirkenes is the final point of call for the Hurtigruten coastal steamer before it returns south to Bergen.

BELOW: postboxes
brighten up the
winter landscape.
RIGHT: winter in
Kautokeino.

Unusual border post

The extreme eastern tip of Norway, at **Grense Jakobselv**, has a chapel built on the order of King Oskar II in 1869 as an unusual means of protecting Norwegian interests. The idea of a chapel rather than a fort at this strategic location came about when the Norwegians noticed that the Russians attended their own Orthodox church not far over the border. Faced with a Protestant church, the argument ran, the Russians would realise they had strayed into Norwegian territory. This somewhat unusual approach to maintaining the frontier was highly successful.

In the extreme north of Finnmark, Norway is sometimes only a kilometre or two wide between the border and the sea, and a long pocket of the country hangs south between Russia and Finland. Here the **Øvre Pasvik Nasjonalpark** ㉘ includes the largest virgin forest in the country. This comparatively flat area has pine forests, bare rock, swamps and two watercourses which are tributaries of the Pasvik River (the official boundary between Norway and Russia). Wildlife in the park includes moose, reindeer, bear and wolverine; there are whooper swans, great grey owls, bean geese, sea eagles, gyr falcons, spotted redshanks and cranes; the whole area is protected from development and pollution to form a peaceful border, 122 km (76 miles) long between East and West. ❑

SVALBARD

Nearly as close to the North Pole as to Norway, the Svalbard archipelago (with its main island of Spitsbergen) teems with bird, mammal and plant life in the short Arctic summer

Map on page 338

NORWAY

F rom Tromsø in the north of Norway, the big airliner drones almost due north for an hour and a half. Far below is a seemingly empty sea, hidden here and there by banks of clouds. Suddenly the traveller becomes aware that through the clouds, stark, jagged mountain peaks project like huge fangs, and that the clouds in between are in reality great snow-covered glaciers. This is Svalbard, the land of the pointed mountains.

The Svalbard archipelago lies 640 km (400 miles) north of the mainland of Norway and has two main islands, Spitsbergen and Nordaustlandet, with numerous smaller islands dotted around in the seas nearby. In winter, the pack ice of the Arctic is all around and only some 950 km (600 miles) separate the islands from the North Pole. Only three islands are populated: Spitsbergen, Bjørnøya and Hopen.

The smooth asphalt runway lies on the narrow coastal plain between the mountains of Spitsbergen and the sea of Isfjorden. With a minimum of formality, you are through customs and on to a land where the forces of nature are still in control. On the landward side, the mountain slopes darkly up in to the clouds, traversed by a row of pylons; now disused, they carried coal from the mines down to the loading jetties.

PRECEDING PAGES: rock formations on Spitsbergen. **LEFT:** a young polar bear. **BELOW:** the Russian mining settlement of Barentsburg.

Why an airport?

The Svalbard coal mines are rare in that the mine shafts do not go down into the ground but are driven horizontally into the mountains. The township of **Longyearbyen ❶** was built solely to accommodate the people who came north, mainly from Norway, to work at the hard and dangerous job of mining coal from the inside of the mountains.

Coal was first discovered in the early 17th century, but for many years it was used only as a source of fuel for trappers. Only since around 1900 have serious attempts been made to exploit this resource, and the first to claim mining rights was a Norwegian skipper from Tromsø, called Zakariasen. He was followed by others including John Longyear, an American after whom the village is named.

Around 1,800 people live in the village, mainly in modern, well-insulated houses, served by facilities such as shops, a bank, restaurants and bars, a café, and a sports centre with a swimming pool. There is a fine little **museum** which, as well as stuffed examples of typical Spitsbergen birds and mammals, displays many artefacts from the days when the only people to live in these Arctic islands were a few hunters and trappers.

As if to remind you that summer, if sweet, is short: in front of most houses you will see a parked skidoo, a motor scooter with rubber tracks and steer-

One of the characteristically spiky peaks that gave Spitsbergen its name.

ing "skis", which is the only means of transport in the long winter months when snow lies thick on the ground.

Mineral rights

After World War I, Norway was granted sovereignty over the archipelago, though the various countries who agreed to the treaty reserved the right to exploit minerals. Sweden already operated a coal-mining business but sold out to a Norwegian company in 1934.

Today, Russia is the only one of the original signatories to the Svalbard Treaty to retain an interest in coal mining, and has a substantial operation at **Barentsburg ②**, only a few miles further down the fjord from Longyearbyen. Around 850 people, mostly Ukrainians, live in a coal-dusty village on the steep fjordside which, nevertheless, has an indoor farm of dairy cattle and chicken sheds. Kittiwakes scream from their nests on the window ledges and, on an esplanade below, well-dressed fur-hatted groups sell cheap Russian souvenirs and, now and then, a family "treasure" to the occasional summer cruise-ship passenger.

Nature in the raw

Svalbard should not, and is unlikely ever to become, a place for mass tourism: the islands cannot support it and, in any case, the appeal is to people who like to find their own wildlife and explore nature in the raw. However, the cruise ships are beginning to threaten the peace. Longyearbyen has two hotels and hardly a day goes by without a luxury cruise ship depositing its passengers on the shore for a barbecue or a short trip around the area. For safety reasons, visitors are normally accompanied by men with loaded guns and may not leave the

BELOW: cruise ships are an increasingly common sight in summer.

pre-set routes. Thus, the polar bear takes care that mass tourism never spoils the environment and only a few well-equipped campers dare go further afield.

The area around Longyearbyen is a pleasant place during the summer, the stark mountains offset by a valley which has meadows spangled with flowers. Here, you will find the tiny bells of cassiope mixed with purple saxifrage and, perhaps, a patch of boreal Jacob's ladder, *Polemonium boreale*, an Arctic rarity with beautiful flowers. Near the shores where the glaucous gulls congregate, look for the fleshy-leaved *Mertensia maritima*, or oyster plant.

The polar winter is a different matter. The sun does not rise above the horizon and everything is locked in darkness, lit only by the moon and the multi-coloured rays of the **aurora borealis** (northern lights; *see page 311*).

When the sun reappears and gathers strength, the ice pack retreats north, speeded by the warming influence of the Gulf Stream. This warm current flows up the west coast of Spitsbergen and ensures that, in summer, ships can have an ice-free passage right to the north shores of the islands. The sun's return is cause for a week-long Sunfestival in March with concerts and outdoor events.

Spitsbergen is mountainous and glaciated with around 60 percent covered in permanent ice. The highest mountain, **Newtontoppen**, is more than 1,700 metres (5,500 ft) high. Further from the influence of the Gulf Stream, the second-largest island, **Nordaustlandet**, is almost completely covered in ice.

Unknown and unexplored

According to the old Icelandic annals, in 1194 land was found to lie "four days sailing from Langanes, at the northern end of the sea". They called it Svalbard, but then the islands were forgotten for several hundred years. The next mention was in the

Map on page 338

TIP

Svalbard offers a wide range of activities for the outdoor enthusiast including dog sledging and skiing, camping expeditions, walks with packhorses and boat trips. See www.svalbard.net for details.

BELOW: a coal train in Ny-Ålesund.

The Norwegian botanist Hanna Resvoll-Holmsen took this self-portrait in 1908, while camping at Colbay.

journals of the great Dutch explorer, Willem Barents, in 1596. Barents, with two ships under his command, was trying to find a northern route to China when he sighted an island which, from the shape of its mountains, he named Spitsbergen (Dutch for "jagged mountains"). The two ships parted, one to carry news of fjords filled with whales and walrus back to the Netherlands, while the other ship with Barents on board continued eastward, only to become trapped in the pack ice and forced to spend the winter there, during which Barents and many of his crew died.

Story of the whales

By 1612 hunting expeditions had begun to arrive around the coast of Spitsbergen. News of the numbers of whales spread and soon the Dutch **whalers** were joined by English, French, Basques and Danes. Inevitably, trouble flared as they disputed rights and fought pitched battles when warships came north to defend the claims of their whalers.

The English and Dutch at last agreed on a division of hunting territories and some peace was restored. The Dutch set up a shore base on **Amsterdam Island**, which grew to be almost a town with a fort, church and whale-oil refinery, and a summer population of a couple of thousand. They called it **Smeerenburg ❸**, the "blubber town", and you can still find the outlines of stone buildings and the furnaces built to render the whale blubber into oil. The large numbers of bleached whale bones testify to the growing demands for whale oil, and in some places there is further mute testimony in the graves of men who died, either in battles or from natural causes. Under the pressure of all the killing, it was inevitable that the whale stock would decline and by around 1720 whaling ceased.

This intensive whaling was purely a summer activity. In winter the islands were deserted except by accident. In 1630, an English ship was wrecked and the crew managed to cling to life throughout the winter. In 1633, some Dutchmen wintered at Smeerenberg, but the following year those who attempted to stay on all died of scurvy. The English had intended to colonise the archipelago but even prisoners under sentence of death refused to face the prospect of the Arctic night.

BELOW: taking a really close look at an Arctic skua.

Tough life

The Russians were made of sterner stuff, however, and in the early part of the 18th century a number of hunting parties built houses on Svalbard and continued to hunt bear, fox, walrus and seals throughout the winter darkness. Not until the late 18th century did Norwegian hunters first arrive. They too overwintered and today their cabins still lie along the shores of many fjords. Though mainly deserted, scientists and explorers often make use of the huts and many are kept in a good state of repair.

A trapper led a tough and rigorous life. He had to set his traps, mainly for Arctic fox whose beautiful pelts were most valuable in winter, in a hunting territory that covered many square kilometres. He also shot or caught polar bears in baited "fell traps" and hunted seals, not just for food and skins, but for the oil which he extracted from the blubber.

Ever since its discovery Svalbard has attracted

scientific expeditions. The first on record was in 1773 and included no less a personage than Horatio Nelson, then a midshipman. In 1827, the first Norwegian geological expedition took place under Professor B.M. Keilhau, and this was soon followed by expeditions from many nations. Today, the **Norsk Polarinstitut** is the clearing house for all expeditions to this Arctic outpost.

Map on page 338

Natural laboratory

Svalbard offers a splendid environment for the study of ecology and **natural history** by scientist and amateur alike. Almost every visitor who makes the long journey north has more than a passing interest in wildlife in general and birds in particular, and Svalbard's short Arctic summer offers a rich feast. For though the archipelago can seem desperately inhospitable, in the 24-hour days of summer the tundra slopes between the mountains and near the sea offer enough thin soil to encourage and support a surprising number of plants. These, in turn, support other wildlife such as insects, 36 bird species and a few mammals. The surrounding seas, although cold, are rich in fish and invertebrates which attract sea birds and sea mammals who use the shores and cliffs for breeding and resting.

The small yellow blooms of the Svalbard mohn.

Kittiwakes, glaucous and ivory gulls push north as soon as daylight allows and are soon followed by Arctic terns, all the way from the southern hemisphere. The kittiwake is essentially an ocean bird which feeds almost exclusively at sea. At nesting time they set up huge noisy colonies on suitable cliffs, or even on window ledges in some places. Another ocean wanderer is the fulmar. Most of the Svalbard fulmars are in the "dark-grey phase" of development and therefore largely confined to Arctic waters, which at first puzzles some bird-watchers from further south. Four species of auks breed in Svalbard: Brünnich's guillemot, the little auk,

BELOW: soil patterns in Sassendalen.

Map on page 338

The seal hunters who once flocked to Svalbard in the summer months used to refer to ringed seals as "floe rats".

RIGHT: in summer the Arctic ice breaks up under the influence of the warm Gulf Stream.

puffin and black guillemot. While Brünnich's guillemot nest on open but inaccessible ledges, the others seek the safety of crevices or burrows, where predators such as Arctic fox and glaucous gulls have less chance of getting at their eggs or young. There are also some waders.

The large expanses of barren mountains do not offer much in the way of food for land birds, but try the slopes and valleys which are often carpeted in dwarf birch and polar willow, and you will find snow buntings foraging for seeds and singing from the rocks. The Svalbard ptarmigan also uses this habitat and it is the only bird to stay through the winter. Three kinds of geese breed on Svalbard – pink-footed, Brent and barnacle – and the many naturalists who have studied the barnacle geese now realise that the entire Svalbard population travels to Scotland each year, to spend the winter in the Solway area in the southwest, then return in spring to breed. When you spot the plentiful flocks of common eider along the shores, look closely because you may be lucky enough to find a few king eiders, showing off their superior plumage to their less flashy kin.

Arctic monarch

There is only one kind of grazing mammal on the islands and that is the hardy Svalbard reindeer. Smaller than the Samiland reindeer, you come across groups which seem quite tame, living a Spartan life off plants and lichens in the valley bottoms. The only other land mammals are the Arctic fox and the bear. The Arctic fox is a very attractive-looking little animal, with a coat of varying shades of white and grey in summer and pure white in winter. Though it was hunted heavily in the past, it is still remarkably tolerant and curious about humans and is not too difficult to find on the sea-bird cliffs in summer, where it digs out nests or picks up any young birds that have fallen from the ledges.

The undoubted king of the Arctic is the polar bear. Adult males especially lead a nomadic life on the pack ice for much of the year and live mainly on seals, while young males and females with cubs tend to spend the summer on the island feeding largely on a vegetarian diet. Though they were formerly hunted for their skins, polar bears are now protected and can be killed only if they threaten human life. They are not uncommon, especially on favourite breeding islands, such as **Barentsøya** and **Edgeøya**.

The fjords of Svalbard may no longer be "filled with whales and walrus", as they were said to be in the 15th century, but you will certainly find sea mammals around the islands. Though it is now rare to see any of the great whales, species such as the lesser rorquhal or minke whales come into the fjord quite often. The beluga or white whale is easiest to identify with its white body and lack of a dorsal fin. You might be lucky enough to sight the remarkable narwhale, with its spear-like tusk projecting out in front.

The immense herds of walrus which in days past thronged places like **Moffen Island** have never fully recovered from over-hunting, but sometimes small groups appear at Moffen or on the south of Edgeøya, where they feast on the clam beds or rest on the shore: a hopeful sign in an age when Svalbard is visited for its stark natural beauty and summer wildlife. ❏

SVALBARD SEED BANK

In 2007 the Norwegian government pledged to establish a seed bank, effectively a "Noah's ark" for the world's most important plant varieties. The Svalbard International Seed Vault will serve as a repository for crucial seeds in the event of global catastrophe, be it nuclear war, natural disasters or gene pollution from genetic modification.

The bank is to be carved into the permafrost and rock of the remote Svalbard peninsula. Its location ensures the vault will remain below freezing point and the seeds will further be protected by metre-thick walls of reinforced concrete, two airlocks and high security blast-proof doors.

The Svalbard seed bank will be of global importance; local seed banks rely on artificial refrigeration and are prone to local problems – dozens of unique crops were lost during the wars in Iraq and Afghanistan.

✵ INSIGHT GUIDES

T R A V E L T I P S

NORWAY

TRAVEL TIPS

Transport

Getting There 348
  By Air 348
  By Sea 348
  By Rail 349
  By Road 349
Getting Around 349
  Public Transport 349
  From the Airport 349
  Tickets and Info 349
  Norway in a Nutshell 350
  By Air 350
  By Rail 350
  By Bus/Coach 350
  Fjord Tours 350
  Travel Passes 351
  Water Transport 351
  Ferries 351
  Long-distance Ships 351
  Buses and Trams 351
  Underground 351
  Taxis 351
  Road Information........... 351
  Private Transport 352
  By Car 352
  Winter Driving 352
  Breakdown and Accidents 352
  Rules of the Road 352
  Toll Roads..................... 352
  Caravanning 353
  Car Hire 353
  Cycling 353
  On Foot 353
  Hitchhiking 353

Accommodation

Introduction 354
Hotel Chains 354
Breakfast Included 354
Booking in Oslo 354
City Packages 355
Chalets *(Hytter)* 355
Fisherman's Cabins...........355
Camping 355
B&Bs............................... 355
Youth and Family Hostels .. 355
Norway's Historic Hotels.... 355
Hotels 356
  Oslo 356
  Oslo Area 356
  Kristiansand 357
  Bergen 357
  Stavanger 358
  Balestrand 358
  Trondheim 359
  Tromsø........................ 359
  Svalbard...................... 359

Eating Out

What to Eat 360
Where to Eat 360
Drinking Notes 360
Oslo 361
Bergen 361
Trondheim 362
Tromsø 362
Stavanger 362

What To Do

The Arts 363
  Music and Opera 363
  Theatre and Dance 363
  Cinema 363
Nightlife 363
Festivals 363
Shopping 365
  What to Buy 365
  Tax-free Shopping...........365
Outdoor Activities 365
  Boating.......................... 365
  Canoeing 366
  Cycling 366
  Fishing 366
  Golf 366
  Hiking........................... 366
  Horse Riding 367
  Skiing 367
  Swimming...................... 367
  Walking in the National
    Parks 368
  Water Sports 367
Spectator Sports................367
Sporting Events..................367
Children 369

A – Z

Animals 370
Business Dealings.............370
Business Hours.................371
Climate.............................371
Crime and Safety..............371
Coffee 371
Cost of Living 372
Customs Regulations.........372
Disabled Travellers 372
Dogs 372
Embassies in Oslo.............372
Emergency Numbers 372
Electricity 373
Entry Requirements...........372
  Visas and Passports 372
Gay and Lesbian Travellers..373
Health and Medical Care 373
  Doctors and Hospitals 373
  Pharmacies 373
  Dentists 373
Internet Cafés 373
Maps 373
Media 374
  Newspapers...................374
  Bookshops 374
  Radio 374
  Television 374
Money 374
  Credit Cards/
  Travellers' Cheques 374
  Tipping 374
Postal Service 374
Public Holidays................. 374
Religious Services 374
Student Travellers............. 374
Telecommunications 374
Time Zone 375
Tourist Information 375
  Oslo/Oslofjord 375
  East Norway 375
  South Norway 375
  Fjord Norway................. 375
  Central Norway 376
  North Norway 376
Websites 376
Weights and Measures 376
What to Bring/Wear 376

Language

Introduction 377
Useful Words and Phrases 377

Further Reading

Books 378
Other Insight Guides 378

T RANSPORT

GETTING THERE AND GETTING AROUND

GETTING THERE

By Air

Scandinavia's flagship carrier, **SAS** (Scandinavian Airline System), runs a wide range of flights between Oslo Gardermoen Airport and other world capitals (usually involving a feeder service to and from one of the main European hubs – usually London, Copenhagen or Frankfurt), with some direct services to and from Bergen, Oslo, Stavanger, Tromsø and Trondheim.

SAS is joined by other major international airlines – including **British Airways, Lufthansa, Air France**, and **KLM** – in connecting Oslo and other cities with daily flights to Europe.

Approximate flying times to Oslo are: London, 2 hours, Frankfurt, 1 hour 50 minutes, Paris, 2 hours, Budapest, 3 hours 35 minutes, and Warsaw, 3 hours 25 minutes.

SAS offers several daily flights from Heathrow to Oslo and two to Stavanger; there are also flights in and out of Manchester. **BA** operates from Heathrow and Manchester to Oslo. **Ryanair** offers low-cost flights from London Stansted and Glasgow Prestwick to Oslo Torp, near Sandefjord (in fact 130 km/80 miles south of the capital) and from London Stansted to Haugesund.

Wideroe flies to 33 destinations within Norway and has flights from Manchester, Aberdeen, Edinburgh, Newcastle, Copenhagen, Gothenburg and Stockholm. It is based at Oslo Torp airport in Sandefjord, 130 km (80 miles) south of Oslo. **Coast Air** also offers domestic flights plus international services to Copenhagen from its base in Haugesund.

Norwegian Air Shuttle is a low-cost airline operating from 10 airports in Norway; flights go to Oslo from London Gatwick and Edinburgh, and from London Stansted to Kristainsand, Oslo, Bergen and Trondheim. All airports are serviced by buses and taxis. Oslo's Gardermoen Airport has a number of train services *(see page 349)*.

SAS

In UK
World Business Centre
Newall Road
London Heathrow Airport
Hounslow TW6 2RE
Reservations from the UK
Tel: 0845-6072 7727
Fax: 020-8990 7127
www.scandinavian.net

In North America
c/o United Airlines
437 Madison Ave (enter on 50th St)
New York
Tel: 1-800 221 2350

In Norway
Tel (reservations): 81 52 04 00

British Airways

In UK
Waterside
P.O. Box 365
Harmondsworth
UB7 0GB
Tel: 0870 850 9850
www.ba.com

In Norway
British Airways
Dronning Mauds g 1–3
0250 Oslo
Tel: 800-33142 (freephone)
Fax: 22 82 20 49

Coast Air

Information and reservations through
www.coastair.no.

Norwegian Air Shuttle

In UK
Tel: 020 8099 7254
Tel: 00 47 21 49 00 15
In Norway
Oksenøyvein 10A
P.O. Box 115
N-1330 Fornebu
Tel: 81 52 18 15
www.norwegian.no

Widerøe

In Norway
Elvind Lychesuei vei 10
N-1338 Sandvika
Tel: 67 11 60 00
Fax: 67 11 61 95
E-mail: sandvika@wideroe.no
www.wideroe.no

By Sea

DFDS Seaways operate the only direct services from the UK to Norway, with sailings from Newcastle to Bergen, Stavanger and Haugesund. The company also offers a wide selection of holiday ideas for summer and winter, ranging from chalets to resorts and motoring breaks in first-class hotels.

Smyril Line operates a weekly sailing from Torshavn in the Faroe Islands to Bergen via Lerwick, with connections to Aberdeen.

Color Line is the main ferry service linking Oslo to the continent, with big new cruise-ferries sailing to Kiel in Germany, and services to the northern tip of Denmark.

DFDS Seaways

Royal Quays
North Shields
Tyne & Wear
NE29 6EG
Tel: 0871 522 9955
www.dfdsseaways.co.uk

Scandinavia House
Parkeston Quay, Harwich
Essex CO12 4QG
Tel: 0871 522 9955
www.dfdsseaways.co.uk

Smyril Line
Scantours UK Ltd
73 Mornington Street
London NW1 7QE
Tel: 020 7554 3530
Fax: 020 7387 4496
info@scantours.com
www.smyril-line.com

Color Line
P.O. Box 1422, Vika
N-0115 Oslo
Tel: 47 81 00 08 11
www.colorline.com

By Rail

Numerous rail services link Norway with the rest of Scandinavia and Europe. From the continent, express trains operate to Copenhagen, where inter-Scandinavian trains connect to Oslo. There are train connections in Oslo to other cities in Norway. First- and second-class coaches are available on these express trains, plus sleeper coaches on all of the overnight expresses.

Seat reservations are required on all night and long-distance day trains, as well as on express and high speed "Signatur" services.

The Norwegian State Railway (NSB) is part of the InterRail, EuroDomino, Eurailpass and Eurail Youthpass system, which offers various discount tickets (including to students). InterRail: www.interrailnet.com, Eurail: www.eurail.com.

There are frequent connections from Copenhagen, Stockholm and Gothenburg to Oslo.

You can also get to northern Norway from Stockholm, with Trondheim and Narvik the principal destinations, again usually twice daily (the line in Norway terminates at Bodø).

International arrivals and departures are located at Sentral-stasjon (Oslo-S). Gardermobanen, the high-speed rail link to/from Oslo Gardermoen Airport has a terminal at Oslo S, and trains also run to/from Asker via Nationalteatret station. NSB provides train information and also operates as a travel bureau across Norway:

Norwegian State Railways
NSB Reisesenter
P.O. Box 673,
N-5001 Bergen, Norway
Tel: 81 50 08 88
www.nsb.no

By Road

Most major shipping lines to Norway allow passengers to bring cars. But coming by car increases sea travel costs, and petrol is expensive in Norway.

Norges Automobil Forbund
(NAF or Norwegian Automobile Association)
Østensjøveien 14, 0609 Oslo
Tel: 22 34 14 00
Fax: 22 33 13 72
Emergency tel: 810 00 505
www.naf.no

Kongelig Norsk Automobilklub
(KNA or Royal Norwegian Automobile Club)
Cort Adelersgt. 16 Oslo
Tel: 21 60 49 00
Emergency tel: 22 30 30 50
(members only).

GETTING AROUND

Public Transport

There is an excellent network of domestic transport services – a necessity in a country so large and often impassable by land. You may have to use more than one means (for example, train and bus or plane and bus) but if you're travelling beyond Oslo you'll find these services indispensable.

Although covering great distances can be expensive, Norway offers transport bargains through special tourist cards like the Fjord Pass, the Bonus Pass (which covers the whole of Scandinavia), plus some of the pan-European programmes like InterRail and Eurail. Within larger cities, tourist passes cover urban transport and give free entry to many museums.

Tickets and Info

For tickets, routes, times and all other queries about public transport, **Trafikanten** in Oslo offers an information and booking service. Its office is at Jernbanetorvet 1, by Oslo Sentralstasjon (at the bottom of the glass tower at the front of the station). Office open Mon–Fri 7am–8pm, Sat–Sun 8am–6pm. Tel: 81 50 01 76 (lines open Mon–Fri 7am–11pm, Sat–Sun 8am–11pm). Info line: 177.

From the Airport
Gardermoen Airport is 50 km (30 miles) north of Oslo. It is served by the Airport Express Train/Flytoget to Oslo S (the Central Station) every 10–20 minutes and takes 30 minutes. Details at www.flytoget.no. For about half the price, regional and local trains also connect Oslo and the airport and take about 45 minutes; there is normally a train at least every hour. Note that rail passes are not valid on The Airport Express. See also www.nsb.no.

The airport bus departs six times an hour to and from the Radisson SAS Scandinavia Hotel via Oslo Busterminal, Clarion Royal Christina Hotel, Helsfyr and Furuset. It takes 40 minutes.

The regular bus No. 344 from the Radisson SAS Scandinavia Hotel via Oslo S departs three times an hour and takes 50 minutes. Buses 332 and 355 also make the journey. Tel: 177 or 22 80 49 71; www.flybussen.no.

Nor-Way Busekspress. No. 114 stops in Oslo and the Oslo fjord area en route to Gardermoen. There are four departures per hour from the Oslo suburbs. Tel: 81 54 44 44, www.nor-way.no.

BELOW: taking the scenic route on the underground to Frognerseteren.

TRANSPORT

ACCOMMODATION

EATING OUT

ACTIVITIES

A – Z

LANGUAGE

Norway in a Nutshell

One of the most pleasurable ways of seeing Norway is to take a **Norway in a Nutshell** journey *(see page 241)*. The trip uses various forms of public transport and takes you from Myrdal to Flåm, Gudvangen and Voss through some of the country's most beautiful scenery. A selection of packages is on offer. Tel: 81 56 82 22. www.fjord-tours.no

The railway line from Myrdal to Flåm is a masterpiece of engineering. When you have made the 850-metre (2,800-ft) descent you are at the head of one of the longest fjords in the world, Sognefjorden, and on the brink of another scenic high.

The trips can be made in either direction and from any of the stations between Oslo and Bergen. **Norway in a Nutshell round trip:** train from Oslo to Myrdal/Flåm, boat to Gudvangen, bus to Voss, train to Oslo.

Norway in a Nutshell one way: train from Oslo to Myrdal/Flåm, boat to Gudvangen, bus to Voss, train to Bergen.

Tickets are sold at the railway stations in Oslo and Bergen or from travel agencies. See www.norway nutshell for more details.

If you arrive from London Stansted at **Torp Airport** at Sandefjord on the southwest side of the fjord, buses and trains will take up to 2½ hours to reach the capital, depending on traffic conditions.

Bergen Airport is at Flesland, 19 km (12 miles) south of the city. The airport bus goes to the Radisson SAS Royal Hotel at Bryggen, via Radisson SAS Hotel Norge and the bus station. For details, tel: 177.

All other major city airports are serviced by buses and taxis.

By Air

Considering its size, Norway is exceptionally well served by domestic airlines, with about 50 airports and airfields throughout the country.

The main domestic airlines are SAS, Widerøe and Norwegian Air Shuttle. Each offers discount travel passes.

SAS Scandinavian Airlines at Oslo and Bergen airports.
Bookings tel: 815 20 400
Info tel: 67 59 67 19
Main office tel: 67 59 60 50

Widerøe's Flyveselskap ASA
Vollsvien. 6, P.O. Box 131, N-1324 Lysaker, and Bergen Airport.
Tel: 67 11 60 00
Fax: 67 11 61 95
Bookings tel: 81 00 12 00.
Norwegian Air Shuttle
P.O. Box 115, N-1330 Fornebu
Tel: 67 59 30 00.

By Rail

Rail services are far more comprehensive in the south than in the north, and tend to fan out from Oslo, so you will have to supplement your trip with ferries and buses, unless you are travelling strictly in the south or to the major towns.

Oslo S (Oslo Sentralstasjon) is Norway's busiest railway station, located in central Oslo at the eastern end of Karl Johansgate on Jernbanetorget. Long-distance, express and local suburban trains arrive and depart here. It is also the terminal for the Oslo Gardermoen Airport high-speed rail link (some trains continue under the city to Asker via Nationalteatret station).

The end of the line in Norway is at Bodø, but the most northerly railway station is at Narvik, which is reached through Sweden by train or by bus from Fauske. Most of Norwegian State Railways (NSB's) lines run through tourist country, presenting continuous panoramas of unspoiled scenic beauty. The Oslo–Bergen line is hailed as one of the world's most spectacular for its scenery.

Most trains are modern and efficient, but the older rolling stock has a touch of nostalgic luxury. New inter-city express (ICE) trains offer one class only. There is a wide range of special offers that can make your holiday better value for money.

National rail passes from NSB are valid for 3–8 travel days in any month. The rail pass is sold under the name of Norway Rail Pass in the US, while in Europe the offer is called EuroDomino Norway (see www.nsb.no). The ScanRail Pass offers unlimited travel all over Scandinavia, as well as discounts on certain ferries, buses and at hotel chains. Note that ScanRail passes bought outside Scandinavia are more flexible and better value than those bought in Scandinavia. Visit www.scanrail.com for more information.

If you plan to take special fast trains, you must book ahead. Ticket sales are from the main hall of the train station (tickets for ordinary trains may also be bought on board).

For information about timetables, ticket prices and bookings contact Trafikanten, Jernbanetorvet 1, by Oslo S, tel: 81 50 01 76 or 177.

By Bus/Coach

Where the rail network stops, the bus goes further: you can get to practically anywhere you want by bus on an ever-growing number of bus lines. Time Express is a popular one (see www.nettbuss.no). Usually it is not

BELOW: the cross-fjord ferry waiting at Fjaerland in the Fjaerlandfjord.

Fjord Tours

Whether you are planning a short break or a long holiday, many companies offer tours of the fjord, coastal and mountain scenery. Two of the main ones are:
Fjord Tours
Strømgt 4
5015 Bergen
Tel: 47 81 56 82 22
www.fjord-tours.com
Fjord Travel Norway
Østre Nesttunvei 4–6
5221 Nesttun, Bergen
Tel: 47 55 13 13 10
www.fjordtravel.no

Travel Passes

The Oslo Pass, issued for one, two and three days, with half price for children, is your ticket to unlimited public transport (including city ferries) and free entry to many museums. If you want a card for travel only, there are all kinds of passes including a Minikort (four rides at a discount) and Flexikort (eight rides at a discount), plus passes appropriate for longer stays.

The Oslo Pass may be purchased at the Central Railway Station (Oslo S), Trafikanten *(see box on page 349)*, as well as all *Narvesen* kiosks and hotels, camp sites and tourist offices.

Other cities offer similar tourist travel cards: for example, the Bergen Card, a 24-hour or 48-hour pass available from tourist information offices, the railway station, hotels, camp sites and the Hurtigrute terminal.

necessary to book in advance; just pay the driver on boarding. NOR-WAY Bussekspress (bus pass) guarantees a seat for all passengers. On sale only outside Norway through the company's agents, the pass offers unlimited travel within 7 or 14 consecutive days. Children up to the age of 4 travel free, 4 to 16 years pay 75 percent of the adult price.
NOR-WAY Bussekspress AS, Karl Johans gt. 2, NO-0154 Oslo, tel: 81 54 44 44; www.nor-way.no.

Water Transport

Ferries

You are never very far from the sea in Norway. Ferries are an invaluable means of transport that allow short cuts across fjords to eliminate long road journeys; in built-up areas they are crucial to commuters, like the Horten-Moss ferry across Oslofjord between Vestfold and Østfold. Ferries to the fjord islands around Oslo leave from the Vippetangen quay near Akershus Castle.

Almost all town marinas have places for guest boats. A mooring fee is required.

The following company operates the ferries which run between the centre of Oslo and the Bygdøy Peninsula, where many of the main museums are located.
Bygdøfærgene Skibs
Rådhusbrygge 3
Oslo
Tel: 23 35 68 90

Long-distance Ships

Hurtigrute, the Norwegian Coastal Express service, is a vital means of water transport for Norwegians, but also a superb way for visitors to see Norway's dramatic coast. In summer, boats leave daily, travelling between Bergen and Kirkenes in 11 days and putting in at 35 ports.

Special coastal passes are available to 16–26-year-olds. The steamers take cars, and should be booked well in advance. Either contact your local travel agent or:
Hurtigruten
Tel: 81 03 00 00
www.hurtigruten.com
Kystopplevelser (Coastal Experiences)
Tel: 75 54 17 10
www.kystopplevelser.no
One-day cruise to Geiranger from Oslo. Fly to Ålesund, seven-hour cruise from Ålesund to Geiranger and back, then return flight to Oslo. Prices from NOK 1,955.
Two days in Geiranger fjord. Fly to Ålesund, sail to Geiranger, stay overnight and then return to Oslo. Prices from NOK 2,560.

Buses and Trams

Oslo's bus and tram system is comprehensive and punctual; there are detailed timetables at every stop. Trafikanten *(see Tickets and Info box on page 349)* can suggest bus or tram routes to get you where you wish to go. There are night buses on some routes and very early morning buses (starting at 4am) so that public transport is available virtually around the clock. Bergen and Trondheim also have tram systems.

Underground

Oslo's underground is called the T-bane *(see map on page 390)* and is simple to use. There are five lines that converge under the centre of Oslo. A circle line linking the station of Storo with Carl Berners plass was completed in 2006. You can catch any train to any of the far-flung suburbs from any of the stations between Tøyen and Majorstuen. Station entrances are marked with a "T". Trafikanten *(see box on page 349)* has route maps. The most scenic route must be T-bane 1 up to Frognerseteren. From there enjoy panoramic views back down to Oslo.

Taxis

Taxis are widely available, even in many suburban and rural areas, so you need never risk drink driving

ABOVE: Trøndelag.

(for which penalties are severe).

No matter where you are in Oslo, telephone 023 23 and you will be transferred to the nearest taxi rank. Mini-buses and taxis (for up to 16 people) can also be booked on 22 38 80 70. Otherwise, you can take a taxi from one of the many taxi ranks scattered around the city.

In Oslo, taxis are more expensive at night or if ordered by phone. At night there are two things to watch out for: when everyone leaves the bars and restaurants late, long queues build up at taxi ranks. This can be extremely uncomfortable in the winter if you are not dressed correctly. The problem has given rise to a second difficulty: "pirate" taxis. These either cruise up out of the blue or a "dummy" comes and asks you if you want a taxi without queuing. Pirate taxis are a risk, but if you do use one, make sure you agree a price beforehand. They tend to gather at Stortorget, opposite GlassMagasin.

Road Information

Vegmeldingssentralen (The Road User Information Centre) is an office of the *Statens Vegvesen* (Public Roads Administration). Its main function is to monitor and provide information about roads and road conditions. You may also get information about distances and ferry timetables. Open 24 hours all year, tel: 175 or 81 54 89 91.

Private Transport

By Car

Norway's roads are extremely good, particularly in view of the treacherous weather conditions encountered in winter. Be prepared for tunnels, though, as some routes have long lengths of road underground.

EU driving licences are valid in Norway, but drivers from some countries must carry an international driving Licence. Drive on the right.

Traffic regulations are strictly enforced (see Rules of the Road, below).

Winter Driving

With Norway's winters, you should never assume all roads are passable. Small roads in the north are often closed so the authorities can put all manpower into keeping main roads safe, and even the E6 highway from Oslo to Trondheim has been known to close. If you intend to travel on minor roads, seek a local's advice and go prepared for anything. Your car must be equipped with winter tyres.

Snow-tyre Hire

If you're driving in Norway in winter you can hire the appropriate tyres and snow chains by the week. Ask in any petrol station. In the UK contact:

Snowchains Europroducts
Tel: 01732 884408
Fax: 01732 884564
www.snowchains.co.uk

Breakdown and Accidents

The AA and RAC are affiliated to the AIT (Alliance Internationale de Tourisme), so members receive free assistance (with journey planning as well as backup in case of breakdown or accident) from Norway's NAF (Norges Automobilforbund). More comprehensive repairs can be carried out at NAF-contracted garages (for which you will have to pay). NAF also patrol Norway's main roads and mountain passes from mid-June to mid-August. They have emergency phones along the mountain passes.

NAF, Storgaten 2, N-0155 Oslo
Tel: 22 34 14 00
Fax: 22 33 13 72
24-hour emergency service (for members of AIT clubs), tel: 22 34 16 00/81 00 05 05.

If you are involved in an accident where there are no injuries, telephone **Falken Redningskorps AS** on 80 03 38 80/22 95 00 00 or **Viking Redningstjeneste AS** on 22 08 60 00/80 03 29 00. Their offices provide a 24-hour service for all Norway.

In an emergency you can contact **Alarmsentralen** (Air Ambulance), tel: 67 92 74 00.

It is not necessary to call the police for minor accidents, but drivers must exchange names and addresses; leaving the scene without doing so is a crime.

Only call the **police** (on **112**) or an **ambulance** (on **113**) if it's a real emergency.

Rules of the Road

It is essential for visitors to Norway to be aware of Norwegian driving regulations, some of which vary significantly from those In the UK and on the continent. Here are a few tips to help you drive safely, but for further guidance it's worth getting a copy of Velkommen på norske veier (Welcome to Norwegian Roads), which includes an English section and is available at tourist offices.

Speed Limits The maximum speed limit is usually 80 kph (50 mph), though 100 kph (62 mph) is permitted on some roads (mainly motorways). The limit is reduced to 40 kph (24 mph) in built-up areas, and even 30 kph (18 mph) on certain residential roads. On-the-spot fines are given for drivers found speeding (this may be as much as NOK 3,500). Speed cameras and radar traps are both used.

Giving Way This can be very confusing to the visitor. Roads marked at intervals by yellow diamond signs indicate that you have priority. On all other roads you are required to give way to traffic entering from the right. This is further confused by the fact that some roads have a series of white triangles painted across them at junctions, which mean stop and give way, though as you can imagine these easily become obliterated by snow and ice in the winter.

On roundabouts, priority is from the left. Always give way to trams, buses and taxis. Many roads have a right-hand lane exclusively for buses and taxis.

Drinking and driving You are strongly advised not to drink at all if you anticipate driving within at least eight hours. The current permissible limit is 0.02 per ml, and penalties are severe (imprisonment, a high fine and loss of licence are automatic).

Documentation and equipment You must always have the following with

Toll Roads

Road	Toll Area	Price (in NOK)	Road	Toll Area	Price (in NOK)
E6	Trondheim–Stjørdal	25	Str.64	Skålavegen	
E6	Øsfold	20		(Møre og Romsdal)	55
E10	Nappstraumen Tunnel		108	Hvalertunnel (Østfold)	50
	(Nordland)	65	Str.207	Bjorøy (Hordaland)	120
E18	Vestfold	20	562	Askøy Bridge	
E18	Eidangerhalvøya			(Hordaland)	70
	(Telemark)	15	Str.566	Osterøy Bridge	
E18	Aust-Agder	20		(Hordaland)	40
E18	Kristiansand		Str.658	Ålesund-Ellingsøy-	
	(Vest-Agder)	10		Giske/Vigra	
E39	Rennesøy (Rogaland)	90		(Møre og Romsdal)	55
E39	Trekantsambandet		Str.714	Hitra-Frøya, Dolmøy	
	(Hordaland)	80		(Sør-Trøndelag)	75
E39	Nordhordaland Bridge		Str.714	Hitra-Festland, Sandstad	
	(Hordaland)	45		(Sør-Trøndelag)	70
E39	Øysand-Thamshamn		Str.714	Hitra-Fjellværøy, Ansnes	
	(Sør-Trøndelag)	15		(Sør-Trøndelag)	60
E39/	Kristiansund		755	Skarnsund Bridge	65
Str.70	Mainlandconnection		Str.769	Namdalsprojeckt	
	(Møre og Romsdal)	65		(Nord-Trøndelag)	15
E134	Åkrafjord (Hordaland)	40	**Oslo Toll Road**		20
E69	Kåfjord-Honningsvåg		**Stavenger Toll Road**		
	(Finnmark)	140	Work days 6am–6pm		5
Str.4	Oppland		**Bergen Toll Road**		15
	(Gjøvik-Raufoss)	15	**Trondheim Toll Road**		15
Str.5	Sogndal-Fjæland				
	(Sogn og Fjordane)	150	Toll prices are for a private car		
Str.5	Naustdalstunnel		(with trailer of maximum weight		
	(Sogn og Fjordane)	40	3,500 kg/7,700 lb). They are		
17	Helgeland Bridge		subject to change without notice		
	(Nordland)	85	and credit cards are not accepted,		
Str.23	Oslofjordtunnel		so Norwegians tend to keep a		
	(Akershus)	55	stash of change handy in the car.		

you in your car: driving licence, car registration documents, European accident statement form, insurance policy and a reflective warning triangle. A snow shovel and tow rope are also useful in winter. For regularly updated information In the UK, the AA runs a very good fact line for just a small charge on tel: 0870 600 0371; www.theaa.com

Lights It is obligatory to drive with dipped headlights on during the daytime, even on the brightest summer day. This rule applies to all vehicles, including motorcycles and mopeds. We recommend you carry spare bulbs. Do not forget that right-hand drive cars require black adhesive triangles (often supplied by ferry companies), or clip-on beam deflectors, so you don't dazzle oncoming drivers.

Seat belts must be worn, both front and back (again, there are on-the-spot fines for failing to comply). Motorcycle and moped drivers and their passengers must wear helmets.

Tyres It is obligatory to use winter tyres from October to April. These are either tyres with studs (piggdekk) or specially designed tyres for use in ice and snow. Studded tyres are preferred but these may soon be prohibited in urban areas for environmental reasons.

Caravanning

For information contact:
P.O. Box 104
1921 Sørumsand
Tel: 63 82 99 90
Fax: 63 82 99 99
www.caravanklubben.no

Car Hire

Hiring a car in Norway can be expensive, but may be worthwhile if shared between several people. Otherwise, watch for special weekend and summer prices.

Avis Bilutleie-Liva Bil AS
P.O. Box 154, N-1361 Billingstad (near Oslo)
Tel: 66 77 11 11
Fax: 66 77 11 30
Booking tel: 81 53 30 44
www.avis.no

Europcar
Grini Næringspark 10, P.O. Box 173, 1332 Østerås
Tel: 67 16 58 00
Booking tel: 67 16 58 20/
800 41 400
www.europcar.no

Hertz Bilutleie
P.O. Box 331
N-1324 Lysaker/Oslo
Tel: 67 16 80 80
Booking tel: 67 16 80 00
www.hertz.no

ABOVE: cycling is a great way of exploring Norway's countryside.

Cycling

Cycling in Norway is safe, as there is so little traffic on many minor roads. But you must ride with caution as, though there are a few cycle routes, it is not an integrated system. Cyclists are not allowed to go through the larger tunnels, for example (because of car fumes). Out in the countryside you'll find surfaced cycle paths. Cycling is a good way of exploring outside Oslo: bicycles are allowed on most trains and buses for a small charge.

Special cycle trains are laid on during the summer. Pick up a copy of Oslo Guide (download or order free from www.visitoslo.com) and you'll find suggestions for a Nordmarka (Oslo's forest land) route. Tourist offices have details of mountain cycle tours.

The Syklistens Landsforening (Cycling Association) can help plan tours and cycling holidays: Storg. 23C Pb. 8883 Youngstorget, 0028 Oslo. Tel: 22 47 30 30; fax: 22 47 30 31; e-mail: slf-bike@online.no.

To organise cycle routes and transport for bicycles, contact Skiforeningen, Kongeveien 5, 0787 Oslo. Tel: 22 92 32 00; fax: 22 92 32 50; e-mail: ski@skiforeningen.no

Cycle Rental

In Oslo, Bergen bikes can be hired from hotels, camp sites, local tourist offices or sports shops, as well as small cycle-hire shops.

A/S Skiservice, dept. bike, Voksenkollen Stasjon, Tryvannsveien 2, 0394 Oslo.
Tel: 22 13 95 00

Vestbanen Bike Rental
Brynjulf Bulls plass 2, 0250 Oslo
Tel: 22 83 52 08

White Water AS
Grensen 3, Oslo
Tel: 23 10 40 50
White Water AS deals in extreme sports gear. Off-road and mountain bikes are available for hire.

On Foot

There is almost nowhere in Norway you can't go happily on foot; it is a nation of devout walkers, and walking is one of the most popular outdoor activities at weekends.

The law of access to the natural environment, known as "everyman's right", allows you to walk wherever you want in the wilderness such as seashore, forests, mountains and in other non-cultivated regions. This should be done with consideration. Use paths and roads when walking in agricultural and populated areas.

It is preferable to make use of camp sites if you are staying overnight outdoors. If you pitch a tent in the wilderness, it should be situated at least 150 metres (160 yards) from the nearest house or hut. Open fires are prohibited from 15 April to 15 September.

Detailed maps are available from the Norwegian Trekking Association (DNT). Membership gives you rights to use the association's huts. The map and guidebook selection is excellent; survey maps of Norway are sold; sketch maps are free.

The Norwegian Tourist Board publishes a handbook, Mountain Hiking in Norway, which gives suggested itineraries for mountain walks and details of chalets and where to stay. Contact Scandinavia Connection, 26 Woodsford Square, London W14 8DP; tel: 020 7602 0657; www.scandinavia-connection.co.uk.

Den Norske Turistforening, (Norwegian Trekking Association) Storgate 3, P.O. Box 7 Sentrum, 0101 Oslo, tel: 22 82 28 00; fax: 22 82 28 01; www.turistforening.no.

Hitchhiking

Hitching is not as common here as elsewhere in Europe; but it is not impossible. You'll have the best chance on busier coastal roads. Using a sign is recommended.

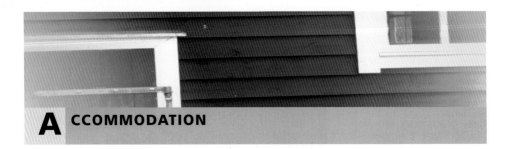

A CCOMMODATION

HOTELS, YOUTH HOSTELS, BED & BREAKFAST

Norwegian hotels can be expensive, but, in common with the rest of Scandinavia, they reduce their rates during the outdoor summer holiday period when business decreases. This makes May to September attractive when compared with standard rates. Weekends are also usually cheaper. Normal weekday rates outside summer are geared towards business occupants, but are generally in line with, sometimes even lower than, hotels elsewhere in Europe or the US.

When it comes to places to stay, Norway has something to suit every requirement. The range covers hotels from the luxurious to the simple, to more modest guesthouses, camp sites, cosy self-catering cottages, and youth and family hostels. Facilities and service are of international standard. A lot of hotels provide luxury attractions like fitness centres and secretarial services, and newer Norwegian hotels are very business conference-oriented.

The British-style bed and breakfast is developing in Norway, and country or farm holidays offer an opportunity to experience day-to-day farm life at close quarters.

Full-board terms are available to guests staying at the same establishment for at least three to five days. Children often go for free, providing the child stays in the parents' room. Guesthouses (pensjonat) offer lower rates and are generally good although many may have shared baths (the bathroom may be down the hall).

The state-run visitors' site, www.visitnorway.com, can be a good starting point for tracking down hotels. See also "useful websites", page 369.

A new online hotel-booking service is available at www.hotels-in-norway.com.

Hotel Chains

Some of the major hotel chains are well-represented in Norway's major cities, but many are not, or they operate through a local brand.

Several local chains, meanwhile, offer passes and discount schemes to help reduce the cost of accommodation. These passes, available for sale at participating hotels, usually involve a modest one-time fee (around NOK 100) and then entitle the holder to discounted rates, mostly in the summer and on weekends. Some passes also offer a free night of accommodation after the pass holder has logged several nights on the programme.

Among the hotel chains in Norway:

Best Western Hotels Norway
Kronprinsens gt 1
0251 Oslo
Tel: 22 94 40 60
Toll-free: 800 11 624
www.bestwestern.no

Choice Hotels AS
Sommerro gt 13-15
0201 Oslo
Tel: 22 40 13 00
www.choicehotels.no

Fjord Tours AS
Norway Fjord Pass
Strømgate 4
5015 Bergen
Tel: 55 55 76 60
www.fjordpass.no

Norlandia Hotels
Skanplus Hotel Pass
Tel: 815 44 144
www.norlandia.no
www.skanplus.com

Radisson SAS Hotels
Tel: 800 160 91
Toll-free from UK: 0800 374411
www.radisson.com

Rica Hotels
Rica Hotellferie Pass
Slependenveien 108
1396 Billingstad
Tel: 66 85 45 60
www.rica.no (Norwegian only)

Scandic Hotels
Sjølyst pl 5
Tel: 23 15 50 00
www.scandic-hotels.com

Thon Hotels
Stenersgate 2
(Skanplus Hotel Pass)
Tel: 23 08 02 00
www.thonhotels.no
www.skanplus.com

Hotels

The hotels are listed geographically, and given a price category. There is a separate box on page 368 with information on booking rooms at some of Norway's historic hotels, many of which are a destination in themselves.

Breakfast Included

Norwegian hotels almost always offer a breakfast buffet that's included in the room rate. All hotel taxes are also included in the quoted rates, so there are rarely any nasty surprises upon checkout (unless you have used the phone in your room to make external calls),

Booking in Oslo

In Oslo, the Tourist Information centres at Fridtjof Nansens Plass 5 (Mon–Sat 9am–5pm), and at the Central Station (daily 8am–11pm; see page 375 for more information) will book accommodation in the capital for those requesting it in person. This service covers private rooms, pensions and hotels.

City Packages

The Oslo and Bergen Packages offer great value for money. They are available at weekends and during the holiday seasons (Easter, summer holidays and Christmas time). The price includes accommodation with breakfast (there are 40 hotels to choose from in Oslo alone) plus the Oslo or Bergen card which includes free entrance to many museums and attractions, free inner city transport and numerous discounts. The packages can be booked through tourist information offices *(see page 375)* in Oslo or Bergen or through a travel agency, but not directly with the hotel.

Chalets *(Hytter)*

There are abundant holiday *hytter* (cabins or chalets) available for rent. These usually house four to six people. If you want to spend just one night in a chalet and then move on, you can stay in one on a campsite without booking ahead. See accommodation guides at www.visitnorway.com, or try the Cultural Heritage Association's website at www.olavsrosa.no/en/.

Fishermen's Cabins *(Rorbuer)*

In the Lofoten islands in northern Norway, and at numerous places elsewhere along the coast, you can rent a traditional former fisherman's cabin, called a *rorbu*. The fishermen used to come to Lofoten from other parts of the coast for the winter cod-fishing season from January to April, and would make these cabins their temporary homes. Most of them have been modernised, and some have their own shower and toilet, but the main appeal is their character.

Lofoten Tourist Office
Tel: 76 06 98 00
Fax: 76 07 30 01

Camping

Norway has more than 1,000 camp sites, classified by 1–5 stars, depending on the standard and facilities available. The fixed charge per plot is usually NOK 80–160, with additional charges per person.

With the Norwegian camping card *(Norsk Campingkort)* you receive a faster checking-in service along with special discount deals. The card is available from participating camp sites. Many camp sites have cabins that may be booked in advance. Some are small and basic, but others are large and well equipped with a sitting room, one to two bedrooms, kitchen, shower and toilet. Ekeberg Camping (tel: 22 19 85 68) and Bogstad Camping – the largest camp site in Norway – also have cabins (tel: 22 51 08 00).

For further information, write to: Norwegian Camping Guide, Essendropsgt. 6, N-0305 Oslo or log onto www.camping.no

B&Bs

British-style bed and breakfasts are catching on in Norway, and they are all of a high standard. You can book at local tourist offices or at Oslo's central railway station. Or look out for signs for *Rom* or *Husrom* outside houses as you drive. A guidebook, *Bed & Breakfast in Norway*, with listings throughout the country, is available from book shops in Norway or from:
Scandinavia Connection
26 Woodsford Square,
London W14 8DP
Tel: 020 7602 0657
www.scandinavia-connection.co.uk

ABOVE: camping in Oppland.

Dalsegg
N-6653 Øvre Surnadal, Norway
Tel: (+47) 99 23 77 99
Fax: (+47) 96 03 56 54
www.bbnorway.com

Youth and Family Hostels

There are approximately 100 youth hostels in Norway, all of a relatively high standard. They are divided into three categories, indicated by a corresponding number of stars.

A night's accommodation costs NOK 75–175, breakfast NOK 60–70 for members of the YHA. Further information can be obtained by contacting *Hostelling International Norway*, or your local YHA office.

Reserving space during the high season is essential, as hostel accommodation is the cheapest way to travel and everyone knows it.
Norske Vandrerhjem
(Hostelling International Norway),
P.B. 53 Grefsen, 0409 Oslo
Tel: 23 12 45 10
Fax: 23 13 93 50
E-mail: hostels@vandrerhjem.no
www.vandrerhjem.no

Norway's Historic Hotels

Tradition runs strong in Norway, and Norwegians are known for preserving their heritage. Massive investment in historic properties has made it possible for visitors to stay in a wide range of them, while enjoying every modern convenience and gourmet meals as well.

A few hotel organisations have been formed during the past decade to keep Norway's historic hotels alive and up-to-date, while maintaining their character and charm. Some of these fairy-tale-like structures are in towns and cities, but many are in the mountains,

along fjords and frankly in relatively obscure but often beautiful locations, making them a destination in themselves. All of the properties are unique, and most include dinner and breakfast as part of the room rate. Overnight accommodation for two including dinner and breakfast generally runs around NOK 2,000, plus drinks. A couple worth trying:
De historiske
PP Box 196 Sentrum
5804 Bergen
Tel: 55 31 67 60
www.dehistoriske.no
This is a group of around 30 historic

hotels, manor houses or timbered lodges and a dozen selected restaurants around Norway, catering to visitors keen on style and good food.
The Great Life Company
Ullern Allé 41, 0311 Oslo
Tel: 24 12 62 10
www.thegreatlifecompany.com
Controlled by a shipowning Oslo family that's made a business out of restoring gracious old lodging establishments. The group consists of around 20 mostly historic inns and restaurants, with a few modern surprises.

TRANSPORT

ACCOMMODATION

EATING OUT

ACTIVITIES

A – Z

LANGUAGE

ACCOMMODATION LISTINGS

OSLO

ABOVE: the Grand Hotel.

Hotel Bristol
Kristian IV's Gate 7
Tel: 22 82 60 00
www.bristol.no
Now part of the Thon
Hotels chain, Bristol
remains a classy place to
stay in the heart of
downtown. Known for its
"Bibliotek (Library) Bar" in
the lobby and its Bristol
Grill restaurant, the hotel is
a popular meeting place for
journalists, politicians and
local celebrities. **$$$**

Hotel Continental
Stortingsgate 24–26
Tel: 22 82 40 00
www.hotel-continental.no
This five-star family-run
hotel often ranks among
the best in northern
Europe, and is famed for

its classic Theater Café, a
Viennese-style café that's
the place to see and be
seen in Oslo. **$$$**

Grand Hotel
Karl Johans Gate 31
Tel: 23 21 20 00
www.grand.no
This is where the Nobel
Peace Prize winner stays
every year, and where the
Nobel Banquet is held.
Located just across from the
Norwegian Parliament, its
venerable Grand Café also
was a favourite haunt of
playwright Henrik Ibsen. **$$$**

Gabelshus Hotel
Gabels Gate 16
Tel: 23 27 65 00
www.choicehotels.no/hotels/no094
This ivy-clad hotel in a
quiet residential
neighbourhood near
downtown is now part of
the so-called Clarion
Collection of hotels. It
opened in 1912. **$$**

Holmenkollen Park Hotel
Kongeveien 26
Tel: 22 92 20 00
www.holmenkollenparkhotel.no
This magnificent wooden
hotel is perched high
above Oslo in the hills
adjacent to the famed
Holmenkollen Ski Jump.
There are outstanding
views over the city and
fjord, with hiking and skiing
trails out the front door.
Rooms are located in a
modern annexe. **$$**

Karl Johan Hotel
Karl Johans Gate 33
Tel: 23 16 17 00
www.norlandia.no/karljohan
Now part of the mid-price
Norlandia chain, this
stately old hotel is a cut
above most of its sister
properties and the location
can't be beaten, right next
door to the Grand and in
the heart of Oslo's
downtown. **$–$$**

First Hotel Millennium
Tollbugaten 25
Tel: 21 02 28 00
www.firsthotels.com
Suite-style family rooms
available in a downtown
location, also popular with
business travellers. **$$**

First Hotel Grims Grenka
Kongens Gate 5
Tel: 23 10 72 00
www.firsthotels.com
Billed as Oslo's first
"design hotel without the
attitude". 42 rooms and 24
suites, rooftop lounge.
Opened in Sept 2007.

Hotel Savoy
Universitets Gate 11
Tel: 23 35 42 00
www.choicehotels.no
A landmark hotel that
recently re-emerged in ultra-
modern style, sporting one
of Oslo's best restaurants
(Restaurant Eik). Part of
the Clarion Collection of
hotels. **$$**

**Radisson SAS
Scandinavia Hotel**

Holbergs Gate 30
Radisson SAS Plaza Hotel
Sonja Henies Plass 3
Toll-free tel (UK): 0800 374411
www.radisson.com
Classic high-rise business-
orientated hotels, with
favourable rates in the
summer. **$$**

Thon Hotel Vika Atrium
Munkedamsveien 45, 0250 Oslo
Tel: 22 83 33 00
www.thonhotels.no/vikaatrium
Mid-range hotel in a great
location near the City Hall
plaza and Aker Brygge. **$**

Coch's Pensjonat
Parkveien 25
Tel: 23-33-24 00
www.cochspensjonat.no
A friendly relatively low-
price alternative with a loyal
following, just at the foot of
one of Oslo's most popular
shopping streets
(Hegdehaugsveien-
Bogstadveien) and a block
from the park around the
Royal Palace. Not all rooms
have private baths. **$**

Perminalen Hotel
Øvre Slottsgate 2
Tel: 23 09 30 81
www.perminalen.no
A recently renovated
hotel near the Parliament
that appeals to young
people on a tight budget.
Simple rooms, where it's
possible to pay just for a
bed in a four-bunk room.
All rooms have private
baths. **$**

OSLO AREA

**Radisson SAS
Airport Hotel**
Oslo Airport Gardermoen
Tel: 63 93 30 00
www.radisson.com
If you need to be near
Oslo's main airport, then
you can't beat this for
convenience. You can walk
from baggage claim to this
elegant and comfortable
hotel in a matter of
minutes. **$$**

Scandic Asker
Askerveien 61
Tel: 23 15 54 00

www.scandic-hotels.com
Suburban hotel near the
main motorway into Oslo,
and a train station. **$**

Thon Hotel Oslofjord
Sandviksveien 184
1337 Sandvika
Tel: 67 55 66 00
www.thonhotels.no
This hotel on the busy E18
motorway in the western
suburb of Sandvika has
been part of several chains
and is now in the Thon
group. It's close to
downtown Sandvika,

Bærum Kulturhus and Ikea
at Slependen. Also close to
the fjord. **$**

Hotell Refsnesgods
Godset 5
1518 Moss
Tel: 69 27 83 00
www.refsnesgods.no
Located right on the Oslo
Fjord on the island of Jeløy,
about an hour south of
Oslo, this is an elegant
getaway spot known for its
wine cellar and art
collection. Several rooms
face the beach. **$$$**

Oscarsborg Festning
1443 Oscarsborg
Tel: 815 51 900
www.nasjonalefestningsverk.no/
oscarsborg
Here you can stay in an
historic fortress on an
island off Drøbak in the
Oslo Fjord. It's good value
for money and open all
year, although arguably
most appealing in the
summer months. The ferry
service is from Drøbak, a
picturesque coastal town in
itself. **$**

KRISTIANSAND

Arnebergs Gjæstgiveri
Dvergsøya
4687 Kristiansand
Tel: 93 08 40 10
www.gjestgiveriet.no
Built by Norwegian architect Arnstein Arneberg in 1917, this carefully preserved guest house sits on the idyllic island of Dvergsøya outside Kristiansand. An exclusive hostelry with emphasis on home-made food. **$$$**

Hotel Norge
Dronningensgate 5
4666 Kristiansand
Tel: 38 17 40 00
www.hotel-norge.no
Stately old hotel in the heart of town, a block off the main shopping street, Markens, and a short walk to the scenic harbour area and fish market. **$–$$**

**Radisson SAS
Caledonien Hotel**
Vestre Strandgate 7, PO Box 339
4663 Kristiansand

Tel: 38 11 21 00
www.radissonsas.com
Large hotel in a central location near the ferry terminal and bus and train stations; all 205 rooms are modern and comfortable, with views of the sea. **$$**

Scandic Kristiansand
Markensgate 39,
4612 Kristiansand
Tel: 21 61 42 00
www.scandic-hotels.com/kristiansand
Though somewhat lacking in character, this hotel is

very conveniently located in the main shopping area of town, and a ten-minute walk from the station.

1-2-3 Hotel
Østre Strandgate 25,
4610 Kristiansand
Tel: 38 70 15 66
www.123-hotel.no
Formally the Syøgløtt Hotel, remodelled into modern budget accommodation. Super location across from the park along the sea front. **$**

BERGEN

ABOVE: sunset over Bergen harbour.

Best Western Victoria Hotel
Kong Oscarsgate 29, 5017
Tel: 55 21 23 00
Fax: 55 21 23 50
E-mail: mail@victoriahotel.no
Once a staging-post inn, this family-run hotel now has 43 comfortable, modern rooms with their own facilities. It's full of character and has an admirable art collection. Fully licensed lobby bar and Greek restaurant. Centrally located. **$$**

Clarion Admiral
C. Sundtsgate 9–13, 5004
Tel: 55 23 64 00
Fax: 55 23 64 64
E-mail: booking@admiral.no
Part of the Choice chain and one of Bergen's finest hotels. There are 210

rooms in varying categories, many of which have superb views over the harbour to Bryggen, while the restaurant has excellent cuisine. **$$**

Golden Tulip Rainbow Hotel Rosenkrantz
Rosenkrantz 7, 5003
Tel: 55 30 14 00
Fax: 55 31 14 76
E-mail: rosenkrantz@rainbow-hotels.no
Comfortable, early 20th-century hotel located in the street behind Bryggen (the wharf) in the heart of the old town; well modernised in light, airy colours. The best rooms have a view of the harbour but get booked up, so plan ahead. There's a restaurant and piano bar. Hotel nightclub entrance is next door. **$$**

Hotel Park Pension
Harald Hårfagresgt 35, 5007
Tel: 55 54 44 00
Fax: 55 54 44 44
E-mail: booking@parkhotel.no
This family-operated hotel with 40 rooms has its own unique flavour and character due to the owner's taste for original antiques. It is located in the university quarter. **$**

Radisson SAS Hotel Norge
Ole Bulls Plass, 5012
Tel: 55 57 30 00
Fax: 55 57 30 01
E-mail: bergen@radissonsas.com
One of Bergen's best-loved hotels and meeting places, right in the centre, with 350 rooms and suites of the highest standard. Four restaurants including gourmet Ole Bull. Winter

garden, swimming pool, nightclub. **$$$**

Radisson SAS Royal Hotel
Bryggen, 5003
Tel: 55 54 30 00
Fax: 55 32 48 08
E-mail: bergen@radissonsas.com
The classic Norwegian architectural style makes this an unusually handsome hotel as it is actually several old warehouses. Upmarket facilities. **$$$**

Scandic Hotel Bergen
Håkonsgaten 2, 5015
Tel: 55 30 90 90
Fax: 55 30 90 91
E-mail: bergencity@scandic-hotels.com
Newly extended and now the biggest Scandic hotel in Norway. Wireless internet access available. Near the city centre. **$$**

Strand Hotel
Strandkaien 2B, 5013
Tel: 55 59 33 00
Fax: 55 59 33 33
E-mail: post@strandhotel.no
Superb harbour views make for a pleasant stay. Family-run hotel with a cosy breakfast room, bar (rated among the five best in Norway) and dinner served in the Lido restaurant. **$**

PRICE CATEGORIES

Price categories are indicated by dollar signs and are per night for two people in a double room with breakfast in high season.
$$$ = More than NOK 1,700
$$ = NOK 1,100–1,700
$ = Less than NOK 1,100

STAVANGER

Radisson SAS Royal Hotel
Løkkeveien 26
Tel: 51 76 60 00
www.radisson.com
Located behind its sister property Atlantic, this is a mid-rise luxury hotel most memorable for its themed floors. **$$–$$$**

Radisson SAS Atlantic Hotel
Olav V's Gate 3
Tel: 51 76 10 00
www.radisson.com
High-rise business hotel in the heart of town, overlooking Lake Breiavatnet. Five-minute walk to the harbour and all its restaurants and bars, with deeply discounted room rates in the summer. **$$**

Victoria Hotel
Skansegate 1
Tel: 51 86 70 00
www.victoria-hotel.no
Historic, first-class, family-run hotel on the harbour, in the heart of the bar and restaurant district yet somehow quietly removed. **$$**

Sola Strand Hotel
Nordsjøvegen
4050 Sola
Tel: 51 94 30 00
www.sola-strandhotel.no
"Strand" means "beach" in Norwegian, and this hotel is located on one of the many windswept beaches along the North Sea, about a 20-minute drive from downtown Stavanger. A classic, traditional hotel with plenty of space to unwind. **$$**

Utstein Kloster Hotel
Mosterøyveien 661
4156 Mosterøy
Tel: 51 72 01 00
www.utsteinklosterhotell.no
Another waterfront hotel, this one is located on an island north of Stavanger near the historic Utstein Cloister. It's connected to the mainland, though, by an underwater tunnel. Excellent area for cycling and seeing historic sites. **$$**

Thon Hotel Maritim
Kongs Gate 32
Tel: 51 85 05 00
www.thonhotels.no/maritim
Tucked into a side-street across from Stavanger's downtown lake, this mid-range hotel participates in the Skanplus Hotel Pass program, offering discounted rates on weekends and in the summer. **$**

BALESTRAND

Innvik Fjordhotel Misjonsheimen
6793 Innvik
Tel: 57 87 42 52
Fax: 57 87 43 95
E-mail: post@innvikfjordhotell.no
This locally owned hotel sits in the heart of the fjord area, with half of the rooms overlooking the fjord, and the other half overlooking the mountainside. The kitchen uses fresh local fruits, meat and fish when in season. There's also a sauna, solarium, café and fitness room. 34 rooms. **$**

Kvikne's Hotel
Kviknevegen 8
Postboks 24
N-6898 Balestrand
Tel: 57 69 42 00
Fax: 57 69 42 01
E-mail: booking@kviknes.no
Owned by the Kvikne family since 1877, this Swiss-style hotel is in a lovely setting on the edge of Sognefjord – most of the rooms have delightful views looking out over the water. The hotel makes a good base for walking, mountain hiking and glacier trips. **$$**

Lavik Fjord Hotel
Lavik, 6947 Lavik
Tel: 57 71 40 40
Fax: 57 71 40 41
E-mail: info@lavikfjordhotell.no
This family-run hotel on the Sognefjord offers beautiful surroundings with fantastic views of the fjord, From here you can fish, swim, row, sail, paddle, cycle or go rock climbing and mountain walking. It's on the coastal highway E39 so can be easily reached by car or bus, or you can take the express boat from Bergen. There's a bar and restaurant. Only 15 rooms. **$**

Midtnes Pensjonat
N-6898
Tel: 57 69 11 33
Fax: 57 69 15 84
E-mail: booking@midtnes.no
A pretty, characterful guesthouse overlooking Sognfjord, with its own pier, bathing-place and rowing boat. Bike hire can be arranged through the tourist office. **$**

Quality Hotel Florø
Hamnegata 7, 6900 Florø
Tel: 57 75 75 75
Fax: 57 75 75 10
E-mail: q.floro@choice.no
Sitting on the waterfront with a view of the fjord, mountains, islands and the sea, this hotel has 79 maritime-style bedrooms and a first-class restaurant. It's not far from the shopping centre and walking trails. **$**

Victoria Hotel
Markegt. 43, 5900 Florø
Tel: 57 74 10 00
Fax: 57 74 19 80
E-mail: kundeservice@hotell.no
The Victoria Hotel, a traditional family-run hotel with spacious rooms, is located in the centre of Florø. There's a bar, nightclub and restaurant, which serves dishes based on local produce from the sea. 164 rooms. **$$**

BELOW: interior of Kvikne's Hotel.

PRICE CATEGORIES

Price categories are indicated by dollar signs and are per night for two people in a double room with breakfast in high season.
$$$ = More than NOK 1,700
$$ = NOK 1,100–1,700
$ = Less than NOK 1,100

TRONDHEIM

Elgeseter Hotel
Tormodsgate 3
Tel: 73 82 03 30
Fax: 73 82 03 31
E-mail: elgeseter.hotell@munken.no
Conveniently located just 10 minutes' walk from the centre. **$**

Grand Olav Clarion Hotel
Kjøpmannsgaten 48
Tel: 73 80 80 80
Fax: 73 80 80 81
E-mail: cc.grand.olav@choice.no
Top-class hotel situated in the heart of Trondheim, close to shops, bars and restaurants. Runs an airport bus. **$$$**

Prinsen Scandic
Kongensgate 30
Tel: 73 80 70 00
Fax: 73 80 70 10
E-mail: prinsen@scandic-hotels.com
A wealth of facilities here including 81 rooms, the fine Pinocchio restaurant, a bistro, bar, grill room, wine tavern and beer garden. **$$**

Quality Hotel Augustin
Kongensgate 26
Tel: 73 54 70 00
Fax: 73 54 70 01
E-mail: hotel-augustin@hotel-augustin.no
Close to the main city square, this huge old brick hotel has 139 comfortable rooms, bar, fitness room, internet access and covered parking. **$$**

Radisson SAS Royal Garden Hotel
Kjøpmannsgt 73
Tel: 73 80 30 00
Fax: 73 80 30 50
E-mail: sales@trdzh.rdsas.com
With 298 well-appointed rooms plus solarium, indoor pool, gymnasium, sauna and several good restaurants. Runs an airport bus every 15 minutes. **$$**

Thon Hotel Gildevangen
Søndre gate 22B
Tel: 73 87 01 30
Fax: 73 52 38 98
E-mail: gildevangen@thonhotels.no
In a grand building in the centre of town, near the bus and train stations, and with a stop for the airport shuttle right outside. All the rooms are a good size and decorated to a high standard. The restaurant, on the second floor, only serves breakfast, Bar, internet access. **$**

BELOW: harbour-side at the Radisson SAS Royal Garden.

TROMSØ

Grand Nordic
Storgt 44
Tel: 77 75 37 77
Fax: 77 75 37 78
E-mail: Resepsjon.gnt@nordic.no
Close to the centre, 4 km (2½ miles) from the airport. Full conference facilities and well-appointed rooms. **$$**

Quality Hotel Saga
Richard Withs plass 2
Tel: 77 60 70 00
Fax: 77 60 70 10
Email: booking@sagahotel.no
Small conference hotel with relaxing atmosphere. **$$**

Rica Ishavshotel
Fr. Langesgt. 2
Tel: 77 66 64 00
Fax: 77 66 64 44
E-mail: rica.ishavshotel@rica.no
First-rate luxury hotel close to the centre, specialising in conferences and comfort. **$$$**

Scandic Tromsø
Heiloveien 23
Tel: 77 75 50 00
Fax: 77 75 50 11
E-mail: tromso@scandic-hotels.com
Modest conference hotel located in Tromsø suburb close to the airport. Outside pool. **$$**

With Home Hotel
Sjøgata 35–37, N-9000
Tel: 77 68 70 00
Fax: 77 68 96 16
E-mail: booking@with.no
A first-class hotel with a difference. Situated by the waterfront in Tromsø's dock district, it offers a beautiful view to the Tromsø bridge and the famous Arctic Cathedral, and has a maritime atmosphere. **$$**

SVALBARD

Kapp Linné/Isfjord Radio
Contact: Svalbard Tourist Office
Tel: 79 02 55 50
Located in a disused radio station, Kapp Linné is situated km km (50 miles) from Longyearbyen and is only approachable by snowmobile or by boat. It offers simple accommodation in 19 rooms in three different buildings from March to May or in summer on request. There is a warm lounge and a dining area. Price includes dinner. **$$**

Radisson SAS Polar
P.O. Box 500, 9171 Longyearbyen
Tel: 79 02 34 50
Fax: 79 02 34 51
E-mail: reservations.longyearbyen@radissonsas.com
The world's northernmost full-service hotel offers views of the snowcapped peaks and the Isfjord. Restaurant, lobby bar and pub are all popular with the locals. Relax room and sauna available. **$$**

Spitsbergen Hotel
P.O. Box 500
9171 Longyearbyen
Tel: 79 02 62 00
Fax: 79 02 62 01
E-mail: spitra@spitzbergentravel.no
Once the meeting hall for the local mining company, this is now a modern hotel. In the cosy lounge you can get freshly baked waffles every afternoon or sit in front of the fire with a book on the Arctic from the library. The Funktionær-messen Restaurant has fantastic views of the town, the Longyear Glacier and Hiorthfjellet. **$$**

Spitsbergen Nybyen Gjestehus
P.O. Box 500
9171 Longyearbyen
Tel: 79 02 63 00
Fax: 79 02 63 01
E-mail: guesthouse@spitzbergentravel.no
A simple guesthouse with a living room and a kitchen for tea-making. The building was erected as part of the post-war reconstruction programme for Longyearbyen and comprised eight accommodation units for miners. Open Mar–Sept. **$**

Thon Hotel Polar
Grønnegata 45
Tel: 77 75 17 00
Fax: 77 75 17 10
E-mail: polar@thonhotels.no
A small and cosy hotel with an informal atmosphere in the centre of Tromsø. Airport bus stops 50 metres/yds from the hotel entrance. With 113 rooms, bar and internet access. **$**

E ATING OUT

RECOMMENDED RESTAURANTS, CAFÉS & BARS

What to Eat

Norwegians eat hearty breakfasts, but light lunches; the size of the evening meal *(middag)* depends on the day of the week and the occasion.

With the abundant supply of seafood and what can be gleaned from forest and field, the Norwegian diet has traditionally been healthy and appetising. For example, white bread is rarely purchased as most Norwegians prefer brown bread or dry crackers for breakfast. However, the younger generation has a tendency to eat frozen pizzas and easily prepared meals.

The hunting season (early autumn) offers some irresistible temptations: pheasant, grouse, elk and reindeer steaks served with peppercorns and rich wild mushroom sauces. It is also a good time of year to make the most of seafood (with cod considered best in months with an R in them).

Outside main meals there are many coffee breaks, often served with pastries, including *bolle* (raisin buns) and *wienerbrød* (lighter pastries laced with fruit or nuts).

Frokost (breakfast) is more or less a variation of the lunch *Kaldtbord*, a spread including breads (try *grovbrød* and *knekkebrød*), sausage, cheese (try the piquant *Gudbrandalsost*, a delicious burnt goats' milk cheese with a dark golden colour), eggs, herrings, *gravlax* (marinated salmon), and coffee and tea.

The lunch version has hot dishes, such as sliced roast meats, meatballs or fish. *Øllebrød* (beef marinated in beer and served inside pitta bread with salad) makes a hearty, inexpensive lunch; an open-faced shrimp or ham sandwich is another staple.

Dinner in a city restaurant can be anything you wish. In someone's home you might eat mutton stew or a fish ragout. Boiled potatoes with dill or parsley usually accompany a hot main course. When dining in more remote places, the menus will invariably be limited by availability. *Smørbrød* is a snack (called *aftens*

when eaten late at night), usually of bread or crackers with butter, cheese and salami or ham.

For dessert, ice cream is a favourite, as is apple pie. In summer there are all kinds of puddings based on the fresh berries that grow profusely in the Norwegian woods.

Where to Eat

There has been a significant increase in what's on offer when you choose to eat out in Norway. Pizza is very popular and the cynic may even describe it as the Norwegian national dish. Asian food has also become a local favourite, although Indian restaurants tend to tone down the spices to suit the more delicate Norwegian palate, so you may wish to tell the waiter to beef it up a bit. Continental European dishes have always played a role in Norwegian cuisine (such as Viennese- and French-style dishes), but pride in native foods and an interest in "new Scandinavian" cuisine is prevalent.

At lunch time many restaurants offer special fixed-price menus. More casual meals can be had from informal establishments, which come under a range of names such as *stovas*, *kros*, *bistros*, *kafés*, *kafeterias*, and *gjæstgiveris* and may sell alcohol as well as coffee and soft drinks. For an even more casual meal buy a hot dog *(pølse)*, kebab or a waffle from a kiosk; these stay open late to catch pubcrawlers. And yes, there is McDonald's.

Restaurants

Restaurants are grouped by area starting with Oslo. They are listed alphabetically in price order, with the most expensive first.

Drinking Notes

No one talks about a trip to Norway without complaining of the high cost of alcohol. For those who can afford the prices, serving hours are long; in Oslo you can drink spirits until midnight and wine or beer until 3am. Outside Oslo, times are less predictable; a conservative Lutheran culture holds sway in many west-coast areas, rendering some counties virtually dry. But there are exceptions to this: in Oslo, for example, there are some no-alcohol hotel/restaurants and in the "dry" counties it is always possible to find a hotel/restaurant

that serves some form of alcohol.

The *Vinmonopolet* (state off-licences/liquor stores) in cities are open Mon–Fri 10am–6pm and Sat 9am–2pm; they are closed on election days, holidays and the preceding day of a holiday.

Most Norwegians drink beer and/or wine. Traditional *Akevitt*, similar in taste to Schnapps, is derived from potato and caraway seeds, and is also a favourite. It can be sipped neat in small glasses at room temperature, or served cold with beer to accompany salty, spicy or pungent dishes.

OSLO

Norwegian Classics

De Fem Stuer
Holmenkollen Park Hotel
Tel: 22 92 20 00
Elegant dining inside the historic timbered salons of this fairy-tale-like hotel overlooking the city and fjord. **$$$**
Det Gamle Raadhus
Nedre Slotts Gate 1
Tel: 22 42 01 07
Housed in the capital's old city hall from the 1600s, now best known for its *lutefisk* in the months leading up to Christmas. **$$**
DS Louise
Stranden 3
Tel: 22 83 00 60
This was one of the first restaurants to open at the waterfront complex Aker Brygge, and it's still going strong. Nostalgic maritime decor and a wide range of traditional dishes. **$$**
Ekeberg Restaurant
Kongsveien 15
Tel: 23 24 23 00
Take the No. 18–19 tram to Sjømannsskolen and walk up the hill to this recently restored gem. Knockout view over the city and fjord, with a large outdoor terrace complementing the restaurant inside. **$$**

Grand Café
Karl Johans Gate 31
Tel: 24 14 53 00
Henrik Ibsen's former haunt, known for its murals and stylish surroundings just across from the Parliament. **$$**
Kaffistova
Rosenkrantz Gate 8
Tel: 23 21 42 10
Cafeteria-style place dishing up authentic rural Norwegian food. Fast and filling. **$**
Maud's
Tollbugate 24
Tel: 22 83 72 28
Old-fashioned Norwegian-style restaurant, named after Norway's first modern queen, the former Princess Maud of England. **$$**
Solsiden
Sondre Akershus Kai 34
Tel: 22 33 36 30
One of the best seafood restaurants in Oslo, situated right on the harbour under the historic Akershus Fortress. Summer only. **$$**
Sult
Th. Meyers Gate 26
Tel: 22 87 04 67
Named after Knut Hamsun's novel *Hunger*, this was one of the first restaurants to pop up in the newly revitalised Grünlerløkka district.

Simple, fresh food dubbed "neo-Norsk." **$$**
Theatercafeen
Stortings Gate 24–26
Tel: 22 82 40 50
Famed Vienna-style café; classic dishes served with flair, live violin music. The place to see and be seen in Oslo. **$$**

Continental/ International

Alex Sushi
Cort Adelers Gate 2
Tel: 22 43 99 99
The *New York Times* lavished praise on this neighbourhood sushi place. Book well in advance. **$$**
Bagatelle
Bygdøy allé 3
Tel: 22 12 14 40
Simply the best, with the Michelin stars and prices to prove it. **$$$**
Bambus
Kirkeveien 57
Tel: 22 85 07 00
Blend of Thai, Vietnamese and Japanese food in a stylish setting in Oslo's trendy Majorstuen district. **$**
Brasserie France
Øvre Slottsgate 16
Tel: 23 10 01 65
You'll think you're in Paris, but the quality of the shellfish is definitely Norwegian. **$$**

Dinner
Stortingsgate 22
Tel: 23 10 04 66
Spicy Szechuan cuisine, hailed by Chinese aficionados. **$$**
La Rosa Magra
Arbins Gate 1
Tel: 22 56 14 00
Excellent Italian food, from small pizzas to full-course meals, located just under the flat where Henrik Ibsen lived after returning from years in Italy. Splendid view across to the Royal Palace. **$–$$**
Oro Restaurant and Bar
Tordenskiolds Gate 6A
Tel: 23 01 02 40
Elegant dining in the main gourmet restaurant, tapas in the adjacent bar/café. **$–$$$**
Restaurant Eik
Universitetsgata 11
Tel: 22 36 07 10
Arguably the best of Oslo's "menu-based" restaurants, where you select how many courses you want from a carefully planned multi-course meal. **$$**
Statholdergaarden
Rådhus Gate 11
Tel: 22 41 88 00
Danish chef Bent Stiansen is host in the elegant restaurant upstairs and the bar downstairs, in an urban home from the 1700s. **$$$**

BERGEN

Bryggen Tracteursted
Bryggen 6
Tel: 55 33 69 99
Traditional Norwegian fare and great fish dishes. **$$**
Dickens
King Olavvs Plass
Tel: 55 36 31 30
This informal setting is popular and relaxed, serving good meals, light snacks and just drinks. **$$**
Fiskekrogen Fisk and Vilt Restaurant
Fish Market
Tel: 55 55 96 40
The very best of Norwegian

cuisine. Superb fish dishes served by friendly and knowledgeable waiters. **$$$**
Fløien Folkerestaurant
Top of Fløien funicular
Tel: 55 32 18 75
Good, reasonably priced food with intoxicating view. Work up an appetite by walking there. **$$**
Holbergstuen
Torvalmenning 6
Tel: 55 55 20 55
In the heart of the town. Good traditional dishes. **$$**

Louisiana Creole Restaurant
Vågsallmenningen 6
Tel: 55 54 66 60
An intimate restaurant offering first-class Creole and Cajun food, located in the centre next to the tourist information office. **$$**
Mago Café
Neumanns GT.5
Tel: 55 96 29 80
Eco-friendly restaurant that claims to be good for your digestion as well as tasty. Organic vegetables and free-range meat and fish. **$**

Mongolian Barbecue Restaurant
Olav Kyrresgt. 39
Tel: 55 32 39 15
Diners can combine lamb, pork, beef, chicken, vegetables and sauces to

PRICE CATEGORIES

The symbols give an indication of prices, based on a three-course evening meal per head, excluding wine.
$ = Less than NOK 150
$$ = NOK 150–400
$$$ = More than NOK 400

suit their own tastes at this Mongolian barbecue buffet. Best for confirmed meat-eaters. Fully licensed. **$$**
Stragiotti Bar & Ristorante
Vestre Torggate 3
Tel: 55 90 31 00

This family restaurant makes a change from Norwegian staples; it's located in pleasant surroundings and offers authentic Italian food with good service. **$$**

To Kokker (Two chefs)
Bryggen, Bergen
Tel: 55 32 28 16
On the Bryggen in Bergen, this well-known restaurant serves Norwegian and French dishes. Specialities

include game, fish and seafood. **$$$**
Wesselstuen
Ole Bulls plass 6
Tel: 55 55 49 49
Fish and stews are served to a loyal local crowd. **$$**

TRONDHEIM

Athena
Brattørgata 5
Tel: 73 53 50 53
A Greek taverna with traditional specialities and good service. Live Greek music on the weekends. **$$**
Bryggen
Øvre Bakklandet 66
Tel: 73 87 42 42
One of the best and most elegant restaurants in Trondheim right by the River Nidelva. Serves an

international menu using the finest ingredients. **$$$**
Big Horn Steakhouse
Munkegt. 14, Ravnkloa
Tel: 73 50 94 90
Specialises in tasty spare ribs and juicy steaks. **$$**
Chablis Brasseri and Bar
Øvre Bakklandet 66
Tel: 73 87 42 50
Chablis is an informal French restaurant under the same roof as Bryggen Restaurant. **$$**

Credo Restaurant and Bar
Ørjaveita 4A
Tel: 73 53 03 88
International-style restaurant known for its original food and no fixed menu. The wine cellar is one of Norway's best. **$$**
Grenaderen
Kongsgårdsgt. 1e
Tel: 73 51 66 80
In a 16th-century forge with a large terrace. Offers a

traditional menu including fish and reindeer. **$$**
Havfruen
Kjøpmannsgt. 7
Tel: 73 87 40 70
Some of the finest Norwegian fish and seafood, plus meat. Trendy bar. **$$**
Zia Teresa Pizzeria Trattoria
Vår Frue Strete 4
Tel: 73 52 64 22
Pizza with a Norwegian twist. **$$**

TROMSØ

Compagniet
Sjøgata 12
Tel: 77 66 42 22
Gourmet fare. **$$$**
Indigo Restaurant
Storgata 36
Tel: 77 66 11 50
This Indian diner is a favourite with the locals and offers traditional courses in an informal setting. **$$**

Peppermøllen Mat-og Vinhus
Storgata 42
Tel: 77 68 62 60
Menu features about 160 dishes using mainly Norwegian ingredients, with fish being a clear favourite. **$$**
Studenthuset
Skipperg. 44,
Tel: 77 68 44 10

Simple student-style restaurant has reasonably priced pizzas, said to be the best in town, and pastas. **$**
Store Norske Fiskekompani
Storgata 73
Tel: 77 68 76 00
Just fish served here, to the highest quality and taken straight from the

harbour. The seafood is cooked in a variety of styles, from traditional to "New Scandinavian". Meat-eaters need not attend. **$$$**
Vertshuset Skarven
Strandtorget 1
Tel: 77 60 07 20
This popular restaurant serves several varieties of steak. **$$**

STAVANGER

Craig's Kitchen
Breitorget
N-4006
Tel: 51 93 95 90

This transplanted North American cook has a lot of fans, and with good reason. The menu may be limited

but the quality of the food is top-notch. **$$**
Hall Toll
Skansegaten 2
Tel: 51 51 72 32
Housed in a former customs hall on the waterfront, this relatively new restaurant is cavernous with an innovative menu and chic clientele. **$$**
N.B. Sørensens Dampskibsexpedition
Skagen 26
Tel: 51 84 38 20
One of the most traditional restaurants in Stavanger, decorated in nautical style to match its location at the Vågen promenade and

marina. An international menu using fresh Norwegian ingredients. **$$**
Charlottenlund
Kongsgaten 45
Tel: 51 91 76 00
Graceful, Norwegian- and French-inspired cuisine served in a former private mansion on the lake in the heart of town. **$$**

BELOW: a traditional Norwegian trout dish (with cheese).

ACTIVITIES

THE ARTS, NIGHTLIFE, FESTIVALS, SHOPPING, OUTDOOR ACTIVITIES AND CHILDREN

THE ARTS

Music and Opera

In summer the arts take to the outdoors in Norway, and classical music and opera are no exception. For Oslo dates, pick up the *What's On in Oslo* guide. The very active Oslo Philharmonic, founded by Edvard Grieg, is conducted by Jukka-Pekka Saraste, with frequent visits by acclaimed guest conductors and soloists. Den Norske Opera (National Opera) stages big productions such as *La Boheme* and *Don Giovanni* during the year. The opera is set to move to a brand-new opera house on the waterfront east of Akershus in April 2008.

Akershus Fortress and the Henie Onstad Art Centre (Høvikodden) are two other fine settings for summer concerts, and there are several outdoor rock and pop festivals from June through to August.

Whether the performers are Norwegian or foreign, the season winter or summer, Norway has a rich and varied musical and operatic life (consult area guides for festival schedules; some English and American newspapers give a pan-European list of festivals at the start of each summer). This may be your chance to listen to some of the conductors and performers you'd previously only heard on Deutsche Gramophone CDs, or a first opportunity to see Grieg performed by Norwegian musicians.

Theatre and Dance

Theatre is booming in Norway, with small, contemporary theatres springing up everywhere; but performances are in Norwegian. Some plays are held in English during the Ibsen Theatre Festival in August in Oslo.

Dance has also come into its own. Classical ballet is performed at the Oslo Opera House. Traditional folk dances can be seen in many towns on National Day (17 May), and at Oslo's Konserthus.

Cinema

The Norwegians love films, hence the vast number of cinemas; Oslo has around 40 screens including the impressive wide-screen cinema at Coloseum in Frogner. First-run and repertory films are always shown in the original language, with Norwegian subtitles. Kiosks, newspapers, and local city guides have listings. Booking tickets is recommended for Fridays and Saturdays.

NIGHTLIFE

Oslo, once considered a big yawn at night, is now vying with Stockholm and Copenhagen to be Scandinavia's nightlife capital. Loads of new bars, pubs and clubs have come on to the scene, but many can't recoup their investments quickly enough and go out of business (some also close down once they have made a quick killing). So check locally for up-to-date venue listings, or see the official *Oslo Guide* provided free by Oslo Promotion and available on the website www.visitoslo.com. All the major cities have both official and unofficial nightlife guides.

In Bergen, Stavanger, Trondheim and Tromsø nightlife exists to a much lesser extent. But you can guarantee that most large hotels have nightclubs and bars. In small towns, you may be out of luck altogether.

International rock, folk, and jazz musicians often include Oslo on European tours.

There are only two things you need to be warned about before a night out: the high cost of drinking, and age restrictions: some clubs have minimum ages as high as 26 (although 21 and 23 are more common).

FESTIVALS

January

Longyearbyen: Polar Jazz. The world's nothernmost jazz festival, 645 km (400 miles) from the North Pole. Tel: 79 02 61 00.

February

Kristiansund: Opera Festival. Two or three opera productions plus church music, ballet and other concerts. Tel: 71 58 99 60.
Rorosmartnan: The Roros Fair has been an annual tradition since 1854. Markets, concerts, exhibitions. Tel: 72 41 00 00.
Tromsø: Northern (De)lights Festival. Music ranging from baroque to contemporary and from jazz to classical. Tel: 76 14 12 03.

March

Alta: Northern Lights Winter Festival with music, theatre, markets, ski and snowmobile competitions and more. Tel: 95 43 88 10.

Narvik: Winter Festival. Church music, jazz, classical music, markets, carnival and sports events. Tel: 76 94 87 00.
Lillehammer: Blues Festival. International and Norwegian musicians. Tel: 61 28 60 55.
Oslo: Church Music Festival. Concerts in Oslo Cathedral and other churches in the city. Tel: 22 41 81 13.

April

Bergen: Music Festival, including blues, country & western, cajun and rock. Norwegian and international artists perform throughout the city. Tel: 55 21 50 60.
Voss: Vossajazz. Three days and nights of jazz and folk music with international and Norwegian performers. www.vossajazz.no

May

Constitution Day (17 May). Celebrations and parades all over Norway.
Stavanger: International Jazz Festival. Tel: 51 84 66 67.
Bergen: International Festival. One of Norway's artistic highlights. World-class music, dance and theatre in a beautiful setting. Also Nattjazz – an international jazz festival. Tel: 55 21 06 31.
Ål: Norwegian Folk Music Week with concerts, song and dance. Competition between the best fiddlers and dancers in the region. Tel: 32 08 56 45.
Bergen: Dragon Boat Festival in the harbour. Tel: 55 56 05 10.
Bomlo: Mostra spelet. Outdoor historical play. Tel: 53 42 66 20.
Stavanger: Maijazz. Traditional jazz festival. Both international and Norwegian artists perform in more than 30 concerts. Tel: 51 84 66 68.

June

Sarpsborg: Gleng Music Festival. Folk, rock, blues, jazz and classical music. Indoor and outdoor concerts. Tel: 69 15 68 00.
Hardanger: Music and culture from the Hardanger fjord area, with chamber, church and folk music. Tel: 53 67 15 15.
Oslo: Norwegian Wood. Rock music festival with Norwegian and international artists. Tel: 81 55 03 33.
Harstad: North Norway Festival. The region's largest cultural event, with music, theatre, dance and art exhibitions. Tel: 77 04 12 30.
Vinstra: Country and Western Festival. Non-stop country music with international and Norwegian artists. Tel: 61 21 69 39.

June/July

Grimstad. Norwegian Short Film Festival. With around 80 short and documentary films. Tel: 37 04 40 41.
Vestfold: Arts festival – Norwegian and international artists perform in locations all over the county. Tel: 33 37 10 00.

July

Kristiansand. Quart International rock festival. Performers from the US and Europe. Tel: 38 14 69 69.
Forde: Norway's largest folk music festival with more than 250 performers from all over the world. Tel: 57 72 19 40.
Molde: International Jazz Festival. Norway's largest jazz festival, with more than 400 performers, many of them world famous. Tel: 71 20 31 50.
Bo: Telemark Festival with traditional folk, blues and jazz music. Tel: 35 95 19 19.

Bergen Festival

Bergen's International Festival in late May offers music, drama, ballet, opera, jazz and folk arts.
For a festival brochure and further details contact:
Bergen International Festival, P.O. Box 183, 5804 Bergen.
Tel: 55 21 06 30
Fax: 55 21 06 40

July/August

Vinstra: Peer Gynt Festival. Art exhibits, music, processions with national costumes, open-air theatre. Performance of Henrik Ibsen's *Peer Gynt* and Edvard Grieg's music, by Gala Lake. Tel: 61 29 47 70.

August

Oslo: Jazz Festival. Over 60 concerts in six days. Tel: 22 42 91 20.
Bodø: Nordland Music Festival. Classical, jazz, rock and folk music – with national and international artists. Also church concerts, music theatre, art exhibitions. Tel: 75 54 90 40.
Stavanger: International Chamber Music Festival. Renowned soloists and new talents perform chamber music in various ensembles. Tel: 51 84 66 70.
Hammerfest: Music and Theatre Festival focusing on culture in northern Norway. Tel: 78 41 21 85.

September

Stavanger: International literature festival. Symposiums, readings, poetry, concerts and plays with Norwegian and international writers. Tel: 51 50 79 40.

October

Oslo: Ultima Contemporary Music Festival. Norway's largest. Tel: 22 42 99 99.
Lillehammer: Jazz Festival. Mainly Norwegian performers. Tel: 61 05 08 00.

November

Fagernes. Salt-cured trout in the Valdres manner. You can sample many versions of this local favourite on the first weekend of the month.

December

Oslo: Parade past the Grand Hotel to honour the winner of the Nobel Peace Prize plus a Nobel concert in the Spektrum Theatre. Tel: 22 12 93 00.

BELOW: one of Oslo's many outdoor festivals.

ABOVE: Aker Brygge shopping centre.

SHOPPING

What to Buy

Popular souvenirs from Norway include knitted jumpers, cardigans, gloves and mittens, pewter, silver jewellery and cutlery, hand-painted wooden objects (like bowls with rose designs), trolls and fjord horses carved out of wood, goat and reindeer skin, enamel jewellery, woven wall designs, furs, handicrafts, glassware and pottery – to name just a few (see *Tax-free Shopping, below,* on how to reclaim tax).

The major department stores are *Glasmagasinet* and *Steen & Strøm,* both of which have a good selection of most of these items. However, if you

Shopping Hours

Weekdays Generally 9am–5pm, with late Thursday opening for many stores until 7 or 8pm. Stores may close earlier in summer, especially on Fridays.
Saturday Usually 9am–1, 2 or 3pm.
Shopping centres such as Aker Brygge, Palléet and Oslo City in Oslo, Galleriet in Bergen and City Syd in Trondheim are open until 8 or 9pm week nights.
Kiosks tend not to close until 10pm or even 11pm and are usually open all weekend.
Supermarkets Most stay open until 8pm.
Petrol stations are usually open until at least 11pm.

want speciality stores in Oslo, there is a *Where to Shop* guide, as well as a detailed "Shopping" section in the *Oslo Guide* (see www.visitoslo.com). Karl Johansgate, Grensen, and Bogstad-veien are all major shopping streets. With the exception of Oslo, most Norwegian towns are so compact that your best bet is to window shop and go into the places that look most appealing.

Anyone interested in buying Norwegian art will have ample prospects – from south to north, Norway abounds in galleries. Get a local recommendation.

If you are food shopping, fruit and vegetable prices vary considerably throughout the year. Look out for *lavpris* (low-price) shops offering discounts. The first Saturday of each month is "Super Saturday" when shops in Oslo open longer and offer special discounts. Bear in mind that most bottles (whether plastic or glass) have a returnable deposit of NOK 1.

Tax-free Shopping

If you are a resident of a country other than Norway, Sweden, Denmark or Finland, you are entitled to tax-free shopping on purchases in excess of NOK 308 at any of the 3,000 stores connected to the scheme.

The store issues you with a tax-free voucher for the amount of VAT paid. When you leave Norway, a refund of 11–18 percent (depending on the sale price) will be refunded on presentation of the goods, the tax-free voucher and your passport, on condition that the item has not been used while in Norway.

Global Refund has its own representatives at a total of 100 refund places, including airports, international ferry terminals and at the main border crossings. Check opening times, as they are not open

24 hours, and make sure there is a refund desk if you are using a small border crossing. Customs officials cannot refund VAT. For details, contact Global Refund Norge, P.O. Box 48 N-1332 Østerås, tel: 67 15 60 10; fax: 67 15 60 29.

OUTDOOR ACTIVITIES

If Norwegians can contrive a sport as an excuse to be outdoors, they'll do it. That's why there are such great facilities here; all Norwegians love sport. (For a full listing of the range of sports and sports facilities in the Oslo region, see the Outdoor Activities pages of the *Oslo Guide*; www.visitoslo.com.) There is a Forest Safari programme, where for a half or whole day you can partake in a range of activities in Marka (Oslo's forest) in between which you are carted around by Land Rover. Visit the main tourist information office for details.

Boating

Foreign visitors are always welcome in boating circles, and there are hundreds of sailing and boating clubs and associations throughout Norway. The national organisation for recreational and competitive motor-boating is: Kongelig Norsk Båt Forbund, Vågebyveien 23, 0569 Oslo, tel: 22 35 68 00, fax: 22 35 68 11.

The most popular volumes of the six-volume *Den Norske Los* ("Norwegian Pilot"), the meticulously detailed manual of all navigable waters, is available with Norwegian and English texts. Volume 3 covers the southwest coast from south of Stavanger to north of Bergen; Volume 2 the Oslo Fjord and the south coast. If you are planning a sailing holiday, obtain a copy of *Guest Harbours in Norway* (available from tourist offices, *see page 375*), which provides valuable information, including place

BELOW: coming ashore in Trøndelag.

descriptions, sketch maps and details of the coastguard escort service. *Cruising in Norwegian Waters* is another useful boating book.

Canoeing

Numerous rivers and lakes in Norway offer canoeing and kayaking. Some of the best include the Femund area, Østfold, Aust and Vest Agder, Telemark and suburban Oslo. Contact the local tourist office for details, or **Norges Padleforbund** (Norwegian Canoe Association), Service Boks 1, Ullevaal Stadion, 0840 Oslo
Tel: 21 02 98 35
Fax: 21 02 98 36
www.padling.no.

Cycling

As a particularly popular method of transport in Norway, cycling is considered relatively safe. Special routes exist during summer and special cycle paths can be found in rural areas. For further details on planning a cycling holiday and renting bicycles, see *Getting Around, page 353.*

Fishing

With a coastline of 21,465 km (13,330 miles), as well as countless fjords, lakes and rivers, Norway is a fisherman's paradise. In summer there are many boat cruises, and in some fjord towns groups can charter boats for fishing or pleasure.

The fishing is excellent in Norway, whether you're at sea or on a fjord, lake or river; enquire locally about

Winter Norway

Norway is often dubbed the "Cradle of Skiing". What we today know as a sport is the way Norwegians used to get around, and Norway is said to be responsible for the invention of ski waxing and the laminated ski.

But skiing is just one of Norway's winter attractions. There are snowmobile trips to the North Cape, reindeer safaris and dog-sled races over the plane of Finnmarksvidda.

You can go on horse-drawn sleigh rides, or try your hand at sledding, ice fishing, snow boarding or ice skating. Several companies offer winter train journeys along the spectacular coast.

For details of tour operators who specialise in winter holidays in Norway, see *Specialist Tour Operators* on page 375. Or contact the Norwegian Tourist Board, which has a list of holiday agents offering packages.

Night Skies

Midnight sun In some parts of Norway the sun does not sink below the horizon for several weeks in the summer. The best time to see the "midnight sun" is mid-May to late July. Longyearbyen on Svalbard has the longest period of midnight suns, from about 20 April to 20 August.

Aurora borealis The northern lights, or aurora borealis, are most likely to occur from November to February. You need to go north of the Arctic Circle, which cuts through Norway just south of Bodø on the Nordland coast. There is, unfortunately, no guarantee they will occur every year.

short-term permits. To fish sea char, salmon, sea trout or inland fish, you must be over 16. A fee is payable. See *Angling in Norway* (available from tourist offices, *see page 375*) for full details.

Golf

This popular sport has only recently caught on in Norway and many landowners, be they farmers or municipal authorities, have turned over land to developing golf links. The few Norwegian golf courses are by and large difficult and challenging. Ninety-nine percent of them require either a Green Card or a handicap under 20. Green fees are more expensive than at other European golf courses.

In the Oslo region professional competitions are held at Bogstad, Larvik, Borre and Vestfold golf clubs, but by far the most beautifully situated is the Tyrifjord golf links. For further information and club details, contact:
Norges Golfforbund, P.O. Box 163, Lilleaker, 0216 Oslo
Tel: 21 02 91 50
E-mail: post@golfforbundet.no
www.ngf@golf.no

Hiking

One of the country's favourite pastimes, hiking can be done anywhere and combines well with

other activities such as berry-gathering or swimming in a lake. The country's mountain ranges and high plains make ideal walking terrain. The most popular areas include the Jotunheim mountain range; the Rondane and Dovrefjell mountains; the Hardangervidda plateau in the Trollheimen district; and the Finnmarksvidda plain. Mountain cabins are open from the end of June until mid-September, and at Easter.

The Norwegian Trekking Association (DNT) runs about 300 guided hikes of varying difficulty during the summer, and glacier walks in winter. It also has a wealth of information on hiking and maps for the whole of Norway and can recommend cabin-to-cabin hiking holidays. Foreigners can write requesting membership, which gives you certain free publications and hut access.
Den Norske Turistforening (The Norwegian Trekking Association)
P.O. Box 7 Sentrum, 0101 Oslo
Tel: 22 82 28 00
Fax: 22 82 28 01
www.turistforeningen.no/english

Glacier Hiking

Not for the lily-livered, glacier hiking is an exhilarating and exciting experience – which should only be attempted with an experienced local

BELOW: the Northern lights over Kvaløya in Tromsø.

ACTIVITIES ◆ 367

TRANSPORT

ACCOMMODATION

EATING OUT

ACTIVITIES

A – Z

LANGUAGE

ABOVE: glacier walking on the Briksdalsbreen.

guide. Several Norwegian tour companies offer guided glacier walks *(breer)*, most particularly in the following areas:

Fjords: Hardangerjøkulen, Folgefonna, Buarbre, Bondhusbre, Smørstabbre, Fannaråkbre and Nigardsbre.

Oppland: Styggebre.

Norland: Svartisen and Engenbreen.

Alternatively, you could contact one of the **Glacier Information Centres** in western Norway at Oppstryn (tel: 57 87 72 00), Fjærland (tel: 57 69 32 88) and Josterdalen (tel: 57 68 32 50).

Horse Riding

Norway offers a wide range of opportunities for the rider, whether you wish to hire a pony for trekking or take lessons. Enquire at the local tourist office or at your hotel or camp site for further information or visit www.elveli.no.

Skiing

Along with hiking, this is the primary participant sport in Norway. Even in the summer Norwegians

Glaciers

One of the highlights of Norway is seeing the glaciers, but every year there are fatalities, when tourists are careless. Glaciers are in motion, so crevasses several metres wide and 30–40 metres (33–43 yards) deep occur, often covered with snow. Never climb or venture onto or under a glacier without a guide.

Glacier Information Centres at the following places show films and exhibitions about the glaciers, and offer tours:
Oppstryn (tel: 57 87 72 00)
Fjærland (tel: 57 69 32 88)
Jostedalen (tel: 57 68 32 50)

take to the slopes in the country's mid-north (as a rule from June to September), and the sight of people swooping down the slopes wearing bikinis or trunks is something to behold.

There is both downhill and cross-country skiing available. The main ski resorts are at Lillehammer, Trysil, Geilo, Hemsedal, Norefjell (the nearest to Oslo) and Voss, but there are many more; all tourist offices can advise on local ski facilities for cross country and slalom.

Ask the Norwegian Tourist Board for a copy of the *Winter Travel Planner* for details of ski operators and resorts, or log on to www.skiinfo.no or www.skioslo.no

Swimming

Temperatures at beaches along the coast and inland reach 24°C (68°F,) and even in the north it can be warm enough to swim. Nude sunbathing beaches are to be found in Oslo, Moss, Halden, Drammen, Tønsberg, Larvik and Molde.

Most larger hotels have pools and there are numerous leisure centres throughout Norway.

Water Sports

There are several possibilities for waterskiing and windsurfing along the coast, as well as on Norway's numerous lakes.

White-water rafting is available on the following rivers: Sjoaelva in Oppland, Trysilelva in Hedmark and Driva in Sør-Trøndelag.

The Norwegian coast offers very good conditions for diving. Cave and wreck diving are popular in Norway and there are many dive centres in the north, such as in Narvik and Lofoten, where the water visibility is extremely high. There are several diving centres along the west coast, particularly in the counties of Møre and Romsdal.

Spectator Sports

Annual skiing competitions, such as the Holmenkollen Ski Festival *(see page 105)* and Bislet Games, are the primary spectator sport in Norway. Check local guides.

There are several horse-trotting and race tracks in Norway.

Other popular spectator sports include marathon running, football (soccer), ice hockey and boat races. Again, check the *Oslo Guide* (www.visitoslo.com) or a local area guide or tourist office for further details.

Sporting Events

January

Geilo: World Kick-sledding Championships.
Hamar: European Speed Skating Championship. www.n-s-f.no/em2006

February

Oslo: Holmenkollen Ski Marathon. Cross country 42 km (26 miles) through Nordmarka, Oslo's vast outdoor park. Also Biathlon World Cup.

March

Oslo: Holmenkollen: Ski Festival with world cups in cross-country skiing, Nordic combined and ski jumping.
Lillehammer: World Cup Alpine Skiing Finals. Downhill, slalom, giant slalom and super G at the Kvitfjell and Hafjell.
Hemsedal: Winter Golf Tournament. Norway's only winter golf tournament on snow ("whites" instead of "greens").
Oslo: Holmenkollen: the world's largest ski competition for children 4 to 12 years old. Including cross-

BELOW: taking on the rapids, Sørlandet.

Walking in the National Parks

The Ministry of Environment has set up more than 20 national parks to ensure the protection of the country's distinctive characteristics. **Børgefjell** 1,107 sq. km (427 sq. miles), on the border between Nord-Trøndelag and Nordland. Fishing and hunting (licences required) for hare and grouse is available. The western part of the park has high peaks with cirque glaciers and steep-walled ravines. Many birds inhabit the wetland areas, while Arctic foxes and wolverines live in the park.

Dovrefjell 256 sq. km (100 sq. miles), in central Norway, comprising a chain of valleys. The western part of the park is dominated by precipitous slopes, with Snøhetta rising to 2,286 metres (7,500 ft). The east has calcareous bedrock; this is northern Europe's richest mountain in terms of plant life.

Femundsmarka 390 sq. km (150 sq. miles), between Hedmark and Sør-Trøndelag. Lakes and streams make Femundsmarka a dream for anglers. Domesticated reindeer graze in Femundsmarka and a few musk oxen, introduced to Norway from Greenland, inhabit the area parts of the year.

Gressåmoen 182 sq. km (70 sq. miles), in Nord-Trøndelag. This was established to protect ancient and almost undisturbed spruce forest. The park has lakes abounding in trout and burbot. Wading birds, with the whimbrels as a characteristic species, thrive in the wetland areas.

Gutulia 19 sq. km (7 sq. miles) directly south of Femundsmarka, bordering with Sweden. The undisturbed forest supports numerous species of birds. 250-year-old spruce trees and 350-year-old pine trees can be found in Gutulia.

Hardangervidda 3,422 sq. km (1,320 sq. miles), covering parts of the Hordaland, Telemark and Buskerud regions in southern central Norway. The park is the home of the largest herd of wild reindeer in Europe, and also the southern limit of many Arctic plants and animals, such as the Arctic fox and snowy owl. The largest mountain plateau in northern Europe.

Jostedalsbreen 1,230 sq. km (475 sq. miles), situated between the Sognefjord and the Nordfjord, is the largest glacier in mainland Europe, being 80 km (50 miles) long. Many wild reindeer inhabit the western part of the park, whereas domesticated reindeer can be found in the Lom-Vågå district.

Jotunheimen 1,145 sq. km (442 sq. miles), extends over parts of Oppland and Sogn and Fjordane. Jotunheimen features Norway's highest mountains. It also has cabins.

Ormtjernkampen 9 sq. km (3 sq. miles), just northwest of Lillehammer, in the county of Oppland. Ormtjernkampen is Norway's smallest national park. It was protected because it represents a typical eastern Norwegian old-growth spruce forest undisturbed by logging activities.

Rago 167 sq. km (65 sq. miles), approximately 25 km (15 miles) north of Fauske in Nordland. Rago is dominated by a wild mountain landscape with deep ravines. The unique watercourse landscape is characterised by waterfalls and rivers flowing over polished rock.

Reisa 803 sq. km (310 sq. miles), in Nordreisa in Troms, about 60 km (37 miles) from Finnmark. Consists of narrow valleys and ravines, mighty waterfalls, river gorges and potholes. The national park is dominated by Reisadalen – a canyon in northern Troms formed by the cutting action of the River Reisaelva into the mountain plateau.

Rondane 580 sq. km (225 sq. miles), just south of Dovrefjell Park, in Oppland. Known as the last outpost of the vulnerable wild reindeer. The vegetation is sparse because of altitude and climate. Most of the area is characterised by impressive, barren mountains, narrow gorges and deep cirques. Among the animal species who can survive the climate are wild reindeer, stray wolverines, snow bunting, rock ptarmigan and wheatear.

Saltfjellet – Svartisen 1,840 sq. km (710 sq. miles) in the county of Nordland. Svartisen glacier (370 sq. km/140 sq. miles) is the largest ice sheet in northern Scandinavia. Glomdalen offers polished marble, caves and underground rivers. Stormdalen's mountain-birch forest has an unusually high plant production.

Stabbursdalen 98 sq. km (38 sq. miles), south of Porsanger peninsula in Finnmark. The world's northernmost pine forest. The Stabburselva, which runs through the entire length of the park, is a famous salmon river.

Øvre Anarjåkka 1,399 sq. km (540 sq. miles), in the south of Finnmark. This remote area is characterised by an ancient rolling landscape of birch forest, sparse pine, bogs and lakes.

Øvre Dividal 743 sq. km (287 sq. miles), in the region of Troms, bordering Sweden. The park has a rich mountain flora, with square-stemmed heather and Arctic rhododendron growing abundantly. A large number of domesticated reindeer graze in the park. Norway's four large animals of prey – brown bear, wolverine, wolf and lynx – are found in the area.

Øvre Pasvik 67 sq. km (26 sq. miles), the easternmost corner of Norway in Finnmark, bordering Finland and Russia. The largest area of primeval forest in the north. The area has a brown bear population. The watercourses are rich in fish, especially pike and perch.

Ånderdalen 69 sq. km (27 sq. miles), on the island of Senja in Troms. Undisturbed mountain-birch forests and wetlands dominate the park, but some coastal pine forests can be found. Stunted and contorted pine trees lend an air of wilderness to the park.

On Svalbard

Nord-vest Spitsbergen 3,560 sq. km (1,375 sq. miles), covers the northwestern corner of Spitsbergen. Large colonies of sea birds, reindeer and walrus; plus areas of cultural and historical interest. The park includes the Moffen nature reserve and areas of cultural-historical value, for instance Danskøya and Amsterdamøya, where archaeological excavations have brought to light several whaling stations and graveyards from the 17th century.

Forlandet 640 sq. km (247 sq. miles); a long, thin island with flat beaches, high mountain peaks and small glaciers. The warming effect of the Gulf Stream makes this the nesting place of many bird species.

Sør Spitsbergen National Park 5,300 sq. km (2,046 sq. miles), covers the southern parts of Spitsbergen. Glaciers and permanent snow and ice cover about 65 percent of the total area. The Arctic landscape is varied. There is a rich bird life, including several sea-bird colonies and important breeding sites for eider ducks and barnacle geese.

For more information

Contact regional tourist boards or the Directorate for Nature Management, N-7485 Trondheim. Tel: 73 58 05 00; e-mail: direktoratet@dirnat.no; www.dirnat.no

ABOVE: Hunderfossen familiepark.

country races and family games.
Tel: 22 92 32 00.
Svolvaer: World Cod Fishing
Championships. Up to 300
competitors from near and far.
Lillehammer: Birkebeineren.
International cross-country ski race
with historical roots, covering the
distance between Lillehammer and
Rena, a 53-km (33-mile) trek.
Tel: 41 77 29 00.

May

Oslo: Holmenkollstafetten Street
relay race.

June

Oslo: Esso/Mobil Bislett Games.
International track and field
competition with some of the best
athletes in the world.
Trondheim: Midnight Golf Tournament
over 18 holes. Every night until 2am.
Telemark: Bicycle race from Skien to
Rjukan and back.
Spitsbergen Marathon. The world's
northernmost marathon. Also half
marathon and 10-ks.
Tromsø: Midnight Sun Marathon.
Marathon and other competitions at
midnight. Concerts and other
entertainment.
Trondheim: The Great Challenge.
Bicycle race from Trondheim to Oslo.
Also shorter distances:
Lillehammer–Oslo and Eidsvoll–Oslo.

July

Ekebergsletta: Norway Cup: World's
largest international football
tournament for children
Lofthus. Fédération Aéronautique
Internationale Paragliding
Competition.
Stavanger: World Tour Beach

Volleyball. One of the world's largest
beach volleyball tournaments.
Tel: 51 97 16 80.

August

Rena/Lillehammer: international
bicycling race from Rena to
Lillehammer.

September

Oslo: half marathon.
Suldalslagen: international salmon
fishing competition.

October

Oslo: horse show. Competitions,
Grand Prix. Tel: 22 51 87 58.

December

Lillehammer: Ski Festival. Opening of
the world cup season.

CHILDREN

Norway is a welcoming and safe
place for children; this is one reason
why you will see them out on their
own here at a young age. You can
usually get child rates for travel and
accommodation.
Family attractions include:

In and around Oslo

International Children's Art Museum
(exhibits and workshops), Lille Frøens
vei 4, tel: 22 46 85 73 (open all
year, entrance fee).
**Horse riding, minigolf and Minizoo
Ekeberg** near Ekeberghallen, tel: 22
68 26 69.
Puppet Theatre Frognerveien 67, tel:
22 34 86 80 (open May–Sept).
Tusenfryd Amusement Park Ås,
Østfold. Open June–Aug (May–Sept
times vary). Transport by bus 541
from Oslo-S or Rådhuset, tel: 64 97
64 97; www.tusenfryd.no. Attractions
include: roller-coaster, Spaceshot,
flume ride, carousel, magic carpet,
climbing wall and so on. Height
restrictions apply on some rides.
VikingLandet (adjacent to Tusenfryd,
open May–Sept, times vary),tel: 64
97 64 97. Live like a Viking for a day.
VikingLandet gives you an authentic
picture of the Viking Age. Experience
the buildings, the market place,
smithy, farm animals and fields. Not
to be missed is **Plus Toktet**, a Viking
voyage deep in a mountain cave.
Combination tickets with Tusenfryd
are available, but you need two days
to do the lot.

Around Norway

The Troll Family Park near
Lillehammer, tel: 61 27 55 30;
www.hunderfossen.no. Main attractions

are: river rafting, the fairy-tale
castle, the world's largest troll, fairy
tale cave, Supervideograph, the
Photo Adventure, Energy Centre
(exhibition centre for oil and gas),
Wax Museum and Experience Centre
for Ice Cream. Outdoor
entertainment twice daily throughout
the summer season.
Kongeparken near Stavanger, tel: 81
52 26 73; www.kongeparken.no. Over 40
attractions, including life-sized model
of The Giant Gulliver (85 x 7.5
metres), riding tracks, bob track,
farm, car track, Wild West City, birds
and fun fair.
Telemark Sommarland Bø in
Telemark, tel: 35 06 16 00;
www.sommarland.no. Norway's biggest
water park with various wet and dry
attractions, including many water-
slides and Stuka, a 26-metre/80-ft
high water chute; Flow Rider, said to
be the world's biggest surf wave, and
a floating river. Plus live
entertainment, pony rides, Wild West
City and children's playground.
Kristiansand Dyrepark
tel: 38 04 97 00; www. dyreparken.com
(open all year, times vary). Norway's
largest wildlife park and most-visited
tourist attraction. The park has a
wide range of other attractions:
amusement park, water park, show
and entertainment park, leisure park
and Kardemomme by a tiny village
from a well-known children's book by
the Norwegian author Thorbjørn
Egner.
Youth Information in Oslo provides
information on all subjects for young
people:
Møllergata 3, Oslo
Tel: 24 14 98 20; www.unginfo.oslo.no
Open Mon–Fri 11am–5pm.

BELOW: Holmenkollen.

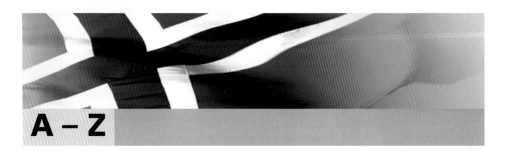

A – Z

A HANDY SUMMARY OF PRACTICAL INFORMATION, ARRANGED ALPHABETICALLY

A Animals 370
B Business Dealings 370
Business Hours 371
C Climate 371
Crime and Safety 371
Customs Regulations 372
D Disabled Travellers 372
Dogs 372
E Embassies in Oslo 372

Entry Requirements 372
Emergency Numbers 372
G Gay and Lesbian Travellers 373
H Health and Medical Care 373
I Internet Cafés 373
M Maps 373
Media 374
Money 374
P Postal Service 374

Public Holidays 374
R Religious Services 374
S Student Travellers 374
T Telecommunications 374
Time Zone 375
Tourist Information 375
W Websites 376
Weights and Measures 376
What to Bring/Wear 376

Animals

See under Entry Requirements on page 372.

Business Dealings

Norwegians have all the props when it comes to doing business. Don't be caught out without possessing a firm handshake, mobile phone, business card and, if possible, a laptop.

Like all Scandinavians, Norwegians take their summer holiday very seriously as a time for retreating to a fjord or mountain *hytte* (usually a log cabin). During the common holiday in July, offices and factories empty, and it is virtually impossible to arrange an appointment or do any business. May, with its holidays, can also be a difficult time.

Business matters can take a lot longer to complete in Norway and government services are notoriously slow. People take work seriously, but also know how to maintain a pleasantly relaxed business atmosphere. Norwegians dress for business much as they do elsewhere; although in summer dress codes are relaxed slightly.

Norwegians are rarely deceitful. They may well mention the bad points of something first, to get them out of the way; then it's on to the

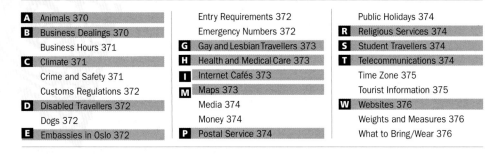

Visiting a Norwegian Home

Norwegians usually eat dinner around 5 or 6pm, but dinner parties generally start later, at around 7.30pm. An invitation for any other time of the day usually means coffee and cake (if in doubt call the host and make certain). Let's say you've been invited to dinner and you want to make a good impression. Norway is not a "drop-in" society so you can expect the food to be well planned and of high quality. You could do far worse than taking note of the following protocol:
1 Norwegians are very punctual and expect others to be. Guests usually arrive exactly on time, jokingly called

Norsk time, sometimes even early. Make sure you dress correctly for the occasion (again, if in doubt ask the host in advance).
2 When entering a room, shake hands with everybody present, unless a large function makes that impossible. Introduce yourself to those you have not met before; give a friendly greeting to those you do know, but still shake hands.
3 If it's your first visit to someone's home it is customary to take a small gift along (usually flowers, a plant or chocolates).
4 Dinner parties in Norwegian homes follow a fixed pattern and include

short speeches even on family occasions. After tapping his glass, the host will always give a welcome speech and then propose a *skål*. It would be discourteous to touch the wine *before* this initial toast (but expect a liberal helping of *skåls*!).
5 Second helpings (*annen servering*) are so much the rule in Norwegian homes that the host will specifically point out if the dish is only to be passed round once. The secret is not to take too much the first time.
6 Every meal in Norway is concluded with a *takk for maten* (thank you for the food) and, if it's dinner, a general *skål*.

sell. In other words, you won't be drowned in a sea of hype, and the honesty can be a little hard to get used to. Ultimately you'll appreciate not having to figure out the pitfalls for yourself.

If you are looking up someone's number in a phone book, you'll find his or her profession listed next to the name; not only is this a matter of professional pride, but a real help in a country with a limited number of surnames. Amazingly, you can also find a person's yearly taxable income, the details of which are freely available on government internet sites. Norwegians take freedom of information quite literally.

So much for generalisations; there will always be exceptions. The only really important things to remember are that liquid lunches are unusual, and the work day often ends at 3.30 or 4pm.

Most Norwegian consulates and embassies have commercial attachés. Three organisations in Oslo deal with tourism, business and trade:

Innovation Norway (Trade Council)
(Innovasjon Norge)
P.O. Box 448 Sentrum, N-0104 Oslo
Tel: 22 00 25 00
The Norwegian Tourist Board
P.O. Box 722 Sentrum, Stortorvet 10
NO-0150 Oslo
Tel: 24 14 46 00
Fax: 24 14 46 01
E-mail: norway@ntr.no
www.visitnorway.com
Oslo Promotion AS
Grev Wedels plass 4 0151 Oslo
Tel: 23 10 62 00
Fax: 23 10 62 01
E-mail: oslo@oslopro.no
www.oslopro.no

ODIN, the central web server for the Norwegian government, office of the prime minister and the ministries, can be found at:
www.odin.dep.no

Bergen Convention Bureau – Bergen Tourist Board
P.O. Box 4055, Dreggen
NO-5023 Bergen
Tel: 55 31 38 60
Fax: 55 31 56 82
E-mail: convention@visitbergen.com

Business Hours

Office hours are 8 or 9am–4pm; lunch is taken early, usually 11.30am–12.30pm, or noon–2pm for a restaurant lunch or lunch meeting, which are business-like affairs. Shopping malls open
Shops open Mon–Fri 9am–5pm, Thurs until 8pm, Sat 9am–1, 2 or even 3pm.
Shopping centres open Mon–Fri 10am–9pm, Sat 9am–6pm and are closed on Sundays.
Banks weekdays only 8.30am–4pm.
Pharmacies open Mon–Fri 9am–5pm, Sat mornings and on a rota basis in larger cities.

Climate

In Oslo the January average daytime high is -2°C (28°F) and the night-time low is -7°C (19°F); Bergen is less cold (high 3°C/37°F, low -1°C/30°F). Further north sub-zero temperatures can last for months and a good number of roads shut over winter due to long-term snow, although right on the coast it is usually a little milder. February and March are the best skiing months. March and April and sometimes even early May are the wet spring months when skies are grey, and roads are buckled due to thaws and refreezes; during this time the daily high temperature slowly lifts from about 4°C (39°F) to 16°C (61°F).

Come summertime and the season of the midnight sun, Oslo can enjoy daily temperatures averaging 20–25°C (68–77°F), while the sunlight-bathed north has a perfect

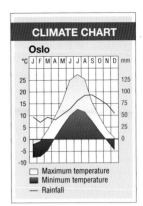

CLIMATE CHART
Oslo

Maximum temperature
Minimum temperature
Rainfall

hiking temperature, hovering around 17°C (63°F). October sees temperatures dip below 10°C (50°F), then continue their slide towards zero. The first snow can be expected any time from mid-October to early December, depending on the location.

Independent travel during the winter months of November to February should be treated with caution, especially away from coastal cities to inland, colder regions.

May and September are very popular with visitors. Transport, hotels and museums are often crowded in these two months. The Easter ski break is a time of mass exodus from schools and jobs to the slopes and trails. Otherwise, Norwegians mainly holiday from mid-June to early August. The traditional common holiday is in July *(ferietide)* when some businesses shut down.

Crime and Safety

The streets of Oslo are relatively safe compared with the bigger cities of Europe and North America, even though the tabloids report an abundance of muggings, stabbings and other crimes of violence, as they do everywhere.

Crime against tourists is rare, however. Take the same precautions here as anywhere: park safely and hide valuables out of sight. The same applies when out on the town. Simply

Coffee

Coffee is the national stimulant and served whenever people meet. But the real difficulty is coping with the mounds of pastry often served with the coffee; if you must refuse, do so politely, especially if you are turning down home-made pastries.

BELOW: beautiful Norway in winter.

TRANSPORT
ACCOMMODATION
EATING OUT
ACTIVITIES
N–Z A–I
LANGUAGE

The Cost of Living

Norway has a name for being expensive, and certainly this is true in some respects: the price of a cup of coffee in a smart city café can be exorbitant and even the smallest of items like toiletries can be double the amount they are elsewhere in Europe. Look out for "Lavpris" shops, which offer lower prices. It is true that the cost of alcohol is enough to make even heavy drinkers think twice about another bottle of wine; beer is a cheaper alternative and can be bought from supermarkets at good prices. Discount cards on accommodation *(page 354)* and public transport *(page 349)* are available, plus Norway offers tourists tax-free shopping *(page 365)*. The Oslo Youth Information Centre publishes a budget guide to the capital, *Streetwise*. It is available from tourist offices.

stick with the happy crowds and avoid the sleazy joints.

Norwegian cities late at night are usually full of young people, many of them drunk: this is mainly because of the lengthy opening hours and the Nordic drinking culture (a Norwegian often drinks to get drunk).

Most bars have good bouncers, so alert them if you're having trouble. Police patrols are now outnumbered by private-sector security personnel and *Nattravene* (Night Ravens, a Guardian Angel-type patrol).

Another potential threat can be drug abusers. However, they are usually placid and in Oslo generally gather around Jernbanetorget (central station). There is no strict rule here; a no-go area today could be tomorrow's in place.

Customs Regulations

The following can be brought into Norway by visitors:
Money Notes and coins (Norwegian and foreign) up to NOK 25,000 or equivalent. If you intend to import more, you must fill in a form (available at all entry and exit points) for the Customs Office.
Alcohol Permitted imports for people aged 20 and over include 1 litre of spirits (up to 60 percent vol.) plus 1 litre of fortified wine (up to 22 percent vol.) or 3 litres of wine (if no spirits) and 2 litres of beer, or 5 litres of beer.
Tobacco European residents over the age of 18 may bring 200 cigarettes or 250 g of other tobacco goods.

Sweets 1 kg (2.2 pounds) duty-free chocolate and sweets.
Meat and dairy products Meat, meat products, cheese and foodstuffs except dog and cat food, totalling 10 kg (22 pounds) altogether from EEA (European Economic Area) countries. From countries outside the EEA, it is prohibited to bring meat, meat products, milk and milk products with you in your luggage.
Sundries Other goods (excluding articles for personal use) may be brought in duty-free up to a value of NOK 6,000.
Prohibited goods Narcotics, medicines (except for personal use), poisons, firearms, ammunition and explosives. Note: the mild narcotic leaf *khat* is illegal in Norway.
Agricultural produce This comes under strict surveillance. If it concerns you, get specific details beforehand.

Disabled Travellers

Visitors in need of assistance should contact **Norges handikapforbund**, Schweigaardsgt. 12, 0185 Oslo, tel: 24 10 24 00, fax: 24 10 24 99, www.nhf.no

Hotel listings in accommodation guides have symbols designating disabled access and toilets. In the *Oslo Guide* (see www.visitoslo.com) under Handicap Information you'll find some listings that specially mention capacity for disabled visitors, such as the Bogstad ski area in Nordmarka, Oslo.

It is becoming more usual for hotels to adapt their furnishings to the needs of people with physical disabilities. These hotels are indicated in *Accommodation in Norway* (available from the Norwegian Tourist Board). The Norwegian State Railways (NSB) have carriages specially furnished for the disabled, and the new Coastal Express ships have lifts and cabins for disabled people. The **Euro Terra Nova AS**, at Grensen 8, 0159 Oslo, offers brochures on coach tours around Norway especially for wheelchair users. They also provide hotel bookings and hire cars, tel: 22 94 13 50, fax: 22 94 13 61 www.euroterranova.no. Guidebooks for Nordland county (north Norway) can be ordered free of charge from Nordland Reiseliv.

The Society for Accessible Travel and Hospitality (SATH) provides information and advice for travellers with disabilities. Their website is: www.sath.org.

Dogs

All dogs in Norway are required by law to wear a name tag clearly showing the telephone number of the owner (these are available from pet shops). Dogs must be kept on a leash between 15 April and 15 August while walking in forests and fields, to protect the environment and the local wildlife.

During the winter months, special notices are posted in public places, to inform you of whether or not dogs have to be placed on leads.

Note that it is illegal for a dog to foul a public place – you are expected to pick up the mess using a plastic bag and to deposit this in a litter bin. Failure to do so may result in a fine. Dogs are not allowed in restaurants; shops and other public buildings usually show a sign if dogs are not welcome. Guide dogs are an exception to this rule.

Embassies in Oslo

Canada
Wergelandsvn 7
Tel: 22 99 53 00
www.canada.no
UK
Thomas Heftyesgate 8
Tel: 23 13 27 00
www.britain.no
US
Henrik Ibsensgate 48
Tel: 22 44 85 50
www.usa.no
Australia/NZ (in Germany)
Wallstrasse 76–79,
Berlin 10179, Germany
Tel: (49-30) 880088-0
Fax: (49-30) 880088-210

Entry Requirements

Visas & Passports

A valid passport is all that is necessary for citizens of most countries to enter Norway. Visas are not required. Norway is a member of the Schengen agreement, allowing citizens of other Schengen countries to enter without passports.

Emergency Numbers

Fire 110
Police 112
Ambulance 113
Medical problems For emergency medical treatment in Oslo *(legevakt)* ring 22 11 80 80.
Internal directory enquiries 1881/1880
International directory enquiries 1882

Electricity

220 volts AC, 50 cycles. Plugs have two small round pins, so you may need an adapter for appliances you bring with you.

If you enter from another Nordic country (Denmark, Finland, Iceland, or Sweden), you won't get a new entry stamp. Tourists are generally limited to a three-month visit; it is possible to stay longer, but you must apply for a visa after the initial three months (Scandinavian passport holders are exempt from this requirement) or if you plan to work in Norway.

Animals

Dogs, cats and ferrets from all EU countries except Sweden must have pet passports, ID marking, a valid rabies vaccination, and valid blood-test documentation (this does not apply to ferrets). Dogs and cats must also be given approved tapeworm treatment during the week before and the week after they have been brought into the country.

G ay and Lesbian Travellers

In common with the rest of Scandinavia, Norway has a very relaxed attitude to homosexuality. There is very little open hostility to gays and lesbians in general society and, partly as a result, the commercial gay scene is relatively small. Tourist offices (see page 375) carry details of the main places and events, including the Gay Pride

BELOW: newspaper kiosk.

celebrations in Oslo and Bergen and the annual Oslo Gay Film Festival.

The main bars and clubs include:
London Pub, Hambros Plass 5, Oslo. Tel: 22 70 87 00.
Finken Café and Bar, Nygardsgate 2a, Bergen. Tel: 55 32 13 16.

H ealth and Medical Care

The are no major health hazards in Norway. No vaccinations are necessary to enter Norway and the tap water is (generally) good. A degree of common sense is required when travelling in remote areas, especially during the winter. When hiking/skiing in the mountains always let someone know of your travel intentions, and use guides wherever possible.

Treatment

Norway has reciprocal treatment agreements with the UK and many other European countries; your own National Insurance should cover you to receive free treatment at public hospitals. EU citizens should obtain the relevant documentation to entitle them to this (for British citizens an EHIC, European Health Insurance Card, is available from post offices). People from countries without such agreements, and those without an EHIC card, will have to pay a small fee. If you are concerned whether you need extra cover, check in your own country before you go. The EHIC card only covers the basics and does not include the cost of medicine, so it is advisable to take out additional medical insurance. You will need to take out extra cover if you are going skiing or doing any other dangerous sports.

Doctors and Hospitals

The standard of health provision in Norway is very high, and even in remote areas you should have no problem getting medical help. Just about all doctors and nurses speak good English, and if they don't they'll soon find someone who does.

In medical emergencies EU members will receive free treatment at state hospitals (see above for reciprocal arrangements), but have to pay towards the non-hospital costs and for prescriptions.

If you are ill, ask your hotel, tourist office or a pharmacy for the address of an English-speaking GP. Private doctors are listed in the directory under Leger (doctors). Make sure you keep receipts if you have medical insurance.

Pharmacies

For minor problems, head for a pharmacy, or Apotek (for opening hours, see page 371). Most larger cities have all-night pharmacies (see below). In other cities enquire at your hotel, or try the emergency number in the phone book under Legevakt (doctor on duty).

Where there is a rota of 24-hour pharmacies in a city, a list will usually be posted on the door of each one.

Oslo
Jernbanetorvets Apotek, across from Central Station, Jernbanetorget 4B. Tel: 22 41 24 82. Open 24 hours.
Bergen
Apotek Nordstjernen, Strømgata 8. Tel: 55 21 83 84. Open Mon–Sat 8am–midnight, Sun 9.30am–midnight.
Stavanger
Loeveapoteket, Olav V's gt 11. Tel: 51 91 08 80. Open daily until 11pm, Christmas, New Year, Easter and Whitsun 9am–8pm.
Trondheim
St Olav Vakt-apotek, Beddingen 4. Tel: 73 88 37 37. Open Mon–Sat 8am–midnight, Sun 10am–midnight.

Dentists

Emergency dental treatment in Oslo, outside regular dentists' office hours, is available from:
Oslo Kommunale Tannlegevakt, Tøyen Senter, Kolstadgata 18, (near Tøyen T-bane station). Tel: 22 67 30 00. Open Mon–Sat 7am–10pm, Sun and public holidays 11am–2pm.

I nternet Cafés

Free internet access is available at most public libraries in Norway. Screen time is limited and you may need to reserve your slot in advance. The Oslo Tourist Information Service, Oslo Promotion, publishes a list of internet cafés in the capital. These include: **Arctic Internet**, Oslo Central Station. Open daily 8am–midnight. Tel: 22 17 19 40;
Coffee and Juice Netcafé, Nedre Slottsgate 12. Open 10am–1am, Sun noon–midnight. Tel: 22 41 21 90;
Qba, Olaf Ryes Plass 4. Open weekdays 8am–1am, Sat 11am–1am. Closed Sun. Tel: 22 35 24 60.

M aps

For tourist maps, contact:
Den Norske Turistforening
Postboks 7 Sentrum, 0101 Oslo
Tel: 22 82 28 00
www.turistforeningen.no

Media

Newspapers

Most larger kiosks (like the *Narvesen* chain) and some bookshops sell English-language newspapers. Norwegian news in English is found on the website of Norway's main newspaper *Aftenposten*: www.aftenposten.no.

Deichmanske Bibliotek, the main public library, is at Henrik Ibsen's Gate 1 in Oslo; you'll find a selection of international papers and periodicals in its reading rooms, as well as free internet access.

Bookshops

There are several bookshops in Oslo with English-language sections, including; **Erik Qvist** at Drammensveien 16, tel: 22 54 26 00; **Tanum Karl Johan** at Karl Johansgate 37/41, tel: 22 41 11 00; and **Norli** at Universitetsgaten 20–24, 0162 Oslo, tel: 22 00 43 00.

Radio

English broadcasts on short wave can be picked up if atmospheric conditions are favourable. Best results can usually be heard on short-wave frequency 9410.

During the winter months **BBC radios 1**, **2**, **3** and **4** can sometimes be received on AM but reception is often distorted. **Radio 5** can be picked up on 909 and 693 medium wave (best reception in the evening). On Sundays **Radio Norway** (93 FM) broadcasts the news from Norway in English in *Norway This Week*, a 30-minute programme at 5pm. For local frequencies of the **BBC**

BELOW: Norwegian krone.

World Service enquire at the nearest tourist office.

Television

Norway has four main television stations: **NRK1**, **NRK2** (Norsk Rikskringkasting), **TV2** and **TV Norge** (TVN). Cable TV is common here and allows you to pick up a variety of channels, including **BBC Prime**, **BBC World**, **CNN**, **Swedish TV1** and **TV2**, **Discovery**, **MTV**, **French TV5**, **Eurosport**, **TV3** and so on, depending on the distributor. Most hotels have pay channels in addition to the above. English films on Norwegian television are subtitled, not dubbed.

Money

The Norwegian krone (NOK) is divided into 100 øre. Notes come in denominations of NOK 50, 100, 200, 500 and 1,000 and coins are 50 øre and NOK 1, 5, 10 and 20.

You can change currency at post offices, the Oslo S train station, international airports, some hotels and commercial banks. The relatively new FOREX offices have good rates and no fees. It is always useful to carry a certain amount of cash with you in case of emergency.

Credit Cards/Travellers' Cheques

Use of credit cards is widespread in Norway, with Eurocard, Visa, Mastercard, American Express and Diner's Club the most common. Check with your own credit card company about acceptability and other services.

Travellers' cheques are not very widely used now, but they are accepted in the bigger hotels and should be purchased before travelling to Norway. In most banks you can generally get cash on a debit card or a Visa or Mastercard.

Tipping

Tipping is quite straight forward in Norway. Hotels include a service charge and tipping is generally not expected. Restaurants usually have the service charge included, in which case it's your choice to add anything (5–10 percent is customary). The same applies to taxis. Table service in bars (particularly outdoor tables) requires tipping. With hairdressers a tip isn't quite as customary, but again 5–10 percent would be appropriate – and appreciated. Cloakrooms usually have a fixed fee of about NOK 5–10; if not, leave a few krone for the attendant.

ostal Services

Post offices in Oslo open Mon–Fri 9am–5pm and Sat 9am–3pm.

Letters and postcards cost the same price to send to the UK and continental Europe, slightly more to send to North America. Post takes 2–3 days to Europe and 7–10 days to North America.

eligious Services

The Lutheran church is Norway's state church, with around 86 percent of the population registered as Lutherans. Oslo has many Lutheran places of worship, including one American Lutheran church (Fritzners g. 15, tel: 22 44 35 84, fax: 22 44 30 15).

Services are held in English at the **American Lutheran church** and the **Anglican/Episcopalian church** (St Edmund's, Møllergate 30, tel: 22 69 22 14).

Minority religious groups are Pentecostalists, Baptists, Seventh Day Adventists, Evangelical Lutherans, Methodists, Catholics, Jews (the **synagogue** is at Bergstein 13, near St Hanshaugen, tel: 22 69 65 70) and Moslems. The **Oslo Cathedral** (Protestant), Domkirke at Storgate, tel: 23 31 46 00, puts on interesting concerts for tourists at 8pm every Wednesday. For up-to-date information, consult the daily press, the tourist office or the *Oslo Guide* at www.visitoslo.com.

tudent Travellers

There are numerous opportunities for reduced student rates, especially for travel; contact the following for more information:

Ung Info (Young info)
Møllergata 3
N-0179 Oslo
Tel: 24 14 98 20
Fax: 24 14 98 21
E-mail: use-it@ung.info
or log onto: www.isic.org

Time Zone

Central European Time, 1 hour ahead of Greenwich Mean Time, 6 hours ahead of Eastern Standard Time. The clock is set forward an hour to summer time at the end of March, and back an hour at the end of September.

Telecommunications

Calls abroad can be made from hotels – with a hefty surcharge – or from phone booths or the main telegraph office at Kongensgate 21 (entrance Prinsensgate), Oslo. You can also send faxes from this office.

Norwegian payphones take 1, 5, 10 and 20 kroner pieces. Phonecards, which can be used in the green phone booths, can be bought in *Narvesen* kiosks and at post offices. Credit cards are accepted in card phones.

When calling from Norway to foreign countries always dial 00 first. Cheapest calling times are outside business hours: 5pm–8am. Extra-cheap international calling cards, such as Eurocity, can be purchased from a variety of kiosks (corner shops) in most major towns.

Telephone directories have a page of instructions in English in the index. When looking up names, remember the vowels æ, ø, and å come at the end of the alphabet, in that order.

Some US phone companies have their own international access numbers, to allow US citizens cheaper calls, as follows:
Sprint 800-19 877
AT&T 800-19 011
WorldPhone 800-19 912

Tourist Information

There are around 350 local tourist offices around Norway, as well as 18 regional tourist offices. For general information, contact:
The Tourist Information Centre
Fridtjof Nansens Plass 5, Oslo
Tel: 24 14 77 00
Fax: 22 42 92 22
Email: info@visitoslo.com
www.visitoslo.com

Regional Information
Regional tourist offices are experts in the county they cover. They are usually open to personal callers, and will also supply advice and informa-tion in writing or over the phone.

Oslo/Oslofjord
The Tourist Information Centre
(details as above)

Akershus Tourist Board
Kultur- og næringspark
NO-2060 Gardermoen
Tel: 64 82 22 99
Fax: 64 82 22 98
E-mail: info@akershus.com
www.akershus.com
Destinasjon Vestfold AS
Thor Dahls Gate 1–5
N-3210 Sandefjord
Tel: 33 48 60 00
Fax: 33 46 61 01
E-mail: info@vestfold.com
www.visitvestfold.com

East Norway
Buskerud Opplevelser BA
Engene 44
N-3015 Drammen
Tel: 32 89 02 50
Fax: 32 89 17 73
E-mail: info@buskerud.no
www.buskerud.no
Fjell og Fjord Ferie
Gamlevegen 6
N-3550 Gol
Tel: 32 02 99 26
Fax: 32 02 99 28
E-mail: fjellogfjord@online.no
www.eventyrvegen.com
Hedmark Reiseliv BA
Grønnegate 11
N-2317 Hamar
Tel: 62 55 33 20

Fax: 62 55 33 21
E-mail: post@hedmark.com
www.hedmark.com

South Norway
Arendal Turist Kontor
Lanbrygga 5, Pollen
4803 Arendal
Tel: 37 00 55 44
Fax: 37 00 55 40
www.arendal.com
Destinasjon Sørlandet
Vestre Strandgate 32
4612 Kristiansand
Tel: 38 12 13 14
Fax: 38 02 52 55
E-mail: destinasjon@sorlandet.com
www.sorlandet.com
Telemarkreiser
P.O. Box 3133 Handelstortget
N-3707 Skien
Tel: 35 90 00 30
Fax: 35 90 00 21
E-mail: info@telemarkreiser.no
www.visittelemark.com

Fjord Norway
Bergen
Vagsallmenningen 1
N-5014 Bergen
Tel: 55 55 20 00
Fax: 55 55 20 01
E-mail: info@visitbergen.com
www.visitbergen.com

Specialist Tour Operators in the UK

Activity Holidays
Inntravel
Nr Castle Howard
York YO60 7JU
Tel: 01653 617 949
Scantours
73 Mornington St, London NW1 7QE
Tel: 020 7554 3530
Fax: 020 7387 4496

Arctic Voyages/Dog-sledging/Whale Watching
Arctic Experience & Discover the World
29 Nork Way, Banstead,
Surrey SM7 1PB
Tel: 01737 214214
Arcturus Expeditions
PO Box 41, Hereford
HR1 9DP
Tel: 01432 850886

Christmas Holidays
Page & Moy
136–140 London Road,
Leicester LE2 1EN
Tel: 0870 833 4012

Norway specialists
Norsc Holidays
1 The Lawns, Charmouth DT6 6LR
Tel: 01297 560033

Taber Holidays
P.O. Box 176, Tofts House
Tofts Road, Cleckheaton,
West Yorkshire BD19 3WX
Tel: 01274 875 199

Skiing/Walking
Crystal Holidays
King's Place, Wood Street,
Kingston, Surrey KT1 1JY
Tel: 0870 166 4971
Exodus Travel
Grange Mill, Weir Road
London SW12 0NE
Tel: 0870 240 5550
Mountain & Wildlife Ventures
Brow Foot, High Wray, Ambleside
LA22 0JE
Tel: 015394 33285

Tours
Explore Worldwide
1 Frederick Street, Aldershot,
Hampshire GU11 1LQ
Tel: 01252 760000
ScanMeridian
73 Mornington St, London NW1 7QE
Tel: 020 7554 3530
Great Rail Journeys
Saviour House, 9 St Saviourgate,
York YO1 8NL
Tel: 01904 521900

TRANSPORT · ACCOMMODATION · EATING OUT · ACTIVITIES · A – Z · LANGUAGE

Tourist Info Abroad

Australia
The embassy deals with tourist information.
17 Hunter Street, Yarralumia, Canberra ACT 2600
Tel: 2 62 702700
UK
Norwegian Tourist Board
Tel: (brochure line, calls cost 50 pence per minute) 0906 302 2003
Fax: 020 7839 6014
E-mail: infouk@ntr.no
www.visitnorway.com
US/Canada
Norwegian Tourist Board
Tel: 212 885 9700
Fax: 212 885 9710
E-mail: usa@ntr.no
www.goscandinavia.com

Fjord Norge AS
Lodin Leppsgt 2B
NO-5003 Bergen
Tel: 55 30 26 40
Fax: 55 30 26 50
E-mail: info@fjordnorway.no
www.fjordnorway.com
Hordaland Reiseliv
P.O. Box 416 Marken
NO-5828 Bergen
Tel: 55 31 66 00
Fax: 55 31 52 08
E-mail: info@hordalandreiseliv.no
www.hordalandreiseliv.no
Møre og Romsdal Reiselivsråd
Fylkeshuset
N-6404 Molde
Tel: 71 24 50 80
Fax: 71 24 50 81
E-mail: mr-reiselivsrad@eunet.no
www.visitmr.com
Rogaland Reiseliv
P.O. Box 130
NO-4001 Stavanger
Tel: 51 51 67 88
E-mail: gen@rogfk.no
www.rogaland-f.kommune.no
Sogn and Fjordane Tourist Board
P.O. Box 370
NO-6782 Stryn
Tel: 57 87 40 40
E-mail: mail@nordfjord.no
www.sfr.no

Central Norway

Trøndelag Reiseliv AS
P.O. Box 65
N-7400 Trondheim
Tel: 73 84 24 40
E-mail: turistinfo@mnr.as
www.visitcentral-norway.com

North Norway

Finnmark Tourist Board
Sorenskrivervn 13
NO-9511 Alta
Tel: 78 44 00 20
Fax: 78 43 51 84
E-mail: post@visitnorthcape.no
www.visitnorthcape.com
Nordland Reiseliv AS
P.O. Box 434
N-8001 Bodå
Tel: 75 54 52 00
Fax: 75 54 52 10
E-mail: nordland@nordlandreiseliv.no
www.visitnordland.no
Svalbard Reiselivsråd
P.O. Box 323
N-9171 Longyearbyen
Tel: 79 02 55 50
Fax: 79 02 55 51
E-mail: info@svalbard.net
www.svalbard.net
Troms Reiseliv
P.O. Box 326
NO-9305 Finnsnes.
Tel: 77 60 80 40
Fax: 77 60 80 41
E-mail: post@visittroms.no
www.visittroms.no

W ebsites

Norway's official travel website
State tourism officials compile this portal offering information on everything from attractions to special events to accommodation, with links to regional sites all over the country. www.visitnorway.com
Oslo's official travel website
The capital's visitor's bureau compiles this site full of information about what's happening in Oslo, accommodation assistance and general tourist tips. Similar sites are available for Bergen, Stavanger and most other cities in Norway – just change "oslo" in the address to the name of the city. www.visitoslo.com
The Oslo Pass
For visitors intending to use a lot of public transport and visit lots of museums, this pass from the visitors' bureau can come in handy. www.visitoslo.com/the-oslo-pass.49104.en.html
The Norwegian Trekking Association (DNT)
This national organisation manages hiking and skiing trails all over the country, runs lodges and cabins in the mountains and other scenic areas and its staff are experts on hiking and outdoor life in Norway. www.turistforeningen.no/english/
Foundation Norwegian Heritage (Norsk Kulturarv)
The foundation seeks to preserve Norway's history through "historical vitality," that is, opening historic farms and other sites to the public. It offers listings of historic sites, lodging and attractions around the country, using the St Olav's Rose as its symbol for quality. www.olavsrosa.no/en/
News in English
For a look at domestic and international news from Norway's perspective, log onto: www.aftenposten.no/english

What to Bring/Wear

You're in for a pleasant surprise if travelling to Norway in summer. As it is protected by the Gulf Stream it can get even warmer than some of its southern neighbours. In the south, temperatures above 25°C (77°F) are not unusual. The average temperature for the country as a whole in July, including the far north, is about 16°C (60°F), 22°C (71°F) in Oslo. Bring swimming gear, as the water in most fjords, except northern Norway, is 20°C+ (68°F+) in midsummer.

Pack the clothes you would normally wear in northern Europe, including jumpers and a raincoat, and bring some strong walking shoes.

The mountains can be cold, so bring some warmer garments. You are not usually required to dress formally for dinner at Norwegian resort hotels. Spring and autumn are rainy (an umbrella is always useful), and nights can be chilly. It is rainy year-round on the west coast.

In winter bring very warm clothing and dress in layers (cotton against the skin and then wool). Woollen mittens or gloves and hats (covering the ears) are strongly advised (and face cover and goggles, if you are skiing). In the far north, temperatures drop to below -20°C (-4°F). In January, the average daytime temperature in Oslo is -2°C (28°F) and -7°C (19°F) at night. Inland areas are generally colder than the coast.

A first-aid kit is recommended for those who plan to make any trips to remoter parts. And be sure to include medicines for preventing and treating mosquito bites, as from midsummer into early autumn biting insects are rife, especially in Finnmark.

Weights and Measures

Metric. Distances are given in kilometres (km) but Norwegians often refer to a *mil* which is 10 km (thus 10 mil = 100 km). When talking about land area you will often hear the word *mål*. This old measure of 984.34 sq. metres has been rounded up to 1,000 sq. metres (or 1 decare).

LANGUAGE

UNDERSTANDING THE LANGUAGE

Introduction

Germanic in origin, Norwegian is one of the three Scandinavian languages, and is closely related to Danish and Swedish. There are two official forms of Norwegian, *bokmål* and *nynorsk*. The former reflects Norway's 400 years of Danish domination, while *nynorsk* is built on native Norwegian dialects. The Sami population (Lapps) in north Norway speak Lappish. English is widely understood.

Useful Words and Phrases

Yes *Ja*
No *Nei*
Good morning *God morgen*
Good afternoon *God eftermiddag*
Good evening *God kveld*
Today *I dag*
Tomorrow *I morgen*
Yesterday *I går*
Hello *Hei*
How do you do? *Står det til?*
Goodbye *Adjø/Ha det bra/Hadet*
Thank you *Takk*
How much is this? *Hvor mye koster det?*
It costs *Det koster...*
How do I get to...? *Hvordan kommer jeg til...?*
Where is...? *Hvor er...?*
Right *Høyre*
To the right *Til høyre*
Left *Venstre*
To the left *Til venstre*
Straight on *Rett frem*
Phrase book *Parlør*
Dictionary *Ordbok*
Money *Penger*
Can I order please? *Kan jeg få bestille?*
Could I have the bill please? *Kan jeg få regningen?*
What time is it? *Hvor mye er klokken?*

It is (the time is...) *Den er (Klokken er...)*
When? *Når*
Where? *Hvor?*
Could I have your name please? *Hva er navnet?*
My name is *Mitt navn er...*
Do you have English newspapers? *Har du engelske aviser?*
Do you speak English? *Snakker du engelsk?*
I only speak English *Jeg snakker bare engelsk*
May I help you? *Kan jeg hjelpe deg?*
I do not understand *Jeg forstår ikke*
I do not know *Jeg vet ikke*
It has disappeared *Den har forsvunnet*
Chemist *Apotek*
Hospital *Sykehus*
Doctor *Lege*
Police station *Politistasjion*
Parking *Parkering*
Department store *Hus/Stormagasin*
Toilet *Toalett/WC*
Gentlemen *Herrer*
Ladies *Damer*
Vacant *Ledig*
Engaged *Opptatt*
Entrance *Inngang*
Exit *Utgang*
No entry *Ingen adgang*
Open *Åpent*
Closed *Stengt*
Push *Skyv*
Pull *Trekk*
No smoking *Røyking forbudt*
Breakfast *Frokost*
Lunch *Lunsj*
Dinner *Middag*
Eat *Spise*
Drink *Drikke*
Cheers! *Skål!*
Hot *Varm*
Cold *Kald*
Aircraft *Flymaskin*
Car *Bil*

Train *Tog*
Ticket *Billet*
Single/return *En vei/tur-retur*
To rent *Leie*
Free *Ledig*
Room to rent *Rom til leie*
Chalet *Hytte*
Can we camp here? *Kan vi campe her?*
No camping *Camping forbudt*
Grocery store (in countryside) *Landhandel*
Shop *Butikk*
Food *Mat/kost*
To buy *Kjøpe*
Sauna *Badstue*
Off licence/liquor store *Vinmonopol*
Clothes *Klær*
Overcoat *Frakk*
Jacket *Jakke*
Suit *Dress*
Shoes *Sko*
Skirt *Skjørt*
Blouse *Bluse*
Jersey *Genser*

Days and Months

Sunday *søndag*
Monday *mondag*
Tuesday *tirsdag*
Wednesday *onsdag*
Thursday *torsdag*
Friday *fredag*
Saturday *lørdag*

January *januar*
February *februar*
March *mars*
April *april*
May *mai*
June *juni*
July *juli*
August *august*
September *september*
October *oktober*
November *november*
December *desember*

TRANSPORT • ACCOMMODATION • EATING OUT • ACTIVITIES • A–Z • LANGUAGE

FURTHER READING

Snorri Sturluson

The Prose Edda, Penguin Classics, 2005.
Heimskringla, History of the Kings of Norway, University of Texas Press, 1991.
King Harald's Saga (an excerpt from the *Heimskringla*), Penguin Classics, 1976.

Miscellaneous

Garrison Keillor's Lake Wobegone Series.
A Happy Boy, Bjørnson Bjørnstjerne.
Constance Ring, Amalie Skram, Northwest University Press, 2002.
Shyness and Dignity, Dag Solstad, 2006.
Kristin Lavaransdatter, Sigrid Undset, Penguin, 2005.
Writing on the Wall, Gunnar Staalesen, Arcadia, 2002.
Punishment, Anne Holt, Time Warner, 2006.

Henrik Ibsen

A Doll's House
Peer Gynt, Oxford Classics.

Edvard Munch

Edvard Munch: Behind the Scream, Yale University Press, 2005.

Arctic Explorers

Farthest North, by Roland Huntford about Fridtjof Nansen's polar exploration.
Scott and Amundsen: Last Place on Earth, Roland Huntford, Abacus 2000.
The South Pole: An Account of the Norwegian Antarctic Exploration in the Fram, 1910–1912, Roald Amundsen, Cooper Square Press, 2001.
Kon Tiki: Across the Pacific by Raft, Thor Heyerdahl, Simon and Schuster Press, 1995.
Kon Tiki Expedition, Flamingo 1996.
In the Footsteps of Adam, Heyerdahl's autobiography, Abacus, 2001.
No Horizon is So Far, Ann Bancroft, Da Capo, 2003. About Liv Arresen's journey.

Knut Hamsun

Hunger, Canongate Books, 2006.
Mysteries, Souvenir Press, 1992.
The Growth of the Soil, Souvenir Press, 1989.
Wanderer, Souvenir Press, 2001.
In Wonderland, IG Publishing, 2004.
Wayfarers, Souvenir Press, 1994.
Women at the Pump, Souvenir Press, 1978.

Jostein Gaarder

Orange Girl, Phoenix, 2005.
Sophie's World: A Novel about the History of Philosophy, Phoenix, 1996.
Ringmaster's Daughter, Orion, 2003.

Feedback

We do our best to ensure the information in our books is as accurate and up-to-date as possible. The books are updated on a regular basis, using local contacts, who painstakingly add, amend and correct as required. However, some mistakes and omissions are inevitable and we are ultimately reliant on our readers to put us in the picture. We would welcome your feedback on any details related to your experiences using the book "on the road". Maybe we recommended a hotel that you liked (or another that you didn't), or you'd like to tell us about new attractions, or facts and figures you have found out about the country itself. The more details you can give us (particularly with regard to addresses, e-mails and telephone numbers), the better. We will acknowledge all contributions, and we'll offer an Insight Guide to the best letters received.

Please write to us at:
Insight Guides
PO Box 7910
London SE1 1WE
United Kingdom
Or send e-mail to:
insight@apaguide.co.uk

Other Insight Guides

Europe is comprehensively covered by over 200 books in Apa Publications' three series of guidebooks.
Insight Guides provide the reader with full cultural background and top-quality photography. Titles in this part of Europe include: *Denmark, Finland, Iceland, Sweden* and *Scandinavia*.

Insight Pocket Guides are written by local hosts and contain tailor-made itineraries to help users get the most out of a short stay. Each title comes complete with a pull-out map that can be used independently from the guide. Scandinavian destinations in the series include *Oslo & Bergen, Stockholm* and *Denmark*.

Apa also publishes **Insight Compact Guides**, mini encylopaedias which give you the facts about a destination in a very digestible form, supported by maps and colour photographs. Titles in the series include *Iceland, Finland, Denmark* and *Copenhagen*.

ART & PHOTO CREDITS

AKG-images London 124
Alesund Tourist Board 134/135, 277
Snorre Aske/Fjord Norway 219T
Aslak Aarhus 69, 73, 103
Mick Barnard/Nor-Ice back cover right, spine, 40, 98/99, 104, 132, 133, 165, 171, 173, 177T, 180, 185, 191, 197, 198T, 199, 202, 206, 216, 229, 230/231, 233, 244/245, 257, 266, 271, 276, 282, 286, 288/289, 304, 305, 326
Bergen Tourist Board 249T, 254
Bergen Tourist Board/Willy Haraldsen 357
Trygve Bølstad 29, 68, 72, 100, 119, 154, 155, 177, 184, 217, 284
Espen Brathe/Samfoto 164
John Brunton 90, 327
Knut Bry/Fjord Norway 227T
Pål Bugge/Innovation Norway 353
Nancy Bundt/Innovation Norway 6BL, 9TR, 349, 356, 365T, 369B
Camera Press/Björn Sigurdsön/Scanpix 82
Courtesy of Cannery Museum 7TR
J. Corbett/Leslie Garland 330T, 331
Ole Didriksen/Fjord Norway 285T
Fritz Dressler 12/13, 84/85, 89, 189, 196, 227, 274/275, 279, 312/313, 333
Hauke Dressler 147, 166/167, 194R, 198, 268, 270, 329
Per Eide/Fjord Norway 278T
Tor Eigeland back cover left, 32, 121, 186, 214, 246, 249, 253, 255, 256, 269, 270T, 294
R. K. Evans/Mark Azavedo Photo Library 172
Mary Evans Picture Library 189T
Fjord Norway 126, 235T
Fløibanen as/Pål Hoff 247
Leslie Garland Picture Library front flap top, back flap top, 37, 96, 102, 149, 158, 158T, 190, 192, 208, 211, 228R, 273, 293, 293T, 297, 300, 326T, 344
Paul Gogarty 118, 193
Blaine Harrington 2/3, 14, 62/63, 64/65, 95, 123, 142, 150T, 150, 151, 153T, 159, 207, 212/213, 250T, 260, 261, 263, 264T, 264, 265, 291, 309, 319T, 323
Stefan Hauberg 41, 59, 67, 92, 93, 161, 163, 175, 187, 200/201, 203, 210, 258/259, 290, 295, 298/299, 303, 308, 314, 315, 316T, 319, 320, 321, 322, 332
Johannes Haugan/NN/Samfoto 18
Ola Heining 225
Herheim Foto/Fjord Norway 238T
Pål Hermansen/NN/Samfoto back flap bottom, 66

Frank Heuer/Laif/Camera Press 6T
Marie Holstein 31, 38, 114/115
Hordaland Tourist Board 236, 238, 241
Hans-Peter Huber/4Corners 8BL
Hunderfossen/Innovation Norway 369T
Michael Jenner 146, 152, 162T
Per Jonsson/Fjord Norway 218
Ottar Johansen/Fjord Norway 239
Bjørn Jørgensen/Innovation Norway 367
Erik Jørgensen/Innovation Norway 371
Gerold Jung 263T, 295T, 325T
Hans Klüche 130, 235, 251, 252, 269T, 337, 338, 339, 340, 341T, 343
The Kobal Collection 54
Marte Kopperud/Innovation Norway 368T
Jens-Uwe Kumpch 57T
Janos Jurka/Bruce Coleman 306, 307T
Øystein Klakegg/Billedbryået 108
Arne Knudsen 19, 68, 109, 176, 226, 308T
Courtesy of Kongsvold Fjeldstue 9CL
Kvikmes Hotel - Balestrand 358
Bard Løken/NN/Samfoto 4/5
Vincent Lowe/Leslie Garland 307, 341
Mats Lindén 232, 318
K. Marthinsen/Leslie Garland 287
Olympia Utvikling back cover centre
Robert Meyer Collection 24, 26, 27, 43, 44, 46, 47, 48/49, 50, 94, 120, 325R, 340T
Anna Mockford & Nick Bonetti/Apa 7BR, 8TR, 9BR, 364, 373, 374
Reidar Munkejord/Fjord Norway 221, 220T
Dag Myrestrand/Fjord Norway 228T
NHPA 174
Phil Nixon/Leslie Garland 329T
Norway Tourist Office 184T, 197T
Norwegian Literature Abroad 127
Richard Nowitz front flap bottom, 1, 20, 23, 153, 161T, 251T
Per Nybø/Fjord Norway 254T
David Paterson/Mira.com 350
Radisson SAS 359
Terje Rakke/Nordic Life/Innovation Norway 351, 355, 362, 365B
Rex Features 58, 83, 122, 136/137, 138/139
Riksforsatlingen 172T
Rogaland Tourist Board 30, 219, 222
O. Roksvag/Fjord Norway 282T
Galen Rowell/Corbis 105
David Simson 87
Robert Spark 301, 324, 328
Stavanger Tourist Board back cover bottom, 30, 224
Destinasjon Stavanger/Fjord Norway 228L

Swedish Institute 160
Topham Picturepoint 10/11, 16/17, 21, 25, 33, 34, 35, 36, 39, 42, 51, 52, 53, 55, 56, 60/61, 70, 71, 74/75, 76, 77, 78, 79, 82, 86, 88, 91, 97, 107, 110, 112, 117, 131, 144/145, 162, 178/179, 181, 188, 194L, 195, 209, 223, 267, 272, 280, 281, 285, 294T, 325L, 330
Pascal Tournaire/DPPI/Rex Features 111
Bobby Tulloch 57, 250, 334/335, 336, 338T, 342
Mikael Utterstrom/Alamy 6BR
Pål Visnes/Fjord Norway 283
Voss Tourist Board 237, 240
Werner Forman/Corbis 8BR
Johan Wildhagen/Innovation Norway 7TL, 368B
Odd Inge Worsoe/Fjord Norway 220

PICTURE SPREADS

Pages 80/81 *Top row*: Leslie Garland; Leslie Garland; Christian Skredsvig/Mary Evans ; Eric Werenskjold/Mary Evans; *Centre*: Leslie Garland. *Bottom row*: Richard Nowitz; Leslie Garland; Leslie Garland; Theodor Kittelsen/Mary Evans.
Pages 128/129 All Leslie Garland except: Blaine Harrington 128BL & Cephas/StockFood 129BR.
Pages 247/248 *Top row*: Staffan Widstrand/Bruce Coleman (BC); Colin Varndell/BC; Dr Eckhart Pott/BC; Steve Morgan/Environmental Images. *Centre*: Robert Maier/BC; Mark Carwardine/BC. *Bottom row*: Hans Reinhard/BC ; Werner Layer/BC; Stephen Krasermann/BC; Christer Fredricksson/ BC.
Pages 310/311 *Top row*: Leslie Garland; Hans Klüche; K Marthinson/ Leslie Garland; N. Rosing/Topham. *Centre*: Leslie Garland. *Bottom row*: all Leslie Garland.

Cartographic Editor Zoë Goodwin

Map Production: Lovell Johns Ltd
© 2008 Apa Publications GmbH & Co. Verlag KG (Singapore branch)

Picture Research: Tom Smyth & Celia Sterne
Production: Linton Donaldson

※INSIGHT GUIDE
NORWAY

Cartographic Editor **Zoë Goodwin**
Production **Linton Donaldson**
Design Consultants
Klaus Geisler, Graham Mitchener
Picture Research **Hilary Genin**

INDEX

Numbers in italics refer to photographs

A

Aak 280
Aasen, Ivar 71
accommodation 354–9
  Balestrand hotels 358
  Bergen hotels 357
  Kristiansand hotels 357
  Oslo hotels 356
  Tromsø hotels 359
  Trondheim hotels 359
  Stavanger hotels 358
  Svalbard hotels 359
  Fjord Pass 13, 354
  budget hotel chains 354
Adolfkanonen (Adolf Cannons) 320
Agatunet 238
air services/transport 96, 348–9
airports 349–50
Akershus 169
akevitt (aquavit) 129
  Løiten Brænderi (Distillery) 183
Aksla 278
aktiv 107
alcohol 131–3, 155, 360
Alfheim 286
Alghazal 25
Alstahaug 308
Alsten 308
Alta 325
Altmark affair 53
Alvsson, Knut 37
America, North 26, 77
Amsterdam Island 340
Amundsen, Roald 77, 79, 176
Andøya 41, 319
angling *see* fishing
aquariums *see under*
  nature centres
arboretums *see under*
  nature centres
Archer, Colin 177, 284
architecture *31*, 124, 126
Arctic Circle *see* Polarsirkel
Arendal 206
Arnesen, Liv 79
art 125–6
  monuments to artists 240
art galleries/collections/
  exhibitions 126
  see also under museums
  Bergen 255
  Oslo fjord 173, 174
  Ulvik 238
Art Nouveau architecture 277
arts 45, 363
  traditional 117–20
Asbjørnsen, Per Christen 81
Askøy 240
Astrup, Nikolai 270
Astruptunet 269–70
Aulestad 184
Aurlandsvangen 198
Aurora borealis
  (Northern Lights) 263,
  311, 337, 366

Ausevik 271
Austråtborgen 296
Avaldsnes 222
Averøya *282*, 282–3
Å 317
Åkrehamm 222
Ål 194
Ålesund 95, 262, 277–8, *279*
Åndalsnes 280
Åsane 256
Åsgårdstrand 176

B

Balestrand 267
Balsfjord 321
Barents, Willem 339, 340
Barentsburg *337*, 338
Barentsøya 342
Baroniet Rosendal (Rosendal
  Barony), Sunde 235
Båtsfjord 330
beaches 177, *162*, 218, 317
bears 242
  see also polar bears
Beitostølen 197
Bergen *244–5*, 247–56
  art collections 255
  bathing areas 252
  shopping 255
  tours 252
  Bergen Akvariet (Aquarium) 252
  Bergen Kunstmuseum
    (Art Museum) 255
  Bergen Travpark
    (trotting course) 257
  Bergenshus 250
  Botanisk Hage
    (Botanic Garden) 252
  Bryggen (Tyskebryggen)
    249, 250
  Bryggens Museum 249
  Domkirke (Cathedral) 249
  Fantoft Stavkirke 254
  Fløibanen *247*
  Fløyen 247
  Fredriksborg 252
  Gamle Bergen (Old Bergen)
    251–2
  Gamle Rådhuset (Old Town Hall)
    252
  Gamlehaugen 253
  Grieghallen 255
  Håkonshallen 250
  Hansa houses 250–1
  Hanseatisk Museum 250–1
  Historisk Museum (Cultural
    History) 252
  Hotel Victoria 252
  Johanneskirken (St John's
    Church) 252
  Korskirken (Holy Cross) 249–50
  Lehmkuhl 252
  Lille Lungegårdsvann 255, 256
  Mariakirken (St Mary's
    Church) 249

Naturhistorisk Museum
  (Natural History) 252
Den Nationale Scene
  (National Theatre) 253
Rosenkrantztårnet 249, 250,
  252
Sailors' Monument 252
Sjøfartsmuseum (Maritime) 252
Sydneshaugen 252
Theta Museum 249
Torgalmenningen 252
Torget (market) *130*, 247,
  251, 252
Vågen 249
Berlevåg 330
Bernadotte, Jean-Baptiste 41
Bindalen 304
biodiversity *see* wildlife
birds 242
  Ekkerøya 331
  Lofoten Islands 263
  Rogaland 218, 219, 220
  Runde Bord Rock 278–9
  Sogn og Fjordane 271
  Svalbard 341, 342
Bjørnson, Bjørnstjerne 50, 124,
  125, 253
  birthplace 184
  home, Aulestad 184
Bjørnsund 282
Blixgård 308
boat trips *see* Hurtigruten
boating 365
boats and boat-building 27, 72,
  236, 284, 285
Bodø 307, *309*
Bognes 319
Boine, Mari 88, *90*
bokmål (book language) 71, 124,
  125
Bonaparte, Napoleon 40
Borgund *29, 32*, 198
botanic gardens *see under*
  nature centres
Botn 306
breakfast 128, 130, 154
Bremangerlandet 271
Bremsnes 283
Brimnes 238
Brufoss 177
Brundtland, Gro Harlem 57
Bud 282
Bugøfjord 332
Bugøynes 332
Bulle, Ole 127, 235, 253
  home on Lysøen 254, *255*
bunads (costume) 72, *119*, 120,
  186, 282
burial mounds *see* prehistoric
  monuments
buses 95, 349, 350, 351
business hours 371
Bygdin 197
Bymarka 296
Bøge, Kari 125
Bømlo 233

C

camping 355
car hire 353
car transport 349, 352
cathedrals see under churches
and major towns
caves 304, 320
Chancellor, Captain Richard 328
children's attractions 369
Christian Frederick 41
Christiania 38, 43, 48–9
Christianity 24, 30, 31, 33, 374
and St Olav 233, 291
Battle of Stiklestad 297
in Ryfylke 219
missionaries 31
Pietism 39
churches and cathedrals
see also under major towns
stave churches (stavkirke) 31–2,
117–18, 194, 198
Atlanterhavskatedralen (Atlantic
Cathedral), Kristiansund 285
Borgund Stavkirke 29, 32, 198
Dolstad 304
Drøbak Kirke 172–3
Egersund 217
Grip 285
Hadsel Kirke 318, 319
Heddal Stavkirke 121, 209
Hemsedal 195
Hopperstad Stavkirke, Vik 268
Hove Kirke, Vik 268
Kaupanger Stavkirke,
Sogndal, 269
Kinnøy 271
Kinsarvik (stone) 238
Kvernes (stave church) 283
Kvinnherad Kirke, Sunde 235
Lom (stave church) 80
Mosterhamm (stone) 233
Nidaros Domen 262
Ringebu Stavkirke 189
St Olaf Kirke, Avaldsnes 222
St Olav's Kirke, Balestrand 267
Sami chapel, Skaidi 326
Nordmøresdomen, Tingvoll 286
Torpo Stavkirke 194
Trollkirka (the Troll Church),
Bud 282
Trondenes 319
Urnes Stavkirke, Luster 269
Vangskyrkja, Voss 238, 239–40
cinema 127, 363
climate 21, 163, 371
coastal express steamers 93,
261–4
Constitution Day 373
copper mining 188
costs 13, 130–3, 372, 374
costume 12–13
see also bunads
Sami 84–5, 88, 89
crime 371
culture 34, 123–7, 363–4
Sami 89
currency 374
customs 372
cycling 218, 366

D

Dahl, J.C. 123, 152
Dass, Petter 308
disabled travellers 372
Djupevåg, Kristian 236
Dragsvik 268
drinking 70, 129, 131–3, 360
driving regulations 352
Drøbak 169, 172–3
Oscarsborg Festning (fort) 172
Dønna Manor, Dønna 308

E

Edgeøya 342
Egersund 217
Eid 272
Eidsvoll 41, 42, 172
Eidsvollsbygningen 172
Eikesdalsvatnet 281
Eiriksson, Leiv 77, 78
Ekkerøya 331
Elden, Asbjørn 125
Elverum 185
Elveseter 198
embassies 372
emergency numbers 372
Engelbrektsson, Olav 37
Erik the Red 78
Espevær 222
Estenstadmarka 296
Etasjegrotten 304
EU 58, 349
events diary 363–4
explorers 77–9

F

Fagernes 197
family/children's attractions
369–70
Ferieparken (amusement park),
Kinsarvik 238
Hunderfossen Familiepark,
Øyer 184
Kongeparken, Ålgård 218, 219
Kristiansand dyrepark/
Kardemomme By
(Cardamon Town) 205
Lilleputhammer, Øyer 184
Sommarland (family park),
Bø 210
Fana Folklore 256
Faroes 43
Farsund 206
fauna 242–3
see also national parks,
nature centres
Fauske 306, 307
Fedje 239, 241
Fehn, Sverre 126, 183, 268
Ferkingstad 222
ferries 348, 351
festivals 363–4
Åsgårdstrand Festival 176
Bergen International Festival of
Music 255, 364
Emigration Festival,
Stavanger 226

Gjøglerne Kommer (The Clowns
are Coming), Oslo 151
Holmenkollen Ski Festival 105,
108
international jazz festival,
Oslo 151
International Trad Jazz Festival,
Haugesund 222
Molde International Jazz Festival
282
Norwegian Film Festival,
Haugesund 222
Rosendal Music Festival 235
St Olav Festival 296
Fetsund 171
Fimreite, Battle of 269
Finnmark 87, 324
Finnmarksvidda (Finnmark plain)
90, 324
Finse 102
Firdariket, Eid 272
fishing 8–9, 112–13, 366
see also fishing rivers
angling licences 112, 113, 222
fishing (commercial) 217, 226,
241, 315, 326
fishing rivers
Driva 286
Jøstra 270
Måselv 321
Namsen/Sandøla 302
Nidelva 296
Rauma 280
Suldalslågen 220
Surna 286
Vosso 239
fisker 112
Fiskeravgift (fishing fee) 112
Fjærland 94, 268
fjell see mountains
fjording (fjord horse) 271, 272
fjords 6–7, 215, 267
tours 350
Aurlandsfjord 310
Bjørnafjord 240
Borgundfjorden 136–7
Eidfjord 238
Eidfjorden 233
Geirangerfjorden 276, 279
Hafrsfjorden 218
Hardangerfjorden 233, 235
Lyngenfjorden 323
Lysefjorden 219
Nærøyfjorden 241, 269
Nordfjorden 272
Oslofjorden 169–177
Sognefjorden 267, 268
Sørfjorden 237–8
Storfjorden 279
Todalfjorden 286
Trollfjorden 212–13, 263, 318
Trondheimsfjorden 291
flag, Norwegian 69
Flakstad 317
Flakstadøya 317
Flåm 241, 266, 269
Flekkefjord 206
flora 88, 218, 306, 339, 341
see also national parks
Florø 270

folk arts 117–20
  dance 120, 256
folktales 80–1
Folldal 187
food 128–9, 360–2
  fish 112, 128, 129, 278
  prices 130
Förde 270
Fosna Culture 283
Foyn, Svend 176
Fram 74–5, 77, 79, 284
  museum 162
Fredrikstad 174
Frognerseteren
  Restaurant 118

G

Gaarder, Jostein 125
Galdesand 198
Gamlehaugen 134–5
Garborg, Hulda 120
Gardermoen 171
Geilane, Lars Larsen 44
Geilo 193–4
Geiranger 279–80
Gilja 218
Gille, Harald 24
Gimle Gård, Kristiansand 205
Gjevilsvassdalen 190
Gjesvær 329
glaciers 101, 103, 367
  hiking 374
  Briksdalsbreen 272, 273, 311
  Folgefonn Glacier 233, 311
  Grovebreen 270
  Hardanger Glacier 238
  Jostedalsbreen 103, 268, 311
  Nigardsbreen 269
  Sulitjelma 307
  Svartisen 304
  Øskfjordjøkelen 324
Glomfjord 308
Glomma river 185
Gloppedalsura 217
Gloppen 272
Gokstadhaugen (burial site) 176
Gokstad Viking ship 14, 20, 22,
  176
Greenland 26, 35, 43, 77, 78
Grefsen 164
Grense Jakobselv 332
Grieg, Edvard 124, 253
  and cultural traditions/customs
    235, 253
  museum 253
  Peer Gynt Suite 190
  Troldhaugen (summer home)
    124, 253–4
Grimstad 206
Grip 285
Grong 302
Grønnligrotta 304
Grorud 164
Grotli 196
Gudbrandsdalen 189
Gudbrandsjuvet 280
Gude, Hans Frederick 152
Gyldenløve, Ulrik Frederick 39
Gynt, Peer (Per) 189, 190

H

Hadseløya 318
Hafjell 181, 183
Hafrsfjord, Battle of 218
Halden 173, 174
  Fredriksten Festning 174
Hallingskarvet 193
Hamar 181, 183
Hammerfest 264, 326, 326–7
  Isbjørnhallen (Polar Bear
    Hall) 327
  Meridianstøtta (Meridian Column)
    327
  museum (polar bear) 327
  Skansen 327
Hamningberg 331
Hamsun, Knut 124, 173, 262
Hangurfjell 239
Hankø 174
Hanseatic League 35, 249
  houses in Bergen 250–1
Haraldsen, Sonja 83
Hardanger fiddle 237, 240
Hardangervidda 193, 233
Haugesund 222
health 373
Heddal 210
Hegra Festning 301
Helgøya 181
Hell 301
Hella 268
Hellesylt 279
Hellviktangen Manor 162
Hemsedal 195
Henie, Sonja 107
Henningsvær 316
heritage centres see museums
Herjulfsson, Bjarni 77, 78
Heyerdahl, Thor 19, 77, 162, 177
hiking 366
Hinnøya 319
history 18–58
  constitution 41
  World War II 52–3
  Danish rule 36–41, 70
  emigration 44, 45, 225
  prehistory 21
  Swedish rule 41, 43–7, 69
  20th century 50–9
  Vikings 23–7
Hjemmeluft (rock carvings) 325
Holberg, Ludvig 40
Holmenkollen
  March 105
  Ski Festival 105
  ski-jump 105, 161
  Skimuseet (Ski Museum) 161–2
Honningsvåg 328
Hordaland 233–41
Hornindalsvatnet 273
horse riding 367
Horten 175
hospitality 67–8, 370
Hotel Utsikten Bellevue,
  Geiranger 279
Hurtigruten 93, 212–13,
  261–4, 351
  museum 319
Huseskogen bob track 184

hydro-electric power stations
  Kvilldal 220, 221
  Lysebotn 219
  Sima Kraftverket 238
  Sudalen 221
  Ulla Førre 221
Hyperboreans 21
hytter 72, 102, 102–3, 118, 355

I

Ibsen, Henrik Johan 46, 47, 68,
  122, 124
  childhood home, Skien 207
  memorabilia, Grimstad 206
  museum, Oslo 152
  Peer Gynt 190
Ice Age 21
Ice Fishing Festival 113
Iceland 26, 30, 35, 43, 77
idrett 107
Ingstad, Helge 78
Innlandet 285
internet cafés 373

J

Jeløy 174
Jenstadjvet 286
Jondal 236
Junkerdalen 306
Jærstrendrene Landskaps
  vernområde 218, 229

K

Kabelvåg 315
  Lofotakveriet (aquarium) 316
kalesjevogn 94
Karasjok 329
  Sámpi (theme park) 329
Karmøy 221–2
Kaupang, 169
Kautokeino 325, 332
Kielland, Alexander 124
kings
  Alfred the Great of England
    23, 26
  Canute, King of Denmark
    33, 297
  Christian I 36
  Christian II 37
  Christian III 37
  Christian IV 38, 89, 161, 203,
    285
  Erik Bloodaxe 30
  Erik of Pomerania 36
  Frederick I 37
  Håkon den Gode (the Good)
    30, 32, 241
  Håkon Håkonson 176, 222, 250
  Håkon VII 50, 82, 83
  Halvdan the Black 29
  Harald Hårdråde 33, 34, 161
  Harald Hårfagre (Fair Hair)
    29, 30, 218, 222, 297
  Harald V 83
  Karl Johan 41, 43
  Olav Haraldson (St Olav) 32, 33,
    233, 240, 262, 291, 297

Olav Kyrre 247
Olav Tryggvason (Olav I) 32, 291, 297
Olav V *56*, 57, 82, 83, 105, 107
Oscar I 45, 162
Oskar II *47*, 332
Øystein 31, 34
Svejn, King of Denmark 297
Sverre 132, 269
Kinnøy 271
Kinsarvik 238
Kirkenes 264, 330, 332
Kjeåsen 238
Kjerringøy 262, 308
Kjøllefjord 330
klippfisk 129, 278
town 283
Knudsen, Knut 71
Kongelige Seilforening (the Royal Norwegian Sailing Association) 284
Kongelige Slottet (Royal Palace) 150
Kongens Utsikt 171
Kongsberg 38
Kon-Tiki
expedition 77
museum 162
Kopervik 222
Kragerø 207
Kringen 190
Kristensen, Monika *79*
Kristiansand 38, 203, 205
Kristiansund 283, 285
Krokkleiva 171
Kuli 286
Kvamskogen 235
Kvernes 283
Kvinnfoss (waterfall) 268
Køltzow, Live 125, *127*

L

lakes
Gjende 197
Eikesdalsvatnet 281
Hornindalsvatnet 272
Jølstravatnet 269
Maridalsvatnet 171
Mjøsa 172, 181
Ørdalsvatn 217
Sognsvann 171
Vangsvatnet 239
Lakseslottet Lindum (Salmon Castle), Lindum 221
Laksestudioet (salmon observation studio) 220
landsmål see nynorsk
Langøya 319
language(s) 38, 59, 70–1, 123, 124, 125, 377
haddock English 329
Sami 87, 89, 90, 124
useful words and phrases 377
Lapps of Finnmark *see* **Sami**
Larvik 177
Lærdalsøyri 269
Norsk Villakssenter (wild salmon centre) 269
League of Nations 51

legends 80
Leirvik 233
Leka 309
Leknes 316
Lie, Trygve 57, 58
lighthouses 220, 235, 241
Lindesnes 205, *210*
Tungenes Fyr 218
Verdens Ende 176
Lillehammer 183–4
Winter Olympics *178–9*, 183
Lillesand 206
Lillomarka 164
Lindesnes 205
Lindisfarne, Northumberland 117
literature 124–5
see also **folktales**
Loen 273
Lofoten Islands *142*, *212–13*, 262, 315–18
Lom 198
Longyearbyen 337
Luster 269
Lyngsalpene 323
Lysebotn 219
Lysekloster 254
Lysøen 254
Lærdalsøyri 269
Løkvika Fiskehytte og Partisanhule (Fishing Cabin and Partisan Cave) 330
Løveid, Cecilie 125
Løvøy 175

M

maelstroms
near Bodø *300*
Moskenstraumen 317
Saltstraumen 308
Saltstraumen Opplevelsessenter (Experience Centre) 308
Mandal 205, *209*
maps (walking) 171, 373
Maridalsvannet 171
Markland 78
Mathisen, Oscar 107
medical services 373
Melbu 318
Mellomverftet 285
Michelsen, Christian 50, 253
Midnight Sun 262, 366
Land of the 310
Milde 256
mineral rights 338
Mjøsabyen 181
Mo i Rana 304
Moe, Jørgen 81
Moffen Island 342
Molde *280*, 281–2
monarchy
see **Royal Family**
money 372, 374
Morgedal 104, 108, 209
Mosjøen 304
Moskenstraumen 318
Mosterhamn 233
Mosterøy 219
Mostraspelet 233
mountain railway 269

mountains and mountain ranges
Bleia 270
climbing/mountaineering 103
Dalsnibba 280
Dovrefjell *190*
Galdhøpiggen 103, 195, 198
Glittertind 103, 195
Jotunheimen (Home of the Giants) *101*, *195*, 195–6
Kjerragbolten 219
Kjerragfjell 219
Krossbu 198
Kvflnangsfjellet 324
Lofotensveggen 317
Lyngsalpene (Lyngen Alps) 323
Newtontoppen 339
Reka 319
Skagastølstindane 195
Stetind 320
Storsteinen 264, 294, 323
Sunnmøre mountains 279, 282
Torghatten 309
Tosenfjellet 304
Trollheimen (Home of the Trolls) 286
Trolltindane 280
Trollveggen 280
Ulriken 247
Munch, Edvard 123, 124, 158
and Oslo 147, 150
Åsgårdstrand 175–6
in Bergen art collection 255
Munchmuseet 158
Munchs Lille Hus 176
Skrik (*Scream*) 158
summer home *207*
The Vampire 124
museums, heritage centres and other attractions
see also **family/children's attractions**
Allied Monument, Måløy 271
Anders Svor Museum, Grodås 273
Archaeological Museum, Ullandhaug 229
Arendal Bymuseum (Town Museum) 207
Arkeologisk Museum (Archaeological Museum), Stavanger 229
Astrup Fearnley Museet for Moderne Kunst (Modern Art), Oslo 151
Ålesund Museum 277
Bergen Kunstmuseum (Art Museum) 255
Borgarsyssell Museum, Sarpsborg 175
Bryggens Museum, Bergen 249
Dalane Folk Museum, Egersund 217
Edvard Grieg Museum, Troldhaugen 254
Egersund Fayance Museum 217
Eidsvoll Bygdetun (Rural Museum) 172
heritage sites, Espevær 222
Falstad Museum, Levanger 301

Fetsund Lenser (Log Floating Museum) 171
fisheries museum, Sund 317
Fishery Museum, Molde 282
Folldal 187
Follo Museum (Heritage Museum), Drøbak 172
Forvarsmuseet (Armed Forces Museum), Oslo 149
Fossheim Steinsenter (Stone Centre), Lom 198
Frammuseet, Oslo 162
Gamle Lensmannshuset (Sheriff's House), Jondal 236
Glomdal Museum, Elverum 185
Grimstad Bymuseum (Town Museum) 206
Hallingdal Folkemuseum, Nesbyn 195
Hanseatiske Museum/ Schøtstuene, Bergen 250–1
Hardanger Fartøyvernsenter (Hardanger Ship Conservation Centre), Norheimsund 236
Hardanger Folkemuseum, Utne 237
Heddal Byydetun (Farmhouse) 210
Hedmarksmuseet, Hamar 126, 183
Hermetikmuseet (Canning Museum) 227
Historisk (Historical Museum), Oslo 169
Historisk Museum (Cultural History), Bergen 252
Hjemmefrontmuseet (Resistance Museum), Oslo 149
Hjertøya Fishery Museum, Molde 282
Hol Bygdemuseum (Hol Rural Museum), Geilo 194
Holmenkollen Skimuseet (Ski Museum), Oslo 161–2
Hurtigruten Museum, Stokmarknes 319
Ibsen Muséet, Oslo 152
Ingebrigt Vik Museum, Øystese 236
Jernbanemuséet (National Railway Museum), Hamar 183
Kolbeinstveit Museum, Suldal 220
Kon-Tiki Museum, Oslo 162
Krigsminnemuseum (War Museum), Narvik 321
Kunstindustrimuséet (Museum of Applied Art), Oslo 152
Kunstmuseum (Art Museum), Lillehammer 184
Kystmuseet i Sogn og Fjordane (Coastal Museum), Florø 271
Leikvin Kulturminnepark (Heritage Park), Grøa 286
Lillesand (Town Museum) 206
Lofotmuséet (Lofotens Museum), Kabelvåg 315
Longyearbyen 337
Maihaugen (open-air museum), Lillehammer 183–4, 191

Marinemuseet (Naval Museum), Horten 175
Munchmuseet (Munch Museum), Oslo 155
Museet for Samtidskunst (Museum of Contemporary Art), Oslo 151
Måbødalen Kulturlandskaps museum (Måbødalen Cultural Landscape Museum) 238
Mælandsgården Museum, Skudeneshavn 221
Nasjonalgalleriet (National Gallery), Oslo 152
Naturhistorisk Museum (Natural History), Bergen 252
Nesch Museum, Ål 194
Nord Trøndelag (Dampsaga), Steinkjer 302
Nordenfjeldske Kunstindustri-museum, Trondheim 291
Nordfjord Folkemuseum, Sandane 272
Nordkapphuset (North Cape Museum), Honningsvåg 329
Nordkappmuséet (North Cape Museum), Honningsvåg 329
Nordmøre Museum, Kristiansund 283, 285
Nordnorsk Kunstnersentrum (North Norwegian Artists' Centre), Svolvær 315
Norsk Arkitekturmuseum (Museum of Architecture), Oslo 151
Norsk Bremuseum (Norwegian Glacier Museum), Fjærland 268
Norsk Fiskevaersmuseum (Norwegian Fishing Village Museum), Å 317
Norsk Fjellmuseum (Mountain Museum), Lom 198
Norsk Folkemuseum (Norwegian Folk Museum), Oslo 162
Norsk Industriarbeidermuseum (Norwegian Industrial Workers Museum), Rjukan 210
Norsk Luftfartsmuseum (Norwegian Aviation Centre), Bodø 307, 308
Norsk Oljemuseum (Oil Museum) 227
Norsk Skogsbrukmuseum (Forestry Museum), Elverum 185
Norsk Teknisk Museum (Museum of Technology), Oslo 152
Norsk Telemuseum (Museum of Telecommunications), Oslo 152
Det Norske Utvandrersenteret (Emigration Centre), Stavanger 225
Norsk Veg Museum (Museum of Vehicle History), Lillehammer 184
Olavsgruva (Olav mine), Røros 187, 188

Oslo Bymuséet (City Museum) 161
Oslokunstersenter (contemporary and applied arts) 158
Petter Dass Museum, Alstahaug 308
polar bear, Hammerfest 327
Polarmuséet (Polar Museum), Andenes 319
Polarmuséet (Polar Museum), Tromsø 322
Polarsirkelsenteret (Arctic Circle Centre) 305
Resistance Museum, Hegra Festning 301
Ringve Museum (Museum of Musical History), Trondheim 295
Romsdals Museum, Molde 282
Rustkammeret (army museum), Trondheim 293
Saltdal Museum, Rognan 306
Saltdal Bygdetun Blodveimuséet (Blood Road Museum), Rognan 306
Samisk Museum, Kautokeino 325–6
De Samiske Samlinger (Sami Museum and Library), Karasjok 329
Selbu Strikkemuseum (Knitting Museum) Selbu 296
Setesdalmuséet (Heritage Museum) 210
Setesdalsbanen (Setesdal Railway Museum) 205
Sjøfartsmuséet (Maritime Museum), Trondheim 294
Sjøfartsmuseum (Maritime Museum), Oslo 162
Sjøfartsmuseum (Maritime Museum), Bergen 252
Sjøfartsmuseet (Maritime Museum), Stavanger 227, 228
Skimuseet (ski museum), Oslo 161
Skimuseet, Trondheim 295
Smelthytta, Røros 187, 188
Smøla 285
Sogn og Fjordane Kystmuseet (coastal museum) 270–1
Sogn Folkemuseum, Sogndal 269
Son Kystkultursenter (Coastal Heritage Centre) 173
Stavanger Museum 229
Sternersenmuséet (contemporary arts), Oslo 152
Stiklestad Nasjonale Kultursenter (Stiklestad National Arts Centre) 301
Stjørdal open-air museum, Værnes 301
Strikkemuseum (Knitting Museum), Selbu 296
Sunndal Museum, Grødalen 286
Sunnfjord Museum, Førde 270
Sunnhordland Folkemuseum, Leirvik 235
Sunnmøre Museum, Ålesund 277
Sør-Varanger Museum, Neiden 332

Telemark Museum 207–8
Theta Museum, Bergen 249
Tromsø University Museum 322
Trøndelag Folkemuseet (Folk
    Museum), Trondheim 294
Trøndelag Kunstnersenter
    (Academy of Art) 295
Trondhjems Kunstforening/
    Trøndelag Kunstgalleri
    (Trondheim Art Gallery) 295
university museum,
    Trondheim 291
Valdres Folkemuseum,
    Fagernes 197
Varanger Samiske Museum 330
Vardøhus Museum, Vardø 331
Vefsn open-air museum,
    Mosjøen 304
Versterålen Museum, Melbu 318
Vestvågøy Museum, Fygle 316
Vigeland-musèet, Oslo 155, 161
Vikingskipshuset (Viking Ship
    Museum), Oslo 20, 162, 176
Vitenskapsmusèet (Museum of
    Natural History and
    Archaeology), Trondheim 294
Voss Folkemuseum 240
music 127, 150–1, 256, 363
    see also **yoik**
    monuments to musicians 240
Myrdal 96, 241
Måbødalen 238
Måløy 271
Møre og Romsdal 277–86
Møstrevåg 235

N

Namdalen 303
Namsen Laksakvarium (aquarium)
    303
Nansen, Fridtjof 50, 77
    Nansen Passport 51
    statue 268
Narvik 53, 320
national parks 242, 368
    Borre Nasjonalpark 175
    Børgefjell Nasjonalpark 303, 368
    Dovre Nasjonalpark 190, 368
    Gressåmoen Nasjonalpark 302,
        368
    Hardangervidda Nasjonalpark
        193, 368
    Jotunheimen Nasjonalpark 195,
        368
    Øvre Dividal Nasjonalpark 321
    Øvre Pasvik Nasjonalpark 332
    Rago Nasjonalpark 320, 368
    Ravnedalen Nasjonalpark 205
    Rondane Nasjonalpark 187, 368
NATO 57, 58, 59
nature centres, aquariums,
    arboretums, botanic gardens
    Bergen Akvariet (Aquarium) 252
    Botanisk Hage (Botanic Garden),
        Bergen 252
    Lofoten Akvariet (Aquarium),
        Kabelvåg 316
    Namsen Akvariet (Aquarium),
        Fiskumfossen 303

Norsk Villakrssenter (Wild Salmon
    Centre), Lædalsøyri 269
Norwegian Arboretum, Milde 256
Ringve Botaniske Hage
    (Botanic Gardens) 295
Slettnes Nature and Heritage
    Reserve, Gamvik 330
Stavanger Botanisk Hage
    (Botanic Gardens),
    Ullandhaug 229
Svinivik Arboret (Arboretum) 286
Tøyenhagen (Tøyen Botanical
    Gardens), Oslo 158
Nærøyfjorden 269
Neiden 332
Nelson, Horatio 40, 340, 341
Nerdrum, Odd 126
Nesch, Rolf 194
Nesodden 162
Nesseby 330
Nesset 281
Nevlunghavn 177
new Norse *see* **nynorsk**
Nidaros 291
nightlife 363
    Oslo 152–4
Nobel, Alfred 160
Nobel Peace Prize 160
Nordnes 269
Nord Trøndelag 301
Nordaustlandet 339
Nordfjordeid 272
Nordhordland 240–1
Nordkapp (North Cape) 264, 327,
    328–9
Nordkapphallen (North Cape Hall)
    329
Nordland 262, 303
Nordmarka 70, 164, 171
Nordnes 269
Norges Idrettsforbund (NIF)
    (Norwegian Confederation of
    Sports) 107
Norheim, Sondre 104, 108, 208–9
Norheimsund 235
Norsemen 23
Norsk Polarinstitut 341
North Cape *see* **Nordkapp**
northern lights *see* **aurora borealis**
Northmen 23
Norway in a Nutshell 350
Norwegian Rose marble 306
Norwegian University of Science
    and Technology (NTNU),
    Trondheim 291
Nusfjord 317
Nygaardsvold, Johan 52
nynorsk 71, 72, 124, 125, 377
Nøtterøy 176

O

Oarddojokke 330
oceanography 77
Ogna 218
oil 97, 225
Olden 273, 274–5
Olympic medals 110
opening hours 371
Oppdal 190

Opsvik, Peter 126
Orkney Islands 24, 30, 34, 35, 37
Oseberghaugen (burial mound) 176
Oseberg ship 29, 176
Oslo 33, 43, 147–64
    bus/trams 349
    eating out/nightlife 152–4
    Oslo Pass (Oslokortet) 149, 376
    Oslo Guide 152
    outdoor life 163–4
    shopping 164
    underground (T-bane) 351
    Aker Brygge 147, 149, 164
    Akershus Slott (Castle) 37, 148,
        151
    Astrup Fearnley Museet for
        Moderne Kunst (Modern Art)
        151
    Aula 150, 160
    Basarhallene 150, 164
    Bygdøy peninsula 162, 163
    Christian IV's gate 150
    Christian IV's town 151, 161
    Christiania torv 161
    Domkirke (Cathedral) 150
    Eidsvollplass 150
    Forvarsmuseet (Armed Forces
        Museum) 149
    Frammuseet 162
    Frognerparken (park) 159, 161
    Grünerløkka 158
    Historisk (Historical Museum)
        169
    Hjemmefrontmuseet (Resistance
        Museum) 149
    Holmenkollen Skimuseet
        (Ski Museum) 161–2
    Ibsen Musèet 152
    Kampen 159
    Karl Johans gate 67, 149, 150
    Kongelige Slott (Royal Palace)
        150
    Konserthuset 151
    Kon-Tiki Museum 162
    Kunstindustrimuseet
        (Museum of Applied Art) 152
    Kvadraturen 151, 161
    Markveien 158
    Monolitten 146, 161
    Munchmuseet (Munch
        Museum) 155
    Museet for Samtidskunst
        (Museum of Contemporary
        Art) 151
    Nasjonalgalleriet (National
        Gallery) 152
    Nationaltheatret (National
        Theatre) 150
    Norsk Arkitekturmuseum
        (Norwegian Museum of
        Architecture) 151
    Norsk Folkemuseum
        (Norwegian Folk Museum) 162
    Norsk Teknisk Museum
        (Museum of Science and
        Technology) 152
    Norsk Telemuseum (Museum of
        Telecommunications) 152
    Oscarshall Slott (Castle) 162
    Oslo Bymuseet (City Museum) 161

Oslo Sentralstasjon (Oslo S
  station) 150, 164
Oslokunstersenter (contemporary
  and applied arts) 158
Rådhus (City Hall) *123*, 147–8,
  149
Sjøfartsmuseum (Maritime
  Museum) 162
Slottsparken (Palace
  Gardens) 149
Sternersenmuseet
  (contemporary arts) 151
Stortinget (Parliament) *46*,
  144–5, 150
Tøyenbadet (swimming baths)
  158
Tøyenhagen (Tøyen Botanical
  Gardens) 158
Tryvannstårnet (Observation
  Tower) 162
university 150
Vigeland-museet *155*, 161
Vigelandsparken (sculpture park)
  159, 161
Vikingskipshuset (Viking Ship
  Museum) *20*, 162, 176
Oslofjorden *166–7*, 169
Oslomarka 171
Osterøy 240
outdoor pursuits *98–9*, *100*,
  101–5, 164
  see also **sports**
Outdoor Recreations Act
  (*Lov om friluftslivet*) 101, 171

Ø

Ørnesvingen 280
Ørneveien 280
Ørsta 279
Østerdalen 185
Østfold 173
Øye 279
Øystese 235

P–Q

passenger ferry service 348, 351
passports 372
Peerson, Cleng 44
peoples 67–70
  see also **Sami**
  early 21, 22
  longevity 21, 22
pharmacies 373
Pietism 39
pilgrimages/pilgrim routes
  291, 292
polar bears 242, *336*, 342
  museum, Hammerfest 327
Polasirkel (Arctic Circle) 262, 305
police 371
population 24, 38
postal services 374
power stations *see* **hydro-electric
  power stations**
**prehistoric burial mounds and
  monuments**
  see also **rock carvings**
  Alsten 309

Borre 175
Doøa Hill 222
De Fem Dårlige Komfruer (Five
  Bad Virgins), Haugesund 222
Gokstadhaugen 176
Helgøya 181
Horgsteinen (Stone of Horg),
  Averøya 283
Hunn 174
Jærstrendene Landskaps
  vernområdet 218
Kuli 286
Oseberghausen 176
Raknehaugen 171
Sigarshaugen 320
Storbåthallaren 317
Svanøy 271
Trondenes 319
Ullandhaug 229
Vang 190
Vanse 206
Preikestolen *216*, 217, 219, *311*
prisoners of war 309
  museum 306
prohibition 132–3
public holidays 374
public transport 13, 95–6, 348–51
  tickets 13, 349
puffins *308*, 242
Quisling, Vidkun 52, 55, 56

R

Ra expedition 77, *78*, 162
Ragnhild 30
railway, mountain
  (Flåm to Myrdal) 269
Raumen 218
Red Maiden 24
reindeer 87, 90, 219, 242,
  306, 342
Reine 317
religion 374
  Sami 89
restaurants 360–2
Restauration 44, 226
Resvoll-Holmsen, Hanna 340
Ridderspranget (Knight's Leap)
  196, 197
Riegel cemetery 309
Ringebu 189
Ringve 295
Risør 207
Rjukan 54, 210
roads 93–5, 352–3
  Atlanterhavsveien (Atlantic Road)
  282–3
  Ferieveien (holiday road) 296
  Kopperveien (Copper Road) 187
  Mossveien 172
  old mountain road, Rogaland 221
  Oldtidsveien (Highway of the
    Ancients) 174
  Opplevelserute (Discovery Route)
  221
  Ørneveien (Eagle's Road) 280
  Peer Gyntveien 190
  Rondevegen 186
  silver road 306
  Utsiktsveien (Panorama Way) 195

rock carvings
  Ausevik 271
  Balsfjord Kirke 321
  Bognes 320
  Bolø 302
  Bremanger 271
  Farsund 206
  Frostatinghausen 301
  Herand 236
  Hjemmeluft 325
  Leirfall *81*
  Sagelv 320
  Rodøy Man 104
  Rogaland 217–22
  Romsdalen 280
  Rondane 186
  rorbuer 314, 315, *316*, 355
  rosemaling (**rose painting**) *38*,
    114–15, 118–19, 238, 256
  royal family 19, 82–3
  Runde 278
  runic inscriptions 25, *33*, 35
  Ryfylke 218, 219
  Råggejavie 320
  Røldal 221
  Røros *10–11*, *40*, 118, 187, 188
  Røst 312–13, 318
  Røvær 222
  Røyrvik 303

S

sagas 29, 80
Sagas of the Norse Kings
  (*Heimskringla*) *26*, 29
sailing 284, 348, 351
**St Mary's Sewing Needle,
  Avaldsnes** 222
St Olav *see under* **kings**
St Sunneva Kloster, Selje 271
Saltfjell 305
Sametinget (Sami parliament) 90
Sami 22, *84–5*, *86*, 87–90, *91*,
  264
  Finnmark 325–6
  museums 325, 329, 330
  Nordkapp 329
  Snåsa 302
Samiland 87
samnorsk 71
Sand 220
Sandane 272
Sandefjord 22, 176
Sandemose, Aksel 68
Sandnes 218
Sandnessjøen 308
Sarpsborg 175
Saur, the dog king 31
Scandinavia 22, 59
Schengen Agreement 58
sculptures 126
security 371
seed bank 342
Seim 241
Selje 271–2
Setergrotta (caves) 304
Setermoen 321
Setesdal 210
Shetland 30, 35, 37
Shetland Bus 55

ships *20*, 22
  see also **boats and boat building**
Viking *14*, *20*
shopping 164, 255, 365
  hours 371
siddis 226
Silda 271
silver 38
SINTEF 291
Sivle, Per 240
Skaidi 325
skalds 29
skiathlon 108
Skien 207–8
skiing 103–4, 110, 367
  Telemark 108
  Folgefonn Summer Ski centre,
    Jondal 236
  Norwegian Skiing Adventure
    Centre, 209
  Snowland (summer ski
    centre) 196
  Stryn (summer skiing) 273
  Svarsted Ski Centre 177
ski-jumping 104, 105, 108
  see also *Holmenkollen*
Skudeneshavn *221*, 221, 222
sloopers 44
Slottsfjellet 176
Smeerenburg 340
Smøla 285
Snåsa 302
Sogn og Fjordane 267
Sogndal 269
Sognefjell *270*
Solstad, Dag 125
Son 173
  Son Kystkultursenter 173
Sortland 319
Sortland Bridge 319
Sotra 240
souvenirs 365
Spitsbergen see **Svalbard**
sporting events 367–9
sports 101–5, 107–10, 366–9
  see also **cycling, fishing,
    skiing, walking**
  federations 107
  individual sports 366–9
  international competitions 109
  sport/idrett/aktiv 107
  winter 184, 186, 195, 197
sports centres
  see also *under* **skiing**
  Aak 280
  Gloppen Camping &
    Fritidssenter (adventure
    centre), Sandane 272
sportsfisker 112
SS concentration camp 301
Stalheimskleive 240, *241*
Stamsund *314*, 316
standard of living 130–3
statues 107, 126
Stavanger *225*, 225–9
  markets 225
  Arkeologisk Museum
    (Archaeological Museum) 229
  Aviation Museum 229
  Breivatnet 228

Cathedral School 228
Domkirke (Cathedral) 226,
  228, 229
Gamle Stavanger (Old
  Stavanger) *227*
Hermetikmuseet (Canning
  Museum) 227
Norske Utvandrersenteret
  (Emigration Centre) 225–6
Sjøfartsmuseum (Maritime)
  227, 228
Stavanger Botanisk Hage
  (Botanic Gardens),
  Ullandhaug 229
Stavanger Museum 229
Vågen 226
Valbergtårnet (Valberg tower) 228
stave churches (*stavkirke*) *see*
  under **churches**
Steinkjer 302
Stiklestad 301
  Battle of 291, *296*, 297
Stødi 305
Stokmarknes 318–9
stolkjaerrer 94, 272
Stord 233
Struensee, Friedrich 39
Stryn 273
Sturluson, Snorri 24, 29
Suldal 220
Sulitjelma 306–7
Sunde 235
Sunndalen 286
Sunnhordland 233
Sunnmøre mountains 279
Surnadalen 286
Svalbard *334–5*, 337–42
Svanøy 271
Svinvik Arboret (arboretum) 286
Svolvær 315
Svor, Anders 273
swimming 367
Sætergrotten 304
Sødorp 189
Sørlandet 203
Sørumsand 171

T

Tamokdalen 321
Tana Bru 329
taxes 130, 133
Telemark *71*, 203
  heroes of 54
  skiing 108
Telemarkkanal 208
Terboven, Joseph 55
**Tertitten narrow-gauge railway,
  Sørumsand** 171
theatre 363
Thor the Thunderer 24
Tidemand, Adolph 152
Tingstua 190
Tingvoll 286
tipping 374
Tjeldsundet *92*, 320
Tjøme 176
Tjøtta 308
Todalfjorden 286
toll roads 352

tolls 95, 133
Tordenskiold, Peter Wessel 39
Torvik *282*
tour operators, specialist 375
**Touring Association (Den Norske
  Turistforening)** 164
tourist board/information 375
tours
  glacier (Jostedalsbreen) 268
  Norway in a Nutshell (railway)
    241, 350
trails 102, 103, 104
trains 96, 349, 350
transport network 93–6, 348–53
Treaty of Kiel 43
Troldhaugen 124, 253–4
trolls 80
**Trollstigen (Trolls' Ladder/Trolls'
  Causeway)** 280
Trolltindale 280
Troms 321
Tromsø *138–9*, 264, 321–4
  Domkirke (Cathedral) *322*, 323
  Ishavskatedralen (Arctic Ocean
    Cathedral) 264, *323*
  Polarmuseet (Polar Museum) 322
  Tromsø Bymuseum (City
    Museum) 264
  Tromsø University Museum 322
Trøndelag 288–9
Trondenes 319
  Trondenes Church 264
Trondheim 291–6
  Trondheim Aktivum (local tourist
    office) 293
  Austråtborgen (ancient manor
    house) 296
  Bakklandet 294
  Erkebispegården
    (Archbishop's Palace) 292
  Fosenkaia 293
  Hospitalsløkka 294
  Kristiansten Festning
    (Kristiansen Fort) 293
  Lyngsalpan 323–4
  Munkholmen 294
  Nidarosdomen (Cathedral)
    262, *263*, 291–2
  Nordenfjeldske Kunstindustri-
    museum 291
  Ravnkloa fish market 293
  Ringve 295
  Ringve Botaniske Hage
    (Botanic Gardens) 296
  Ringve Museum (Museum of
    Musical History) 295
  Rustkammeret (army museum)
    293
  Sion 294
  Sjøfartsmuseet (Maritime
    Museum) 294
  Skansen 294
  Stiftsgården 293
  Strikkemuseum (knitting
    museum) 296
  Trøndelag Folkemuseet
    (Folk Museum) 294
  Trøndelag Kunstnersenter
    (Academy of Art) 295
  Trøndelag Teater 294

Tyholttårnet 296
university museum 291
Vår Frues Kirke (Church of Our
   Lady) 293
Vitenskapsmuseet (Museum
   of Natural History and
   Archaeology) 294
Trysil 186
tunnels 94, 95, 96
Turtagrø 198
Tysnesøy 233
Tønsberg 176

U

Ullandaug 229
Ulvik 238
Undset, Sigrid 184
UNESCO World Heritage sites
   Bergen 250
   Hjemmeluft 325
   Nusford 317
   Røros 188
   Urnes Stavkirke, Luster 269
universities 150, 291
Utne *236*, 237
Utsira *222*
Utstein Kloster 220

V

Vadsø 330, *331*
   Innvandrermonumentet
      (Immigration Monument) 331
   uftskipsmasta 331
Valdres 196
Valen, Fartein 235
Valevåg 235
Varangerbotn 330
Varden 281

Vardø 95, 331
Vassbø 217
VAT 130
Venstop *see also* **Telemark**
   Museum
**Vesteraalens Dampskibsselskab
   (Steamship Company)**
   93, 261, 318
Vesterålen Islands 318
Vesterøy 176
Vestkapp 272
Vigeland, Gustav 159, 161
Vigra 95, 278
Vik 268
Vik, Ingebrigt 236
Vikings 23–7
   burial 27
   folk arts 117, 118
   Gokstad ship *14*, *20*, 22
   gold *16–17*
   in Britain 26
   longships 117
Vikna 309
Vinland 78
Vinmonopolet 133
Vinstra 189
visas 372
Voss 239, 240
Våg 308
Vågar 315
Vågen 285
Vågsøy 271
Værnes 301
Værøy 318

W

Waitz, Grete 107
walking trails 102, 103, 164, 190,
   218, 256, 280, 368

   in national parks 368
waterfalls 235, 305
   Brudesløret (Bridal Veil) 279
   Fiskumfossen 303
   Formofossen 303
   Fotlandfossen 217
   Kjosfossenen 241
   Kvinnfoss
      (Lady's Waterfall) 268
   Laksfossen 304
   Mardalsfossen 281
   Målselvfossen 321
   Månofoss *218*
   Skykkjedalsfossen 238
   De Syv Sostre (The Seven
      Sisters) 279, 286
   Valursfossen 193
   Vrangfossen 208
   Vøringfossen *235*, 238
water sports 367
Weidemann, Jacob 302
Wergeland, Henrik 123, 235
wergild 24
whales/whaling 242, 243, 340
   Oksevåg whaling station 330
   safaris 318, 319
wildlife 242–3
Wilhelm II, Kaiser 272
With, Richard 318
wood carving 117
World War II 52–6, 82, 149
   Finnmark 324
   monument 185
   museum 306
   Narvik 320–1
   resistance 54, 249

Y

yoik 88, 89

INSIGHT GUIDES
The classic series that puts you in the picture

☒ INSIGHT GUIDES
www.insightguides.com

Alaska
Amazon Wildlife
American Southwest
Amsterdam
Athens
Argentina
Arizona & the
  Grand Canyon
Asia's Best Hotels
  & Resorts
Asia, East
Asia, Southeast
Australia
Australia & New Zealand's
  Best Hotels & Resorts
Austria
Bahamas
Bali
Baltic States
Bangkok
Barbados
Barcelona
Beijing
Belgium
Belize
Berlin
Bermuda
Boston
Brazil
Bruges, Ghent, Antwerp
Brussels
Budapest
Buenos Aires
Bulgaria
Burgundy
Burma (Myanmar)
Cairo
California
California, Southern
Canada
Cape Town
Caribbean
Caribbean Cruises
Channel Islands
Chicago
Chile
China
China, Southern
Colorado
Continental Europe
Corsica
Costa Rica
Crete
Croatia
Cuba
Cyprus
Czech & Slovak
  Republics
Delhi, Agra & Jaipur

Denmark
Dominican Republic
  & Haiti
Dublin
East African Wildlife
Ecuador
Edinburgh
Egypt
England
Finland
Florence
Florida
France
France, Southwest
French Riviera
Gambia & Senegal
Germany
Glasgow
Gran Canaria
Great Britain
Great Gardens of
  Britain & Ireland
Great Railway Journeys
  of Europe
Great River Cruises
  of Europe
Greece
Greek Islands
Guatemala, Belize
  & Yucatán
Hawaii
Holland
Hong Kong
Hungary
Iceland
India
India, South
Indian Wildlife
Indonesia
Ireland
Israel
Istanbul
Italy
Italy, Northern
Italy, Southern
Jamaica
Japan
Jerusalem
Jordan
Kenya
Korea

Kuala Lumpur
Laos & Cambodia
Las Vegas
Lisbon
London
Los Angeles
Madeira
Madrid
Malaysia
Mallorca & Ibiza
Malta
Marine Life in the
  South China Sea
Mauritius, Réunion
  & Seychelles
Mediterranean Cruises
Melbourne
Mexico
Mexico City
Miami
Montreal
Morocco
Moscow
Munich
Namibia
Nepal
Netherlands
New England
New Mexico
New Orleans
New South Wales
New York City
New York State
New Zealand
Nile
Normandy
North American &
  Alaskan Cruises
Norway
Oman & the UAE
Orlando
Oxford
Pacific Northwest
Pakistan
Paris
Perth & Surroundings
Peru
Philadelphia
Philippines
Poland
Portugal

Prague
Provence
Puerto Rico
Queensland & The
  Great Barrier Reef
Rajasthan
Rio de Janeiro
Rockies, The
Romania
Rome
Russia
St Petersburg
San Francisco
Sardinia
Scandinavia
Scotland
Seattle
Shanghai
Sicily
Singapore
South Africa
South America
Spain
Spain, Northern
Spain, Southern
Sri Lanka
Sweden
Switzerland
Sydney
Syria & Lebanon
Taipei
Taiwan
Tanzania & Zanzibar
Tasmania
Tenerife
Texas
Thailand
Thailand's Beaches
  & Islands
Tokyo
Toronto
Trinidad & Tobago
Tunisia
Turkey
Turkish Coast
Tuscany
US National Parks West
USA On The Road
USA New South
Utah
Vancouver
Venezuela
Venice
Vienna
Vietnam
Wales
Washington D.C.
The Western
  United States

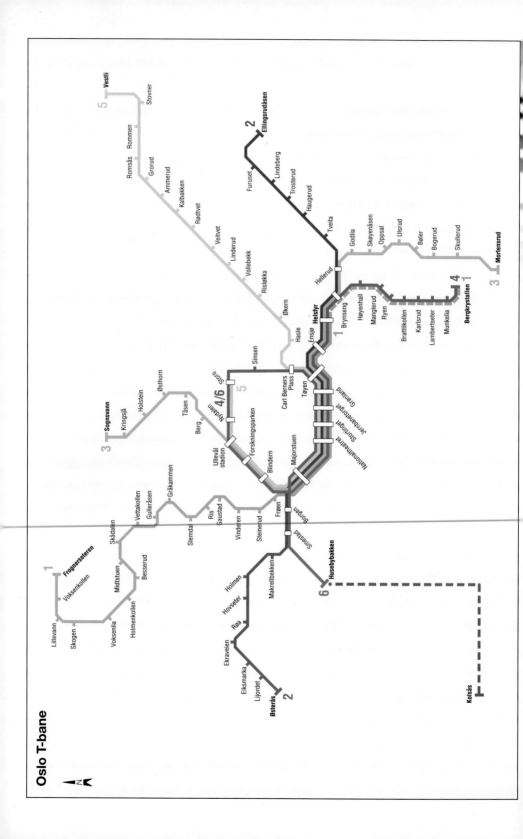

Oslo T-bane

Holmenkollen area

Tryvannstårnet
Øvresetertjern
Frognerseteren
Lillevann
Voksenkollen
Holmenkollen
Skøyen
500
Voksenkollveien
Litleåsveien
Voksenkollveien
Holmenkollveien
Bogstad campingplass
Voksenlia
Skimuseet
Holmenkollen kapell
Holmenkollbakken
Bogstad Manor
Midtstuen
Holmenkollen
Ankerveien
Oslo
Besserud
Sørkedalsveien

750 m
750 yds

Grefsen
Fysikk
Diakonhjemmet
Barnekunstmuseet
Lille Frøens
Fjernsynshuset
N.R.K.
BLINDERN
Kringkastingen
Fabritiusalléen
Damplassen
Borgenveien
Sørkedalsveien
Apalveien
Wilhelm Færdens vei
VESTRE
GRAVLUND
Borgen
Frøen
Suhms gate
Gydas vei
Trudvangveien
Gardeveien
Kirkeveien
Majorstuen
Sporveismuseet
Misjons-kirken
168
Colosseum senter
Fridtjof Nansens vei
Colosseum kino
Sørkedalsveien
Valkyrie
Majorstuen
Jacob
Aalls vei
Ole Vigs gate
Sørkedalsveien
Schønings gate
Hammerstads gate
Industrigata
MAJORSTUEN
Bogstadveien
Ole Vigs gate
Rosenborggata
HEGDEH
168
VIGELANDS-PARKEN
Monolitten
Dammene
Frogner stadion
Kirkeveien
Jacob Aalls gate
St. Dominikus
Gjørstad gate
Industrigata
Bogstadveien
FROGNERPARKEN
Frogner
R2
Professor Dahls gate
Fagerborggata
Fearnleys gate
Uranienborgveien
Prof. Dahls gate
HOMANSBYEN
Gustav Vigelands vei
Jonsrudveien
Oslo Bymuseum
Kirkeveien
Munthes gate
Briskebyveien
Undr
Hegdehaugsveien
Josefines gate
Thomas' vei
Drammensveien
Frognerelva
Halvdan Svartes gate
Vigelandmuseet
Nordraaks gate
Gydenløves gate
Tidemands gate
FROGNER
Eckersbergs gate
Arno Bergs plass
Uranienborg
Josefines gate
Uranienborgveien
Matserud
Sørhellinga
Kristinelundveien
Harald tordveien
Nobels gate
Sølheimgata
Frognerveien
Løvenskiolds gate
Gyldenløves gate
Eilert Sundts gate
Hotvedt
Oscars gate
Camilla Colletts vei
Oscars gate
Incognitogata
SLOT
Olav Kyrres plass
Bygdøy allé
Eckersbergs gate
Thomas Heftyes gate
Gimleveien
Odins
Elisenbergveien
President Harbitz gate
Niels Juels gate
Skovveien
Riddervolds plass
Riddervolds gate
Parkveien
Slottet
Frøyas gate
Tostrups gate
Bygdøy allé
Frogner
Gimle kino
Bygdøy allé
Gabels gate
Niels Juels gate
Skovveien
Meltzers gate
Colbjørnsens gate
Oslo Energi
Incognitogata
DRONNIN PARKEN
Bygdøy alle
American Lutheran Church
Sophus Lies gate
Mogens Thorsens gate
Bygdøy allé
Hydro
Drammens
Drammensveien
Thomas Heftyes gate
Gyldenløves gate
Frogner
Frederik Stangs gate
Gabels gate
Niels Juels gate
Universitetsbiblioteket
Solligata
Colbjørnsens gate
Adelers gate
Huitfeldts gate
Folkveien
Kirkeveien
RUSELØKKA
Drammensveien
Observatorie Terrasse
Prof. Aschehougs gate
Reichweins gate
Oslou
Munkedamsveien
Observatorie
Rikstrygdeverket
Munkedamsveien
Frognerkilen
SKILLEBEKK
Framnesveien
AKER BRYGGE

Bygdøy

Oscarshall slott
Oscarshallveien
Oscarshallveien
Dronninghavnveien
Båthavn
Kongen
Ferry port
Tjuvholmkaia
Filipstadveien
FILIPSTAD
Filipstadkaia
Tjuvholmen

Norsk Folkemuseum
Wedels vei
Langviksveien
åveny
Hux
Christian Bennechies vei
Båthavn
Dronningen
Bygdøynesveien
Filipstadutstikker

Vikingskiphuset (Viking Ship Museum)

Langviksbukta

Kon-Tiki museet
Frammuseet
Norsk Sjøfartsmuseum

Oslofjorden

Oslo

500 m
500 yds

Denmark, Germany

Hellviktangen Manor, Nesoddtangen